£14.95

Privatization: An Economic Analysis

MIT Press Series on the Regulation of Economic Activity

General Editor
Richard Schmalensee, MIT Sloan School of Management

Privatization: An Economic Analysis

John Vickers and George Yarrow

The MIT Press
Cambridge, Massachusetts
London, England

This book was set in Times Roman
by Method Ltd
and printed in Great Britain by
Galliard (Printers) Ltd, Great Yarmouth

Library of Congress Cataloging in Publication Data

Vickers, John, 1958–

Privatization: An Economic Analysis/by John Vickers and George Yarrow

   p. cm.—(MIT Press series on the regulation of economic activity; 18)
   Bibliography: p.
   Includes index.
   1. Privatization—Great Britain.
2. Privatization—Great Britain—Case studies.
I. Yarrow, George K. II. Title. III. Series.
HD4145.V53   1988   338.941—dc19   88–2080
ISBN 0–262–22033–4.   ISBN 0–262–72011–6 (pbk.)

Dedication

To our parents

Contents

Note   Some sections of chapters 2, 4, and 5 are marked with asterisks. These sections contain more technical material and may be omitted without loss of continuity.

List of Tables and Figures

Tables

Government regulation of economic activity in the United States has changed dramatically in this century, radically transforming the economic roles of government and business as well as relations between them. Economic regulation of prices and conditions of service was first applied to transportation and public utilities and was later extended to energy, health care, and other sectors. In the early 1970s explosive growth occurred in social regulation, focusing on workplace safety, environmental preservation, consumer protection, and related goals. Regulatory reform has occupied a prominent place on the agendas of recent administrations, and considerable economic deregulation and other reform has occurred. But the U.S. economy remains highly regulated, and the aims, methods, and results of many regulatory programs remain controversial.

The purpose of the MIT Press Series, Regulation of Economic Activity, is to inform the ongoing debate on regulatory policy by making significant and relevant research available to both scholars and decision-makers. Books in this series present new insights into individual agencies, programs, and regulated sectors, as well as the important economic, political, and administrative aspects of the regulatory process that cut across these boundaries.

Industries that have been subjected to economic regulation in the United States have more commonly been government-owned in other nations. Just as an active deregulation movement in the United States has sought, with some success, to reduce the scope of economic regulation, strong privatization movements abroad have sought in recent years to transfer the ownership of government enterprises to the private sector. In some cases privatization replaces government ownership by economic regulation; in others it produces unregulated markets.

In this book John Vickers and George Yarrow provide both a useful overview of the economic theory relevant to privatization, much of which has been developed only recently, and a comprehensive examination of the far-reaching privatization program of the Thatcher Government in the U.K. This important "microeconomic experiment" will fundamentally change market and regulatory structures in a number of important sectors of the U.K. economy. Vickers and Yarrow present the most comprehensive and rigorous analysis of privatization—both in general and in the U.K.—that has appeared to date. This important book should be of interest to scholars and policy-makers concerned with industries that have been included in the U.K. "experiment" and, more generally, to all concerned with economic regulation, public enterprise, and comparisons between them.

Preface

The end of 1987 is in many ways a fortunate time to complete a book on the economics of privatization in Britain. We can look back on the record of the first two terms of Mrs Thatcher's Conservative Government and, following her election victory in June, we can look ahead to the privatizations of the electricity and water industries which are planned to occur about two years from now. The past 12 months or so has been a particularly active period. Since December 1986, about £15 billion worth of state assets—British Gas, British Airways, Rolls-Royce, the British Airports Authority, and the Government's remaining shareholding in BP—have been sold to private investors. With the next major privatizations likely to be some way into the future, now is an opportune moment to reflect on what has happened so far.

But the world does not stand still. In the few months since our manuscript went to the publishers in September, privatized companies have continued to be at the center of events. British Airways successfully fought with SAS for control of British Caledonian, BP made a bid for Britoil, the intention to privatize British Steel was announced, and British Gas's industrial pricing policies were referred to the Monopolies and Mergers Commission. There was also the stock market crash in October, right in the middle of the BP sale. Our publishers kindly allowed us to add a word or two on some of these events, but with each day's news it would always be possible to say a little more. However, we have tried throughout to emphasize the longer-term economic issues connected with privatization in Britain.

It is a pleasure to thank those who have helped us in the writing of this book. Sara Connolly, Simon Cowan and Ian Preston gave us valuable research assistance. Julia Gibert unselfishly gave of her time to ensure deadlines were met. Colin Mayer, Francis McGowan, Shirley Meadowcroft, Al Phillips, David Starkie, Jeffrey Wheatley and Hyun Shin were among those who commented on draft chapters. Alison Hook typed large portions of the manuscript with great skill and remarkably good cheer. Christine Sharrock of Omega Scientific organized the typesetting speedily and efficiently. Robert Bolick of MIT Press was a pleasure to work with. We are extremely grateful to them all. Responsibility for remaining errors alas remains with us.

Finally, we would like to thank Oxford University and our respective colleges for giving us the opportunity to write this book.

John Vickers
Nuffield College, Oxford

George Yarrow
Hertford College, Oxford

Chapter 1

Introduction

Privatization policies are currently in progress the world over—in Europe, North America, Japan, and numerous developing and newly industrialized countries—but nowhere are they being carried out as vigorously and extensively as in Britain. When Mrs Thatcher came to power in 1979, about 11.5 percent of gross domestic product was accounted for by state-owned enterprises. By the time of her third election victory in June 1987, that figure was down by over a third to about 7.5 percent. In the process over half a million employees were transferred to the private sector, of whom around 90 percent acquired shares in their companies, and the total number of private shareholders in Britain roughly trebled. And much more is to come.

Privatization, then, is high on the political agenda, but what of its economic consequences? Answers to this question are as old as the subject of economics itself. In the *Wealth of Nations* Adam Smith (1776) argued that:

"In every great monarchy in Europe the sale of the crown lands would produce a very large sum of money, which, if applied to the payment of the public debts, would deliver from mortgage a much greater revenue than any which those lands have ever afforded to the crown . . . . When the crown lands had become private property, they would, in the course of a few years, become well improved and well cultivated."

This view of the issue has not gone uncontested. Apart from the Marxist critique of private ownership of the means of production, it is perfectly possible to argue within an orthodox microeconomics framework that in many contexts (of which natural monopoly conditions are the most obvious example) public management will do better in terms of economic efficiency than private management.

Despite the long history of debate, it would be wrong to conclude that the issue of ownership has occupied a central place in the development of economic analysis. On the contrary, although there have been a number of distinguished contributions to the subject, mainstream economic theory has tended to bypass the issue: most microeconomics textbooks, for example, contain little or no discussion of *positive* theories of public enterprise. This might be considered a somewhat surprising outcome in view of the prominence frequently afforded to the question of ownership in political life: differences in attitudes to public and private ownership are frequently some of the main distinguishing characteristics of political parties. It may, however, simply be a reflection of beliefs either that the ownership of firms is a factor of relatively little economic importance and/or that public policy in this area is influenced much more by political philosophy and political expediency than by the niceties of economic analysis.

Our own view is that both the latter beliefs are misguided.In the first place, there are good reasons for thinking that the ownership of a firm will have significant effects on its behavior and performance, since changes in property rights will alter the structure of incentives faced by decision makers in the firm. Second, although economic analysis may have little direct impact on particular policy decisions, it does, over time, affect the climate of public opinion within which those decisions are made. Keynes (1936) was no doubt (deliberately) exaggerating the position when he claimed that "Practical men, who believe themselves to be quite exempt from any intellectual influences, are usually the slaves of some defunct economist," but it is not necessary to go this far to believe that ideas, analysis, and evidence do, ultimately, have a substantive bearing on the evolution of public policy.

Apart from the obvious and important point that extensive privatization programs are under way in many countries, we would argue that, for at least two further reasons, now is a particularly timely moment to re-examine the implications of the structure of ownership for the behavior and performance of firms. First, over the past decade there have been a number of important advances in areas of economic theory that are of immediate relevance to the ownership question, including the study of principal–agent relationships, imperfect competition, and regulatory theory. Second, technological and structural changes in a number of industries where public ownership is common indicate that a re-evaluation of policy options is in order.

It is these three factors—the significance of current privatization policies, developments in economic analysis, and technological and structural change—that motivate our book. The 11 chapters that follow are divided into two major parts. Part I (chapters 2 through 4) presents a number of theoretical perspectives on the topics of ownership, competition, and regulation, which have a direct bearing on the issue of the relative performance of publicly owned and privately owned firms, while part II (chapters 5 through 11) aims to give a comprehensive assessment of the privatization policies that were implemented in Britain between the summer of 1979 and the autumn of 1987—a period that approximately coincides with the first two Thatcher Governments.

We commence, in chapter 2, with the question: does ownership matter? The analysis is concerned chiefly with the effects of ownership on allocative efficiency in the marketplace and on the internal efficiency of firms. We conclude that the allocation of property rights does matter because it determines the objectives of the "owners" of the firm (public or private) and the systems of monitoring managerial performance. Public and private ownership differ in both respects. As a result, changes in property rights will materially affect the incentive structures, and hence the behavior, of managements.

The efficiency implications of these changes in incentives depend very much upon the competitive and regulatory environment in which a given firm operates. Indeed, it can be argued that the degree of product market competition and the effectiveness of regulatory policy typically have rather larger effects on performance than ownership *per se*. Chapters 3 and 4, therefore, are respectively devoted to evaluations of the roles played by competitive forces and regulation in determining managerial incentives, behavior, and performance.

With respect to competition we stress three themes: the role of potential competition, the properties of product market competition when viewed as an incentive mechanism, and competition issues that arise in connection with networks and vertical relationships. These themes have been selected because of their importance to the ownership question in general and to the British privatization program in particular. In each case, we are primarily interested in the relationships between market structures and economic efficiency.

In chapter 4 we seek to provide a theoretical perspective on the economics of regulation that will underpin our assessment of British regulatory policy in part II of the book. Regulation is viewed as a game between the policy agency and the firm(s), and the focus is on the incentive properties of various regulatory mechanisms to encourage both internal and allocative efficiency. As a consequence of imperfect information, there is necessarily a trade-off between the two components of efficiency and we examine ways in which this trade-off can be handled. Other issues that are emphasized include the dynamics of regulation and the strategic interactions between firms and regulators that can occur over time.

Since the British privatization program has partly been motivated by dissatisfaction with the economic performance of publicly owned firms, and since we need to establish benchmarks against which the records of newly privatized firms can be judged, part II of the book begins, in chapter 5, with an examination of the framework of control for nationalized industries in Britain, together with an assessment of the past performance of these industries.

In chapter 6 we move on to present an overview of the British privatization program. We argue that, although a number of policy objectives have been set forth in connection with the program, many of the stated goals (e.g. wider share ownership) could better be attained by means of alternative policies and, therefore, that privatization policies should primarily be judged on their contribution to economic efficiency. Chapter 7 examines some financial aspects of the sale of state assets.

While the smaller asset sales are assessed, albeit briefly, in chapter 6, the larger privatizations are singled out for much more extensive evaluations in the later chapters of the book. For convenience, these are grouped according to industrial sector: telecommunications (chapter 8); energy (chapter 9); transport (chapter 10); and water (chapter 11). Under these headings we take the opportunity to discuss planned privatizations (electricity and water) and possible future privatizations (e.g. coal and rail transport), as well as the asset transfers that have already taken place.

In each case, we first outline the main characteristics of the industry or industries concerned and then proceed to evaluate the policy changes that have recently been implemented or are planned for the near future. A number of themes emerge that are common to several of the chapters, including the role of new entry and potential competition, the network characteristics of the various industries, and the similarities among the regulatory structures and policies that have been adopted or are proposed. The common themes serve to link the case-by-case evaluations back to the theoretical perspectives developed in part I of the book.

In chapter 12 we conclude by drawing together the various threads of argument to give an overall assessment of the British privatization program. We stress the lessons that it contains for the future development of economic policy, including the importance of increasing effective (actual or potential) competition and improving the longer-term effectiveness of regulatory policies to contain monopoly power.

We began by quoting Adam Smith's advocacy of the sale of the crown lands (and note that farming is a competitive business). We will end by giving another quotation from Adam Smith which also bears on a central theme of this book:

"Monopoly, besides, is a great enemy to good management, which can never be universally established but in consequence of that free and universal competition which forces every body to have recourse to it for the sake of self-defence."

Part I

THEORETICAL PERSPECTIVES

Ownership and Incentives

2.1 Introduction

Transfer from the public to the private sector (or vice versa) of entitlements to the residual profits from operating an enterprise necessarily implies a change in the relationships between those responsible for the firm's decisions and the beneficiaries of its profit flows. In general, the change in the allocation of property rights leads to a different structure of incentives for management and hence to changes in both managerial behavior and company performance. This chapter therefore analyzes some of these immediate incentive effects of privatization in the context of U.K. market arrangements and political institutions.

The relationships between managements and the proximate or ultimate recipients of residual profit flows can be viewed as giving rise to a particular set of agency problems. The general agency problem can be characterized as a situation in which a principal (or group of principals) seeks to establish incentives for an agent (or group of agents), who takes decisions that affect the principal, to act in ways that contribute maximally to the principal's own objectives. The difficulties in establishing such an incentive structure arise from two factors: (a) the objectives of principals and agents will typically diverge, and (b) the information available to principals and agents will generally be different (for example, the former might not be able to observe some of the decisions of the latter).

Within this framework managements of firms can be regarded as agents acting (in the case of private ownership) for shareholders or (in the case of U.K. public ownership) for the department of government to which they are responsible. Alternatively, in the latter case, government departments may themselves be considered to be agents acting for the ultimate principals, the voting public. Either way, an immediate consequence of privatization will be some shift in the objectives of principals. In addition, it is also to be expected that the transfer of ownership will be associated with some change in the types of incentive systems that can be offered to managements. Thus, under private ownership, rewards can be linked to the company's share price via share ownership or options schemes, while poor financial performance might be penalized by the threat of a takeover by another firm.

The implications of these differences in principal–agent relationships will be considered in sections 2.2 and 2.3 below. Of particular interest are the possible effects of ownership on economic efficiency, and, in examining this issue, it is useful to distinguish between allocative efficiency in the market, which depends upon the output levels of firms with given cost structures, and internal efficiency, which depends upon the total costs to the firms of producing given bundles of outputs.

In public policy debate in Britain, it has often been claimed that the privatization of firms with market power tends to improve internal efficiency, but at the risk of worsening allocative efficiency unless some of the effects of profit-seeking behavior are held in check by sufficiently rigorous competitive and/or regulatory constraints. As will be seen in sections 2.2 and 2.3, this view, while not necessarily incorrect as an empirical summary of final outcomes, rests upon a number of specific assumptions about the incentive structures associated respectively with private and public ownership. Thus, to explore further the nature of the trade-off between allocative and internal efficiency that exists when a firm is transferred from public to private ownership, section 2.4 of the chapter sets out a simple formal model that incorporates changes both in objectives and in the effectiveness of the system for monitoring managerial performance. In this example it turns out that unit costs are lower under private ownership if and only if the private monitoring and incentive system is significantly better than the public system.

Section 2.4 also serves to highlight a very important point in the economics of privatization. Ownership arrangements are only one of a variety of factors that influence managerial incentive structures and economic performance, and, in particular, the competitive structure of the industry in which the firm is operating and the regulatory constraints that it faces will each have significant effects on incentives (and hence on both allocative efficiency and internal efficiency). Moreover, the impact of changes in any one of these three sets of influences (ownership, competition, and regulation) on efficiency will, in general, be contingent upon the other two.

Competitive forces and regulatory policies will be examined in detail in chapters 3 and 4 and, for the moment, it need only be noted that the theoretical analysis indicates that the effects of privatization cannot properly be assessed in isolation from these additional influences on incentives. This conclusion is also supported by empirical studies of the relative performance of public and private industry in the U.K. and elsewhere, some of which are summarized and discussed in section 2.5.

Although somewhat uneven in quality and scope, the empirical literature does at least serve to counter the simplistic view that the effects of ownership on performance are uniform and independent of other economic conditions.

2.2   Private Ownership

2.2.1   Principal–Agent Theory

Economic analysis of the behavior of privately owned firms most frequently rests upon the assumption that the aim of decision makers is the maximization of profit, where the latter is defined to encompass both current and future financial flows. However, while it is likely that privatization will indeed lead managers to place greater weight on profit goals, the changes involved are rather more complex than a straightforward shift to profit maximization. It will therefore be useful first to consider some general features of the underlying principal–agent problem, together with their implications for the behavior of a "typical" company that has been transferred to the private sector.

A general description of the agency problem runs as follows. There exists a principal and an agent—the owner and the manager of a firm, for example—who do not share the same objectives. The principal wants to induce the agent to act in his (the principal's) interests, but he does not have full information about the circumstances and behavior of the agent, and so he has a monitoring problem. This prevents the principal from successfully telling the agent what to do, for he cannot fully observe what is happening. In any event, he would usually want the agent's behavior to depend on circumstances that perhaps only the agent can observe. Principal–agent theory is concerned precisely with this problem of information and incentives. It addresses the central question: what is the optimal incentive scheme for the principal to lay down for the agent?

There are two versions of the basic principal–agent model. Let W and π be the utility functions of the principal and agent respectively, let a be the agent's action (which might be his level of effort), and let θ represent the state of the world. The principal cannot observe a or θ individually, but he can observe the outcome $x(a, \theta)$ of the agent's action given θ, and he makes his own action (e.g. a payment to the agent), denoted y, a function of that observed outcome. Thus the principal's problem is to choose $y(x)$, the *incentive scheme* for the agent. In doing so he must recognize two constraints. First, the agent will behave in a self-interested way given the incentive scheme. Second, the incentive scheme must be attractive enough for the agent to be willing to participate in the venture with the principal.

The two versions of the basic model differ according to whether the agent can or cannot observe θ at the time when he chooses his action. If he cannot, the agent chooses a to maximize his expected utility given $y(x)$. Much now depends upon the agent's attitude to risk. If he is risk-neutral, the optimum incentive scheme takes a simple form: the principal receives a flat amount from the agent whatever happens. That is, the agent bears all the risk (but being risk-neutral he does not mind that), incentives are "perfect," and there is no monitoring problem. However, if the agent is averse to risk, optimality requires the principal to offer the agent some insurance in bad states of the world. This dulls the agent's incentives, because he gains only part of the benefit resulting from extra effort on his part. The asymmetry of information can therefore give rise to "slack."

In the second version of the model the agent *can* observe θ before deciding on his action. His strategy in the face of incentive scheme $y(x)$ will then be a function $a(\theta)$, since the best action will depend upon circumstances (i.e. on θ). As before, the principal must also ensure that the incentive arrangement is sufficiently attractive for the agent to want to take part in it. (This "participation constraint" can take a variety of forms depending on whether it needs to hold for all θ, on average, or whatever.)

There are numerous applications of principal–agent theory in economics, including relationships between regulators and managers (see section 4.3), employers and workers, lenders and borrowers, landlords and tenants, insurers and the insured, and tax authorities and households. A fuller exposition of the theory and some of its uses is given by Rees (1985), whose bibliography contains detailed references. In what follows, however, we will initially be concerned only with the relationships between the shareholders and managers of a privately owned company.

The decisions in such a company will be taken by professional managers whose payoffs will not exclusively be dependent upon profit flows. At the simplest level, it can be assumed that managerial utility is a function of income and effort levels, although several other relevant variables have been suggested in the literature, including the sales revenue of the firm, its growth rate, and the level of discretionary managerial expenditures. The inclusion of one or more of these additional variables is usually motivated by a desire to capture the implications of managerial preferences for greater power and increased prestige.

The typical large company will have many shareholders, each of whom possesses a relatively small fraction of the total equity of the firm. In addition the shares in the company will be marketable. Hence, at any time, a shareholder can transfer his property rights to another investor and thereby terminate his direct relationship with the company. As a consequence, substantial changes in the number of principals and in the distribution of shareholdings can occur quite rapidly (see Alchian and Demsetz, 1972).

In these circumstances the pursuit of its own objectives by the management of the firm will be constrained by three groups of participants in capital markets:

(i) the firm's shareholders, seeking contractual arrangements with management that maximize their own payoffs;

(ii) other investors or their agents (e.g. managers of other companies), who might purchase the firm's shares as a prelude to attempting to alter existing contractual arrangements;

(iii) the firm's creditors (including lenders at fixed interest), who could seek managerial changes in the event of threatened or actual default.

The impact of these three groups on managerial incentives will be analyzed under the headings of shareholder monitoring, takeovers, and bankruptcy.

2.2.2 Shareholder Monitoring

Before examining the problems faced by principals in specifying and enforcing managerial contracts, it is necessary first to consider shareholders' objectives. The working assumption that will be made is that shareholders seek to maximize their expected financial return (profit) from the company. One justification for this approach is that, if shareholders hold diversified asset portfolios, it is reasonable to suppose that in respect of their returns from any one individual firm they will be approximately risk-neutral. There are, however, a number of possible objections to the assumption, and since some of them may be significant in the context of the U.K. privatization program they should be noted explicitly.

First, in a world of uncertainty, asymmetric information, differential taxation, and incomplete markets, the interests of different shareholders will not coincide. Even if it were true that each sought to maximize his expected financial return from the firm, in general there would be a lack of unanimity in shareholders' rankings of alternative managerial policies. For example, an institution such as a pension fund might prefer a higher dividend payout ratio than an individual investor faced with a somewhat different tax position. This is, of course, a general problem in the theory of the firm that can only be dealt with at the cost of a substantial increase in the complexity of the analysis (see Ekern and Wilson, 1974).

Second, if shareholders are also consumers of the firm's products, their interests in decisions will not be confined to the effects of managerial actions on financial returns. To illustrate, while a higher price might contribute positively to shareholder welfare through an accompanying increase in company profits, it would have the additional effect of reducing welfare derived from the shareholder's consumption of the final output. The point is particularly relevant where consumers of a monopolist's products hold a substantial fraction of its share capital (e.g. a newly privatized utility company such as British Telecom or British Gas).

Third, for a variety of reasons, many of the shareholders of a company transferred to the private sector may not in fact have diversified asset portfolios. Thus, by encouraging wider share ownership in general, and employee share ownership in particular, the U.K. privatization program has created a large class of small shareholders with interests in only a very limited number of companies. In such circumstances the risk-neutrality assumption may well be inappropriate.

We will return to some of these points later when we come to analyze the detail of privatization policies in Britain. Initially, however, our focus will be on other aspects of the agency problem surrounding privately owned firms, and, for the moment, the assumptions that shareholders are expected-profit maximizers and are unanimous in their rankings of managerial actions will suffice.

Given this assumption, then, the first issue to be considered concerns the implications of dispersed share ownership for the effectiveness of shareholder monitoring of management. If there existed only one, risk-neutral, shareholder, we could hypothesize a benchmark optimal contract between the firm's owner and its management. The terms and conditions of such a contract would depend upon factors such as the relevant production function, managerial preferences, and the information structure of the problem (who knows what and when, and the methods and costs of acquiring more information). At this stage the precise details of the optimal contract are not important; all that needs to be assumed is that there are nonzero specification and enforcement costs. A single owner would bear all these costs but, in return, would receive all the residual profit flow from the firm.

When the ordinary share capital of a firm is divided amongst many investors, the activity of specifying and enforcing managerial contracts confers external benefits on others. If one of the shareholders engages in this task, he bears the full cost of the activity but receives only a fraction of the total gain. For example, if the increase in expected profit resulting from an incremental increase in monitoring by i, assumed to cost c_i, is equal to $\Delta\pi$, the individual shareholder will only receive a benefit of $\mu_i\Delta\pi$, where μ_i is the fraction of the shares held by i. In such circumstances there is a danger that, from the perspective of shareholders as a whole, the intensity with which managers are monitored will be suboptimally low. If that is the case managers can be said to have discretion to pursue their own objectives and it may not be appropriate to base analysis of company behavior on the expected-profit-maximization assumption.

A second reason why dispersed shareholdings might lead to suboptimal monitoring of managements emerges from possible characteristics of the monitoring technology. As a result of factors such as economies of scale in the acquisition of information, it could be more cost effective to have monitoring activities concentrated in a single pair of hands, thereby avoiding the possible duplication of effort associated with multiple shareholdings. In other words, cost conditions might be such as to make monitoring of management a natural monopoly.

The problems associated with dispersed shareholdings, and in particular their implications for assumptions about the objectives of the firm, have long been recognized in the economics literature. Nevertheless, profit maximization, together with its variants that allow for risky profit flows, has continued to maintain a dominant position in the formal analysis of company behavior. One defense of this standard position rests upon the takeover threat which will be discussed in section 2.2.3. Other arguments include the following.

First, company law establishes a framework in which monitoring activities can be centralized via a board of directors for the firm. Directors are elected by shareholders, and serve as agents for the latter in specifying and enforcing managerial contracts. For example, the directors can establish incentive structures that link managerial remuneration to financial performance through such mechanisms as profit-related bonuses and share option schemes. While this arrangement introduces a further layer of principal–agent relationships (with attendant monitoring problems), it is at least arguable that the existence of nonexecutive directors partially attenuates the discretion of managements.

Second, it is sometimes claimed that, for many firms, the degree of dispersion of shareholdings has been exaggerated. Thus, when the holdings of various members of the same family are consolidated it frequently turns out that, for medium-sized firms at least, there exists a group that accounts for a significant fraction of the share capital. Again the point is not that external effects in monitoring activities are absent, but rather that such effects are smaller than is sometimes supposed.

Third, to reduce risk, the typical investor will hold a diversified portfolio of shares. For large institutional investors such as pension funds and insurance companies, the holdings may be spread over hundreds of companies and in total may amount to billions of pounds. The principal–agent relationship between a given investor and a given management should not therefore be viewed in isolation from other similar relationships elsewhere. In deciding upon the appropriate level of monitoring activity in respect of one company, the shareholder will take account of any secondary effects that such an activity will have upon the value of his holdings in other firms, since, in conditions of imperfect information, actions will send information signals to other managements that tend to affect the latter's behavior (cf. Kreps and Wilson, 1982). Thus, active monitoring of one management may help to create or maintain a reputation for toughness that in turn serves to restrict the discretion of the managers of other firms in which the investor has an interest. Put more formally, the incremental benefit of an increase in monitoring of one management can be expressed as $\Delta\bar{\pi} + \mu_i\Delta\pi$, where $\Delta\bar{\pi}$ is the increase in expected profit from other companies in the portfolio. Hence, even if μ_i is relatively small, there might still be substantial incremental payoffs from monitoring, and hence the suboptimalities implied by the earlier analysis could be relatively small.

Finally, even accepting the existence of managerial discretion at the senior management level, the implications of this phenomenon for profit performance may not be clear cut. The existence of larger rewards at the top of the hierarchy serves as a prize that intensifies internal competition for the acquisition of senior management positions, with associated benefits for company performance. That is, when the managerial function is viewed as a whole, the existence of large prizes at the top may serve as a relatively satisfactory incentive structure for shareholders. Moreover, in conditions of oligopolistic competition it will not generally be optimal for shareholders to have profit-maximizing managers acting as their agents. Thus, if managers derive utility from higher sales or market shares, the existence of discretion arising from dispersed shareholdings will influence the decisions of rivals and will thereby have an indirect effect on the profits of the firm in question. It is therefore possible to envision circumstances in which, via its effects on the behavior of rivals, more dispersed share ownership is associated with *higher* realized profit flows (cf. Vickers, 1985c).

In conclusion, it can be seen that, because the principal–agent relationships between managements and shareholders exhibit a number of subtleties, it would be premature to conclude that models of company behavior embodying one or other variant of the profit-maximization hypothesis should be abandoned when shareholdings are dispersed. However, uncritical acceptance of the notion that the managers of privately owned firms will *always* be constrained to act in the best interests of their shareholders is an equally unacceptable position. What is indicated is a more case-specific approach to the incentive problem that allows for some quantification of the various factors that are relevant to the principal–agent relationships.

2.2.3 Takeovers

Thus far we have been considering situations in which the management of a newly privatized firm is confronted by a large number of shareholders who seek to introduce incentive structures aimed at maximizing expected profit. Since shares are marketable, however, the size distribution of shareholdings can change quickly as a result of investors' buying and selling decisions. In particular, at any time, one individual or institution can seek to purchase *all* of the shares by making a takeover bid for the company. If successful, the bid would concentrate ownership and eliminate the externalities associated with multiple holdings. It can therefore be argued that, as a consequence of marketability, dispersion of shareholdings is not a factor of great significance for managerial incentives.

Consider, for example, a management that was not maximizing expected profit. A takeover raider could purchase all the shares of the company and then proceed to specify and enforce the optimal contract appropriate to the new single-shareholder situation. Suppose that the shares of the target company can be acquired at a price p, and that the value of each share following the introduction of the optimal contract is p^*. Suppose further that there are n shares in the target company on the market and that the transactions cost of the acquisition is f. Then the capital gain available to a successful raider is equal to $n(p^* - p) - f$ and, assuming that potential acquirors are profit maximizers, a takeover will occur when this expression is positive. Alternatively, the condition for a profitable takeover can be rewritten as $p < p^* - f/n$.

The argument is now straightforward. If the management of a firm fails to act in ways consistent with the optimal contract, the share price of the company will fall and the cost of purchasing shares will decline relative to np^*, the value of the firm contingent upon the existence of the optimal contract. As the deviation between p^* and p increases, the management will at some point become vulnerable to a takeover raid. The existence of this perceived threat of takeover in turn acts as an incentive mechanism that deters management from the pursuit of policies that are substantially at variance with the interests of its shareholders.

The effectiveness of the takeover mechanism in establishing incentives for good financial performance is a matter of some importance for the analysis of privatization policies. When a firm is transferred from the public sector the introduction of shares creates a market for corporate control, and if this market functions in the way described in the preceding paragraphs it can be argued that, whatever the implications of privatization for allocative efficiency, the transfer of ownership will produce powerful incentives toward internal efficiency. Thus, if the firm's internal efficiency is poor, its share price will be relatively low and management will be vulnerable to a hostile bid. The argument does not, of course, imply that *any* deviation from maximum internal efficiency will be punished in this way: some degree of managerial discretion will exist, if only because the transactions costs of takeovers are finite. If, however, the latter are low, management's performance will be heavily constrained by the threatened loss of control.

Detailed economic research on takeovers has revealed several reasons, some theoretical and some empirical, why the above line of argument might lead to a misleading perspective on the efficiency of the market for corporate control. Following Grossman and Hart (1980), consider first the decision faced by a shareholder who receives an offer to buy from a raider intent on increasing the market value of the target company. Let the value of the offer be p per share and assume that, because shares are widely held, each investor believes that his own sell/hold decision has a trivially small effect on the outcome of the bid. If the offer is expected to succeed, the value of the shares will rise to p^*, and it will be better for the shareholder to decline the offer and free-ride on the performance improvement that it is anticipated the raider will generate. In such circumstances all shareholders will decline the offer and the bid will fail. Hence, in equilibrium (where expected outcomes coincide with actual outcomes), there can be no successful takeovers at an offer price less than p^*. However, transactions costs imply that raids are unprofitable at offer prices greater than or equal to p^*. It follows that there is no equilibrium price at which successful takeovers will occur.

The stark simplicity of the free-rider argument's implications are contradicted by the historical record of takeover activity in the U.K. Between 1964 and 1970, for example, approximately one in three of all companies quoted on the London Stock Exchange disappeared as a result of acquisition, and a "mistake" theory of takeovers is clearly incapable of providing a satisfactory account of this and similar episodes. There are a number of possible explanations of the discrepancy between theory and evidence, including the following:

(i) strategic behavior by holders of diversified portfolios who accept offers in order to establish reputations as willing sellers and thereby put greater pressure on the managements of other companies in their portfolios;

(ii) the lack of protection afforded to minority shareholders under U.K. company law, which leaves them vulnerable to oppression by the controlling interest (e.g. via profit transfers out of the target company) in the event that they do not sell and the bid succeeds;

(iii) the compulsory acquisition provisions of U.K. company law—once an acquiror has obtained acceptances in respect of 90 percent of the ordinary share capital the remaining 10 percent (or less) can be compulsorily purchased at the offer price accepted by the majority—which can be used by the raider to eliminate the payoffs from free-riding strategies.

The first of these points is another version of the reputation argument outlined in section 2.2.2 above. The second has been developed by Grossman and Hart, who treat the post-raid level of oppression of minority interests as a control variable that can be set *ex ante* by the shareholders of the target company. Suppose, for example, that an acquiring company can transfer an amount γ (> 0) per share from minority shareholders to itself. If a raid is expected to succeed, the maximum post-acquisition value of a share to a minority holder then becomes $p^* - \gamma$. Thus, if $\bar{p}$ is the value of each share if the raid fails, selling is the optimal decision (irrespective of expectations of success and failure) if the offer price satisfies the two "acceptance" conditions: $p > p^* - \gamma$ and $p > \bar{p}$. However, the "profitability" condition for a successful bid is, as before, $p < p^* - f/n$. The three acceptance and profitability conditions can therefore simultaneously be satisfied, and hence equilibrium takeover bids can occur, if $\gamma > f/n$ and $p < p^* - f/n$. That is, provided the per-share level of oppression exceeds f/n, the effectiveness of the takeover constraint on the behavior of incumbent managements is restored.

There are considerable obstacles, however, to the precise specification of the level of oppression of minority interests, and there is little evidence that the instrument has been widely used by individual groups of shareholders as a mechanism of managerial control in Britain. Rather, protection of minority interests has been determined by the general provisions of company law and the regulations of bodies such as the City of London Panel on Takeovers and Mergers. In practice, U.K. company law offers only extremely limited protection for minority holders, and, although this eliminates the payoffs from free-riding strategies, it does so at the risk of creating incentives for socially excessive rates of takeover activity: partial takeovers become attractive as a result of the prospective returns from oppression of minority interests, and, if a bid is expected to succeed, there is the possibility that shares could be acquired at a price *below* the pre-bid market level because of the threat of partial expropriation. The provisions of company law have therefore been buttressed by regulations set out in the City Code on Takeovers and Mergers, several of which are designed to protect shareholders against these two outcomes (see Yarrow, 1985). However, as its name implies, the City Code is a form of self-regulation and the associated Takeover Panel has only limited powers of control. Hence, the question of whether or not the existing regulatory framework does in fact provide a level of shareholder protection commensurate with effective functioning of the takeover mechanism continues to be vigorously debated.

The compulsory acquisition provisions of section 209 of the Companies Act 1948 represent a more direct policy response to free-rider problems associated with takeover bids. If an offer is contingent upon acceptances in respect of at least 90 percent of the shares of the target company, the incentives to hold shares in the hope of participating in post-acquisition performance improvements are removed, since, if the acceptance level is attained, the successful raider has a right to purchase all the remaining shares. The vast majority of mergers and acquisitions in Britain are, in fact, characterized by offers that are contingent upon a 90 percent acceptance rate (see Franks and Harris, 1986a).

The compulsory acquisition solution to the free-rider problem is not entirely straightforward, however. Unless accompanied by a sufficiently damaging threat of oppression, the cost of declining an initial offer, even if it is expected eventually to succeed, may be relatively small. Then, if shareholders anticipate that, if the bid is not initially successful, an improved offer will be made (possibly as a result of competition from a second bidder), incentives to hold shares may be restored. Nevertheless, we believe that, taken as a whole, the British regulatory and legal framework does successfully overcome many of the adverse consequences of free-rider strategies, and therefore permits the threat of takeover to act as a potentially important constraint on managerial behavior. Although the solution is not perfect, and many residual problems remain, any major deficiencies in the market for corporate control are more likely to be the result of other influences that are at work in the market, to some of which we now turn.

Thus far it has been assumed that the objective of the acquiring firm is expected-profit maximization and that takeovers are triggered by deviations in the target management's behavior from that implied by its optimal incentive contract. Both assumptions are open to question. In the first place, raids may be motivated by a desire to increase managerial utility rather than to increase shareholder welfare. Thus, takeovers should be viewed as a potential *instrument of* managerial-utility maximization as well as a *control on* such behavior. Given this point, it is by no means clear that high levels of takeover activity will always be in the interests of shareholders. Second, even if raiders *are* profit seekers, takeovers may be motivated by factors such as the gains from increased market power or from reductions in tax liabilities. King (1986), for example, has argued that British merger activity has historically been correlated with stock market prices as a result of a tax-induced distortion in the pricing of financial assets. The implications of these factors are that even an efficient management may be vulnerable to takeover bids and, more generally, that the link between internal efficiency and the takeover threat may be weakened.

One consequence of this last point is illustrated by the following model of the incentive effects of takeover threats. Suppose that managerial utility is given by $U(x)$, where $U_x < 0$, $U_{xx} < 0$, and x can be interpreted as either the level of managerial effort or a measure of the internal inefficiency of the firm. Let x^* be the effort level associated with the optimal contract. Without loss of generality, $U(x^*)$ can be set equal to zero, and for simplicity we assume this also to be the utility of management in the event that the firm becomes a takeover victim. It is further assumed that the market value of the firm is an increasing function of effort, and that higher effort therefore reduces the perceived probability of takeover. In particular, suppose that the probability of takeover in the period $(t, t+dt)$, conditional upon the firm having survived until time t, is equal to $h(x; \theta)\, dt$, where $h_x < 0$ and θ is some parameter affecting the relationship between effort and the likelihood of takeover. (In reliability theory, the function $h(.)$ is called the hazard rate.)

In these circumstances the discounted present value of expected managerial utility is given by

$$\int_0^\infty U(x)\exp[-(r + h)t]\, dt = \frac{U(x)}{r + h(x; \theta)}, \tag{2.1}$$

where r is the discount rate. Maximizing this expression with respect to x yields the first-order condition

$$\frac{U_x}{U} = \frac{h_x}{r+h} \,.$$

(2.2)

The equilibrium level of effort is therefore determined by the condition that the marginal proportionate increase in utility consequent upon a reduction in effort is equal to the present value of the marginal increase in the probability of takeover, where the latter is calculated at a discount rate equal to $r + h$. Thus, as can be seen more directly from (2.1), one effect of the takeover threat is to increase the discount rate that managers apply to future utility (from r to $r + h$). Determination of the equilibrium effort level, denoted $\bar{x}$, is illustrated graphically in figure 2.1.

Consider next the effect of a change in the parameter θ which leads to an increase in the conditional probability of takeover at effort level x (θ can be interpreted as reflecting conditions in the market for corporate control). As can be seen from figure 2.1, the implications of the change for the equilibrium effort level depend upon whether the function $h_x/(r + h)$ is shifted upwards (effort decreases) or downwards (effort increases). In general the effect is ambiguous, depending upon the relative magnitudes of two counteracting forces. First, the increase in the conditional probability of takeover raises the denominator in the expression on the right-hand side of (2.2), leading, other things being equal, to an upward shift of the function. Intuitively, managerial discount rates are raised, producing

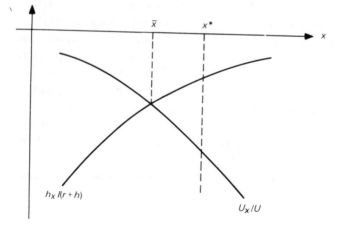

Figure 2.1   Takeover threats and managerial effort

greater incentives for shirking while the incumbent management is still in control of the firm ("making hay while the sun shines"). Second, greater takeover activity can be expected to increase the sensitivity of the probability of takeover to changes in effort or internal efficiency. That is, the absolute value of the derivative h_x can be expected to increase. Other things being equal, this shifts the function $h_x/(r + h)$ downwards, leading to greater effort being applied. In this case the intuition is that increased shirking is punished more heavily by a greater increase in the probability of takeover.

The model therefore demonstrates the possibility that a more active market in corporate control may be associated with lower internal efficiency. The effectiveness of the takeover threat depends upon the strength of the link between managerial effort and the probability of takeover. However, since raids may be motivated by factors other than the potential capital gains resulting from the correction of poor managerial performance, the creation of freely transferable property rights associated with privatization does not have uniformly benign implications for internal efficiency. One potentially adverse effect is an increase in managerial discount rates. In the model above this feeds through into an incentive to reduce effort levels, but it is easy to see how an increased emphasis on shorter-term payoffs could also have adverse implications for other decision variables (e.g. investment) in more elaborate analyses.

It can also be noted that, since acquisition of other firms may be one of the favored methods of increasing managerial welfare, an increase in the threat of takeover could produce a positive feedback effect by encouraging potential target companies to become raiders themselves, thus exacerbating the control problem. This is one example of a more general class of problem connected with the incentives for incumbent managements to engage in defensive actions to counteract the takeover threat, which actions may themselves have undesirable effects on shareholders' interests. Particularly in countries such as the U.K., where shareholders have very little direct influence on acquisition decisions, an unconstrained market in corporate control could easily generate an excessive level of takeover activity.

We conclude, therefore, that theoretical analysis of takeovers indicates a number of possible limitations to the effectiveness of this form of capital market constraint on the performance of managements. That is not to say, however, that takeover threats have no role to play in promoting internal efficiency. Indeed, in general we believe that raiders can, and often do, perform a useful function in this regard, particularly where they have better information about the performance of incumbent managements than the latter's own shareholders (see Scharfstein, 1986). The point is simply that the impact of the takeover threat depends heavily upon the precise characteristics of the relevant capital market, including factors such as the extent of shareholder protection afforded by the regulatory and legal frameworks, the constraints imposed by competition law, and the relevant fiscal system. Since these vary from country to country, we should not be surprised to find that the role played by the takeover constraint also shows marked international variations. Given our concern with privatization in Britain, it will therefore be useful to examine briefly some of the available U.K. evidence on the effectiveness of the market for corporate control.

The most extensive empirical work on U.K. acquisitions has been conducted by Singh (1971, 1975) who has sought, among other things, to estimate the empirical relationship between company performance and the likelihood of takeover (which relationship is the cornerstone of the argument that takeovers generate incentives for managers to act in the interests of owners). Singh found only small differences in profitability and other measures of financial performance between companies that became takeover victims and companies that did not, casting doubt on the notion that relatively poor performance leads to a sharp increase in the threat of takeover. In contrast, the data did suggest that the likelihood of takeover diminished significantly for firms above a certain size, suggesting that the most effective defense against unwanted bids is for potential targets themselves to seek rapid growth by means of acquisitions. Although later experience indicates that very large companies have now become more vulnerable to unsolicited takeover bids than in the periods studied by Singh, it remains true that the sizes of newly privatized firms such as British Telecom and British Gas provide incumbent managements with substantial protection against takeover threats. In these cases, therefore, there must be considerable doubt as to the efficacy of the takeover constraint on managerial performance.

Meeks (1977) examined the other side of the capital market discipline argument: if raids are motivated by the capital gains that can be realized from improving the performance of an inefficient company, it is to be expected that the financial performance of successful acquirors will itself improve following the takeover. In his sample, however, he could find no evidence of general post-raid increases in the profitability of acquirors, and, if anything, there was a slight, though not statistically significant, deterioration in profitability relative to industry averages.

Unfortunately, the findings of Singh and Meeks cannot be regarded as decisive evidence against the hypothesis that the probability of takeover is strongly linked to company financial performance. Suppose, for example, that such a relationship exists, but that the management of each firm chooses to act in a way that leads to a probability of takeover that is constant across firms. In equilibrium there would then be no observed differences in the average profitabilities of firms that were and were not takeover victims in a given period. Moreover, competition among potential acquirors might ensure that, where takeover bargains were accidentally available, the gains were appropriated by the targets' shareholders. That is, competition in the market for corporate control might drive the returns from acquisition down to approximately normal levels, implying that no significant net gains could be expected to accrue to successful raiders.

The results of later studies by Firth (1979, 1980) are less ambiguous. Firth found that, although on average the combined market values of acquirors and acquirees in his sample were not materially affected by the takeovers, the average share prices of acquirors fell significantly upon the announcement of the bid while the share prices of acquirees increased substantially. In other words, on average the takeovers led to supernormal losses for the acquirors' shareholders, in line with the hypothesis that takeovers tend to be used as an instrument for improving managerial welfare. Although these results are quite consistent with the view that managers are also constrained by a link between performance and the threat of takeover, taken in conjunction with the theoretical model outlined above they do illustrate the point that shareholder interests may not always be well served by a highly active market for corporate control.

Firth's results have recently been challenged by Franks and Harris (1986a, 1986b) who, using a larger sample and a longer sample period, concluded that acquisitions *did* increase the aggregate market value of the companies involved, and that on average there was no evidence of supernormal losses to acquirors' shareholders. The Franks and Harris results are in line with those of the majority of U.S. studies of the issue (e.g. Halpern, 1973; Mandelker, 1974; Asquith, 1983), although it should be noted that there are dissenting voices (e.g. Malatesta, 1983). Since a large fraction of U.K. takeovers have been of a broadly horizontal nature, to the extent that they do actually exist, such gains may, of course, simply reflect increases in market power rather than improvements in internal efficiency. Where researchers have specifically tried to uncover efficiency improvements attributable to takeovers, the results have not been very encouraging for the capital market incentives argument. Thus, Cowling *et al.* (1980) found no evidence for the proposition that mergers had led to significant improvements in the internal efficiencies of the companies in their sample, while Newbould (1970) concluded that both *ex ante* appraisals of acquisitions and *ex post* plans to realize potential efficiency gains were, in a high proportion of the cases he studied, extremely limited in scope.

To summarize, although theoretical analysis and empirical evidence do not yield unambiguous conclusions about the strength of the managerial incentives generated by the existence of a market for corporate control, they do indicate certain imperfections in the market that may limit the impact of capital market disciplines on internal efficiency. One problem is the relative lack of shareholder influence on acquisition decisions, over which managers continue to have considerable discretion. Acquisitions therefore appear frequently to have been used to promote managerial interests at the expense of shareholders, and the consequent high level of takeover activity may, by raising managerial discount rates, have had negative consequences for both internal and allocative efficiency. Another potential limitation, which is of some importance for the policy evaluations contained in chapters 8 through 11, is that the takeover constraint may be relatively weak in cases where the target firm is very large.

2.2.4 Bankruptcy

Bankruptcy can be viewed as another means by which managers may lose control of the company, and can therefore be regarded as leading to an alternative version of the takeover constraint. In discussing the implications of bankruptcy, however, the analysis of the previous section has to be modified to take account of a number of special features of control loss that occurs via this mechanism, including (a) the circumstances in which bankruptcy is likely to occur, (b) the fact that proceedings may be initiated by a different group of economic agents (creditors, for example), and (c) the legal and regulatory framework governing the process.

At the simplest level, bankruptcy can be assumed to occur when the market value of the firm's assets falls below the value of its outstanding liabilities. It therefore sets a floor value for the market capitalization of the firm. If it is assumed that managerial utility is a decreasing function of effort, that there is no uncertainty, and that bankruptcy is the only operative constraint, utility-maximizing managers would choose an effort level such that the total market value of the firm is exactly equal to the value of its debt. In these circumstances, while the value of the firm might be increased by raising its debt level, shareholders would derive no benefits from the change: the value of equity would always be zero.

Once uncertainty is introduced, however, it is easy to see how the threat of bankruptcy affords some protection to ordinary shareholders. To illustrate, let the market value of a firm with debt level D be $\pi(x) + \theta$, where θ is now a random variable with zero mean. The probability of bankruptcy is then the probability that $\pi + \theta < D$, which can be rewritten as $\theta < D - \pi$. It is therefore equal to $F(D - \pi)$, where $F(.)$ is the cumulative distribution function of θ and $F'(.) > 0$.

If $F(.)$ is reinterpreted as a hazard rate, a straightforward adaptation of the model in section 2.2.3 leads to the assumption that managers will seek to maximize

$$\int_0^\infty U(x) \exp\{-[r + F(.)]t\}\, dt \;=\; \frac{U(x)}{r + F(.)}$$

where managerial utility in the event of bankruptcy has again been normalized to zero. The first-order condition for the optimal effort level is

$$\frac{U_x}{U} = -\frac{F' \pi_x}{r + F(.)}. \tag{2.3}$$

If θ^m is the maximum value of θ, the market value of the ordinary shares of the company will be positive provided that the solution of equation (2.3) is such that $0 < \pi(x) + \theta^m - D$ since there will then be states of nature in which the total value of the firm exceeds D and in which shareholders will therefore receive positive returns.

Condition (2.3) is similar in form to equation (2.2) in section 2.2.3. The numerator of the expression on the right-hand side of (2.3) is the marginal reduction in the probability of bankruptcy resulting from increased effort, while the denominator is the effective managerial discount rate. As before, it can be seen that a finite probability of bankruptcy raises this discount rate and that, in general, the overall impact of an increase in the probability of bankruptcy on the effort level is ambiguous in sign.

It can be expected that the tightness of the bankruptcy constraint will largely be dependent upon the difference between the maximum expected value of the firm, denoted π^*, and the firm's debt level. The impact of the constraint on managerial decisions is likely to be greater where market conditions are such as to reduce the value of this spread. Thus, when the relevant industry is experiencing a period of recession or of more intense product market competition, the role of the bankruptcy threat as a control mechanism is likely to be enhanced. However, in boom conditions its role, relative to the other constraints on managerial behavior, will tend to be more limited.

If shareholders are able to control the level of debt of the firm they will be able to use this instrument to influence managerial behavior by varying the incentive structure that faces the management. This can be seen by noting that, since the level of debt is a parameter of the managerial-utility maximization problem set out above, the equilibrium effort level will be a function of D, denoted $x(D)$. Hence, via changes in D, shareholders can, in principle, influence the internal efficiency of the firm.

There are at least two limitations, however, on the strength of the incentives that can be established in this way. The first emerges as a consequence of the effects of increased debt on the managerial discount rate. Thus, particularly when probabilities of bankruptcy are relatively high, increasing debt may have a relatively greater impact on the denominator of the right-hand side of (2.3) than on the numerator, in which case the effort level becomes a *decreasing* function of D. In effect, if managers believe that the firm has a good chance of going out of business whatever decisions they take, this will lead them to the conclusion that they should enjoy more managerial discretion in the short run. If this occurs, on the criterion of promoting internal efficiency there will usually be a finite optimum debt-to-equity ratio. At this point the usefulness of the bankruptcy constraint as a control mechanism will have been exploited to the fullest possible extent, and further improvements in efficiency will not be feasible via reliance on this mechanism alone.

The second limitation of the bankruptcy constraint is that, in practice, determination of the firm's level of debt is a decision that is most frequently delegated to managements. Hence, managers can ease the constraint, and thereby simultaneously weaken the incentives for internal efficiency and increase their own utility, by choosing lower debt levels than shareholders would wish to see. It is, of course, true that managers will have regard to the consequent negative effects on the market value of the firm's equity. The extent of the concern with valuation effects, however, will be governed by the constraints on managers arising from the threats of shareholder intervention or takeover. Hence, in very many circumstances it is the latter that will be the effective control mechanisms. Only when market values are low as a result of factors such as depressed demand or intense product market competition is it likely that the threat of bankruptcy will play a substantial role. Thus, for example, it is unlikely that this particular control mechanism will have much effect on the incentives for internal efficiency in privately owned monopoly utilities.

2.3   Public Ownership

For publicly owned firms the task of monitoring managerial performance is entrusted to government. Compared with private ownership, the most obvious differences in the relationships between managers and their immediate principals arise from the facts that (a) the principals do not typically seek to maximize profits, (b) there are no marketable ordinary shares in the firm, and hence no *market* for corporate control, and (c) there is no direct equivalent to the bankruptcy constraint on financial performance.

Even more than in the case of private ownership, the precise detail of the principal–agent relationships surrounding public industry is heavily influenced by the institutional structures of the relevant economy. Since chapter 5 will be devoted to an examination of the nature and record of public ownership in Britain, the discussion in the current section will be restricted to the broader economic issues and problems associated with the specification of objectives and with the framework of control.

2.3.1   Public Interest Theories

Public interest theories are based upon the assumption that, in their dealings with industry, government departments seek to maximize economic welfare. The rationale for this approach is that such bodies are themselves agents for, and therefore properly should act in the best interests of, the wider public. Put another way, public interest theories abstract from the incentive problems associated with this agency problem by implicitly assuming that a first-best solution to it can be attained. We will return to this issue in section 2.3.2.

The usual approach is to assume that the objectives of government departments are defined by some form of social welfare function—thereby also begging questions connected with the aggregation of individual preferences—and the most frequently adopted specification is that social welfare is equal to the sum of consumers' and producers' surpluses, denoted S and π respectively. In other words, it is assumed that government departments seek to maximize a partial equilibrium measure of economic efficiency. There are, however, two "public interest" reasons why, in practice, governments might want to attach differential weights to consumers' and producers' surpluses in their objectives.

The first arises from *distributional* objectives. In the case of a privately owned firm, if shareholders are typically more wealthy than the average taxpayer a government concerned with redistribution might wish to reduce transfer payments from taxpayers to shareholders. Moreover, irrespective of the type of ownership, low income households often account for a substantial fraction of the sales of some utility industries (because income elasticities of demand for the goods are low), in which case the government might attach extra weight to consumer interests for distributional reasons. In addition to these possible "egalitarian" motives for distributional objectives, a government concerned only with domestic welfare would discount the proportion of a (wholly or partially) privately owned firm's profits accruing to overseas shareholders (a factor that is relevant in the telecommunications and gas privatizations discussed in chapters 8 and 9).

A second reason why a government would not be indifferent to transfer payments to the firm arises from the costs of raising public funds. For example, the payment of a subsidy to the firm requires raising tax revenue from elsewhere in the economy or extra government borrowing or money creation. But higher taxes will add to the distortion of economic decisions in other markets (for example, higher income tax would affect the trade-off between work and leisure). Similarly, borrowing or money creation would cause costs to be incurred elsewhere. In short, the payment of an additional £1 subsidy to the firm would impose upon the rest of the economy a cost that is in excess of £1.

The simplest way to incorporate distributional considerations is to write the government's objective as $W = S + \alpha\pi$, where $0 < \alpha < 1$. The cost of public funds can be represented by stating the objective as $W = S + \alpha\pi - \lambda T$, where $\lambda > 0$, T is the transfer paid to the firm, and λT captures the cost of the extra distortions created elsewhere in the economy. Although these versions of a government's objective function have the virtue of simplicity, it must be remembered that they are very crude when viewed in the light of the complex general equilibrium effects that should ideally be taken into account. The shortcomings of the partial equilibrium approach are well known, but it does at least provide a useful starting point from which the analysis can proceed.

Given a welfare-maximizing government, and assuming for the moment that monitoring of management is equally effective under both types of ownership, it is immediately obvious that public ownership has some potential advantages over the private alternative. In particular, it provides government with additional policy instruments to correct any deviations between social and private returns that arise from failures in goods and factor markets. To give just one example, profit-maximizing monopolists may engage in a variety of business practices that run counter to the public interest, and, while it may be feasible to limit such behavior via the provisions of competition or regulatory policies, the complexities of this type of exercise in conditions of asymmetric information may render public ownership the preferred framework in which to tackle the problems.

The market failure argument can also be applied to the market for corporate control: government monitoring does not encounter the public good problems associated with dispersed shareholdings and avoids the transactions costs of share purchases that are incurred by takeover raiders seeking to gain control of a firm. In contrast with a shareholder who owns only a small fraction of the outstanding shares, government departments can directly intervene in managerial decision making or can set appropriate incentive structures for the managers of publicly owned firms. Thus, for example, government can, *in principle*, provide profit-related bonuses and/or fire personnel when performance is poor.

The loss of some instruments of control (e.g. takeover and bankruptcy threats) that results from public ownership does not necessarily imply, therefore, that monitoring is thereby made less effective. For privately owned firms, Williamson (1975) has argued that hierarchical arrangements can, in appropriate circumstances, produce more efficient monitoring than capital markets. Indeed, it is difficult to understand why firms of any size should exist at all if hierarchical solutions to the control problem were not more efficient than market solutions in a wide range of economic conditions.

Determination of the balance of advantage between hierarchical and market control systems, however, is a complex exercise. One of the major aspects of performance monitoring is the acquisition of relevant information about the firm. Under public ownership this information-gathering role is effectively entrusted to a single body, whereas private ownership typically involves the participation of many individuals and institutions that are frequently specialists in the given task. While there may be scale economies in the acquisition of information, it is also likely that competition among independent monitors will lead to the discovery of a greater volume of relevant information. The possibility remains, therefore, that, even from the idealized perspective of public interest theories of governmental policy, private monitoring may provide the more effective method of control.

2.3.2 Government Incentives

The assumption that the public interest can be represented by a well-defined function which governments seek to maximize is clearly rather heroic. In one sense it can be regarded as the obvious counterpart of the assumption that privately owned firms are profit maximizers, since the latter is based upon the notions that shareholders' interests are well defined and that managers act in the best interests of their shareholders.

Nevertheless, just as in the case of private ownership, an examination of the relevant principal–agent relationships is required to assess whether or not the assumption is likely to provide a sound basis for analysis of the behavior of publicly owned enterprises.

The position is complicated by the fact that two distinct groups of public officials are involved in monitoring activities: politicians and civil servants. The full monitoring hierarchy is therefore made up of the general public, its elected political representatives, nonelected civil servants, and the managers of the publicly owned firms. Hence, it is necessary to analyze a number of separate principal–agent problems.

Consider first the relationships between the general public and its elected representatives. As in the case of managers, it is unlikely that preferences of politicians can accurately be captured by a simple and general objective function. The variables upon which utility might be assumed to depend are numerous and include factors such as monetary rewards, effort levels, and power. One feature of the problem does stand out, however, and that is the relative insecurity of tenure enjoyed by politicians: the period spent by one individual as head of a department responsible for the control of a particular public enterprise is frequently rather brief, and may be ended by electoral failure or by promotion or demotion. Since the politicians of a given party have a common interest in electoral success, it is likely that promotion and demotion within the period of office of a given administration will in turn depend heavily upon the individual's contribution to the electoral prospects of his own party. If it is assumed (a) that the utility of politicians is much higher in office than out of office and (b) that the effects on utility of changes in other variables are substantially smaller in magnitude, this suggests that a useful starting point for the analysis of political behavior is the hypothesis that decisions are taken with a view to maximizing the probability of electoral success.

Given this hypothesis, it might still be maintained that, with respect to the behavior of publicly owned firms, politicians will seek to achieve economic efficiency. For, if resources were not allocated in an efficient manner, there would be scope for improving the welfare of some sections of the public without making others worse off, which should have a positive, or at least nonnegative, effect on the electoral prospects of the political party in power.

The argument does depend, however, upon voters being well informed about both the decisions made on their behalf and the eventual consequences of those decisions, and in practice there will be very considerable informational asymmetries between politicians and voters. Consider, for example, the position of a typical member of the public. He or she will have an opportunity to vote once every four or five years and will face an almost zero probability of influencing the outcome of the election. Further, the election will be concerned with a wide range of issues, not just with the question of the stewardship of any one publicly owned firm. In these circumstances, the average voter has very little incentive to acquire costly information about the performance of elected representatives in monitoring particular firms.

Furthermore, the benefits and costs of political decisions are often not evenly spread throughout the population. Those groups that are substantially affected by monitoring activities (the workers in a publicly owned firm, for example) will therefore have greater incentives to acquire information than the average voter, with the result that informational asymmetries between different groups of voters will also emerge.

The latter asymmetries imply that politicians responsible for the monitoring of public industries may no longer derive electoral benefits from improvements in economic efficiency. To illustrate, suppose that improvements in the internal efficiency of an enterprise are possible but that, in the absence of compensatory transfer payments, they would lead to a·fall in the welfare of workers in the industry. Political action to encourage managers to reduce unit costs would be observed by workers who suffer materially as a consequence, but the benefits from lower taxes and/or lower prices, if widely spread throughout the population, might not be visible to the recipients. On the other hand, if workers in the industry *were* compensated for their losses, this would draw the attention of taxpayers to the magnitude of the benefits from efficiency improvements that they (the taxpayers) would be required to forego so that workers can continue to enjoy the fruits of the earlier inefficiency. Thus, whether or not compensation is actually paid, informational asymmetries indicate that an efficiency improvement could sometimes lead to a worsening of electoral prospects. In a similar vein, there could be electoral benefits in setting politically sensitive prices (e.g. domestic telephone rates, electricity and gas prices) at levels below marginal cost, since the direct positive impact on consumers is more visible than the indirect negative effects arising from the accompanying changes in fiscal policy.

To summarize, in addition to suggesting that consumers' and producers' surpluses will be accorded differential weights in government objectives, the asymmetric information arguments imply that payoffs to workers in publicly owned firms will also be a factor that affects the utility of elected officials. Thus, an appropriate specification of the *political* objective function might be

$$GW = S + \alpha\pi - \beta x - \lambda T$$

where x is some measure of the effort applied to cost reduction in the industry. The negative weight attached to x in this equation captures the electoral payoffs from easing the pressures on the wage rates and effort levels of workers in the industry.

In the context of public ownership in Britain there is one further point about the role of politicians in the monitoring hierarchy that is worth making at this stage. Until recently, the option of linking managerial rewards to performance in relation to underlying political objectives has been eschewed. This may have been due in part to the difficulties of measuring some of the components of the underlying objective function (consumers' surplus and workers' rents, for example) but also probably reflects an unwillingness explicitly to reveal those objectives. Whatever the cause, the result has been that control of public enterprises has frequently involved political intervention in the detail of the managerial decision process itself, rather than the "arm's length" relationship between departments and managers that was envisioned when many of the enterprises were first nationalized (see chapter 5). The consequent confusion of roles is therefore an additional source of potential inefficiencies in the control of nationalized industries.

Turning to the civil servants who, in support of their ministers, undertake much of the detailed monitoring work, it can be expected that insecurity of tenure will play a less central role in explaining behavior than in the case of elected politicians. The two most commonly cited variables that are likely to affect utility in this case are the size of the relevant government department or subdepartment and the rents accruing to the officials (see Niskanen, 1971). Thus, if y is a variable measuring the output of the department, z is the actual unit cost level (assumed to be a decision variable), and c^* is the efficient unit cost level, the utility of officials might be assumed to be given by a function $U[y, (z - c^*)y]$ which has positive first-partial derivatives. An economic model of bureaucratic behavior could then be constructed by assuming that this function is maximized subject to a fixed budget constraint of the form $yz = B$.

Suppose, for example, that $U(.) = y^2(z - c^*)$. In that case it can easily be shown that equilibrium activity and unit cost levels will be equal to $B/2c^*$ and $2c^*$ respectively. The activity of the department is therefore an increasing linear function of the budget, while unit costs are always equal to twice their optimal level. Substituting back into the utility function we find that maximized utility is equal to $B/4c^*$, so that, as is to be expected in general, the payoffs to officials are an increasing function of their departmental budget. (Some models of bureaucratic behavior, which are more concerned with the process of budget determination than with output/efficiency choices, simply assume that officials aim to maximize an indirect utility function $U(B)$.)

The activities of civil servants are, of course, monitored by the politicians who are in charge of their departments. As the above example shows, however, if the size of budget is the only instrument of control, the resulting outcomes may be far from satisfactory: unit costs in the model are twice their optimal levels. More direct monitoring of bureaucratic activity will therefore be required if effective performance is to be achieved, but there are a number of reasons for believing that the results will not be entirely satisfactory. First, there is the problem of asymmetric information between civil servants and departmental ministers which, in countries such as the U.K., is exacerbated by the relatively brief periods of tenure of particular ministerial offices by given politicians. Lacking good information about departmental performance, and in particular lacking suitable benchmarks against which such performance can be evaluated, ministers may find it extremely difficult to improve efficiency. Second, the incentives for ministers to search for performance improvements are generally fairly weak since the resulting payoffs are unlikely to have much of an impact on electoral prospects. Third, the factors that increase the welfare of civil servants are likely, other things being equal, to have positive effects on ministerial welfare: ministers can also be assumed to favor increases in the size of their departments and to derive some benefits from higher rents to the civil servants who surround them. Indeed, U.K. departmental ministers are frequently notorious for the tenacity with which they seek to increase or defend their own budgets.

Although it can be expected that a given level of bureaucratic activity will be conducted at greater than minimum unit cost, it is not clear whether the level of activity itself is likely to be suboptimally high or low in relation to either political or social objectives. The key factor is the size of the budget: whichever of the two objectives is used as the benchmark, the higher the budget expenditure the more likely it is that the departmental activity level will be excessive, as can be seen from figure 2.2.

In the diagram, the line MB shows the marginal benefit of departmental activity, and it is assumed that the budget is set at a level where the total benefit of the activity is equal to its total budgetary cost (i.e. that

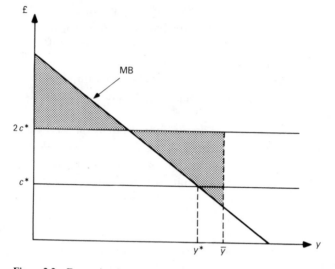

Figure 2.2 Determination of bureaucratic activity level

bureaucratic activity absorbs all the potential surplus that is available). The equilibrium activity level is therefore $\bar{y}$, which is determined by the condition that the two shaded triangles are equal in area. The optimal activity level, given by the condition that marginal benefits are equal to (efficient) marginal costs, is y^*, which is less than $\bar{y}$. Equilibrium output $\bar{y}$, however, is directly proportional to the size of the budget so that, if the latter were reduced, it could easily turn out to be the case that bureaucratic activity is suboptimally low ($\bar{y} < y^*$).

To conclude, judged in terms of public interest criteria, we have identified four potential sources of suboptimality in the framework of control for publicly owned industries: displacement of social objectives by political objectives; a preference for direct political intervention in managerial decisions over an "arm's length" relationship that would restrict government departments to the task of setting appropriate managerial incentive structures; internal inefficiencies in bureaucracies; and inefficient levels of bureaucratic activity. The implications of these factors for the performance of publicly owned firms will vary with the precise institutional details of differing frameworks of control, and we will have more to say on this issue in chapter 5. However, as a matter of general principle, it can safely be concluded that incentive structures for public enterprises will tend to exhibit significant imperfections at each level of the monitoring hierarchy and, in particular, that public interest theories of political decisions are unlikely to provide an adequate conceptual basis for the analysis of behavior in nationalized sectors of the economy.

2.4*   Ownership and Economic Efficiency: A Benchmark Model

As noted in the introduction to this chapter, it is possible to argue that the privatization of a firm that enjoys substantial market power will tend to improve internal efficiency, but at the risk of worsening allocative efficiency unless profit-seeking behavior is held in check by an appropriate framework of competition and regulation. The purpose of this section, therefore, is to examine this possible trade-off between internal and allocative efficiency in the context of a very simple model in which a monopoly firm is privatized. The assumptions underlying the analysis are intended to capture (albeit in a highly stylized way) a number of the features of private and public ownership that have been discussed in sections 2.2 and 2.3. A more extensive treatment of the issue has been provided in a recent paper by Bös and Peters (1986).

Consider therefore the situation of a private monopolist supplying a homogeneous good, and suppose that, by virtue of the principal–agent problems outlined in section 2.2, managerial incentives to engage in cost-reducing activity are imperfect. That is to say, the manager is rewarded only partially for the benefit that the owners receive from cost reduction. To reflect this assumption it is postulated that the manager maximizes

$$A(q,x) = \pi(q,x) - (a-1)x$$
$$= [p - c(x)]q - ax,$$

where q is the output level, x is expenditure on cost-reducing activities, p is price, $c(x)$ is unit cost, and a measures the cost of effort to the private manager relative to the benefit to him of greater profit. If $a = 1$ he would have the "right" incentives for effort (i.e. he would be a profit maximizer), but in general we shall assume imperfect incentives, in which case $a > 1$.

Under public ownership the manager of the firm is assumed to maximize

$$B(q,x) = S(q,x) + \pi(q,x) - (b-1)x$$
$$= V(q) - cq - bx,$$

where $V(q)$ is consumer utility from output q. For simplicity, in this specification consumers' surplus and producers' surplus have been assumed to have equal weights in the political objective function, and the resource costs of any transfers to or from the firm have been assumed to be zero. The parameter b measures the cost of effort to the public manager relative to the benefit to him of greater social welfare (= $S + \pi$). Imperfections in the public monitoring system, including any weight given to the rents of workers in political objective functions, are reflected in the assumption that $b > 1$ (workers' rents can be taken to be negatively related to managerial effort). If public and private monitoring systems were equally effective, we would have $a = b$, but if incentives are keener under private ownership, as many would contend, then we have $a < b$.

In summary, the effects of privatization in this simplified setting are to change the (ultimate) principal's objective from welfare maximization to profit maximization and to alter monitoring and incentive arrangements (as represented by the change from b to a in the managerial objective function). The resulting trade-off is clear. Public managers choose the socially optimal level of output for a given cost level, whereas private managers do not, since they seek monopoly profits. Thus allocative efficiency under public ownership is better than that under (unregulated) private ownership. However, if $a < b$, then, for given output, private managers achieve greater internal efficiency than public managers. The overall balance of advantage will therefore depend upon the relative magnitudes of these two effects.

In what follows we denote outcomes under private ownership by a circumflex and those under public ownership by an asterisk. When public monitoring arrangements are no less efficient than private mechanisms we have the following result:

if $a \geqslant b$, then $q^* > \hat{q}$

$$p^* < \hat{p}$$
$$x^* > \hat{x}$$
$$c^* < \hat{c}$$
$$W^* > \hat{W}. \tag{2.4}$$

That is, public ownership is superior in terms of both internal and allocative efficiency. The (straightforward) proof of the proposition is omitted, but the intuition is as follows. Public managers produce more output and set a lower price than private managers with similar cost levels because they set price equal to marginal cost rather than marginal revenue equal to marginal cost. Since they produce more, public managers also have a greater incentive to reduce costs because the resulting savings are enjoyed across a larger volume of output. Therefore public managers both produce more *and* make more cost-reducing effort, and social welfare is unambiguously higher.

It follows from considerations of continuity that public ownership is also superior when $a < b$ in a neighborhood of b. Hence, a necessary condition for the superiority of private ownership is that a should be distinctly less than b. In other words, private incentive systems must be significantly better.

Matters can be taken a little further by postulating isoelastic functional forms for $p(q)$ and $c(x)$:

$$p = \sigma q^{-\varepsilon}, \quad \sigma, \varepsilon > 0;$$
$$c = \beta x^{-\alpha}, \quad \beta, \alpha > 0.$$

Thus, ε is the inverse elasticity of demand and α is the elasticity of unit cost with respect to the relevant expenditures. Under the given demand conditions $V(q)$, which is the integral of the inverse demand curve from 0 to q, is $\sigma q^{1-\varepsilon}/(1 - \varepsilon)$, and is therefore equal to the revenue of the firm multiplied by $1/(1 - \varepsilon)$. We require $1 > \varepsilon$ for this to be well defined, in which case the effect of the change in objectives is equivalent to a proportionate outward shift in the firm's demand curve.

The resulting maximization problems are now fairly straightforward. For example, in the private ownership case the first-order conditions yield

$$\sigma(1 - \varepsilon)\hat{q}^{-\varepsilon} - \beta \hat{x}^{-\alpha} = 0$$
$$\alpha\beta\hat{x}^{-\alpha-1} - a = 0.$$

For the publicly owned firm, the output term in the first equation becomes $\sigma q^{-\varepsilon}$ and b replaces a in the second equation; otherwise the expressions are similar. It can be shown that the second-order conditions are satisfied in both cases if, as we will assume, $\varepsilon > \alpha/(1 + \alpha)$.

Solving the two models and comparing the equilibria, we find that

$$\hat{q} \gtreqless q^* \text{ according as } (1 - \varepsilon)^{(1 + \alpha)/\alpha} \gtreqless a/b. \tag{2.5}$$

This shows how outputs (and hence prices) under the two regimes depend upon the demand elasticity and the sensitivity of cost to effort, as well as the relative effectiveness of the monitoring schemes. As demand becomes more elastic (i.e. ε becomes smaller), the monopoly mark-up of the private firm is reduced, quantity increases, and price becomes lower. This enhances the incentive for cost reduction, and it may be the case that costs are reduced so much that, even with the monopoly mark-up, the price is lower under private ownership. Condition (2.5) also brings out the importance of α, which measures the scope for cost reduction. If α is small enough, public ownership certainly implies lower prices.

With respect to the comparison between cost-reducing activities we have that

$\hat{x} \gtrless x^*$ according as $(1 - \varepsilon)^{1/\varepsilon} \gtrless a/b.$ (2.6)

Again, the elasticity of demand is found to be of central importance. For any a and b, if the elasticity is sufficiently low (ε close to 1), then $x^* > \hat{x}$ and costs are lower under public ownership. The limit of $(1 - \varepsilon)^{1/\varepsilon}$ as ε approaches zero is $1/e = 0.3679$, and therefore a must be *much* smaller than b for it to be true that $\hat{x} > x^*$, no matter how elastic demand may be.

Conditions (2.5) and (2.6), together with the assumptions that $a < b$ and $\varepsilon > \alpha/(1 + \alpha)$, imply that

$\hat{q} \geqslant q^*$ implies $\hat{x} > x^*.$

This is entirely natural. If the private firm produces more than the public firm, then it achieves more cost reduction because the private incentive system is keener. Conversely, if $x^* > \hat{x}$, then $q^* > \hat{q}$: if the public producer has lower costs, then it produces more than the private firm.

A detailed comparison of aggregate welfare under public and private ownership involves messy expressions, but some relatively simple results can be derived from the above propositions. For example, if $a/b \geqslant (1 - \varepsilon)^{1/\varepsilon}$, condition (2.6) implies that $x^* > \hat{x}$. Hence, $q^* > \hat{q}$, and it follows that $W^* > \hat{W}$. Thus, $a/b \geqslant (1 - \varepsilon)^{1/\varepsilon}$ is a sufficient condition for social welfare to be higher under public ownership. By similar reasoning it can also be shown that $a/b \leqslant (1 - \varepsilon)^{(1 + \alpha)/\alpha}$ is a sufficient condition for social welfare to be higher under private ownership.

The cases involving intermediate values of a/b lead to much more cumbersome expressions, but the above analysis of sufficient conditions at least indicates some of the principal features of the problem, and in particular the importance of α and ε, the fundamental parameters of technology and demand. Thus, for example, if ε is interpreted as a measure of the degree of competition faced by the firm and if α is interpreted as a measure of the the rate of technical progress in the industry, the analysis tends to support the notion that the merits of privatization are greater in technologically progressive industries where competition is effective. However, given both the static nature of the analysis and the assumption of only one firm, it would be wrong to stretch the interpretations too far.

It should also be stressed that only unregulated private enterprise has been considered. The incorporation of regulation would introduce a new policy instrument into the model, involving a further trade-off between internal and allocative efficiency (see chapter 4), and can generally be expected to lead to results that are more favorable to private ownership than are those derived above. Nevertheless, the possibility of regulation is unlikely to affect the central implication of the analysis, which is that privatization is likely to improve social welfare only if it provides significantly keener managerial incentives than does the control system for public enterprise.

2.5   Performance under Public and Private Ownership: The Evidence

Given that the relative performance of publicly and privately owned firms in respect of allocative and internal efficiency will depend upon a range of factors that includes the effectiveness of the respective monitoring systems, the degree of competition in the market, regulatory policy, and the technological progressiveness of the industry, evaluation of the welfare implications of privatization necessarily depends upon empirical assessment of the role and significance of each of these various factors. Much of the second part of the book will be devoted to this task for cases that have arisen in the context of the U.K. privatization program. At this stage, however, it will be useful to take a preliminary look at the findings of the more general literature that has been concerned with empirical comparisons of the performance of public and private firms.

Unfortunately, despite the large number of studies that have been conducted, the results of this empirical literature are less informative than might be anticipated. In the first place, many studies focus almost exclusively upon the ownership variable and fail to take proper account of the effects on performance of differences in market structure, regulation, and other relevant economic factors. In part, this is simply a consequence of data problems: the limited number of observations available renders it difficult to conduct complex multifactor analyses. It is also attributable, however, to theoretical failures: even where sufficient data are available, statistical tests have rarely been sophisticated enough to take account of the interacting (nonseparable) effects of ownership, competition, and regulation on incentive structures, and hence on the performance of firms.

Second, in measuring performance there has been a tendency in the empirical literature towards reliance upon variables that are easily observable. Thus, rather than attempting to estimate the sum of producers' and consumers' surpluses, the more usual approach is to examine factors such as profitability, factor productivity, and unit cost levels. As a consequence, in some studies the methodology leads to a bias in favor of private ownership. Given some degree of market power, it might be expected that private firms will tend to be the more profitable, but this in itself has no direct bearing on the question of economic efficiency.

Similarly, a finding that private firms have lower unit costs than their public counterparts does not necessarily imply that their contributions to social welfare are greater; questions relating to allocative efficiency and to the quality of goods or services provided also need to be taken into account.

In the light of this second set of comments it is perhaps surprising that, in surveying the empirical literature up to around 1980, Millward (1982) concluded that there appeared to be no general ground for believing that managerial (i.e. internal) efficiency was lower in public firms. However, a closer examination of the material on which Millward based his article, taken in conjunction with the results of later work, suggests a slightly different conclusion, namely, that privately owned firms tend, on average, to be the more internally efficient when competition in product markets is effective. Thus, subject to the latter condition about competition and provided that other allocative inefficiencies associated with market failures are not substantial, we would argue that the available evidence supports a presumption in favor of private enterprise. However, when market power is significant, and particularly when company behavior is subject to detailed regulation, there is little empirical justification for a general presumption in favor of either type of ownership, and case-by-case evaluation of the various trade-offs is therefore in order.

Investigation of the relative performance of public and private enterprises has been most active in the United States, where the two types of ownership frequently coexist in similar market conditions. The industries that have been most extensively covered include electricity generation and distribution, water, and refuse collection; see Millward (1982), Yarrow (1986), and Boardman and Vining (1987) for bibliographies. With respect to electricity supply, a number of economists (Meyer, 1975; Pescatrice and Trapani, 1980; Fare et al., 1985) have concluded that, after allowing for differences in output mixes and input prices, public sector utilities typically have lower unit costs than privately owned utilities. However, the results are not entirely convincing. As in Europe, public electric utilities have access to cheap capital and, given the capital intensity of the industry, their relative unit costs are highly sensitive to the adjustments made to allow for this factor. Thus, one recent study (Edison Electric Institute, 1985) has argued that earlier papers failed to make adequate allowances for the lower input prices facing public utilities and that, once the appropriate corrections are made, the evidence indicates that ownership has little effect on internal efficiency. Nevertheless, it can safely be concluded that the evidence does not establish the clear-cut superiority of private ownership in respect of cost efficiency.

Analysis of the pricing behavior of public and private electric utilities in the United States also serves as a warning against the presumption that allocative efficiency is necessarily improved by public ownership. Both Peltzman (1971) and De Alessi (1977) found that time-of-day pricing (which, in electricity supply, can be expected to lead to higher allocative efficiency) was more common in private utilities. Tariff structures, however, are heavily influenced by the regulatory environment, and there is evidence suggesting that this is the more important determining factor: jurisdictions in which the quality of regulation is generally regarded as high have been pioneers in the introduction of time-of-day pricing. Moreover, the publicly owned electricity industries in both Britain and France were early proponents of sophisticated peak-load pricing structures.

Work on the U.S. water industry suggests similar conclusions. For example, Crain and Zardkoohi (1978) found that, although regulated private water utilities exhibited over-capitalization (see section 4.2.1), their higher labor productivity implied that, on balance, their unit costs were lower than in public utilities. In contrast, a later paper by Bruggink (1982) found in favor of public enterprise on unit cost criteria. Taken in conjunction with the research on U.S. electric utilities, we are therefore led to the conclusion that, where firms face little product market competition and are extensively regulated, there is no generally decisive evidence in favor of one or other type of ownership.

Research on refuse collection in the United States highlights a different point. Here the findings are much more supportive of the proposition that private firms exhibit greater internal efficiency (see Kitchen, 1976; Savas, 1977; Stevens, 1978), but the more important factor in determining performance may be competition rather than the type of ownership *per se*. The incidence of private firms will tend to be correlated with the existence of competitive tendering for contracts, and the effects of the latter may incorrectly be ascribed to the ownership variable. Thus Savas (1977) found that the gap between the unit cost levels of public and private firms was closed by competitive tendering arrangements.

This last result is not altogether surprising. Competition acts as a selection mechanism that weeds out the less efficient firms: enterprises that survive are those that have passed the selection test and, provided that the competition between the different types of enterprises is fair (which is, of course, a major proviso), substantial differences in the internal efficiencies of the survivors are not to be expected. Confirming evidence of the importance of competition can be found in the study by Caves and Christensen (1980) of the relative performance of the two Canadian railroad companies, one privately owned and the other publicly owned. On the basis of their findings, Caves and Christensen argue that "public ownership is not inherently less efficient than private ownership," and that the "oft noted inefficiency of government enterprises stems from the isolation from *effective* competition rather than public ownership *per se.*" It should be stressed, however, that in this context effective competition presupposes equitable treatment of publicly and privately owned enterprises and that in practice this condition will not always be satisfied. Thus, the tendency of governments to subsidize public firms may account for the rather different findings of Boardman and Vining (1987), who conclude that private companies exhibit significantly better performance in competitive environments.

It would also be wrong to interpret the results of Savas and of Caves and Christensen as implying that, even when markets are effectively competitive in the full sense, there is absolutely *no* link between internal efficiency performance and the type of ownership of the firm (i.e. that ownership does not matter). Supposing, for example, that private firms generally *are* the more efficient, it is to be expected that this will show up in the frequency with which they win contracts. That is, although the unit costs of surviving public firms may, on average, be as low as the costs of their private rivals, we would expect to see far fewer of them in competitive markets. Since this is exactly what we do observe, the evidence, although not conclusive, is at least consistent with a general presumption in favor of private ownership in these conditions. Moreover, in practice, it is often difficult to envision the practical development of greater competition in product markets, and of more effective franchise bidding systems, without allowing actual or potential entry of private firms. Ownership and competition may conceptually be distinct, but that is not to say that changes in the pattern of ownership have no implications for competitive behavior. Thus, in industries where public ownership predominates and where one of the goals of public policy is to promote greater competition (see chapter 3), the available evidence offers some support for certain types of privatization policies.

Evaluation of the relative performance of private and public firms in the U.K. has been much less systematic than in the United States. The existence of state monopolies in utility industries such as electricity, gas, telecommunications, and water has meant that there are no immediate domestic benchmarks against which the performance of the public enterprises can be assessed. As a consequence, most empirical work has focused upon more competitive market structures where the two types of ownership have coexisted.

A good example of this type of study is the paper by Pryke (1982), which compares economic performance in three industries: airlines, ferries and hovercraft, and the sale of gas and electricity appliances. Pryke analyzed a range of productivity, profitability, and output variables, and concluded that, in each case, the private firms tended both to be more profitable and to exhibit greater internal efficiency than their public sector rivals. These findings have been reinforced by later work on airlines (Forsyth *et al.*, 1986) and ferries (Bruce, 1986). Similarly, Rowley and Yarrow (1981) found a slight deterioration in the productivity performance of the British steel industry following nationalization in 1966, coupled with more significant declines in market share and in the rate of diffusion of new steelmaking processes. With respect to refuse collection, a U.K. study by Hartley and Huby (1985) supports the earlier conclusions of U.S. research: the introduction of competitive tendering appears to have promoted reductions in unit costs.

However, each of the U.K. papers is open to objections of one form or another. For example, in the Pryke studies it is not clear that like is always compared with like: in respect of the sales of electricity and gas appliances, the public firms are compared with the more efficient of the private companies operating in the market, thereby biasing the results against the former. In the steel industry paper, the sample period ended in 1975, before the dramatic improvements in productivity that occurred (under public ownership) from the late 1970s onwards (see section 5.7.3). Finally, an Audit Commission study (1984) of refuse collection costs discovered wide variations in public sector performance, with the better public enterprises exhibiting lower unit costs than many of the private firms in the sample.

Nevertheless, U.K. research does provide additional backing for our earlier conclusion that, where competition is effective, the available evidence suggests that private enterprise is generally to be preferred on both internal efficiency grounds and, subject to the qualification that other substantive market failures are absent, social welfare grounds. To repeat, this does not mean that, in competitive markets, we believe that public enterprise is always and everywhere the less efficient type of ownership. Relatively efficient public enterprises can and do survive, but, on average, we would expect the frequency of this occurrence to be lower than for private enterprises.

2.6   Concluding Remarks

In this chapter we have examined some of the implications of different types of ownership for managerial incentive structures and enterprise performance. Broadly speaking, it can be concluded that "ownership matters" in the sense that changes in the structure of property rights are likely to have significant effects upon firm behavior. At this level of abstraction, however, it is hard to be very precise about the detailed implications of changes in the ownership of a firm, since the latter depend upon factors such as the relevant institutional environment, including the framework of regulation for firms with market power, and the market structures of the industries in which the firms operate. The main message, therefore, is simply that managerial incentive structures are determined via a complex set of interactions among factors that include the type of ownership, the degree of product market competition, and the effectiveness of regulation.

Given the incentive problems associated with the control of publicly owned firms, it is likely that public monitoring systems are generally less effective than their private counterparts. It has been shown, however, that this in itself does not imply that, judged against social welfare criteria, the performance of public industry will be inferior, since allowance also has to be made for the effects of the shift in the objective functions of principals. Where product markets are competitive, it is more likely that the benefits of private monitoring systems (e.g. improved internal efficiency) will exceed any accompanying detriments (e.g. worsened allocative efficiency), a view that is generally confirmed by empirical studies of the comparative performance of public and private firms. In the absence of vigorous product market competition, however, the balance of advantage is less clear cut and much will depend upon the effectiveness of regulatory policy.

3.1 Introduction

The next step in our analysis of the economic effects of privatization is to consider how competitive and regulatory constraints influence company behavior under public and private ownership. In the previous chapter we examined the discipline on managers of private firms that is sometimes provided by competition in the market for corporate control, and now we turn to the role of competitive forces in product markets. Regulatory constraints will be the subject of chapter 4.

It is important at the outset to underline the obvious fact that *privatization*—the transfer of ownership—and *liberalization*—the opening up of competitive forces—are logically quite distinct concepts. Public ownership does not imply state monopoly, and private ownership does not entail competition. Nevertheless privatization and liberalization are frequently intertwined in policy debate and public perception. The political presentation of privatization policies has emphasized the stimulation of competitive forces, and the privatization of companies such as British Telecom (BT) was indeed accompanied by some important liberalizing measures. Although there is no logical connection between public enterprise and the absence of competition, there are several practical reasons why the two have often gone together.

First, public ownership is one of the main solutions to the problems of market failure that arise in industries where competition is impossible or undesirable, or where major externalities exist. Much of the postwar nationalization in Britain was motivated, at least in part, by the belief that competitive solutions were unsuitable in the markets in question, and there were particular concerns about natural monopoly in industries such as gas, electricity, railways, water, and telecommunications. Although many of these concerns were—and still are—well founded, the danger exists that competitive forces become too neglected, and are assumed to be irrelevant, when perhaps they have a useful role to play. Conditions of demand and technology may change so that yesterday's natural monopoly no longer persists, and the difficulties of efficiently controlling public enterprise may turn out to be such that competitive forces have significant advantages despite being imperfect.

A second possible link between public enterprise and monopoly has to do with the interests and influence of public sector managers and related civil servants. In the spirit of the "capture" theories of American-style regulation (see section 4.5 below) some would contend that managers of Britain's nationalized industries have successfully resisted the advent of effective competition by their influence on political decision making, institutional inertia, and the support of employees. In contrast, consumers and potential competitors have a relatively ineffective voice. On this view privatization is connected with liberalization insofar as it breaks the anticompetitive institutional blockage. However, as we shall see later, it can equally be argued that managers of companies being privatized—such as BT and British Gas—have been quite successful in limiting the competitive threats that they subsequently face in the private sector.

In any event, it is important to try to understand the costs and benefits of attempted competitive solutions to the market failure problems in the industries in the privatization program, and the aim of this chapter is to present some of the pertinent theories of competition. The recent economics literature on industrial organization has made several important (and sometimes controversial) contributions, and we shall emphasize three themes in particular.

First, and most important, is the role of *potential competition*, which we discuss in section 3.3. The main question here is whether liberalizing conditions of entry into an industry creates entry threats of sufficient power to impel the incumbent firm or firms to behave efficiently and in accordance with consumer preferences. In their theory of contestable markets, Baumol and others examine free entry in its purest form—in which case the answer is in the affirmative. But the economics of strategic entry deterrence and predatory behavior shows that in many circumstances incumbent firms may be able to thwart potential competitors by anticompetitive tactics. The economics of potential competition is therefore highly pertinent to the problems of regulating privatized industries. Do the forces of potential competition operate with such effectiveness as to remove or diminish the need for regulation? Or do policies of liberalization actually require public intervention to ensure that potential competition is effective?

Our second theme is competition as an *incentive mechanism*, which we consider in section 3.4. The problems of monitoring and rewarding managers' effort and efficiency arise under both public and private ownership. The asymmetry of information that exists between the managers of the firm and the government ministry or regulatory agency is at the heart of the matter. The competitive process and the results it delivers (especially in the form of comparisons between rivals' performances) can reveal information in a most economical fashion, and it therefore acts as a natural and useful incentive mechanism. Thus the competitive process provides a spur to *internal* efficiency and the elimination of X-inefficiency, as well as serving as a mechanism conducive to *allocative* efficiency.

Thirdly, in section 3.5, we look specifically at competition issues that arise in connection with *networks* and *vertical relationships*. These have been important in several of the industries where privatization has occurred, of which telecommunications is a good example. If a subscriber in town A wishes to call another in town B, he must use three elements of the telecommunication system—the local networks in A and B, and the long-distance link between the towns. In effect he demands a composite commodity consisting of local and long-distance links. The local networks are monopolized by BT, the dominant firm, but there is scope for competition in the supply of the long-distance link, which BT also offers. Unless constrained from doing so, BT will thwart competition in the long-distance market. This is the crucial *interconnection* issue. It has parallels in the gas and electricity industries, where rival producers rely on the transmission networks of the dominant firms. The economics of vertical relationships therefore bears on U.K. regulatory policy and the wider question of whether vertical separation of a privatized company is appropriate.

Before proceeding to these questions, however, we first outline some relevant welfare economics of actual and potential competition, with particular reference to industries with economies of scale.

3.2   Some Relationships between Competition and Welfare

There is of course a vast literature on the welfare properties of industrial competition, and this is not the place to attempt a survey. Instead we shall briefly discuss two issues of particular relevance to the privatization program. The first is the trade-off between allocative efficiency and scale economies, and the related question of whether free entry can lead to undesirable losses of cost efficiency. The second issue concerns the role of public enterprises in markets where they compete with private firms. We consider how public firms should behave, and what objectives their managers should be given, in those circumstances.

3.2.1   The Trade-Off between Allocative Efficiency and Scale Economies

An argument often advanced for restricting entry into industries with economies of scale is that entry leads to undesirable duplication of fixed costs, and that it is better to have a few (or even just one) large firms than to have more smaller ones. However, the problem is that market power is greater when there are fewer firms, and monopolistic behavior worsens allocative efficiency. The trade-off between allocative efficiency and scale economies is central to many problems in competition policy (e.g. mergers), and precisely the same question—albeit in a much more complex form—arises for example in relation to the licensing of network operators to compete with BT. Two questions can be asked about the trade-off. First, what number of firms maximizes social welfare? Second, does free entry lead to the existence of too few or too many firms at the market equilibrium?

As to the ideal number of firms, the *first-best* outcome when there are economies of scale is to have a single firm operating where price equals marginal cost. This is optimal because the cost of an extra unit of output is equal to consumers' willingness to pay for it. The first-best outcome attains allocative efficiency *and* productive efficiency (no duplication of fixed costs).

However, there are two difficulties with this outcome. First, the firm makes a loss. If lump-sum transfers were feasible, the government could costlessly make good the loss, but otherwise it could not. If such transfers were costly enough, the problem would be to maximize W subject to $\pi \geqslant 0$. The solution to this *second-best* problem would be to have a single firm producing where price equals average cost. The second difficulty is that the firm is unlikely to want to operate where price is equal to marginal (or average) cost, especially if it is privately owned. Regulatory constraint might somehow compel that outcome, but our present concern is with competitive forces unfettered by regulation.

The following simple model illuminates the trade-off between scale economies and allocative efficiency. (For more detailed treatments the reader is referred to Williamson (1968), von Weizsäcker (1980), Perry (1984), Mankiw and Whinston (1986), and Suzumura and Kiyono (1987).)

Suppose that we have an industry consisting of n similar firms each supplying the same homogeneous good. Let $V(Q)$ be consumer utility and $P(Q) = V'(Q)$ be the inverse demand curve for the good, where Q is the sum of the firms' outputs.

Let $q(n)$ be output per firm when there are n firms in the industry, and let $C(q)$ be the cost function of each firm. We shall suppose for simplicity that social welfare is equal to the sum of consumer and producer surplus. As a function of the number of firms, social welfare can then be written as

$$W(n) = V[nq(n)] - nC[q(n)].$$ (3.1)

We must now specify how the market equilibrium depends on the number of firms, i.e. how q depends on n. For example, we could assume that there is Cournot behavior at market equilibrium. That is to say, firms operate at an equilibrium in which none has any incentive to alter its behavior given the output decisions of its rivals. But rather than specifying any particular oligopoly solution concept, we shall simply assume that $dq/dn < 0$, i.e. output per firm falls as the number of firms increases. This assumption holds true in a wide range of circumstances, including Cournot behavior in normal cost and demand conditions. In the model the assumption implies that the market equilibrium number of firms will not be too small, and tends to be excessive (see Mankiw and Whinston, 1986; Suzumura and Kiyono, 1987). The reason is as follows.

If we were allowed to treat the number of firms n as a continuous variable, then the socially optimal number of firms n^*, given market equilibrium behavior, would be such that

$$\frac{dW(n^*)}{dn} = 0.$$ (3.2)

In fact the number of firms must be an integer, and there is little chance that n^* is an integer. But if $W(n)$ is single-peaked (when n is regarded as a continuous variable) then the optimal number of firms is one of the two integers closest to n^* as defined by (3.2).

The market equilibrium number of firms when there is free entry is given by the condition that further entry would be unprofitable. Let $\pi(n)$ be profit per firm as a function of n. If n was a continuous variable, the equilibrium number of firms $\hat{n}$ would be given by

$$\pi(\hat{n}) = 0.$$ (3.3)

If we take the equilibrium number to be one of the integers neighboring $\hat{n}$, we can now compare n^* and $\hat{n}$ to see whether there will be too much or too little entry at the market equilibrium. Differentiating W with respect to n in (3.1) we obtain

$$\frac{dW}{dn} = \left(q + n\frac{dq}{dn}\right)V' - C - n\frac{dC}{dq}\frac{dq}{dn}.$$ (3.4)

Recalling that $V' = P$ and rearranging terms we obtain

$$\frac{dW}{dn} = n\left(P - \frac{dC}{dq}\right)\frac{dq}{dn} + (Pq - C). \tag{3.5}$$

The second term on the right-hand side of (3.5) is profit per firm, which is zero at free-entry equilibrium. As regards the first term, imperfect competition implies that $P > dC/dq$ (i.e. price exceeds marginal cost), and the assumption that $dq/dn < 0$ therefore implies that $dW/dn < 0$ at $\hat{n}$. It follows that social welfare (as defined) would be increased at the margin by reducing the number of firms below the free-entry equilibrium level. If n is treated as a continuous variable, the optimal number n^* is less than the equilibrium number $\hat{n}$. Thus there is a tendency for excessive entry in the context of the model.

In other words, if output per firm falls with n, then the entry of a new firm is good for consumers, bad for existing firms, and approximately neutral at equilibrium for the new firm, but the benefit to consumers is outweighed by the detriment to existing firms. The result might be different if social welfare gave more weight to consumer surplus than to producer surplus. For example, if no weight is given to producer interests, all that matters is the sign of dQ/dn, which is the response of industry output to changes in n. Under plausible assumptions this is positive, and there is too little entry at the market equilibrium.

Of course it would be foolish to draw any policy conclusions from preliminary analysis of the kind described above. For one thing, policy measures designed to influence the number of firms in the industry (e.g. licensing of entry) must be considered alongside policies (such as regulation) that are intended to affect firm behavior more directly. Secondly, the *threat* of entry can itself have a major influence on industry conduct—n firms surrounded by unsurmountable entry barriers are likely to behave very differently from n firms facing entry threats from potential competitors. It is partly for this reason that the liberalization of entry conditions has been so central to the debate on privatization in Britain. We will return to the important theme of entry threats and potential competition in section 3.3 below, where we consider a number of nonprice aspects of company behavior, including product differentiation, investment, advertising, and research and development (R&D). Thirdly, there are major informational advantages from having more competitors, and incentives for internal efficiency can be enhanced. These important effects are omitted from analysis above, but we discuss them further in section 3.4 below.

3.2.2   Public Enterprise in Competition

We began this chapter by saying that public ownership and competition are perfectly compatible with each other. Indeed, we believe that it would often be advantageous to confront public enterprises with competitive forces even where privatization is not taking place. Legislation in Britain in 1981–1983 opened up the (legal) possibility of some competition with public enterprises in the telecommunications, gas, and electricity industries, and although privatization has since occurred in two of those three sectors, it did not necessarily have to follow liberalization.

There are several reasons why competitive forces might improve industry performance when public enterprise exists. First, internal efficiency might be enhanced by the disciplining effect of competitive threats upon the managers of public firms. It has been said that the greatest of all monopoly profits is the quiet life, and if that is so, there is a case against public monopoly. This case is all the stronger if mechanisms for regulating public enterprise—whether they are explicit or implicit—have serious weaknesses, as both empirical and theoretical evidence suggests. In particular, competitive forces break the "monopoly of information" about industry conditions that may otherwise exist, and which tends to hamper the effectiveness of the regulatory regime. Note that competition need not be an alternative to regulation—it can instead be a useful supplement to it.

A second advantage of opening up the possibility of competition with a dominant public firm is that it creates opportunities for innovation. Rival firms might have the incentive to introduce new products or processes into parts of the public firm's market which the public firm had little incentive to introduce or perhaps had not even thought of. This in turn acts as a spur to the public firm to be more innovative itself, which takes us back to the point in the previous paragraph.

These points will be amplified when we come to consider entry threats and the role of competition as an incentive mechanism. But first we briefly consider some of the questions addressed in the (relatively small) literature on competition in "mixed markets"—i.e. markets in which private and public firms compete.

The simplest case to study is a homogeneous goods duopoly with a welfare-maximizing public firm and a profit-maximizing private firm. If it is assumed that marginal cost is an increasing function of output, the Nash equilibrium in quantities involves the public firm's operating where its marginal cost equals the market price and the private firm's operating where its marginal revenue equals marginal cost. However, if the public firm is a Stackelberg leader (i.e. has first move), it can obtain a better outcome because it can choose any point on the private firm's reaction function (instead of just the Nash outcome). Welfare is enhanced by the public firm's producing less than its Nash output in order to induce a beneficial expansion in the output of the private firm (given that it has a downward-sloping reaction function).

Beato and Mas-Colell (1984) reverse this move order by giving the public firm the second move. Since the public firm will choose to operate where price equals marginal cost, this is equivalent to the public firm's being committed in advance to a marginal cost (MC) pricing rule. The private firm is then the Stackelberg leader and will optimize given the reaction function (i.e. the MC pricing rule) of its public competitor. Beato and Mas-Colell find that the outcome implied by the MC pricing rule compares favorably with the result obtained when the public firm is the Stackelberg leader. Harris and Wiens (1980) also give second move to the public firm but allow it to commit itself to any strategy in advance. With such powers of commitment, it is best for the public firm to promise to behave in such a way that the competitive price comes about. Then the private firm is induced to act so that price equals marginal cost. However, unlike the MC pricing rule, this commitment by the public firm lacks credibility.

De Fraja and Delbono (1986) consider what objective should be given to the managers of a public firm faced by a number of profit-maximizing competitors. They find that, if the number of firms is large enough, it may be better for the public firm to have profit maximization, rather than welfare maximization, as its objective. Even if there is only one private competitor, Nash equilibrium social welfare is increased if the public firm's managers give some weight to profit in their calculations. The reason is that the Nash equilibrium is then shifted towards the outcome that results when the public firm is the Stackelberg leader (see above).

Finally, Cremer et al. (1987) ask whether social welfare would be improved by changing the ownership—or, more precisely, the objective—of some firms in an industry of n firms producing a homogeneous good under increasing returns to scale. They show in their framework that it is often optimal to nationalize a single firm, but that complete nationalization may be desirable.

The literature on competition in mixed markets is not extensive, although we believe that the topic is important. The approaches reported above do not consider the effects of competition upon incentives for internal efficiency (see section 3.4), but they do show how public enterprise can have a positive role in improving allocative efficiency in imperfectly competitive markets. The results of the analysis are sensitive to assumptions about move order and objectives, but the simple MC pricing rule emerged as an attractive guideline in markets where competitors are few. However, it can be desirable for public enterprises to attach more weight to profits where competition is stronger.

3.3   Potential Competition and Entry Threats

Privatization of firms in competitive markets raises few problems for industrial policy because competition between firms in the market effectively regulates company behavior and provides reasonably good incentives for internal and allocative efficiency. But the mechanism of competition between existing firms cannot be relied upon if the incumbent firm being privatized has a preponderant market share and if it is not being split into units that will subsequently compete with each other. It is then only the entry and growth of new rivals—or at any rate the threat of it—that can provide competitive disciplines for the incumbent firm. If these do not exist, regulation of the incumbent's pricing behavior will be needed to check monopolistic abuse. Regulation in the form of policies to prevent anticompetitive behavior may be needed to make entry threats properly effective.

In this section we examine the theory of contestable markets and recent theories of strategic entry deterrence and predatory behavior. Two of the main questions that we have in mind were stated in the introduction to this chapter. Do the forces of potential competition operate with such effectiveness as to remove or diminish the need for regulation? Or do policies of liberalization actually require regulation to ensure that potential competition is effective?

3.3.1   The Theory of Contestable Markets

In a contestable market the threat of potential competition is at its most potent. The incumbent firm or firms are compelled to meet consumers' wishes with maximum efficiency, for otherwise new entrants will simply take their business away. The theory of contestable markets proposed by Baumol and his colleagues was developed in a series of articles beginning in the late 1970s and was expounded in the book by Baumol et al. (1982) and in Baumol's (1982) presidential address to the American Economic Association. The theory has provoked great academic controversy and has featured prominently in public debate on regulation and antitrust. An evaluation of the theory is essential for an understanding of the role of competitive forces in constraining the behavior of apparently dominant firms, and hence it is at the heart of much debate on privatization policy.

One of the main contributions of contestability theory has been to illuminate the economics of multiproduct industries and to introduce important cost concepts (such as economies of scope and trans-ray convexity). However, we shall begin by focusing on its contribution to the theory of potential competition in the context of an industry supplying a single product. Our plan is first to define what is meant by "contestability," then to infer what properties must hold in a contestable market, and finally to discuss the implications of the theory for practical policy making in the light of the criticisms that have been made of it. More extensive discussions of contestability theory are provided by Baumol and Willig (1986), Brock (1983), Schwartz (1986), Sharkey (1982), Shepherd (1984), and Spence (1983).

A contestable market is one in which existing firms are vulnerable to hit-and-run entry. All firms—actual and potential—have access to the same production methods, and hence their *cost functions are identical*. Moreover, entry involves *no sunk costs*: a firm can enter the market without making irrecoverable expenditures, and so there are no barriers to exit. Therefore

"Even a very transient profit opportunity need not be neglected by a potential entrant, for he can go in, and, before prices change, collect his gains and then depart without cost, should the climate grow hostile." (Baumol, 1982, p. 4.)

The distinction here between sunk costs and fixed costs should be noted. Fixed costs are costs that do not vary with the level of output; they are not always sunk. For example, a firm that leases a photocopier for a short period of time incurs a fixed cost but not sunk costs. It is perfectly possible to have a contestable market with high fixed costs, so long as there are no sunk costs, and indeed a natural monopoly market can in principle be contestable and vulnerable to hit-and-run entry.

If equilibrium exists in a contestable market, the following properties hold.

(i)   Price P equals average cost AC. That is to say, all firms make zero profits. If $P > AC$ there would be an incentive for a new firm to enter the market and displace an incumbent firm by slightly shading its price. If $P < AC$ a firm would do better to leave the market, which can be done cost-lessly in view of the assumption that sunk costs are absent. It follows that $P = AC$ at equilibrium.

(ii)   There is no inefficiency in production. If an existing firm was producing its output at more than minimum cost, rivals would find it profitable to enter the market, take the other firm's business, and produce more efficiently.

(iii)   Price is at least as great as marginal cost. If some firm was operating where $P <$ MC, a new firm could profitably enter the market producing slightly less than the other firm and take that firm's business by shading price infinitesimally. This strategy would be profitable because the marginal revenue lost by reducing output, which is approximately equal to P, is less than the saving of MC.

(iv)   If there are two or more firms at equilibrium in the market, then price is no greater than MC. If one of the existing firms was operating where $P >$ MC, a new firm could come in and produce slightly more than that firm. The entrant's marginal revenue MR ($= P$) would exceed his MC, and so he would make more profit than the firm displaced. The entrant could (and would) also take some of the business of other incumbent firms by an arbitrarily small price reduction. This argument does not go through if initially there is only one firm in the market, because then the only way for a firm to increase sales volume is to lower price. Figure 3.1 shows how $P >$ MC is possible at equilibrium in a market characterized by natural monopoly cost conditions. (Note that (iii) and (iv) together imply that $P =$ MC if there are two or more firms at equilibrium.)

(v)   The number and configuration of firms at equilibrium is such that industry output is produced at minimum cost. Therefore there is productive efficiency at the industry level as well as the level of the firm (see

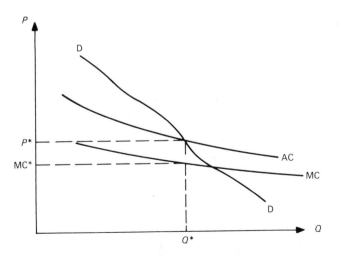

Figure 3.1   Equilibrium with price greater than marginal cost

(ii)). If this property did not hold, a new entrant producing at minimum average cost could profitably enter the industry by taking business from firms producing at higher cost levels. This result about productive efficiency at the industry level implies that market structure is endogenous in a contestable market.

Results (i) through (v) above were stated in the context of a single-product industry in order to show as clearly as possible why they hold. The arguments generalize naturally to multiproduct industries, where (i) through (v) also hold. We shall state two more results about equilibrium in contestable multiproduct industries.

(vi)   There will be no cross-subsidies between products. This follows from the fact that price must be at least as great as marginal cost for all products in the industry. Otherwise a new firm could profitably enter producing slightly less of the product in question than some existing firm. This profit opportunity is ruled out only if cross-subsidy is absent.

(vii)   Under certain assumptions about cost conditions (trans-ray convexity and declining ray average costs), a natural monopolist deters entry by charging Ramsey prices. Ramsey prices maximize welfare subject to a minimum profit constraint. (The basic reason for this result can be outlined as follows. If firm B wants to take the business of firm A, it will seek to maximize its profits subject to the constraint of offering consumers a more attractive deal than firm A. The dual of this constrained optimization problem is to maximize consumer wellbeing subject to a minimum profit constraint. That is essentially the same as the Ramsey optimization problem.)

By now it will be evident that the properties that hold at equilibrium in a contestable market are highly desirable by the yardsticks of traditional welfare economics. There is internal efficiency, because firms—individually and collectively—are compelled by the entry threat to produce at minimum cost, and there is allocative efficiency because $P = \text{MC}$, except possibly in a natural monopoly (in which case pricing is optimal subject to the nonnegative profit constraint).

The theory has been proposed as a competitive benchmark that is in a sense more general than the traditional textbook model of perfect competition. Instead of a huge number of very small firms being the hallmark of competition, it is entry threats that make for competition in a contestable market, even though only one or two firms might exist at equilibrium. Indeed market structure is determined endogenously by the

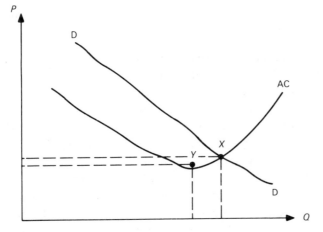

Figure 3.2   An example of nonsustainable natural monopoly

fundamental parameters of technology and demand. It is sunk costs (as opposed to fixed costs) that are of central importance—a point which has implications for policy.

The desirable properties stated above rest on the assumption that equilibrium in a contestable market exists. Unfortunately it need not do so, as the following examples show. Figure 3.2 depicts a natural monopoly industry—cost and demand conditions are such that single-firm production is most efficient. However, the price–output combination X is not an equilibrium, because it is vulnerable to entry by a firm operating at point Y. The entrant can undercut the firm and still make a profit. This is an example of the *nonsustainability* of natural monopoly. A generalization of this example is an industry with textbook U-shaped average cost curves. If P^* is the minimum average cost and if q^* is the associated level of output, equilibrium exists in the contestable market only if demand at price P^*, denoted by $D(P^*)$, is an integer multiple of q^*. The chance of this happening is effectively zero. This problem can be avoided by supposing that cost curves are flat-bottomed, but that is perhaps a rather artificial step to take.

A second important reason for nonexistence can arise in multiproduct industries (see Faulhaber, 1975). Suppose that there are three products in the industry and that there is demand for one unit of each product. Let $C(k)$ be the cost of producing k of the products ($k = 1, 2$, or 3). It is quite possible that

$$\frac{3}{2}C(2) < C(3) < C(2) + C(1), \tag{3.6}$$

for example if $C(1) = 6$, $C(2) = 8$, and $C(3) = 13$. There is a natural monopoly because the most efficient way to produce the three products is for one firm to produce all of them. But that state of affairs is vulnerable to entry by a firm producing two out of the three products. A three-product firm could cover its costs provided that the sum of the prices of the products was no less than 13. In that case the sum of the prices of the two most expensive products could not be less than $8\frac{2}{3}$. But then a new firm supplying only two products could undercut the first firm and still make a profit.

This multiproduct example of the nonsustainability of natural monopoly is sometimes associated with "cream skimming" and "destructive competition." Cream skimming occurs when a rival takes a profitable component of the incumbent's business, leaving the incumbent with a loss on the rest. The (alleged) undesirability of cream skimming is sometimes offered as a justification for restrictions on entry.

Although the nonsustainability of natural monopoly is a theoretical possibility, we would urge that arguments for restrictions on entry based on grounds of cream skimming or destructive competition should be treated with the greatest caution. First, there is a broad class of natural monopoly cost conditions that imply sustainability (see Sharkey (1982) for a full discussion). Secondly, natural monopoly conditions are not as widespread as is often claimed. Thirdly, the vested interests of incumbent firms are such that they should bear a heavy burden of proof when arguing for restrictions on entry. Fourthly, the sustainability problem—and existence problems in general—are of little or no consequence in industries that are not contestable.

At this point it is appropriate to address some of the main criticisms (apart from the existence problems just discussed) that have been leveled against the theory. We shall focus on claims that the theory has minimal relevance to real-world industries and that it is therefore devoid of practical policy implications. If the theory can withstand such criticisms, it has very important consequences, for it suggests that opening industries to potential competition (even industries that are highly concentrated in terms of current market shares) does away with the need for regulatory policies, because the force of potential competition itself produces desirable results.

The first major criticism is that the theory assumes an unnatural sequence of events when entry occurs. In particular, it assumes that the entrant can establish itself, undercut the existing firm(s) on price, and take as much of their business as it likes, all before the existing firms respond

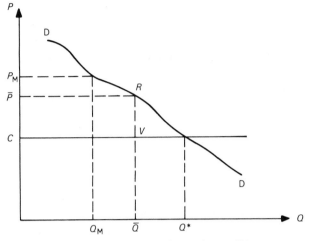

Figure 3.3   Nonrobustness: illustrative market conditions

by lowering their own prices. The criticism is that this implicit assumption—that entry can occur more quickly than price changes by existing firms—is precisely the *reverse* of what it is realistic to suppose.

The second criticism is that the assumption of zero sunk costs is *nonrobust* (see Schwartz and Reynolds, 1983; Dasgupta and Stiglitz, 1985). Proponents of contestability theory can reply to the objection that the assumption of zero sunk costs is never strictly *true* by saying that no theory can be more than an approximation to the truth. But the claim of nonrobustness is more damaging, because it implies that the theory is not useful even as an approximation to reality.

Both criticisms can be illustrated with the aid of figure 3.3. The diagram concerns a market for a homogeneous product. The demand curve is labeled DD, and the constant level of unit costs is denoted by C. Social welfare would be maximized when price $P = C$ and output is Q^*. Suppose the entry into the industry involves sunk cost S, which can be regarded as an entry fee. Suppose that firm A is currently in the market and that firm B is contemplating entry. Let T_A be the time that it would take for firm A to respond to B's decision to enter, and let T_B be the time that it would take B to set up at full scale. Thus, if $T_A > T_B$, then B can set up before A responds to B's entry. But if $T_A < T_B$, then A responds to B's entry before B has set up at full scale. Suppose that, once A has responded to B's entry, competition between them rapidly drives price down to the cost level C. Note that this does not involve firm A's reducing its price below the level of costs. Define T as follows:

$$T = \begin{cases} T_A - T_B \text{ if } T_A > T_B \\ 0 \text{ otherwise.} \end{cases} \tag{3.7}$$

Thus, T is the amount of time that B would have at full scale before A's response drove prices down to level C.

Suppose that A is currently charging price $\bar{P}$. Should B enter the market? If he entered and charged a price just below $\bar{P}$, he would earn a profit flow of almost

$$\pi(\bar{P}) = (\bar{P} - C)D(\bar{P}), \tag{3.8}$$

i.e. the rectangle $\bar{P}RVC$. This profit flow would last for T units of time, at which point profits would be driven down to zero. Entry is worthwhile if this profit flow covers the sunk cost S, i.e. if and only if

$$T\pi(\bar{P}) > S. \tag{3.9}$$

Now, if sunk costs are zero ($S = 0$) and the entrant can set up before the incumbent firm responds ($T > 0$), then any price P in excess of C is vulnerable to entry. This is the case of a contestable market.

If, however, the incumbent can react faster than (or just as fast as) the entrant can establish himself at full scale, then $T = 0$. This is usually the realistic case. Now, if sunk costs are positive—no matter how tiny—then $S > 0$, and from (3.9) it follows that no price would attract the entry of firm B. Therefore A could charge the monopoly price P_M without inducing entry. In this case, even though sunk costs might be miniscule, the threat of entry is nonexistent, and the incumbent can behave as a monopolist with impunity.

The remaining case is that in which $T > 0$ and $S > 0$. The incumbent will deter entry if he charges a price P such that

$$\pi(P) \leqslant S/T. \tag{3.10}$$

Even if S is rather small, this constraint on the behavior of the incumbent firm will be very weak if T is small. It may well be that the monopoly price P_M satisfies (3.10). S must be infinitesimal if the entry threat is to promote anything remotely like competitive behavior in this model.

In short, any departure from the strict assumptions of contestability theory ($S = 0$, $T > 0$) leads to an outcome that may be radically different from the outcome predicted by the theory.

Contestability theory is important insofar as it provides a valuable framework for thinking about a number of problems of industrial organization: it has led to several important lines of research on multiproduct industries; it has introduced important concepts and analytical tools; it allows for the endogenous determination of market structure; it highlights the importance of sunk costs; and it underlines the beneficial role that potential competition can play in improving industrial performance.

However, we have grave doubts about the empirical applicability of contestability theory, especially to major industries of the kind being privatized in Britain. The entrenched dominant positions of companies like BT and British Gas, and the inevitably sunk nature of many costs, are such that entry threats *on their own* cannot remotely be expected to compel the dominant firm to behave benignly. Entry threats are usually very desirable, but they will be impotent unless supplemented by effective competition policies that strike at anticompetitive behavior against potential entrants by incumbent firms. Moreover, there are a number of markets and submarkets where the threat of entry simply does not exist and cannot be made to exist. Direct regulation of the dominant firm is then required.

3.3.2   Strategic Entry Deterrence

In this section we consider in more detail how an incumbent firm with market power might act so as to stifle potential competition. This is a central question for privatization policies in the U.K., because major enterprises such as BT and British Gas have entered the private sector with positions of great dominance, and it is not clear to what extent measures to liberalize entry into their industries will promote truly effective competition. This depends partly upon the nature of policies to guard against anticompetitive behavior designed to thwart potential entrants. A theoretical perspective on this issue is provided by the recent literature on *strategic entry deterrence* (see Vickers (1985a) for a survey). In this section we outline some of the main elements of that literature, and we consider the problem of designing policies against predatory behavior. We postpone until later in the chapter our discussion of competition and entry deterrence in networks and vertically related markets.

The key to strategic entry deterrence by an incumbent dominant firm is to make credible the threat of responding to entry—for example by very aggressive pricing—in such a way that the rival would regret having entered the market. The threat is credible if and only if it is believed to be in the interests of the incumbent to carry it out when entry actually occurs. In order to assess the danger of strategic entry deterrence thwarting potential competition and to consider appropriate policy measures, we must focus precisely on this question of credibility. One school of thought (often associated with the University of Chicago) has it that predatory pricing is irrational, and therefore unlikely to occur, because it hurts the incumbent as much as the entrant. In that case threats of predatory pricing are not credible. But others have recently contended that predatory and entry-deterring behavior of various kinds is entirely possible, and that policy measures are vital if dominant firms are not to choke off the threat of potential competition.

For simplicity, we shall focus on the case where one incumbent firm is seeking to deter the entry of one potential rival. The entry decision of the rival depends upon his beliefs as to the likely profitability of being in the market. Entry will occur if and only if the expected profits exceed the expected costs of entry. How can the incumbent influence those beliefs in such a way as to deter entry? We shall address this question in two steps. First, we shall suppose that each firm is fully informed about the behavior, opportunities, and motivation of the other. Secondly, we shall relax these assumptions about the information available to the firms, and examine the roles of signaling and reputation in entry deterrence.

The best known traditional analysis of entry deterrence is the Bain–Sylos limit pricing model (see Hay and Morris, 1979, pp. 185–190). In that analysis it is assumed to be common belief that the incumbent would not change its pre-entry output level in the event of entry. Although it makes for tractability, that assumption is not credible, because the incumbent almost certainly would wish to change its behavior when faced with a rival. More generally, as Friedman (1979) has observed, in a game of complete and perfect information, and with no intertemporal interdependences of cost or demand conditions, the incumbent's output level before the entry decision ought to make no difference to the rival's assessment of the profitability of entry. Once entry occurs, a new game begins, and the parameters of that game are independent of previous behavior. This suggests that flexible instruments such as price or quantity are less likely to be the means of entry deterrence than instruments that have a more lasting effect upon cost or demand conditions. The key is for the incumbent to *commit* himself to a course of conduct that would be detrimental to an entrant. A large amount of literature, from which but a few items will be mentioned, is devoted to this theme. Figure 3.4 sketches a simple schema.

First, the incumbent chooses the level of some strategic variable K. Numerous interpretations can be given to K, but for the moment regard it as the incumbent's capacity level. If the rival chooses not to enter, he gets zero and the incumbent gets $I^0(K)$, as shown at the foot of the right-hand branch. Note that the incumbent's payoff depends on K even if entry does

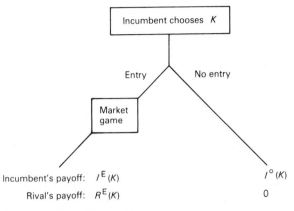

Figure 3.4   Strategic entry deterrence

not occur. If entry does take place, a duopoly exists. Without examining the details of the duopolist's interactions, let us assume that the upshot of the "market game" between them is that the incumbent gets $I^E(K)$ and the rival gets $R^E(K)$ in the event of entry. The schema is broad enough to allow for the rival also to choose some strategic variable after the incumbent's choice of K. This would be included in the black box of the market game.

The incumbent's choice of K deters entry if $R^E(K) < 0$. It may be that entry is deterred even by the level of K that would have been chosen by a pure monopolist facing no threat of entry. Then entry is said to be blockaded. Or it may be that the incumbent does better to permit entry than to deter it. But here our concern is with the remaining case, in which strategic entry deterrence is optimal for the incumbent.

What are the likely instruments of entry deterrence? It is useful to distinguish between those that affect costs (the incumbent's and/or the rival's) and those that affect demand. As to the former, Dixit (1980) showed how the incumbent's choice of *capacity* could deter entry, but in Dixit's model excess (in the sense of idle) capacity is not observed. More generally, K can be interpreted as the incumbent's level of *capital input*. Strategic entry deterrence commonly implies overcapitalization, in the sense that the output eventually produced by the incumbent could have been produced more efficiently with a lower level of capital and a correspondingly higher level of variable factors of production (see Spence, 1977). The same holds when K is interpreted as the incumbent's cost-reducing R&D expenditure. In all these examples, the incumbent's commitment of high K promises that he will supply a high output level, or charge a low price, in the market game.

The choice of K is therefore offputting to the rival, not because of its direct effects, but because of its indirect influence upon the outcome of the market game.

In criticism of the Bain–Sylos analysis, it was stated above that the incumbent's pre-entry output would not affect the rival's entry decision if there were no intertemporal interdependences of cost or demand. But such interdependences do hold if the *experience curve* effect operates—i.e. if a firm's cost level is a declining function of its cumulative output. In that case it is possible for the incumbent's choice of output to deter entry strategically (see Spence, 1981; Fudenberg and Tirole, 1983).

As well as the incumbent lowering his own costs, there may be ways for him to *raise the rival's cost* (see Salop and Scheffman, 1983). For example, by setting high wage rates in the industry, the incumbent increases his own costs and those of an entrant. The direct effect of this upon the incumbent is unfavorable, but if the indirect effect is to deter the rival's entry then the ploy may well be beneficial to him in overall terms.

Another way in which entry might be deterred is for the incumbent to deny the rival access to technology that would allow him to compete. Gilbert and Newbery (1982) examine *pre-emptive patenting*—the acquisition of a patent by an incumbent firm with the purpose of denying the patent, and hence an entry opportunity, to a potential rival. An important factor here is that the incumbent's incentive to win the patent is likely to exceed the rival's incentive, even if the patent is for a technology inferior to that already enjoyed by the incumbent. This is because the incumbent's monopoly persists if he denies entry to the rival, whereas competition, which is less profitable than monopoly, occurs in the event of entry. This result has an important bearing on the question of the persistence of monopoly, for the advantage of the incumbent arises from his *strategic position*; intrinsically the incumbent may be no different from the rival. The result also offers an explanation of the phenomenon of sleeping (i.e. unused) patents, because the pre-emption result does not depend upon the patent's being for a technology that is superior to the incumbent's existing technology.

Turning from the cost side to the demand side, there are further ways in which an incumbent firm can make the prospect of entry unattractive for a rival firm. In some circumstances, strategic *advertising* deters entry, although in Schmalensee's (1983) exploration of advertising and entry deterrence it emerged that low advertising was the way to deter entry. The reason was that high advertising would cause the incumbent to have a higher price in the market game. For the rival, the favorable latter effect would outweigh the disadvantage of high advertising and make entry more attractive. *Brand proliferation*—the introduction of numerous new products—can also serve to deter entry (see Schmalensee, 1978). To use the locational analogy common in the analysis of product differentiation, brand proliferation fills up product space in such a way that there are no remaining slots or niches for profitable entry.

Product differentiation was one of Bain's three sources of barriers to entry. Although advertising is often regarded as a measure of product differentiation, Bain did not see it as the heart of the problem. Schmalensee (1982) shows how buyers' uncertainty about the quality of new brands can give established (or pioneering) brands an advantage in a differentiated market. The new brand would have to be priced substantially below the existing brand to induce consumers to experiment with it; part of the cost of the experiment is the loss of surplus currently being enjoyed on the existing brand. (Farrell (1986) develops this point in his analysis of moral hazard as a barrier to entry.) This is again an example where the incumbent has strategic advantage solely because of already being in the market.

To summarize so far, there are numerous ways in which an incumbent firm can influence cost and/or demand conditions by strategic investments in such a way as to discourage entry into his market. Bulow *et al.* (1985) and Fudenberg and Tirole (1984) have examined in general terms various types of entry deterrence. Returning to the schema above, we can ask whether overinvestment or underinvestment in the strategic variable K deters entry. The answer depends of course upon the specification of the market game. In some instances (such as excess capacity deterring entry), the incumbent deters entry by being "large." Fudenberg and Tirole call this the "top dog effect." In other instances, the incumbent deters entry by being "small," and thereby promises an aggressive response in the event of entry. This is the "lean and hungry look." It may be better for the incumbent to accommodate rather than deter entry. Then he will act strategically to influence the nature of entry, by being either "large" (a "fat cat") or "small" (the "puppy dog ploy"). The aim of all these strategic moves is to cause the rival to choose to act more favorably for the incumbent than he would otherwise do.

So far we have supposed that firms are fully informed about each other's opportunities and motivation, but we now turn to the second step in the analysis of strategic entry deterrence by relaxing this assumption. Milgrom and Roberts (1982a) have shown how limit pricing can be used to deter entry when the potential entrant is uncertain as to the cost level of the incumbent firm. The rival's expectations concerning that cost level—and hence his entry decision—are influenced by the price charged by the incumbent before the entry decision is made. Therefore the pre-entry price can act as a *signal* of the incumbent's efficiency. An incumbent with low costs would like to signal that fact, because the potential rival would then be more reluctant to enter his market. By the same token, an inefficient incumbent would like to masquerade as a low-cost firm in order to make entry less likely. This incentive to signal in an uncertain environment means that the incumbent's pricing can be used as an instrument of entry deterrence. Note that consumers benefit from this kind of limit pricing insofar as it tends to lower price. Other interesting issues arise when there is uncertainty about demand as well as the incumbent's cost level. Then a low pre-entry price might signal either low demand or low costs (see Matthews and Mirman, 1983).

Milgrom and Roberts (1982b) and Kreps and Wilson (1982) have explored another context in which uncertainty about the incumbent plays a role in entry deterrence, namely in connection with *predatory pricing* (see Vickers (1985b) for a survey). They examine a game due to Selten (1978) in which an incumbent firm—a chain store—is threatened by entry in each of a number of towns. Intuitively, we would expect that the incumbent would fight entry if challenged in a town early in the sequence, in order to deter later entrants. However, this is not so if the entrants have complete information about the opportunities and motivation of the incumbent, because in that case he would never fight entry. This is because it is common knowledge that he would not fight in the last town, and so he would have no reason to fight in the last but one and so on. But if the assumption of complete information is very slightly relaxed—so that there is a possibility that the incumbent is somehow committed to fighting—then even an uncommitted incumbent would (rationally) fight entry in early towns to keep up the *reputation* of possibly being a committed fighter. This reputation effect is very powerful, in the sense that a very small amount of incomplete information can make it rational to fight on a large number of occasions.

Another, quite different, context in which predatory pricing is rational has been examined by Benoit (1985) in a paper which also covers the case of imperfect information. He supposes that the entrant's financial resources are such that it would go into bankruptcy after a predatory pricing war of some finite length (say T periods). In other words, its "war chest" is not unlimited. The incumbent's war chest is assumed to be larger than that of the entrant. Assume now that the incumbent would prefer (i) *one* period of predatory fighting followed by perpetual dominance thereafter to (ii) duopolistic coexistence forever. It now follows that it would be rational for the incumbent to engage in predatory pricing rather than to accommodate entry, no matter how large is T. Given the incumbent's preference for (i) over (ii), it would clearly fight to drive out the entrant if $T = 1$. Now, if $T = 2$, both firms know that the entrant would leave the market voluntarily if it were forced into a position where it could survive only one more period before going bankrupt, because it has already been established that the incumbent would force the entrant out otherwise. So the incumbent would find it rational to fight if $T = 2$. The argument can be extended inductively for all T. If the entrant would exit voluntarily at $T = t$, then the incumbent would rationally fight at $T = t+1$, in which case the entrant would exit voluntarily at $T = t+1$ and so on. Here the logic of credible threats works powerfully against entry.

It is now time to draw together some conclusions on strategic entry deterrence. First, there are many circumstances in which a dominant incumbent can act so as to make entry appear an unattractive prospect. Secondly, nonprice behavior is important in this regard, particularly as it affects future cost and demand conditions. Thirdly, it is far too hopeful to suppose that predatory pricing is irrational and that threats of it would therefore be disregarded. In short, there is often ample scope for a dominant firm to undermine "freedom" of entry, and it follows that policies are required to make that freedom effective. In this section we have suggested some of the problems which those policies must address, but it would be foolish to advance general policy prescriptions without taking account of the individual circumstances of particular industries. We will therefore return to the application of the economic principles of strategic entry deterrence and predatory behavior, outlined in this section, later in the book.

3.4   Competition as an Incentive Mechanism

One of the main virtues of competition emphasized by proponents of privatization and liberalization is its role as a mechanism that stimulates *internal* efficiency. Indeed, despite the emphasis of textbook competition theory on *allocative* efficiency in a static environment, it has long been recognized that much of the effect of competition on welfare is due to its role as an incentive system and discovery mechanism in a world of imperfect information (see for example the work of Hayek (1945) and Leibenstein (1966) on X-inefficiency). If competition promotes internal as well as allocative efficiency, then it is doubly beneficial in terms of social welfare.

We considered in the previous chapter whether or not competition in the market for corporate control stimulates internal efficiency by reducing managerial slack, and now we turn to product market competition. Recent work, notably that of Hart (1983), shows how product market competition can influence the nature of incentive contracts between the shareholders and managers of a firm. Suppose that the unit costs of a firm depend on managerial effort and upon some exogenous cost characteristic of the firm. If there is a high degree of correlation between the exogenous cost characteristics of firms in the industry, then competition between them reveals information about managers' effort rates. Being better informed about managerial effort, shareholders can make managerial reward more sensitive to effort, and slack and X-inefficiency can therefore be diminished. Reward can be based, a least in part, upon *relative* performance, and so managers are effectively in competition with each other.

Willig (1985) has performed comparative statics analysis of a principal–agent model to illuminate the effect of product market structure on managerial incentives and behavior. As above shareholders can observe the level of unit costs c, but cannot infer managerial effort from their knowledge of c. The asymmetry of information means that shareholders must reckon with an incentive compatibility constraint when designing an incentive mechanism for managers. That is to say, they must allow for the fact that the managers will behave in a self-interested manner given the incentives that they face. This constraint prevents the attainment of the first-best outcome, and X-inefficiency (in a precise sense) results. Managers gain from this situation, relative to the first-best outcome. Willig does not explicitly examine competition between firms. Instead he introduces a parameter b that is intended to capture the nature of product market competition in a "reduced-form" way. Thus gross profit $V(c, b)$ depends on the parameter b as well as on the level of unit costs. In the comparative statics analysis, the effect of b upon effort and welfare depends on $\partial V/\partial b$, which measures how profit varies with b, and on the cross-partial derivative $\partial^2 V/\partial c \partial b$, which measures how the sensitivity of V to c varies with b. If competition increases that sensitivity without greatly reducing profit, then competition does improve internal efficiency, because managerial reward can be linked more closely to effort.

The effect of competition upon incentives and efficiency has only recently been the subject of precise theoretical analysis, and much remains to be done. There are close parallels between this work and the recent literature on regulation under asymmetric information (see sections 4.3 and

4.6.2 below and the references cited therein). Both are branches of the principal–agent literature that examines the optimal design of incentive contracts. Although this literature on incentive theory is technically quite complex, it succeeds in illuminating some basic points. Imperfect information constrains the design of incentive contracts, and inefficiencies result. Information therefore has value insofar as it makes possible incentive schemes that are more sensitive to effort. Competition can act as a source of this kind of information, because rewards can be based on performance comparisons. Thus there is a theoretical underpinning to the idea that competition promotes efficiency within the firm, as well as efficient behavior in product markets.

3.5   Interconnection, Networks, and Vertical Integration

Having looked at some general aspects of competition theory pertinent to the privatization program, we now address the specific question of competition in networks and vertically related markets. In many industries involved in the U.K. privatization program, several distinct economic activities are required to supply the final product to consumers. Gas must be discovered, extracted, and distributed to the user's appliance. Electricity must be generated and transmitted through the grid. A long-distance phone call in effect consists of a trunk link and local links. The supply of a private branch exchange (PBX) telephone exchange involves both manufacture and distribution. A long-distance coach journey can be thought of as consisting of facilities to embark and disembark as well as the conveyance of the passenger from one town to another.

In such industries it is often the case that effective competition is more feasible in some activities than it is in others. For example, in the current state of technology, competition in long-distance telecommunications is possible, whereas in local networks typically there is natural monopoly and inevitable market power. In the energy industries the prospect of effective competition in the distribution and transmission of energy is remote, but there is no reason in principle why it should not exist in the production of gas or in the generation of electricity.

The question for policy in these circumstances is how to promote and maintain effective competition in activities where it is feasible in the face of monopoly in the related activities. In other words, can the problems of dominance be confined to those activities in which competition cannot exist, or can the dominant firm thwart competition throughout the industry? We shall pursue this question by examining an industry in which output is produced by combining two inputs, A and B. The inputs could be thought of as long-distance and local telecommunications links respectively, or as gas production and distribution. We shall suppose that competition is infeasible in relation to input B, perhaps because natural monopoly conditions of supply prevail, but that competition can be effective in relation to input A.

We shall attempt to answer two questions.

(i)   Will the dominant firm in activity B (the "B-firm") find it profitable to thwart competition in activity A?

(ii)   If so, what can public policy do to safeguard competition in activity A?

In regard to (ii) we shall focus on two policy measures in particular—*vertical separation* (i.e. banning the B-firm from the A-sector), and rulings on *interconnection* (i.e. stipulating aspects of the relationship between the B-firm and the A-sector).

3.5.1   The Dominant Firm's Incentive to Thwart Competition

To answer question (i) let us begin by supposing that the B-firm can exclude competitors from the A-sector, for example by charging huge prices for the B input. This would happen if BT were allowed to charge Mercury excessive amounts for the local elements of the long-distance calls of Mercury's subscribers, or if British Gas could charge enormous fees for distributing gas produced by rival firms. Suppose that the B-firm is allowed to operate also in the A-sector. Would it wish to exercise its power to exclude rivals there?

If the B-firm's rivals in the A-sector had no cost advantage and if there were nondecreasing returns to scale, then the answer would certainly be positive. Whatever the level of total industry profits without exclusion, the B-firm could achieve at least that level of profit all for itself by excluding rivals in the A-sector and replicating their behavior. Moreover, the B-firm would probably want to change industry behavior, perhaps by restricting industry output, in order to boost industry profits yet further. Excluding rivals in these circumstances therefore allows a double gain—industry profits increase, and the B-firm obtains all of them rather than just part.

We have been speaking as though the inequalities in the previous paragraph were strict, as in general they are, but there is a famous special case in which they are not. This case, in which the B-firm is indifferent between excluding rivals in the A-sector and not doing so, is as follows. Inputs A and B are combined in fixed proportions, there are constant unit costs, and competition in the A-sector is so severe that price is driven down to the level of cost. It then turns out that the B-firm can extract all the monopoly profit that is to be had—for example by buying the A input (by assumption at cost) from the competitive A-sector and combining it with the B input, or by selling the B input to the A-sector with the full monopoly mark-up.

However, as soon as we relax the assumptions of the special case, there is a strictly positive incentive for the B-firm to exclude rivals from the A-sector. If the A and B inputs are combined in *variable* (as opposed to fixed) proportions, then the B-firm's market power is diminished by the ability of rivals in the A-sector to substitute away from the B input, at least to some extent. Alternatively, if *imperfect competition* exists in the A-sector, so that rivals there obtain positive profits, then the B-firm can appropriate those profits (and perhaps more besides) by excluding those rivals.

These rather straightforward arguments do not go through if the B-firm is at a cost disadvantage in the A-sector, or if returns to scale there are decreasing. The reason is that the average cost of producing the industry's output might increase if competitors were excluded from the A-sector, and industry profit might fall as a result. But this will not necessarily happen, because the B-firm will be able to exert greater market power which will tend to increase industry profits. In addition, the B-firm obtains all—rather than part—of industry profit in the event of exclusion. There is therefore a wide range of circumstances in which exclusion is profitable for the B-firm even if cost conditions do not satisfy the assumptions initially made. The example below concerning interconnection will illustrate this point.

3.5.2 Policy Measures to Safeguard Competition

So far we have shown that the B-firm generally has an incentive to thwart competitors in the A-sector by refusing to supply them the B input at reasonable prices. The possible exception is when the B-firm's rivals in the A-sector have a great efficiency advantage there. We now ask whether policy measures exist that can safeguard competition and improve social welfare. We focus on two such measures:

(i) vertical separation—not allowing the B-firm to own any firm that operates in the A-sector;

(ii) interconnect rulings—to stipulate terms of the relationship between the B-firm and the A-sector.

Telecommunications policies in the United States and in Britain illustrate (i) and (ii) respectively. In America when AT&T was broken up after 1982 the long-distance division was separate from the local operating companies. Therefore the local operating companies, being under separate ownership, had less incentive to thwart competition to AT&T in the long-distance market (although some interconnection questions still arose). In contrast, the U.K. Government kept BT intact when privatization occurred. The ability of Mercury—BT's long-distance rival—to compete in the long-distance sector depends on a ruling by Oftel on interconnection which stipulates the terms on which BT must allow Mercury access to its local network.

Although a policy of vertical separation allows competition in the A-sector, it does not necessarily enhance social welfare by itself. The reason is the "double wedge problem" (see Waterson (1984, chapter 5) for a fuller discussion of this and other problems in vertically related markets). Suppose that A and B are combined in fixed proportions to produce the final product. Unless there is *perfect* competition in the A-sector, so that price is driven down to the level of costs, vertical separation has the effect of *raising* the price charged to the final consumer. If the B firm is "downstream," this happens because the B-firm will operate where marginal revenue is equal to marginal cost plus the mark-up of firms in the A-sector. The latter mark-up is absent if the rivals to the B-firm are excluded. Then marginal revenue is equal to the B-firm's overall marginal cost of supplying the final product and, unless the B-firm is relatively inefficient in the A-sector, price is lower with vertical integration. A similar argument operates if the B-firm is "upstream." Unless the A-sector is perfectly competitive, its demand for the B input will be described by a condition that implies that net price exceeds their unit costs. The demand for B is therefore reduced, and it follows that overall output is lower, and the price faced by consumers is higher, than if B were a vertically integrated firm.

In sum, under fixed proportions, with exogenous common unit costs in the A-sector and with no constraint on the market power of the B-firm, vertical separation has undesirable consequences because it exacerbates the harmful effects of the B-firm's monopoly power. This result can be reversed if we relax any of the stated assumptions. First, the assumption of fixed proportions is important, because under variable proportions the market power of the B-firm is weakened by virtue of the ability of rivals in the A-sector to substitute away from input B so as to cut costs. Secondly, if the B-firm has higher costs than other firms in activity A then vertical integration has an obvious drawback. Thirdly, the same is true if competition in activity A has the effect of stimulating internal efficiency in that activity, since costs are then endogenous (see section 3.4). Finally, this entire analysis has supposed that the B-firm is unregulated. If, however, its market power is constrained by regulation, the merits of vertical separation are much stronger. Market power is held in check where it exists, and the advantages of competition are gained where possible. This issue will be taken further in relation to the industries discussed in later chapters, and with the aid of the theoretical perspective on regulation offered in chapter 4.

We now consider rulings on terms of *interconnection* as a second policy measure to combat the B-firm's desire to exclude competitors from the A-sector. More generally we refer to governmental regulation of the terms, notably the price, on which the A-sector can obtain input B from the dominant firm. We use the term "interconnection" because that is the word used in telecommunications economics, where this is central (see section 8.4.1 below). The same issue arises for example in relation to the licensing of innovations, a subject of antitrust cases (for an outline of the theory of licensing see Shapiro (1985)).

The question is to choose the optimal price at which the dominant firm must make input B available to the A-sector. We have already established that the B-firm would set that price at a prohibitively high level to exclude rivals if it had the discretion to do so. We shall use the following simple model to show the determinants of the optimal interconnection price. For simplicity we suppose that the B-firm has only one rival in the A-sector. This corresponds to the situation in the U.K. telecommunications industry: Mercury is BT's only rival in long-distance networks, and BT dominates local networks. Let a and b respectively be the unit costs of producing the A and B inputs, which we assume to be combined in a fixed one-to-one proportion. We will suppose that the cost of combining the inputs to produce the final product is negligible, so that $c = a + b$ is the marginal cost of supplying that product. (Alternatively, we could interpret either a or b as including the cost of combining the inputs.) Let i denote the "interconnection" charge, i.e. the amount paid to the B-firm by its rival for each unit of input B. Therefore the unit cost of supplying the final product is c for the B-firm and $a + i$ for its rival. Let X and Y respectively be the amounts supplied by those two firms, let $Q = X + Y$ be the industry output, and let $P(Q)$ be the inverse demand function. The profit of the dominant firm is then given by

$$\pi^D = XP(Q) + iY - bQ - aX$$
$$= [P(Q) - c]X + (i - b)Y, \tag{3.11}$$

and the profit of the rival is

$$\pi^R = [P(Q) - (a+i)]Y. \tag{3.12}$$

If there is no government intervention, the dominant firm will set i at a prohibitively high level to exclude the rival and will produce where the marginal revenue equals c. In order to say what happens when i does not deter the rival, we need to specify the nature of the duopolistic interaction between the two firms. To this end we introduce a "conjectural variation" term λ as a summary statistic of the degree of rivalry. This term is often interpreted as each firm's expectation of how the other firm's output will change as a result of a change in its own level of output. (However, we are not committed to this interpretation: λ can simply be regarded as a device that saves repeating algebra, because $\lambda = 0$ corresponds to Cournot behavior, $\lambda = -1$ corresponds to Bertrand behavior, and so on).

From (3.11) and (3.12) we now have the first-order conditions

$$(1+\lambda)XP' + P - c + \lambda(i-b) = 0 \tag{3.13}$$

and

$$(1+\lambda)YP' + P - (a+i) = 0. \tag{3.14}$$

Adding (3.13) and (3.14) we obtain

$$(1+\lambda)QP' + 2P = (1+\lambda)c + (1-\lambda)(a+i) \tag{3.15}$$

Now let

$$\eta(Q) = -P/QP' \tag{3.16}$$

be the elasticity of demand. Then (3.15) can be written

$$P[2 - (1+\lambda)/\eta] = (1+\lambda)c + (1-\lambda)(a+i). \tag{3.17}$$

Optimality requires that price P equals marginal cost c. Substituting $P = c$ into (3.17) implies that the optimal interconnection charge is

$$i^* = b - \frac{(1+\lambda)c}{(1-\lambda)\eta}. \tag{3.18}$$

The terms on the right-hand side of (3.18) are b, the unit cost of the B input, and an adjustment term involving λ and η. For $-1 < \lambda < 1$, optimality requires i^* to be *lower than* b. This is in order to offset the duopoly mark-up arising from the imperfect competition between the two firms. This adjustment factor is greater when competition between firms is less intense (i.e. λ is larger) and when the elasticity of demand is lower. Therefore marginal cost pricing ($i = b$) is *sub*optimal unless there is Bertrand, or price-taking, behavior in activity A. In this simple model, an interconnection charge below the level of cost is better. The dominant firm loses and the rival gains from such a policy.

The basic model is very rudimentary, and it can be extended in several directions, for example to the cases of several rivals, cost differences, nonconstant returns to scale, nonlinear pricing, or other social welfare objectives. As it stands the model does not include investment behavior, but it is important for interconnection policy to specify who pays what for investment, since there are externalities between the dominant firm and its rivals. This issue was part of Oftel's ruling on interconnection, which we shall consider in chapter 8.

A simple way of developing the model, which is relevant to the telecommunications industry, is to add a separate market for B. This is appropriate if A and B are long-distance and local links respectively, because there is a demand for local calls (B only) as well as for long-distance calls (which require A plus B). If price discrimination is disallowed, so that the dominant firm is constrained to charge the rival no more for B than it charges consumers in the separate B market, and if the dominant firm is otherwise unregulated, then it has an incentive to raise its price in the B market above the pure monopoly level. This injures the rival in the A-plus-B market and benefits the dominant firm there. This gain outweighs the loss from diverging from pure monopoly behavior in the B market, at any rate for small changes. A ban on price discrimination is therefore liable to introduce distortions elsewhere, and a ruling on interconnection is a superior policy to adopt.

The analysis becomes somewhat more complex if the dominant firm is also subject to regulatory constraint. BT must keep the price of a basket of its services below a given limit. If that constraint binds, the price of its local calls (B only) is inversely related to the price of its long-distance calls (A plus B). It follows that the dominant firm's incentive to price aggressively in the market where there is some competition is stronger, because revenues can be recouped in the other market. The profit function for the dominant firm stated in (3.11) needs extending to cover the other completely monopolized market, with the price in that market inversely related to P. Thus the regulatory mechanism may have the curious effect of making the dominant firm behave more aggressively towards rivals, because the pricing formula allows it to restore revenues elsewhere. We shall discuss further this possible disadvantage of constraining the price level of a wide *basket* of services in chapter 8 on the telecommunications industry.

Another important feature of that industry (among others) is the presence of *network externalities*. The demand for telecommunications services by any one customer depends upon who else is a customer of the same network, since he can call—and be called by—only those people. Network externalities are important for the nature of competition and welfare (see Katz and Shapiro, 1985, 1986; Farrell and Saloner, 1985). In regard to competition, it is clear that a rival would be at a grave disadvantage with respect to the dominant firm if it were denied access to its network of established subscribers. The interconnection question therefore has a further dimension. As to the welfare implications of network externalities, there is possibly a case for some subsidy to new subscribers to the network, since they provide a positive externality to existing subscribers. Space does not permit a fuller treatment of network economics here, but the issue will recur in later chapters.

3.6   Concluding Remarks

Theories about competitive forces of course account for a large portion of microeconomics, and it is therefore impossible in one chapter to say a great deal about them. Nevertheless it was essential for us to outline some selected aspects of those theories in view of the importance attached to competition in the British debate on privatization. To conclude, and to point forward to later chapters, we shall briefly recap on why we selected the topics described in this chapter. Section 3.2.1 looked at the trade-off that sometimes exists between competition and scale economies. This trade-off is at the heart of the question of how many rivals should be licensed to compete with a dominant enterprise such as BT. It also bears on the issue of desirability of unrestricted free entry. Section 3.2.2 discussed public enterprises as competitors, an important topic given that there is no necessary link between private ownership and competition.

Section 3.3 concerned the forces of potential competition, whose virtues have been widely acclaimed by proponents of deregulation and liberalization. Although we too would generally advocate freedom of entry, we argued that contestability theory was not suitable for the analysis of the major industries considered in this book, and we urged the need for policy measures to contain the danger that a powerful incumbent firm could render freedom of entry ineffective by predatory tactics. Section 3.4 briefly described some ways in which the competitive process can act as a mechanism with good incentives for internal efficiency. Such consider-ations have featured prominently in the debate on privatization and liberalization. Finally, in section 3.5 we examined some aspects of competition in vertically related markets, including the question of interconnection which arises not only in telecommunications but also in such industries as gas and electricity. In the following chapters we shall often have cause to refer back to the analysis of competitive forces described above. But first we must look at the economics of regulatory mechanisms for constraining market power.

Theories of Regulation

4.1 Introduction

We saw in the last chapter that in many circumstances the competitive process provides an incentive system that impels private firms to behave in ways that are broadly consistent with efficient resource allocation. But such circumstances do not always hold, and in some industries the forces of competition are inevitably weak or nonexistent. There is then a need for regulatory policy to influence private sector behavior by establishing an appropriate incentive system to guide or constrain economic decisions. This need has arisen in several major industries involved in the U.K. privatization program, where problems of monopoly power and various kinds of externalities have been central issues. In later chapters we consider in some detail the regulatory frameworks adopted in the U.K. telecommunications, gas, and airports industries, and the framework proposed for the water industry, but the purpose of the present chapter is to examine some of the underlying principles of regulatory policy.

For the most part we will leave aside externality problems in order to focus on regulation to constrain market power. To clarify the analysis further, we will begin by assuming that competition in product and capital markets is absent and cannot be stimulated. In other words, we will suppose that the regulatory system is the only constraint upon the firm's behavior apart from the fundamental conditions of demand and technology. We can then examine how the firm would behave when faced with various regulatory systems, and we can also address the broader question of optimal regulatory policy.

It is useful to regard the problem as a game between the government (or its agency) and the firm. With this perspective we need to specify the players' possible strategies, their objectives, the move order, and the information conditions of the game. As regards *possible strategies*, the firm has to make decisions about prices, outputs, capital investment, product quality, investment in cost reduction, product innovation, and so on. The government might seek to regulate some of these variables (for example prices, product quality, or profits) but, unless it is unusually well informed about industry conditions and behavior, it is unlikely to be able to regulate (as opposed to influence) other aspects of the firm's activities. This information problem is crucial because the government can condition its policy only on what it knows. Indeed the asymmetry of information between government and firm will be a central theme of this chapter.

Turning now to decision-makers' *objectives*, there are several assumptions that can be explored. The traditional approach, which offers many useful insights, is to suppose that the firm is intent upon maximizing profits and that the government seeks to maximize social welfare defined as the (possibly weighted) sum of consumer and producer surplus in partial equilibrium analysis. However, we will also wish to pursue other approaches to company behavior—especially in view of the nature of much of the debate about the effect of privatization upon internal efficiency—by assuming that managers also attach importance to nonprofit objectives, for example the minimization of managerial effort or the enhancement of sales revenues. Similarly, we will not always suppose that governments or their regulatory bodies are imbued with the classical public interest objective. Political concerns affect governments, and the interests of regulatory agencies need not coincide with social wellbeing.

As regards *move order* and dynamics, there are again several analytical perspectives. A natural starting point is to suppose that the government has "first move" by virtue of its ability to design the regulatory framework, and that the firm then behaves as best it can in response to that framework. But this simple leader–follower approach has shortcomings. One is that regulatory policies are often more short-term in nature than some aspects of company behavior, notably investment in capital assets with long lives. In such circumstances government does not begin with a clean slate; rather, it responds to conditions shaped in part by decisions of the firm. A second and related point is that the government and firm each make a series of moves over time, and they interact strategically. Thus the firm may seek to influence the design of future regulatory policy by its current actions. Such behavior would not be surprising when—as in several U.K. privatizations—regulatory policy is explicitly temporary and periodically subject to major review. The dynamic nature of the problem also raises issues of credibility (sometimes known as "time-consistency" problems in other contexts). Thus government could not credibly adopt a policy that required it to act contrary to its interests in some future circumstances.

Finally we come to *information conditions*, in particular the asymmetry of information likely to exist between the regulator and the firm. We believe that this information problem is at the heart of the economics of regulation. A fully informed regulator equipped with suitable sanctions could simply command decision makers within the firm to behave in accordance with the first-best outcome. But in fact there are multifarious practical limitations to what the regulator can know, and hence to what outcomes he can bring about. We will pay particular attention to the case in which decision makers in the firm know more about conditions of technology and demand than the regulator. The problem for regulatory policy is one of incentive mechanism design—how to induce the firm to act in accordance with the public interest (which will depend on the state of technology and demand) without being able to observe the firm's behavior. This problem is precisely what agency theory is about, and below we will examine in detail several recent applications of that theory to the economics of regulation.

It will be clear even from these brief remarks about various objectives, strategies, dynamics, and information conditions, that regulation is a vast subject and that a full treatment of it would take us far beyond our present scope (see Kahn, 1970; Bailey, 1973; Schmalensee, 1979; Fromm, 1981; Breyer, 1982; Crew and Kleindorfer, 1986). This chapter therefore has the more limited aim of discussing a selected set of the problems and principles of regulatory policy towards dominant enterprises. The discussion will be organized under five headings:

(i) investment problems;

(ii) internal efficiency and asymmetric information;

(iii) the regulation of multiproduct firms;

(iv) collusion and capture;

(v) some relationships between competition and regulation.

4.2 Investment Problems

Investment problems pose fundamental problems for regulators in many industries. Although the direct object of regulation is often pricing policy, which is easily measured and readily changed, the effects of regulatory policy upon social welfare depends critically upon the investment behavior that it induces. Investment—whether in capacity, R&D, or whatever—is less easily quantified and typically cannot be altered in the short run because sunk costs are involved. The magnitude of the welfare effects is illustrated by investment in industries such as telecommunications (e.g. on network development and digital exchanges), gas (transmission, exploration, etc.), electricity (power stations, transmission grids, etc.), and water (pipelines, sewers, etc.).

Two general questions arise. First, do incentives exist for productive efficiency in the sense that capital investment minimizes the cost of producing the output(s) supplied? Secondly, is the scale of investment and production appropriate to the conditions of demand and technology? We address these questions by examining the regulatory theory stemming from the famous Averch and Johnson (A–J) (1962) paper on incentives for overcapitalization under rate-of-return regulation, and by analyzing a model in which price regulation cannot credibly be committed in advance of investment decisions. We discuss some dynamic issues, including regulatory lag, and we consider incentives for strategic behavior when regulator and firm interact over time. An example is the RPI − X style of regulation being adopted in the U.K., under which a bound for the path of prices (or an index thereof) is fixed for a given interval of time, at the end of which there is regulatory review. As that time approaches the firm might have an incentive to engage in socially inefficient strategic behavior designed to influence the outcome of the review. We also consider how private and social rates of discount might differ, especially when there exists the possibility of the return of the private firm to the public sector at some later date.

4.2.1   Rate-of-Return Regulation: the Averch–Johnson Effect

The fundamental problem for regulators is that they lack the information to determine what the firm's pricing and other policies ought ideally to be from the point of view of economic efficiency. Rate-of-return regulation offers the solution that price(s) should be such that an allowed "fair" rate of return on capital is earned. Three questions immediately arise. What is a "fair" rate? To what measure of the capital base should the allowed rate be applied? Will the firm make decisions affecting its capital base partly with a view to influencing the price(s) it is allowed to charge, and what distortions will result?

In their classic model of rate-of-return regulation Averch and Johnson (1962) provide an affirmative answer to this last question. Firms have an incentive to expand their capital base so as to achieve a greater absolute profit while staying within the constraint on their profit rate. An excellent review of early contributions to the debate stimulated by Averch and Johnson is provided by Baumol and Klevorick (1970), and in this section we rely heavily on their discussion.

The A–J model concerns a monopoly supplier of a single good produced with two inputs, labor L and capital K, according to production function $Q = F(L,K)$. Inverse demand is $P(Q)$, and $R(L,K) = F(L,K) P(F(L,K))$ in the revenue when the input levels are L and K. Labor and capital are available at factor prices w and r respectively, and profit is therefore

$$\pi(L,K) = R(L,K) - wL - rK. \tag{4.1}$$

The allowed rate of return is denoted by s, which is assumed to exceed r. (Otherwise the firm would wish to close down, at any rate in the long run.) Thus the constraint on the firm's behavior is that

$$[R(L,K) - wL]/K \leqslant s. \tag{4.2}$$

This constraint is assumed to bind—that is, s is not so generous that (4.2) is satisfied by pure monopoly behavior. The firm's problem is to maximize (4.1) subject to (4.2), and we form the Lagrangean

$$\begin{aligned} H(L,K,\lambda) &= \pi(L,K) - \lambda[R(L,K) - wL - sK] \\ &= (1-\lambda)[R(L,K) - wL] - (r - \lambda s)K. \end{aligned} \tag{4.3}$$

From the first-order conditions it follows that $\partial R/\partial L = w$, but that $\partial R/\partial K = r - \lambda(s-r)/(1-\lambda)$, which is less than r. (The second-order condition guarantees that $0 < \lambda < 1$.) Therefore excess capital is employed, and the firm produces its output in a manner that is too capital intensive and hence inefficient. The firm has no direct benefit from cost inefficiency, but it achieves a strategic gain by influencing the permitted price.

A diagrammatic method due to Zajac (1970) usefully illustrates this and related results. Figure 4.1 is a three-dimensional depiction of π as a function of L and K. The plane hinged on the L axis is the set of points such that $\pi(L,K) = (s-r)K$. The points on or beneath the plane are precisely those that meet constraint (4.2). Thus the firm's problem is to be as high as possible on the shaded "profit hill" without being above the "regulatory plane."

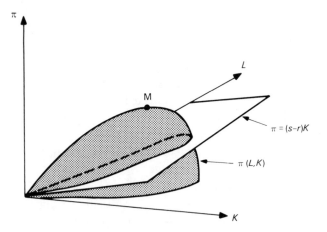

Figure 4.1   Rate-of-return regulation

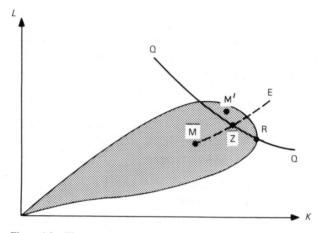

Figure 4.2   The Averch–Johnson effect

The shaded area in figure 4.2 contains the feasible (L,K) combinations that satisfy the regulatory constraint. Since profit is proportional to capital where the constraint binds ($\pi = (s-r)K$), the profit of the regulated firm is greatest at point R, the rightmost point in the shaded area. Curve QQ is the isoquant passing through R. Note that it passes through the interior of the shaded area, which shows that, given output Q, profit and welfare could be higher. The cost of producing output Q is not minimized, because the capital stock is deliberately expanded by the firm. The efficient way to produce Q is at point Z where the "efficiency locus" ME intersects the isoquant. At Z the K/L ratio is lower than at R. Thus the output of the regulated firm is produced in a manner that is too capital intensive. An unregulated monopolist would operate at point M, where efficient production occurs; the unregulated firm has every incentive to minimize production costs.

To summarize, the effect on welfare of rate-of-return regulation in this model has two parts. The level of output is affected, and so too is the efficiency with which the output is produced. If—as is usually the case—regulation increases output, the two effects work in opposite directions, and there is a conflict between internal and allocative efficiency which will appear in several contexts in this chapter.

Without further assumptions on cost and demand conditions it is not necessarily the case that regulation has the effect of increasing output. If, for example, profit were maximized at point M′, output would be higher without regulation. Nor is it necessarily true that the K/L ratio under regulation is greater than that without regulation.

A final observation on the basic A–J model, which Baumol and Klevorick (1970, pp. 175–176) emphasize, is that the amount of capital employed by the regulated firm increases as s is set closer to the cost of capital r. A reduction in s would expand the shaded area in figure 4.2, and so the optimal K would rise. The cost inefficiency due to incentives to overcapitalize may well grow as s is set closer to r. Klevorick (1971) considers the *optimal* choice of s from the point of view of social welfare. Although intuition might suggest that $s = r$ was optimal, this is not in fact so. At $s = r$ the profit-maximizing firm is indifferent between all feasible input combinations that meet the regulatory constraint, because they all involve zero profit. But even if the firm has social welfare as a secondary objective (in the sense of lexicographic preferences) there is a wide range of cases in which some $s > r$ induces a superior outcome than $s = r$. Also, if the firm's secondary objective is to maximize K (e.g. because of managerial satisfaction), then it is generally true that $s > r$ is superior. The reason has already been indicated: s close to r can cause more productive inefficiency.

An extension of the A–J model which remains within its essentially static framework is to replace profit maximization by some other objective for the firm. For example, Bailey and Malone (1970) argue that, under a wide range of conditions, a firm maximizing sales revenue subject to rate-of-return regulation would produce its output in a way that was inefficient by being too labor intensive. This contrasts with Averch and Johnson's finding. However, Atkinson and Waverman (1973) contend that the sales-maximizing firm faces a minimum profit constraint as well as the regulatory restraint, and that various outcomes are possible depending on the interaction of the constraints and the basic conditions of demand. At any rate, this work illustrates that results can be sensitive to assumptions regarding the motivation of the firm.

4.2.2 Regulatory Lag

The A–J model provides a useful starting point, but it can be criticized for being too static in its formulation. Regulation does not occur in a continuous fashion. Typically prices are set for an interval of time, during which the firm is free to choose whatever input combinations it wishes, until the next price review occurs. Review might occur at some time specified in advance—for example the formula governing the pricing of British Telecom's telecommunications services in the U.K. will be reviewed in 1989—or its timing might be uncertain. In the latter case an important distinction must be made between exogenous and endogenous uncertainty. With endogenous uncertainty, the timing of the next review depends partly upon how the firm behaves in the meantime.

Bailey and Coleman (1971) extend the A–J model by supposing that regulators set prices after an interval of T periods. The firm, making its decisions at time zero, faces a trade-off between maximizing profits by producing more efficiently during the next T periods and overcapitalizing to induce a more favorable price when review eventually occurs. The balance is struck where

$$\frac{F_K}{F_L} = \frac{r}{w} - \frac{\rho^T}{1 - \rho^T} \frac{s - r}{w},$$

where ρ is the discount factor. It follows that it is optimal for the firm to overcapitalize to some extent (depending inversely upon T), but not as much as in the basic A–J model. A similar finding is obtained by Davis (1973) for a model in which price adjustment occurs continuously but only partially.

Baumol and Klevorick (1970, pp. 184–188) criticize the approach of Bailey and Coleman, and propose a model of regulatory lag which is of particular relevance to the style of regulation adopted in the major U.K. privatizations. They write (p. 184):

"While Bailey and Coleman regard the period before a regulatory review as a time when the firm suffers a loss because it is carrying an excessive amount of capital, now the period between reviews is regarded as the time when the firm has the possibility of earning a profit rate exceeding that specified by the constraint. When the regulatory review occurs, this excess is eliminated by the regulators' adjustment of the prices the firm can charge."

In our view this point has great force. Regulatory lag allows the firm to appropriate the benefits of improved cost efficiency until the next review occurs. A longer lag increases the firm's incentives to reduce its costs by innovation or superior organization of factors of production, but it delays the time at which consumers benefit from this greater efficiency. On the other hand, a shorter lag means that consumers benefit sooner, but the incentive to cut costs is reduced. This trade-off between static and dynamic efficiency has a close analogy in the literature on optimal patent life, and indeed Bailey (1974) analyzes the problem of innovation and regulatory lag in exactly that spirit (see also the debate between Lesourne (1976) and Bailey (1976)).

There is, however, a further point to consider. In the framework proposed by Baumol and Klevorick, price is brought into line with current costs at the time of each regulatory review. The RPI $-$ X style of regulation implemented in Britain is likely to fit this description. Although such a system provides good incentives for efficiency immediately after a review point, as time passes the firm's calculations will be increasingly affected by the benefit to be gained from influencing the outcome of the next regulatory review. As that time approaches, the firm will have little or no incentive to reduce costs if its future prices are positively related to its current cost level. Indeed, a point would then arise when the immediate gain from cost reduction was so short-lived as to be outweighed by the cost of having to face lower prices for the whole of the period until the following price review. In technical language, the second-order effect would be outweighed by the first-order effect, and the firm would come to favor *higher* costs when regulatory review is close at hand. We shall consider incentives for this kind of strategic behavior further in section 4.4 (see also Sappington, 1980).

These considerations suggest three lessons. First, the incentive effects of regulatory lag are not necessarily always benign. Strategic behavior designed to influence regulatory review could involve substantial losses in terms of allocative and productive efficiency, which would be offset against the initial spur to innovation provided by regulatory lag. Secondly, the potential losses from strategic behavior are reduced when regulatory review is less sensitive to current cost conditions. This points to the importance of the information available to regulators, especially information that is independent of the firm's decisions. We shall return later to this theme of the dangers of the firm's having a "monopoly of information." Thirdly, the timing of regulatory reviews is important—not only in terms of the length of regulatory lag, but also whether regulatory review occurs at regular intervals or stochastically.

We conclude this section by describing two models of stochastic regulatory review. (A discussion of further dynamic analysis is contained in section 4.4.) Klevorick (1973) examines a model in which for every period there is a given probability $\phi \in [0,1]$ of regulatory review. When review occurs, price is set so as to restore the "fair" rate of return s on the current capital stock. If ϕ were equal to 1, we would effectively have the A–J model, albeit in an explicitly dynamic setting, and if ϕ were equal to zero, regulatory lag would be infinite and the firm would have perfect incentives for productive efficiency. The intermediate case leads to overcapitalization, although not to the extent of that occurring in the A–J model.

Bawa and Sibley's (1980) more general model of *endogenous* stochastic regulatory review is more satisfactory. The probability of review in any period is a function $\phi(X)$ of current profit in excess (or deficit) of the level allowed by the rate of return s. Thus X_t is defined as

$$X_t = \pi_t - (s-r)K_t.$$

It is assumed that $\phi(0) = \phi'(0) = 0$, $\phi'(X) > 0$ for $X > 0$, and $\phi'(X) < 0$ for $X < 0$. If review does occur in period t, price is set at the level that yields rate of return s on the capital stock K_t until the next review takes place.

The model captures the idea that the firm has to balance its desire for short-run profits against the risk of jeopardizing future profits by triggering a review of its prices. Bawa and Sibley use techniques of stochastic dynamic programming to establish the following:

(i) the firm will overcapitalize, be efficient, or undercapitalize according to whether the allowed rate of return s exceeds, equals, or is less than the cost of capital r;

(ii) there is continuity in the sense that s close to r leads to approximate efficiency;

(iii) under fairly general conditions there is convergence to the price at which $X = 0$ and to cost minimization.

As well as having a more realistic formulation of the regulatory process, Bawa and Sibley's model yields more intuitive results than the basic A–J model. For example, $s = r$ leads to efficient production and $s < r$ involves undercapitalization, whereas in the A–J model we saw that $s = r$ has an outcome that is indeterminate (and, in terms of capital bias, undesirable) and $s < r$ leads to the shutdown of production. In the richer dynamic setting we therefore escape the welfare trade-off examined by Klevorick (1971) between allocative and productive efficiency as s approaches r: the conflict disappears.

4.2.3   Credibility, Commitment, and Underinvestment

So far we have paid little attention to one of the main features of much capital investment—the presence of sunk costs and adjustment costs. In the A–J model it is as though there exists a rental market for capital equipment that is a freely variable factor of production. But in fact there are typically major adjustment costs when the scale or nature of a firm's operations are changed, and capital costs are often sunk in the sense that the assets have significantly less value in their next alternative use. Much the same is true of certain types of labor when hiring, training, and firing costs are taken into account.

In contrast, variables such as price—the prime instrument of regulatory policy—are usually easier to alter. The resulting asymmetry of adjustment costs can have serious implications for regulatory policy, which we shall illustrate by way of two examples.

The first of these is a "dynamic consistency" problem (see Greenwald,

1984). Suppose for simplicity that the regulation game has three stages: (i) the regulator announces the price that the firm will be allowed to charge, (ii) the firm makes its investment decisions, which involve a large element of sunk costs, and (iii) the regulator reviews the previously announced pricing policy.

At stage (iii) a regulator seeking to maximize consumer benefits would wish to impose the lowest possible prices subject to encouraging the firm to produce (i.e. subject to covering the variable costs of production). Similarly, a regulator intent upon maximizing the sum of consumer and producer surplus would set $P = MC$, which in many regulated industries might imply that price is below (long-run) average cost. In sum there is a range of regulator's objectives for which the firm would be wary of committing large investment expenditures at stage (ii) for fear of what might happen at stage (iii), and the announcement of the price at stage (i) would then lack credibility. (The risk of renationalization on less than fair terms is a related problem, which we consider separately below.)

This credibility problem, which arises from the public interest mandate of the regulator, has the effect of undermining the public interest insofar as it inhibits investment at stage (ii), for example by increasing risk-adjusted private discount rates. The solution advocated by Greenwald (1984, p. 86) is as follows:

"Restricting regulators with an appropriate 'fairness' criterion may, therefore, be essential to the viability of the originally optimal equilibrium. The simplest way to do this would be to require by law that past regulatory promises must be honored in future proceedings. To maintain the flexibility of regulators to respond to unforeseen circumstances, however, the set of legally binding past promises should be minimally constraining. Since investors should be concerned only with future returns, the minimum acceptable set of legal constraints need only guarantee the value of future income implied by past promises."

Greenwald argues that in the United States "properly interpreted, the present structure of rate return regulation corresponds exactly to such a system." The credibility of a commitment to fairness is no doubt enhanced by wider share ownership, because the constituency opposed to "unfairness" is larger and more vocal. But this does not solve the problem completely, because whenever the credibility of the fairness constraint is below 100 percent, there is a risk factor that managers of a profit-maximizing firm would wish to take into account.

We now turn to our second illustration. Returning to the simple schema above, it is clear that the regulator at stage (iii) will be influenced by the investment decisions made by the firm at stage (ii). Thus the firm has an opportunity to influence the regulatory regime that it faces. For simplicity, suppose that expansion of the firm's capital stock is prohibitively costly in the relevant timescale. Assume that the regulator seeks to maximize the sum of consumer and producer surplus, and that there are no externalities. Then the regulator will set $P = MC$ given the cost curve resulting from the firm's prior investment decision.

More formally, let inverse demand be $P(Q)$ and let the cost function be $C(Q,K)$ where Q is output and K is the capital stock. It is reasonable to suppose that marginal cost C_Q is positive, increasing in Q for given K, and decreasing in K for given Q. Thus $C_Q > 0$, $C_{QQ} > 0$, and $C_{QK} < 0$. Also, we assume $C_{KK} > 0$. We are interested in at least two questions. Does the firm choose to operate on a scale that is suboptimally small? Does the firm produce its output in an efficient manner?

The regulator is assumed to impose marginal cost pricing. Thus

$$P(Q) = C_Q(Q,K). \tag{4.4}$$

The firm chooses K and Q to maximize profit $P(Q)Q - C(Q,K)$ subject to (4.4). The Lagrangean is

$$H(Q,K) = P(Q)\,Q - C(Q,K) + \mu[P(Q) - C_Q(Q,K)] \tag{4.5}$$

and the first-order conditions are

$$P + P'Q - C_Q + \mu(P' - C_{QQ}) = 0 \tag{4.6}$$

and

$$- C_K - \mu C_{QK} = 0. \tag{4.7}$$

Equations (4.4), (4.6), and (4.7) imply that

$$C_K = \frac{C_{QK}\,QP'}{P' - C_{QQ}}, \tag{4.8}$$

which is negative. It follows that the regulated firm in this context produces its output inefficiently, and with a capital-to-output ratio (and hence a capital-to-labor ratio) that is too *low*. The firm holds back its capital stock in order to induce a more profitable price from the regulator. The result is undercapitalization. Moreover, the regulated firm produces less output than at the first best.

Figure 4.3 illustrates both points. Isoprofit curves for the firm in (Q,K) space are centered on point F, and isowelfare curves for the regulator are centered on point W. That point is northeast of F, representing the firm's interest in restricting output to the monopoly level. The efficiency locus defined by $C_K = 0$ slopes up and passes through both F and W. The

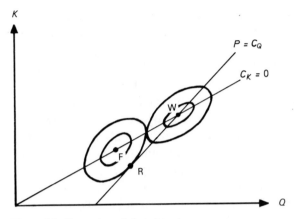

Figure 4.3   Strategic underinvestment

$P = \text{MC}$ locus also has an upward slope; it cuts isowelfare curves where they have a zero slope. The regulated firm operates at point R. Figure 4.3 shows how output is restricted below its optimal level and produced in an undercapitalized manner.

The diagram also suggests—and indeed it can be proved—that the welfare comparison between F and R is ambiguous. The pure monopoly point F is one of allocative inefficiency because $P > \text{MC}$, but the monopoly output is produced at minimum cost. The regulated firm does not produce its output at minimum cost, but R is a point where there is allocative efficiency because $P = \text{MC}$. Once again we see the conflict between internal (productive) efficiency and allocative efficiency.

Both models outlined in this section are rudimentary, but their purpose was simply to illustrate two dangers of underinvestment when considerations of commitment and dynamics are taken into account. In one case investment is inhibited by the fear of "unfair" future regulation. Unless the regulatory and/or political systems provide a credible means of commitment to future fairness, this fear is not entirely unreasonable in view of the objectives of regulators. In the second example, underinvestment was a strategic move by the firm seeking to obtain a more favorable regulatory regime. We will develop this point further, but now we address explicitly a major issue that has so far only been in the background of our discussion—the role of asymmetric information.

4.3   Regulation with Asymmetric Information

If a regulatory agency had as much knowledge about industry conditions and behavior as the firm being regulated, it could simply direct the firm to implement its chosen plan, provided that the agency possessed sufficient powers to do so. Indeed, it would then be better simply to appoint the regulatory agency to run the enterprise rather than to leave decision-making authority with the managers of the firm. But of course decision makers within the firm are generally far more knowledgeable than regulators can be about the circumstances facing them, and the regulator can neither observe nor infer all aspects of the firm's behavior. Thus asymmetric information is one of the main features of the economics of regulation (of both public and private enterprise), and in this section we examine some recent contributions to the literature, notably those of Baron and Myerson (1982) and Laffont and Tirole (1986). An excellent survey of this topic is provided by Caillaud *et al.* (1985). Owing to its more technical nature, some of our discussion is contained in starred sections, which some readers might prefer to omit.

4.3.1   Principal–Agent Theory and Regulation

Principal–agent theory was introduced in chapter 2 as a way of examining the relationship between the (public or private) owners of a firm and its managers. The theory is concerned with the design of incentives for efficiency under conditions of asymmetric information. The principal (i.e. the owners in chapter 2) is less informed than the agent (i.e. the managers) about the conditions facing the firm, and may be unable to monitor the agent's behavior with precision. Asymmetry of information gives rise to imperfect incentives, and inefficiency is the result.

Principal–agent theory can be used in exactly the same fashion to study regulation. In this context the government or the regulatory authority is the principal, and (the management of) the firm is the agent. With this perspective, a system of regulation can be regarded as an *incentive mechanism*. The firm is better informed than the regulator about cost conditions for example, and the regulator seeks to induce the firm to make its pricing, output, and investment decisions in accordance with the public interest given the cost conditions that exist. But the firm is interested in maximizing (say) its profits and, whatever the scheme of regulation may be, it will act in its own interests.

Suppose for example that the government's objective is social welfare W defined as the sum of consumer surplus S and the firm's profit π. Let the firm's objective be to maximize profit. (The firm is taken to be risk-neutral.) Let θ be the unit cost level of the firm, which the regulator cannot observe, and let Q be the firm's level of output. To begin with let us assume that Q is observable by the regulator. He would like Q to be chosen so that price equals marginal cost, but he does not know θ. However, if he can make lump-sum transfers to (or from) the firm, it is in fact possible to bring about the optimal outcome in this example (see Loeb and Magat, 1979). The regulator should undertake to pay the firm an amount equal to the consumer surplus from output Q minus a constant sum. With this incentive scheme the firm receives its profit (i.e. producer surplus) plus the payment equal to consumer surplus minus the constant. It maximizes this objective if and only if it maximizes the regulator's objective. In this special case it is therefore possible to engineer the first-best outcome by an appropriate incentive scheme, even without knowing cost conditions.

Although this decentralized scheme might be neat in theory, it obviously has several overwhelming practical drawbacks (see Sharkey, 1979). First, although the scheme does not require cost information, the government needs to know the magnitude of consumer surplus—a much more demanding task. Although prices provide some information about *marginal* utility, they do not say much about the whole area under the demand curve (let alone income effects etc.). Secondly, the scheme runs the risk of bankrupting the firm when costs are high and consumer surplus is correspondingly low, unless the fixed element of the incentive scheme is so generous as to cushion the firm against any eventuality—in which case the firm will make huge profits in more favorable states of the world. Thirdly, the scheme depends on the government being indifferent to transfers between consumers or taxpayers and the firm, i.e. on its objective being $W = S + \pi$.

However, the government's objective cannot generally be represented simply as the sum of consumer surplus and profit (see section 2.3.2 above, and Caillaud *et al.* (1985, pp. 4–7)). A concern for distribution might cause less weight to be attached to profit than to consumer interests. In that case, an objective of the form $W = S + \alpha\pi$ would be appropriate, with $0 \leqslant \alpha < 1$. Indeed, we shall use that specification of government objectives in the following two sections. Secondly, costs to the economy of raising public funds can be represented by attaching a negative weight to lump-sum transfers to the firm. Thirdly, the interests of employees could be taken into account, although this is less likely to be an important factor for independent regulatory authorities than for politicians.

The next two sections describe versions of the models of regulation under asymmetric information examined by Baron and Myerson (1982) and Laffont and Tirole (1986). Our discussion is far from being rigorous, but it is somewhat more technical than usual. Some readers might prefer to go directly to section 4.3.4, which summarizes the main findings of the analysis.

4.3.2*   Regulation with Unknown Costs

In this section we present a simplified version of Baron and Myerson's (1982) model of regulation with unknown costs. The model is one of asymmetric information. The firm knows its unit cost level, denoted θ, but the regulator does not. We assume that θ is distributed uniformly on an interval $[\underline{\theta}, \overline{\theta}]$.

Consumer utility from output level Q is denoted $V(Q)$, and $P(Q) = V'(Q)$ is the inverse demand curve. Let $R(Q) = QP(Q)$ be the firm's revenue, and let T be the transfer (possibly negative) paid to the firm. Net consumer surplus is therefore $S = V - R - T$, and profit is $\pi = R - \theta Q + T$. The regulator's objective is taken to be $W = S + \alpha\pi$, where $0 \leqslant \alpha \leqslant 1$. We saw above that $\alpha < 1$ can be interpreted as reflecting a concern for distribution.

A regulatory mechanism will induce, for each value of θ, an associated level of output $Q(\theta)$ and transfer $T(\theta)$. The *revelation principle* (see Myerson, 1979; Dasgupta *et al.*, 1979) implies that, without loss of generality, we can consider the regulator's optimization problem as equivalent to the following. The regulator requires the firm to provide a report $\hat{\theta}$ of its cost level, and determines the output $Q(\hat{\theta})$ and the transfer $T(\hat{\theta})$ as a function of that report. The firm must have no incentive to report its cost level untruthfully given that Q and T are determined in that manner.

This truth-telling constraint involves no loss of generality, because if the firm found it optimal to lie by reporting $\hat{\theta}(\theta)$ when the truth was θ, the regulator could simply amend the mechanism to be $\overline{Q}(\theta) = Q[\hat{\theta}(\theta)]$ and $\overline{T}(\theta) = T[\hat{\theta}(\theta)]$, and the firm would then find it optimal to report the truth.

The revelation principle therefore allows us to consider the regulator's problem as one of choosing $Q(\theta)$ and $T(\theta)$ to maximize the expected value of W subject to (i) the firm's finding it optimal to report θ truthfully, and (ii) the firm's always being willing to operate—i.e. receiving nonnegative profits in all states of the world.

More formally, let

$$S(\theta) = V[Q(\theta)] - R[Q(\theta)] - T(\theta)$$

be the net consumer surplus in state θ, and let

$$\pi(\hat{\theta}, \theta) = R[Q(\hat{\theta})] - \theta Q(\hat{\theta}) + T(\hat{\theta})$$

be the profit in state θ when $\hat\theta$ is reported. Define $\pi(\theta) = \pi(\theta,\theta)$. Then we can state the regulator's problem as follows.

Choose $Q(\theta)$ and $T(\theta)$ to maximize

$$EW = \int_{\underline\theta}^{\bar\theta} [S(\theta) + \alpha\pi(\theta)] \, d\theta \tag{4.9}$$

subject to

$$\pi(\theta) \geqslant \pi(\hat\theta,\theta) \text{ for all } \theta \text{ and } \hat\theta \tag{4.10}$$

and

$$\pi(\theta) \geqslant 0 \text{ for all } \theta. \tag{4.11}$$

Conditions (4.10) and (4.11) correspond to (i) and (ii) above. We shall assume that (4.10) is characterized by the first-order condition

$$R'Q' - \theta Q' + T' = 0. \tag{4.12}$$

The constraint (4.11) is binding only at $\bar\theta$, because for $\theta < \bar\theta$ we have

$$\pi(\theta) \geqslant \pi(\bar\theta,\theta) > \pi(\bar\theta). \tag{4.13}$$

The rent accruing to the firm from its monopoly of information derives from this fact.

The Lagrangean associated with the regulator's problem is

$$H = \int [S + \alpha\pi + \mu(R'Q' - \theta Q' + T')] \, d\theta$$

$$= \int [V - (1-\alpha)(R+T) - \alpha\theta Q + \mu(R'Q' - \theta Q' + T')] \, d\theta. \tag{4.14}$$

For notational simplicity in (4.14) we suppress the dependence of Q, T, and the multiplier μ upon θ, and the range of integration $[\underline\theta, \bar\theta]$. Let I be the integrand [.]. Then the Euler optimization conditions are

$$\frac{\partial I}{\partial X} = \frac{d}{d\theta}\frac{\partial I}{\partial X'} \text{ for } X = Q, T \tag{4.15}$$

The condition with respect to Q is

$$V' - (1-\alpha)R' - \alpha\theta + \mu R''Q' = \mu(R''Q' - 1) + \mu'(R' - \theta) \tag{4.16}$$

and the condition with respect to T is

$$-(1-\alpha) = \mu'. \tag{4.17}$$

Since we have a free-boundary problem we can choose $\mu(\underline\theta) = 0$, and (4.17) therefore implies that

$$\mu(\theta) = -(1 - \alpha)(\theta - \underline{\theta}).$$ (4.18)

Using (4.16) to (4.18), and recalling that $V' = P$, we have the central result that

$$P[Q(\theta)] = \theta + (1 - \alpha)(\theta - \underline{\theta}).$$ (4.19)

Under the optimal regulatory mechanism, price is equal to unit (and marginal) cost *plus* a mark-up depending on α and $(\theta - \underline{\theta})$. Note that optimality always involves marginal cost pricing when $\alpha = 1$, in keeping with the Loeb–Magat mechanism described above. But in general, when $\alpha < 1$, there is a loss of allocative efficiency because price exceeds marginal cost, except in the best state of the world $\underline{\theta}$.

It is optimal for the regulator to forego allocative efficiency to some extent because he is also concerned to minimize the size of the transfer T, which has a net cost of $(1 - \alpha)T$. He could induce marginal cost pricing, but only at the expense of a greater expected transfer to the firm. Optimality requires that a balance be struck between allocative efficiency and the minimization of the transfer.

If the regulator were as well informed as the firm—i.e. if he could observe θ—his problem would be to maximize (4.9) subject only to (4.11). The solution to this problem is $P[Q(\theta)] = \theta$ and $T = 0$ for all θ. In that event there is always allocative efficiency, and the firm always exactly breaks even. Therefore the partial loss of allocative efficiency is not the only reason why the regulator is adversely affected by the presence of asymmetric information. He also loses from the fact that the firm obtains a strictly positive payoff (in all but one state of the world). The asymmetry of information therefore causes two kinds of inefficiency to the detriment of consumers and the regulator's objective. However, the firm gains from the regulator's imperfect information because it obtains *money rent* in the form of transfers more than sufficient to meet its break-even constraint.

4.3.3*   Regulation with Unobservable Effort

We now present a model based (somewhat loosely) on the work of Laffont and Tirole (1986) which adds another dimension to the regulatory problem. In the Baron–Myerson model above it was assumed that the level of costs was given to the firm but that the regulator could not observe it. In contrast, we now suppose that costs are influenced by the firm's cost-reducing *effort*, and that the regulator can observe the cost level. However, costs are determined jointly by two factors—the state of nature and the firm's effort—neither of which is observable by the regulator. He therefore cannot tell whether (say) low costs are due to great efforts by the firm or to a favorable state of nature.

More specifically, let unit costs c depend upon the state of nature θ and the level of effort a as follows:

$$c = \theta - a.$$

The cost of effort is denoted $z(a)$, where $z(0) = z'(0) = 0$, $z'(a) > 0$ for $a > 0$, and $z''(a) > 0$. As before, θ is taken to be distributed uniformly on $[\underline{\theta}, \bar{\theta}]$. The notation for consumer utility, price, output, revenue, and the transfer is also as in the previous section. The regulator is again assumed to be concerned with welfare defined as $W = S + \alpha\pi$ with $0 \leqslant \alpha \leqslant 1$.

As before, a regulatory mechanism will induce an output level $Q(\theta)$, a cost level $c(\theta)$, and a transfer $T(\theta)$ for each value of θ. Invoking the revelation principle, we can consider the regulator's problem as choosing the three functions $Q(\theta)$, $c(\theta)$, and $T(\theta)$ to maximize expected welfare subject to (i) the firm's finding it optimal to report θ truthfully, and (ii) the firm's always being willing to operate in the sense of achieving nonnegative profits. It might be thought more natural to view the problem as one of choosing Q and T as functions of observed c, but the revelation principle is more convenient analytically and anyway accommodates the point. For if $\bar{Q}(c)$ and $\bar{T}(c)$ were an optimal regulatory scheme, and if $\bar{c}(\theta)$ was optimal for the firm facing that scheme, then by defining $Q(\theta) = \bar{Q}[\bar{c}(\theta)]$ and $T(\theta) = \bar{T}[\bar{c}(\theta)]$ we would have an optimal scheme satisfying (ii) and expressed in a more convenient form. Therefore no generality is lost.

The net consumer surplus in state θ is

$$S(\theta) = V[Q(\theta)] - R[Q(\theta)] - T(\theta),$$

and the profit in state θ when $\hat{\theta}$ is reported is

$$\pi(\hat{\theta}, \theta) = R[Q(\hat{\theta})] - c(\hat{\theta})Q(\hat{\theta}) - z[\theta - c(\hat{\theta})] + T(\hat{\theta}).$$

Define $\pi(\theta) = \pi(\theta, \theta)$. Then the regulator's problem is as follows.

Choose $Q(\theta)$, $c(\theta)$, and $T(\theta)$ to maximize

$$EW = \int_{\underline{\theta}}^{\bar{\theta}} [S(\theta) + \alpha\pi(\theta)]\, d\theta \qquad (4.20)$$

subject to

$$\pi(\theta) \geqslant \pi(\hat{\theta}, \theta) \text{ for all } \theta \text{ and } \hat{\theta} \qquad (4.21)$$

and

$$\pi(\theta) \geqslant 0 \text{ for all } \theta. \qquad (4.22)$$

We shall assume that (4.21) is characterized by

$$R'Q' - c'Q - cQ' + z'c' + T' = 0. \tag{4.23}$$

Condition (4.21) binds only at $\bar{\theta}$, and $\pi(\theta) > 0$ for all $\theta \neq \bar{\theta}$ (see (4.12) above).

The Lagrangean associated with the regulator's problem is

$$
\begin{aligned}
H &= \int [S + \alpha\pi + \lambda(R'Q' - c'Q - cQ' + z'c' + T')]\,d\theta \\
&= \int [V - (1-\alpha)(R+T) - \alpha cQ - \alpha z + \\
&\quad \lambda(R'Q' - c'Q - cQ' + z'c' + T')]\,d\theta. \tag{4.24}
\end{aligned}
$$

For notational convenience we suppress the functional dependence of Q, c, T, and λ upon θ, and the range of integration $[\underline{\theta}, \bar{\theta}]$.

The Euler conditions with respect to Q, c, and T respectively are given in the following three equations:

$$V' - (1-\alpha)R' - \alpha c + \lambda(R''Q' - c') = \lambda(R''Q' - c') + \lambda'(R' - c) \tag{4.25}$$

$$-\alpha Q + \alpha z' + \lambda(-Q' - z''c') = \lambda[-Q' + z''(1-c')] + \lambda'(-Q + z') \tag{4.26}$$

$$-(1-\alpha) = \lambda'. \tag{4.27}$$

Since this is a free-boundary problem we can choose $\lambda(\underline{\theta}) = 0$, and (4.27) therefore implies

$$\lambda(\theta) = -(1-\alpha)(\theta - \underline{\theta}). \tag{4.28}$$

Equations (4.25) to (4.28) now imply the two central equations

$$P[Q(\theta)] = c(\theta) \tag{4.29}$$

and

$$
\begin{aligned}
z'[\theta - c(\theta)] &= Q(\theta) - (1-\alpha)(\theta - \underline{\theta})z''[\theta - c(\theta)] \\
&< Q(\theta) \text{ except at } \underline{\theta}. \tag{4.30}
\end{aligned}
$$

At the first best, where the regulator can observe effort, we have $P = c$ and $z' = Q$ for all θ. Equation (4.29) states that the optimum with asymmetric information has price equal to marginal cost, which is allocatively efficient *given* the level of costs. But (4.30) implies that cost-reducing effort is generally *less* than that required at the first best. Therefore costs are too high, and so price is higher than at the first best.

The firm in this example also enjoys some rent from its monopoly of information, but this rent comes partly in the form of *slack*—i.e. from suboptimally low levels of cost-reducing effort. Thus there is a precise sense in which the optimal regulatory mechanism involves X-inefficiency (see Leibenstein, 1966).

If the regulator did not have available the possibility of making a lump-sum transfer, he would of course have more problems. Price would have to exceed unit cost in order to cover the cost of effort. This would necessitate a departure from allocative efficiency, and would further attenuate incentives for cost reduction because gains from reducing unit costs would be spread across fewer units of output.

The analysis in the last two sections has been more technical than most of this book, but we must emphasize that it has not been at all rigorous. Our aim has been simply to try to convey the flavor of some of the methods used to analyze asymmetric information. A more exhaustive and rigorous treatment is given by Caillaud *et al.* (1985). Next we summarize the main findings of recent work on regulation under asymmetric information, and discuss some important extensions of the analysis.

4.3.4 Regulation with Asymmetric Information: Conclusions

Asymmetric information is at the heart of the economics of regulation. If the government and the firm's managers had access to the same information about industry conditions and the firm's behavior, then the regulatory problem could be solved by simply directing the managers to implement the socially optimal plan given the (common) information available. In reality, however, managers are much better informed about industry conditions than are the firm's owners and regulators, and their behavior can be monitored only imperfectly. The question is how to motivate managers to exploit their superior information to advantage despite the problem of imperfect monitoring. Note here the very close analogy between (a) the problem that a firm's owners (public or private) have in giving managers incentives to act in the owners' interests, and (b) the problem that government regulators have in giving a regulated firm (or its managers) incentives to act in the public interest.

Chapter 2 on ownership considered problem (a), while the present chapter is concerned with problem (b). Ideally we would like to combine (a) and (b) since the incentives of the managers of a regulated firm are influenced by both its owners and its regulators. However, that would raise very complex issues, and for the present we leave aside problem (a) by supposing that the managers of a regulated private firm act as profit maximizers.

Theories of regulation in the Averch–Johnson tradition do not explicitly take account of asymmetric information. Their purpose is to examine the consequences for firm behavior of given (and not necessarily optimal) regulatory schemes. The recent work reviewed in this section, which explicitly models asymmetries of information, addresses the question of what is the *optimal* regulatory mechanism given the information available. In doing so, it illuminates the trade-offs between internal and allocative efficiency that result from asymmetric information, and it reveals how the effectiveness of regulation depends critically upon the information available to the regulators.

In the model proposed by Baron and Myerson (1982) the government cannot observe the (exogenously given) cost structure of the firm. The government attaches more weight to consumer interests than to producer interests, and a scheme of the type suggested by Loeb and Magat (1979)—in which the firm receives consumer surplus minus a fixed amount—is therefore undesirable on distributional grounds because the firm would tend to make large profits. The government would like price to equal unit (variable) cost, but it cannot observe cost. If it imposed a low price, there would be some circumstances in which the firm would refuse to supply the market. In order to avoid this unpleasant result, the government's regulatory scheme must strike a compromise, and it turns out that price generally exceeds unit costs at the optimal compromise. Allocative inefficiency is the result. Furthermore, the firm generally makes a positive profit thanks to its "monopoly of information."

Laffont and Tirole (1986) extend the model by allowing costs to depend upon the firm's efforts as well as on given circumstances. The government is assumed to be able to observe the level of costs, but not the extent of cost-reducing effort. It cannot tell whether low costs are due to good luck or effort. The trade-off between internal efficiency (i.e. optimal effort given output) and allocative efficiency (i.e. optimal output given effort) is clear. Setting price equal to unit cost gives perfect incentives for allocative efficiency but no incentive for cost reduction. Setting price equal to a given constant gives perfect incentives for internal efficiency but poor allocative efficiency. The optimal compromise involves output being lower, and price higher, than at the optimum with symmetric information. The degree of cost reduction is too low, and so there is internal inefficiency. Once again the firm benefits from its "monopoly of information," and the government is doubly disadvantaged by the asymmetry of information. The outcome is inefficient, and the firm extracts a profit from its informational advantage.

Analyses of this kind can be extended in various ways. Baron and Besanko (1984) introduce the possibility of costly *ex post auditing* of the conditions facing the firm, which can enhance efficiency by diminishing the asymmetry of information between regulator and firm. The same authors (Baron and Besanko, 1987) examine regulation under asymmetric information in a *dynamic* setting. Over time the regulator may be able to learn about the cost conditions facing the firm, and choose a regulatory mechanism that uses the information that emerges. Much also depends on whether the regulator can commit his strategy in advance (see also Freixas and Laffont, 1985). Baron and Besanko examine intermediate degrees of commitment, in particular a "fairness" condition. For an excellent survey of all these matters and more, we again refer the interested reader to Caillaud *et al.* (1985).

4.4 Regulation of Multiproduct Firms

The economics of regulating multiproduct firms is central to an assessment of policy towards companies such as BT, British Gas, and the electricity supply industry (ESI), irrespective of how they are owned. It is obvious that BT supplies a wide range of products (telephone handsets, mobile phone services, private branch exchanges, etc.), and its principal activity (supplying telephone calls) is also a complex business. A call made at 10 a.m. on Monday is a separate product from one made at 4 a.m. on Sunday. A local call within Oxford is a different product from a long-distance call from Oxford to Glasgow (or to Washington). BT's pricing structure must reflect these differences between time and place, and their associated costs. This task is complicated by the fact that many costs are shared between various types of call, and the question arises of which consumers should bear them. Very similar issues are faced by energy utilities such as the electricity industry. Demand fluctuates between times of the day and year, and is influenced by the weather. Given the limitations on capacity and the difficulty of storing output, the electricity pricing structure must be sensitive to demand variation if rationing is to be avoided. Again the question arises of how to cover common costs (e.g. generating and distribution capacity).

Multiproduct pricing and investment problems are of course the subject of a large body of theory on public enterprise, which we have no wish to replicate here (see, for example, Atkinson and Stiglitz, 1980, chapter 15; Baumol and Bradford, 1970; Bös, 1986; Diamond and Mirrlees, 1971; Rees, 1984a,b). Rather, our aim is briefly to describe some work on the behavior of multiproduct profit-maximizing firms subject to regulatory constraint. In particular we will outline the dynamic regulatory adjustment mechanism proposed by Vogelsang and Finsinger (1979), but we begin by looking at the problem in its simpler static form.

Consider a multiproduct firm producing outputs $Q_1, Q_2, ..., Q_n$ for n markets. Let Q denote this vector of outputs. Let $P = (P_1, P_2, ..., P_n)$ be the vector of prices in the various markets. The demand Q_i for product i will depend on the price vector P. The firm's costs $C(Q)$ will depend on the output vector Q, which in turn depends on the prices P. We assume natural monopoly cost conditions. We can write the firm's profit as a function of prices:

$$\pi(P) = \Sigma P_i Q_i(P) - C[Q(P)] \tag{4.31}$$

The first term on the right-hand side is the sum of the firm's revenues in the various markets that it serves, and the second term is its costs. Note that we have not made very restrictive assumptions about the dependence of demand on prices, or the dependence of cost on outputs.

Let consumer surplus (the sum of the areas under each demand curve) plus profit be the social welfare objective. Consumer surplus will depend on the prices charged, and we will denote it by $S(P)$. A useful fact is that

$$\frac{-\partial S(P)}{\partial P_i} = Q_i(P). \tag{4.32}$$

If the price of product i is increased by a small unit, then the loss of consumer surplus is equal to that unit times the quantity of product i demanded.

Which pricing and production plan maximizes social welfare? The ideal solution (the first-best) has marginal cost pricing for each product:

$$P_i = \mathrm{MC}_i = \frac{\partial C}{\partial Q_i}. \tag{4.33}$$

But marginal cost pricing entails losses when there are scale economies. If transfers from the government to the firm are impossible or undesirable, social welfare must be maximized subject to a break-even constraint. The problem then is equivalent to choosing P to

maximize $S(P)$ subject to $\pi(P) \geqslant 0$.

Under fairly mild assumptions about cost and demand conditions, the solution to this second-best problem requires that the term

$$\frac{P_i - \mathrm{MC}_i}{\mathrm{MR}_i - \mathrm{MC}_i} \tag{4.34}$$

is the same in each market (MR_i denotes marginal revenue in market i). This is known as Ramsey pricing. The Ramsey formula implies that price–cost mark-ups are higher in markets where demand is less elastic.

Now let us turn to the profit-maximizing decision of a regulated private firm. Suppose that regulation takes the form of an average price constraint (this is roughly how BT is regulated). Suppose that a weighted average of its prices must be less than a given level $\bar{P}$:

$$\Sigma w_i P_i \leqslant \bar{P}, \tag{4.35}$$

where the w_i are positive weights that add up to unity. The firm maximizes $\pi(P)$ subject to (4.35). Everything now depends on how the weights and the price limit $\bar{P}$ are chosen. An important special case is when they are chosen in such a way that the firm can just break even, and when the weights are proportional to the demands for each product when there is Ramsey pricing. Given some assumptions about cost and demand conditions, it then turns out that *the regulated private firm chooses Ramsey pricing.*

Figure 4.4 attempts to illustrate why this is so in the two-product case. (See Vogelsang and Finsinger (1979) for a more rigorous account. The arguments depend on assumptions (e.g. about concavity) that we do not detail here.) The shaded region contains the price combinations that satisfy constraint (4.35) for a particular choice of the weights w_i and the limit $\bar{P}$. The diagram shows a consumer surplus indifference curve ($S(P)$ = constant) and an isoprofit curve tangential to the line representing the price constraint. Consumer surplus rises, but profit falls, nearer the origin. It is

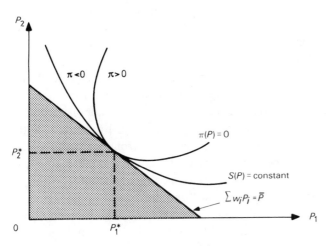

Figure 4.4   Regulation of multiproduct pricing

evident from the way that the diagram has been drawn that the price pair (P^*_1, P^*_2) maximizes consumer surplus subject to $\pi(P) \geqslant 0$. These are the Ramsey prices. The price constraint has been set so that the same price combination maximizes profit subject to prices obeying the regulatory price constraint. Thus the price constraint has induced Ramsey pricing.

How did the choice of w_i and $\bar{P}$ bring this about? The weights w_i determine the slope of the price constraint line, and $\bar{P}$ determines its distance from the origin. For given weights w_i it is easy to choose a level of $\bar{P}$ that causes the price constraint line to be a tangent to the $\pi(P) = 0$ locus. Weights proportional to the quantities demanded at Ramsey prices ensure that this point of tangency is also the point where the consumer surplus indifference curve is a tangent to the price constraint line. That is because the slope of the consumer surplus indifference curve at that point is

$$\frac{dP_2}{dP_1} = \frac{-\partial S(P^*)}{\partial P_1} \div \frac{\partial S(P^*)}{\partial P_2} = \frac{-Q_1(P^*)}{Q_2(P^*)}. \tag{4.36}$$

The first equality in (4.36) follows from totally differentiating $S(P^*) =$ constant, and the second equality follows directly from (4.32). If the weights are chosen so that w_i is proportional to $Q_i(P^*)$, it follows that the points of tangency coincide: maximizing profit subject to the appropriate price constraint delivers the same result as maximizing welfare subject to a break-even constraint.

The general reason why this form of price control produces the (constrained) optimal outcome can be outlined as follows. The problem of maximizing profit subject to the price constraint has the same solution as the problem of minimizing the cost of purchasing the consumption bundle demanded at Ramsey prices subject to the break-even constraint. (This follows from the weights' being proportional to Ramsey quantities.) The latter problem is equivalent to maximizing consumer surplus subject to the break-even constraint, because both involve minimizing the expenditure needed to obtain the consumers' preferred consumption bundle.

To summarize, private ownership of a multiproduct monopolist is no bar to allocative efficiency provided that the price control formula is aptly chosen. This proviso must be emphasized strongly, because the information about cost and demand needed to set the w_i and $\bar{P}$ correctly is very difficult to obtain. If the government possessed the information, it could just as well run the industry itself and implement optimal pricing directly. Before turning to dynamics there is one last point to make about the static case. There is a major difference between the average *price* constraint (4.35) and an average *revenue* constraint of the form

$$\frac{\Sigma P_i Q_i}{\Sigma Q_i} \leqslant \bar{P}. \tag{4.37}$$

The difference is that the weights in (4.35) are exogenous to the firm, whereas the weights (i.e. $Q_i/\Sigma Q_i$) in (4.37) depend on the firm's behavior. The optimality result for the average price constraint does not carry over to the average revenue constraint. In the latter case the firm has an incentive to behave strategically to alter the weights in its price control formula, and allocative inefficiency is the usual result (see section 9.2.4 for a discussion of this point in relation to the average revenue constraint facing British Gas).

The dynamic price control mechanism proposed by Vogelsang and Finsinger (V–F) (1979) is motivated by the limitation on the government's information that was mentioned in the paragraph above (and analyzed at some length in section 4.3). The government simply cannot know enough to design a price control formula that induces Ramsey pricing. Indeed, it does not know what the Ramsey prices are. The V–F mechanism is designed to enforce the eventual adoption of Ramsey pricing despite this lack of information about cost and demand functions.

The V–F mechanism allows the monopoly firm to choose its product prices in each time period subject to the condition that a weighted average of its prices should not exceed a given level. In particular, the prices charged in period t must be such that the revenues from setting the previous period's outputs at those prices must not exceed the total costs incurred in the previous period. In notation, the constraint is that the prices charged in period t must satisfy

$$\Sigma_i P^t_i Q_i (P^{t-1}) \leqslant C[Q(P^{t-1})], \tag{4.38}$$

where the superscripts (t and $t-1$) indicate time periods. It is assumed that the government can observe last period's prices, outputs, and costs, though it does not know the cost and demand functions. For a single-product firm the constraint is that the price in period t must not exceed the average cost in period $t-1$. (It is assumed that there are scale economies. Otherwise the firm would not be able to find a price that meets this constraint and makes a profit. Similarly, in the multiproduct case, it is assumed that there are decreasing ray average costs, i.e. the average cost of supplying a given bundle of goods decreases as the scale of output increases.)

It is assumed that the firm knows its cost and demand functions (which are constant across time), and that it maximizes profits in each period. It follows that its behavior subject to constraint (4.38) leads to an increasing level of social welfare over time. In the limit welfare converges to a level

$W^* = W(P^*)$ such that the optimal (Ramsey) conditions hold at P^*. Thus the V–F mechanism appears to have very desirable incentive properties, despite the limited information available to government. The mechanism gives the firm freedom over relative prices and uses a kind of regulatory lag. In the words of Vogelsang and Finsinger (1979, p. 170) "the regulated firm ... is encouraged to exploit both the potential for cost decreases and the consumers' willingness to pay. The firm converts these into profits. But both these advantages are turned over to the consumers in the next period."

However, the V–F mechanism has weaknesses, and a major problem is analyzed by Sappington (1980). The desirable welfare properties of the V–F mechanism are based on the assumption that the firm is a short-run profit maximizer, but (as Vogelsang and Finsinger themselves recognize) the firm may respond to the V–F mechanism strategically when it has longer-term aims. Sappington (1980, p. 360) argues that "pure waste, inefficient factor utilization, excessive research and development, and overinvestment in demand-increasing expenditures may be employed by a firm to increase long-run profits." Indeed, he shows that V–F regulation can be worse than no regulation at all. Sappington shows that the V–F mechanism can encourage the firm to engage in "pure waste," i.e. the deliberate raising of costs. The strategic advantage of pure waste today is that it increases the permitted level of prices tomorrow. The idea of a firm engaging in pure waste might be thought rather implausible, but the point applies more generally. For example, the firm might strategically slacken its efforts to cut X-inefficiency and there are many instruments that the firm might use in order to manipulate the prices that it can charge under the regulatory scheme.

In this section we have considered the *structure* (as well as the overall level) of prices chosen by a multiproduct monopolist subject to regulation. In a static framework we saw that a profit-maximizing firm can be induced to adopt a desirable pricing structure when regulation takes the simple form of a limit on a suitably weighted average of the prices of the firm's various products. The problem is that the authorities generally do not possess enough information to set the weights and the price limit at the right levels. The ingenious V–F dynamic mechanism can bring about the optimal constraint endogenously over time, but it relies on myopic behavior by the firm. Many regulatory schemes would work well if firms were myopic, but in fact they tend not to be, and the pervasive danger of inefficient strategic manipulation arises once again because asymmetric information rules out its effective prevention.

Many points made in this section are directly relevant to an assessment of the RPI $-$ X method of price control that has been adopted for many privatized firms in Britain. This system essentially lays down a limit on the average price that the multiproduct firm can charge, and there is long regulatory lag. In principle the system could encourage an efficient price structure if the parameters of the allowed pricing formula were set correctly, but the authorities' relative paucity of information prevents this from happening, except perhaps by chance. Secondly, the system is vulnerable to inefficient strategic manipulation of costs by the regulated firm, especially as the time of regulatory review draws near (a problem which is shared by many regulatory schemes).

Finally, regulating a multiproduct firm by the RPI $-$ X method faces further problems when the firm faces competition in some of its regulated product markets. In this section we have assumed that the firm is a pure monopolist, but companies like BT have some competitors even though they enjoy great market power. If the average price constraint covers markets in which there is some actual or potential competition, incentives for an efficient pricing structure can become distorted. The average price constraint encourages the firm to undercut its rivals in the competitive business segments by allowing it to recoup the costs of doing so elsewhere. This problem, which arises from averaging, calls for more product-specific regulation and for safeguards against anticompetitive conduct. These questions go beyond the scope of the present section, and we will return to them when discussing regulation in practice in later chapters.

4.5   Collusion between Regulator and Firm

So far we have discussed what are often called *public interest* theories of regulation. These theories take it as given that the purpose of regulation is the enhancement of economic welfare via improved efficiency in resource allocation, and that the established agencies faithfully pursue the implied allocative objectives. There is a second major strand in the U.S. literature, however, which explicitly challenges these assumptions. Work in this second tradition—often labelled the *economic* theory of regulation (to emphasize that it is concerned with the determinants of the supply of, and demand for, regulatory activities)—has developed from seminal papers by Stigler (1971), Posner (1971), and Peltzman (1976). This work has focused heavily upon the income-distribution consequences of regulatory processes and the incentives faced by the regulators themselves. The theories are intended to be nonnormative, and seek to explain how particular forms of regulation emerge and change by evaluating the gains and losses implied by alternative institutional arrangements for the various interest groups involved.

Some of the interest group pressures on regulators fixing the prices of monopolistic firms are clear enough: consumers benefit from lower prices and producers favor higher prices (up to the unconstrained monopoly level). There are other potentially important aspects of the problem, however, that may be relevant: trade unions may align themselves with management on the pricing issue, hoping to appropriate some of the monopoly returns in the form of higher wages or better working conditions; consumers tend to be less well organized as a lobby group than either management or labor; the greater frequency of contact between management and regulators could, over a period, make the latter more receptive to the firms' arguments; regulators may be influenced by the prospect of remunerative employment in the industry once their public service days are over.

The ways in which these various pressures filter through into regulatory policies are affected by the institutional arrangements of the agencies, and by the constraints placed on the latter in the form of delegated mandates and judicial decisions. In the United States most regulatory agencies have relatively vague mandates (requiring, say, that their rates be "just, reasonable and nondiscriminatory"), thus leaving commissioners with significant discretion as to their interpretation and thereby opening up more opportunities for pressure group lobbying.

The effect of such lobbying will also depend upon the terms of appointment of the commissioners. Factors such as length of service, whether commissioners are appointed or elected, restrictions on re-appointment or re-election, etc. vary considerably from agency to agency in the United States, illustrating the range of alternatives that have been considered appropriate in different circumstances.

There is particular reason to be concerned about the potential influence of producer groups on regulations dealing with new entry into the industry. The effects on consumers of entry restrictions are less visible than the effects of price fixing, and there is a public interest argument in favor of control of entry that could be used in self-serving ways by producer groups. Simply stated, it is that natural monopoly implies that efficiency is improved by having the goods or services in question supplied by a single firm, and that entry prohibition is necessary to guarantee this outcome.

We are, to say the least, highly skeptical of this argument in favor of entry restriction. In the first place, an efficient dominant firm, with significant sunk costs and subject to price regulation, is unlikely to be highly vulnerable to substantial entry threats. More importantly, given the inherent difficulty of actually establishing whether or not a given industry is subject to natural monopoly conditions, it is probable that entry restrictions would in many cases lead to supply by a single firm when the goods or services in question could be more efficiently provided by separate firms. This is particularly significant when technological change is rapid and cost conditions are constantly changing. Finally, if entry threats are removed there will be a corresponding loss of incentives for production efficiency and innovation on the part of the dominant firm.

A theoretical perspective on the possibility of collusion between regulator and firm is provided by work on *hierarchies*, i.e. principal–agent relationships consisting of several levels (see the discussion in chapter 2, and Caillaud *et al.* (1985, section 7)). In the previous section we examined the principal–agent relationship

regulator → firm,

and we supposed that the regulator had the public interest at heart. A generalization is the scheme

government → regulator → firm.

If members of the regulatory agency have interests that do not coincide with the public interest, we should consider the first link in this chain as well as the second. For example, the government might wish to limit the discretion of the regulator. This is what happens under the RPI − X schemes of price regulation being introduced in Britain. The regulator has the duty of seeing that the firm complies with this general formula, but has no duty to intervene on specific pricing decisions.

A further generalization might be appropriate if it was felt that members of government are not necessarily fervent champions of the public interest. Then we might have

voters → government → regulator → firm.

Indeed it has been suggested in connection with the U.K. privatization program that it is government, rather than regulators, which has been partly "captured" by firms when designing regimes of competition and regulation for them. Related criticisms can be made of the control of nationalized industries. In chapter 5 below we will describe how the long-term development of nationalized industries in Britain has often suffered from government intervention and constraints motivated by short-term considerations. One of the advantages sometimes claimed for privatization is that it avoids problems of this kind. Whether or not it is the best way of doing so is another matter, to which we shall return later.

4.6   Competition and Regulation

In this section we examine three respects in which competition and regulation interact. The first is competition *for* monopoly, or franchising, which has indeed been used in a number of areas, for example local authority services in Britain where private operators have opportunities to outbid and displace public suppliers. Franchising has many attractive features especially where the product in question has a simple specification, but in industries of any complexity its merits are likely to be outweighed by problems of uncompetitive bidding, the handover of fixed assets, and contract monitoring. The second theme is competition via regulation, or "yardstick competition," in which regulated units in submarkets that are distinct (e.g. geographically) are brought into competition by the regulatory mechanism. For example, the price increase allowed in region A might be a function partly of cost performance in regions B and C. Thirdly we look at regulation in industries where there is some competition (actual or potential), as in the U.K. telecommunications industry for instance. The presence of competition influences the appropriate form of regulation, and regulation in turn affects the effectiveness of measures to permit or promote competition. Thus it is an important part of the task of regulatory authorities in the U.K. to try to guard against anticompetitive behavior. Here the overlap between regulatory and antitrust policies is most evident, and indeed it should always be remembered that regulatory mechanisms are just one element in the overall combination of public policies toward industrial organization and behavior.

4.6.1   Franchising

The dilemma for policy regarding natural monopolies is how to enjoy the cost benefits of single-firm production without suffering from monopolistic behavior. One answer is to have a competition—in the form of an auction—*for* the monopoly, with several firms competing to be the one that actually operates in the market. We will concentrate on an attractive form of franchising that was originally advocated by Edwin Chadwick, the Victorian social reformer, and developed by Demsetz (1969) in his famous article "Why regulate utilities?" According to the Chadwick–Demsetz (C–D) proposal, the franchise is awarded for a period of time to the competitor offering to supply the product or service at the lowest price(s), or, more generally, the best price–quality package (for a review of franchising in relation to natural monopoly, see Sharpe (1982)).

On the face of it, franchising appears to provide a very attractive way of combining competition and efficiency without any arduous burden for regulators. The competition for monopoly appears to destroy the undesirable monopoly of information that hinders traditional regulation, and price is set by competition, not by administrators. In practice, franchising has been successful in a number of fields. For example, a study in 1986 by the London Business School and Institute for Fiscal Studies showed that local authorities in Britain using private contractors have reduced costs by 22 percent on average while maintaining the standard of services. Local authorities have successfully used competitive tendering, which is a form of franchising, for subsidized bus services (see section 10.4). It goes almost without saying that franchising is widely used within the private sector.

However, there are many industries where franchising cannot work, at any rate in this simple form, and the industries described later in this book (energy, telecommunications, water, etc.) provide leading examples. We shall focus on three sources of difficulty—the danger that bidding for the franchise will be uncompetitive, problems of asset handover, and, most important, the difficulties of contract specification and monitoring.

There are two reasons why bidding for the franchise might fail to be competitive. First, there is a danger of *collusion* between bidders, especially if they are few in number (e.g. because the requisite skills or resources are rare) or if the firms are effectively in a repeated game with one another by virtue of frequent contacts of various kinds.

The second reason is that one firm might enjoy such *strategic advantages* in the competition for the franchise that other firms would be unwilling to compete with it. Suppose, for example, that firm A has recently been the holder of a franchise that is now up for renewal. If the experience gained by A from its past operation of the franchise has had the effect of reducing its costs of operation, then the future franchise is worth more to firm A than to other firms. This fact might deter the other firms even from competing with A for the future franchise because they know that they are unlikely to win the competition.

Another source of incumbent advantage can arise from asymmetries of information. If A is the incumbent operator of the franchise, then A's knowledge of cost and demand conditions is likely to be superior to that of any other firm. This will tend to deter others from competing with A for the future franchise. For if firm B outbids A for the franchise, it is likely that B has bid too much. The fact that the relatively ignorant firm B wins against the knowledgeable firm A is itself an indication that B has paid over the odds. This problem is sometimes known as the "winner's curse." Its effect is to deter competition with the knowledgeable firm, i.e. the incumbent. (Precisely how the effect operates depends, of course, upon the exact nature of the competition for the franchise. Although we do not present a formal model here, we believe that the verbal argument is sufficient to establish the general point. (See further Englebrecht-Wiggans *et al.* (1983) on the value of information in auctions.))

We now turn to problems of *asset handover*. Suppose that A has held the franchise until now, but that B has just defeated A in the competition for the franchise for the next interval of time. What happens to the assets hitherto used by A to operate the franchise? Unless sunk costs are zero (an extremely unlikely event) efficiency requires that B, the new operator of the franchise, takes over these assets from A. Otherwise there will be inefficient duplication of the assets. But how are the assets to be valued for this purpose? Here there is a problem of bilateral monopoly. If A had no alternative, it would accept as little as the scrap value of the assets. If B had no alternative, it would pay as much as their replacement value. The gap between replacement value and scrap value is likely to be large if the assets involve sunk costs, and the expense of bargaining or arbitration regarding the appropriate transfer price might well be considerable.

This fact in turn has implications for the nature of competition for the renewal of the franchise itself. Let X and Y denote the values to A and B respectively of operating the franchise in the future, aside from the cost of transferring the assets and bargaining costs. Let Z be the amount paid by B to A for the assets if B wins the future franchise, and let C_A and C_B be the bargaining costs of the two firms in that event. If A wins the franchise it receives X, and if A loses it receives $Z - C_A$. A's incentive to win is therefore $X - Z + C_A$. If B wins, it receives $Y - Z - C_B$ (which we initially assume to be positive), and if B loses it receives zero. Therefore A has a greater incentive than B if and only if

$$X + C_A + C_B > Y. \tag{4.39}$$

The condition for A to be a more efficient franchise operator than B is simply

$$X > Y. \tag{4.40}$$

A comparison of these two inequalities shows that the costs of bargaining $(C_A + C_B)$ have the effect of giving the incumbent firm A an advantage, because bargaining costs are avoided if the franchise does not change hands.

Note that Z, the amount paid to A for the assets if B wins, does not affect the *difference between* the incentives of A and B in the franchise competition (provided that $Z < Y - C_B$). This is because a higher level of Z reduces A's incentive to win just as much as it reduces B's incentive. However, if $Z \geqslant Y - C_B$, the level of Z *does* effect competition for the franchise, because B cannot make a positive profit whatever it bids and so would not compete. Thus A would be the only contestant. This consideration indicates that some form of regulation of the level of Z may be required.

Moreover the level of Z certainly influences the *level* of the bids that would be made in the auction for the franchise. If B could purchase A's assets at low cost, then B would be prepared to bid more than if the assets were more costly for B to acquire from A. Similarly, the incumbent firm A would compete less vigorously with B if B were required to pay more for the assets. Therefore the level of Z is bound to influence the size of incentives (if not the difference between them) and hence the efficiency of resulting pricing arrangements, especially if the auction is of the C–D type.

The level of Z, the amount paid for the assets of the displaced franchise, is also a critical determinant of the *investment* decisions of an incumbent firm. If it is thought likely that Z will be low (e.g. because the assets are of minimal value to an outgoing incumbent), then the existing incumbent will have an incentive to underinvest if there is any chance that he will fail to win future competitions for franchise renewal. On the other hand, if he were to receive an inflated price for the assets being passed on, he might have an incentive to overinvest.

More generally, there is likely to be considerable *uncertainty* about the level of Z *ex ante*. With risk-averse firms, this will affect investment strategies, bidding behavior, and perhaps even the decision to enter the competition for the franchise.

These numerous problems of asset valuation and handover perhaps suggest that investment decisions should be left to public authority and that the competition should be simply for an *operating* franchise. However, operating franchises allow market forces to act only to a limited extent, and the divorce of investment and operating decisions can lead to undesirable losses of coordination.

Finally we come to the important question of the *specification and administration of franchise contracts* (see in particular Williamson, 1976; Goldberg, 1976). If a franchise contract is for the provision of a well-defined product or service—for example the production of a thousand taxi license plates of a given specification at a given time—then the contract between franchisor and franchisee is a relatively simple affair that requires little effort to administer. But if there is technological or market uncertainty in relation to the product, then the specification of the franchise contract can be a very complex task, and the need to monitor and administer the contract during its life is certain to arise.

Williamson (1976) draws important distinctions between different types of franchise contract. A *complete* contract requires a franchise bidder to specify the terms on which he will supply the product or service at each future date during the life of the contract, and for every future contingency that might arise. A complete contract sensitive to future events would be impossibly expensive to write, negotiate, and enforce if uncertainty is present. But a complete contract does not have to take a complex form. For instance, a contract might simply say that the price charged will be such-and-such in all circumstances—i.e. whatever happens to demand, production costs, inflation, and so on. But an unconditional contract of this form faces two severe problems. First, the firm might be unable to fulfill the contract under some circumstances. The threat of inability or refusal to supply would probably lead to flexibility *ex post*, even though the original contract had been specified unconditionally. Therefore, unconditional contracts, especially if they are longer term, are likely to be infeasible. Moreover, unconditional contracts are undesirable. Considerations of efficiency require that price and quality adapt in response to changes in demand and technology.

Thus we are left with *incomplete* contracts, which do not make explicit what is to happen in every possible circumstance. With incomplete contracts there is a need for administration and monitoring of the (partly implicit) contract as time unfolds; a continuing contractual relationship exists, and this inevitably involves continuing costs. The alternative is for the franchisor to be left at the mercy of the franchisee.

The duration of the franchise contract must also be considered. The difficulties of contract specification and administration alluded to in the previous paragraph perhaps suggest that short-term contracts have advantages, because fewer future contingencies then need to be catered for. But the organization of frequent contests for the franchise also involves major costs. As well as the direct costs of holding more auctions, all the problems of asset valuation and handover (see above) occur more often, and the industry would frequently be in a state of turmoil.

The conclusion to be drawn is that, in industries where there is significant uncertainty about technology and demand, competition for monopoly by franchising does not have many of the advantages over regulation that it superficially appears to possess. Indeed franchising involves an implicit regulatory contract for all but the simplest products and services. As Goldberg (1976, p. 426) writes: "Many of the problems associated with regulation lie in what is being regulated, not in the act of regulation itself."

4.6.2   Yardstick Competition

One of the main themes emphasized in this chapter has been the importance of information for effective regulation. If the regulator is relatively uninformed about industry conditions, and especially if the firm being regulated has a monopoly of information, the regulatory mechanism is liable to become a blunt instrument that is insensitive to the basic parameters of cost and demand. Economic efficiency (in both allocative and internal terms) becomes impaired, and the firm extracts monetary or slack rent from its monopoly of information.

Yardstick competition is a method of promoting competition between regulated units indirectly via the regulatory mechanism. It has been proposed in the Littlechild Report (1986) on regulation of the U.K. water authorities. To take the simplest example, suppose that a national monopolist was split into separately owned northern and southern units, denoted N and S respectively, each with a natural monopoly in its geographical area. Suppose further that cost and demand conditions were very similar in the two regions, although the regulator might not know (say) the scope for cost reduction in either region. The two regional units could be brought into competition by the following kind of regulatory mechanism. The price that N could charge in a given period of time would depend on the level of costs achieved by S, and vice versa for the price allowed to firm S. Provided that N and S face very similar circumstances, and that they do not collude in any way, a method of this kind offers the prospect of combining both internal and allocative efficiency, and therefore of escaping the dilemma that usually exists between the two. Good incentives for internal efficiency exists because N keeps the benefits of its cost-reducing activities, for its price is linked to the cost performance of firm S. Allocative efficiency results if there is symmetry between firms, because industry prices are kept in line with industry costs. The promotion of competition via regulation overcomes the informational disadvantage of the regulator in an economical fashion, and shows again how competition can act as an efficient incentive mechanism.

Yardstick competition illustrates the general proposition that under asymmetric information, when a principal has many agents under his control, it is almost always the case that the optimal incentive scheme involves the reward of each agent's being contingent upon the performance of other agents as well as his own performance. The theoretical literature on this point includes Holmstrom (1982), Mookherjee (1984), and Nalebuff and Stiglitz (1983). It is particularly desirable to make reward contingent partly upon the performance of others when the uncertainties facing different agents are correlated to a high degree. If such correlation is absent, there is no advantage in linking reward to others' performance. Indeed, to do so would serve only to add "noise" in an undesirable way: the risk facing any agent would increase, and he would not be encouraged to behave as his circumstances warranted.

Shleifer (1985) examines a model of yardstick competition. In the basic version of the model there are n identical risk-neutral firms operating in a certain environment. Each faces demand curve $Q(P)$ in its market (the n markets are separate). A firm spending z on cost-reducing effort achieves unit cost level $c(z)$, with $c(0) = c_0$. The lump-sum transfer to the firm (if any) is denoted by T. Profit is therefore given by

$$\pi = [P - c(z)]Q(P) - z + T. \tag{4.41}$$

If the social welfare objective is the sum of consumer and producer surplus (and so is not affected by considerations of distribution or the cost of raising public funds), then the optimum subject to the nonnegative profit constraint has

$$P^* = c(z^*), \tag{4.42}$$

$$-c'(z^*)Q(P^*) = 1, \tag{4.43}$$

and

$$z^* = T^*. \tag{4.44}$$

In sum, price equals unit (and hence marginal) cost, efforts to reduce unit costs occur up to the point where their marginal cost ($= 1$) equals marginal benefit ($= -c'Q$, i.e. degree of cost reduction times volume of output), and the cost of effort is reimbursed by the lump-sum transfer.

However, this first-best outcome cannot be achieved if the regulator does not know the function $c(z)$, which describes the scope for cost reduction. Shleifer supposes that each firm is run by managers who like profits π but dislike effort z. In particular it is supposed that their preference ordering is lexicographic with profits preferred over leisure. This is the minimal extent to which some weight can be given to leisure in managers' preferences. Even so, a regulatory regime in which $P = c$ and $z = T$ (which is sometimes known as "cost of service regulation") induces no cost-reducing effort whatsoever. Profit is the same (i.e. zero) for all z, and so managers prefer to minimize z by setting it at zero, and the cost level is therefore c_0.

The key to efficiency is to break the dependence of the price for firm i upon its cost level. Let

$$\bar{c}_i = \sum_{j \neq i} c_j/(n-1) \tag{4.45}$$

and

$$\bar{z}_i = \sum_{j \neq i} z_j/(n-1) \tag{4.46}$$

be the average cost and effort levels of firms other than i. These provide yardsticks against which to compare i's performance. Shleifer (1985, proposition 1) shows that the following regulatory mechanism for all firms i induces first-best behavior:

$$P_i = \bar{c}_i \tag{4.47}$$

and

$$T_i = \bar{z}_i. \tag{4.48}$$

The profit of firm i is then

$$\pi_i = [\bar{c}_i - c(z_i)]Q(\bar{c}_i) - z_i + \bar{z}_i, \tag{4.49}$$

and the first-order condition is therefore

$$-c'(z_i)Q(\bar{c}_i) - 1 = 0. \tag{4.50}$$

There is a symmetric Nash equilibrium in which all firms choose $c_i = c^*$, in which case $P^* = c^*$ and $T^* = z^*$, and Shleifer shows that there exists no asymmetric Nash equilibrium. Therefore the equilibrium that sustains the first-best outcome is unique. This result in fact holds with pricing rules considerably more general than (4.47), but the simple example suffices to establish the main point. A related result holds even when lump-sum transfers are impossible. Yardstick competition can then induce the second-best outcome, i.e. the social optimum subject to $T = 0$.

The main shortcoming of the version of the model described so far is that it assumes that firms operate in *identical* environments. Of course this is quite unrealistic. The economics of water supply, for example, differs substantially between geographical regions. The water authority operating in the Welsh mountains faces conditions and uncertainties that are correlated by no means perfectly with those encountered by the authority operating in the plains of East Anglia. Shleifer examines the use of regression analysis based on observable characteristics to screen out at least part of the heterogeneity between firms that occurs in practice. *"Reduced-form" regulation* operates roughly as follows. Let θ be the vector of exogenous observable characteristics with respect to which firms differ. The regulator estimates a regression of unit costs against θ. With a linear functional form the regression equation is $c = \alpha + \beta\theta$. With $\hat{\alpha}$ and $\hat{\beta}$ denoting the estimated coefficients, the "predicted" unit cost level for firm i is $\hat{c}_i = \hat{\alpha} + \hat{\beta}\theta_i$, where θ_i is the observable characteristic of that firm. The regulator then imposes the price rule $p_i = \hat{c}_i$ and an associated transfer rule.

Reduced-form regulation works well if θ captures almost all of the variation between firms and if it is truly exogenous. If θ fails to capture the full extent of diversity, reduced-form regulation does not provide perfect incentives, and it causes there to be undesirable noise. The problem is especially acute if characteristics that are correlated with the observed characteristics θ are omitted, because omitted-variable bias is then introduced. Further difficulties arise if firms are able to manipulate the observed characteristics, because incentives then exist for strategic rent-seeking behavior and signaling. Similarly, reduced-form regulation has the disadvantage of encouraging endless argument about the appropriate way to conduct the regression analysis, which variables to include, and so on.

More problems arise if firms are able to collude and thereby frustrate competition via regulation. If firms tacitly agreed to slack to an equal extent, inefficiency would persist. Incentives to cheat might be weak if, as is probable, firms were few in number and well informed about each others' behavior.

Despite these difficulties, however, we believe that competition via regulation can provide good incentive systems in a number of industries. We know that the best regulatory mechanisms will exploit information from comparative performance in some form, but the question is *how* to do so in any particular case. It would be foolish to attempt generalization of this, since the degree of homogeneity between regional units differs from industry to industry, but the benefits to be gained from breaking the monopoly of information of a regulated firm could be substantial in individual cases. This is a factor which should be taken into account when considering the regional break-up of privatized companies.

4.6.3 Regulation to Maintain Effective Competition

Regulation is not only called for when competition is absent. Regulation designed to maintain freedom of *entry* is sometimes essential if threats of potential competition are to have force. We showed in section 3.2.2 that an incumbent firm with market power usually has at its disposal a variety of instruments of strategic entry deterrence, and that incentives for predatory behavior are likely to exist. Unless this sort of conduct (and the threat of it) are checked by suitable policy measures, market "liberalization" in the legal sense can be quite ineffective.

It can be argued that the sanctions of ordinary competition policy are sufficient to strike down anticompetitive behavior of this kind, but we disagree for several reasons. First, competition policy in the U.K. (and elswhere) evolved at a time when dominant utility companies were in public ownership. The competition problems that arise in those industries were therefore not envisaged when policy was made, and so there is little reason why it should be expected to cope with them. Secondly, it can be argued that U.K. competition policy has weaknesses generally (see Sharpe, 1985). Certainly it has usually been less vigorous than U.S. antitrust policy. Thirdly, where the danger of particular anticompetitive practices can be foreseen, it makes sense to legislate against them in advance, and to give the specialist regulatory agency the duty of monitoring and enforcing the policy. This also reduces uncertainty. Finally, the agency has greater knowledge and expertise regarding industry conditions than a generalist competition authority can have. (A separate question, which we do not pursue here, is whether there should be one regulatory authority for all privatized utility companies, or one for each.)

In sum, we believe that the task of "regulation" to promote and maintain competition in industries with dominant privatized firms should belong to the regulatory authority for that industry. This is not to say that the general competition authority (the Monopolies and Mergers Commission (MMC) in the U.K.) has no role to play: the regulator should be able to refer cases to it, but he should also have sufficient power to deal swiftly with anticompetitive conduct if and when it occurs.

In section 3.2.2 we described some of the economics of anticompetitive behavior to deter entry. As regards practical policy measures to combat such conduct, we will pursue this question further when we come to consider the frameworks of competition and regulation that have been established for privatized industries in Britain.

4.7   Concluding Remarks

The purpose of this chapter has been to provide a theoretical perspective on the economics of regulation that will guide our assessment of U.K. regulatory policy in part II of the book.

We have focused on the *incentive* properties of various regulatory mechanisms to encourage both internal and allocative efficiency. We have seen how the regulator's relatively *imperfect information* can lead to an awkward trade-off between the two, and how the firm and its managers can enjoy rewards from their monopoly of information. This suggested that the social return from having better informed regulatory bodies could be high, and it indicated that the benefits from greater competition (potential if not actual) could extend to internal as well as allocative efficiency. We also emphasized the *dynamics* of regulation, and the *strategic interaction* between firm and regulator (or government) that can occur over time. We shall bear in mind all these themes when we come to the case studies of regulation in practice in the following chapters.

Part **II**

THE BRITISH PRIVATIZATION PROGRAM

Chapter 5

Public Enterprise in the United Kingdom

5.1 Introduction

Since the primary aim of this second section of the book is to evaluate the U.K. privatization program as it has developed since 1979, we do not intend to set forth a detailed analysis of the history and evolution of public enterprise in Britain. For the most part we will confine ourselves to brief remarks on this history only when it appears relevant to assessments of privatization in the case studies contained in chapters 8 through 11. Nevertheless, for purposes of comparison, some analysis of the general scope and character of publicly owned enterprises in the period before 1979 *is* required, and the current chapter is therefore devoted to this task.

The most important issue to be considered concerns the nature and performance of the control system for the nationalized industries that emerged in the postwar period. Public ownership is most frequently criticized on the ground that it typically fails to establish efficient incentive structures for decision makers in public sector firms. In chapter 2 we discussed some of the more abstract aspects of this agency problem; here we will focus upon specific features of the problem that have been encountered in the U.K. and upon policies designed to resolve the difficulties within an overall framework of public ownership.

The starting point for the analysis is an examination of the different organizational forms that have been adopted for publicly owned firms. For example, one type of public enterprise rests upon partial or complete state ownership of the shares of a standard joint-stock company. Although a number of such companies have existed in Britain, by far the most significant type of state ownership is based upon the concept of the public corporation. The characteristics of this institution will therefore be explained and discussed in section 5.2.

The general principle underlying the governance of state-owned industry in Britain has been a desire to combine public accountability with managerial autonomy in day-to-day decision making. This has led to the development of a quite elaborate control system for the nationalized industries, the principal features of which are as follows:

(i) statutory duties laid upon public corporations by Acts of Parliament;

(ii) the right of ministers to give directives of a general character to the chairmen of public corporations;

(iii) the ability of ministers to exert "unofficial" pressure on the public corporations;

(iv) investigations conducted by House of Commons committees;

(v) investigations by other official bodies such as the Monopolies and Mergers Commission (MMC);

(vi) guidelines set out in a series of White Papers on the nationalized industries;

(vii) the ability of ministers to impose certain financial constraints on the public enterprises.

We will examine these various dimensions of the control system in sections 5.3 and 5.4. Section 5.3 is concerned chiefly with the relationships between Government and the industries as they have have developed in practice, and covers the first five components of the above list. Section 5.4 deals with the more general questions connected with the framing of appropriate objectives for, and of financial constraints on, the public corporations (components (vi) and (vii) of the list).

The implications of the framework of control that has evolved in Britain are numerous, but in section 5.5 we use a simple economic model to illustrate one or two of the more important points. In particular, we stress the limitations of the prevailing forms of financial constraints when these are used as instruments to promote greater internal efficiency in monopolistic public enterprises. Not only may the financial constraints lead to some loss of allocative efficiency, but also, because of their vulnerability to strategic manipulation by the industries concerned, they may have undesirable effects on investment programs and cost efficiency.

The remaining sections of the chapter are intended to set the scene for our analysis of the British privatization program. Section 5.6 outlines the size and shape of the U.K. nationalized industries in 1979, the year in which the first Thatcher Government came to power, while section 5.7 presents data on the recent performance of the public corporations. Finally, in section 5.8, we draw together our main conclusions about the characteristics of the British approach to the control of public industry, and briefly assess some of the alternative policies that might have been implemented in the absence of privatization.

5.2   Types of Public Ownership

At the national level, three main forms of public ownership have been adopted in Britain. The first involves organization of the industry as a department of state under the direct control of a minister of the Crown. In this case the minister is responsible to Parliament for the day-to-day running of the industry, as well as for more general supervision of the industry's broader strategy. The only significant example of the use of this approach has occurred in the case of the Post Office. In 1969, however, the Post Office was turned into a public corporation, and the features of the "department of state" model are therefore of little relevance in the evaluation of recent U.K. economic policies.

The second type of public ownership involves a sole, or majority, state shareholding in an otherwise normal commercial company. The method has been popular in continental Europe, but less so in Britain. Nevertheless, there are a number of significant British examples, including the following: British Petroleum (BP), in which a controlling interest was acquired by the state before the First World War with the object of securing fuel oil products for the Navy; the British Sugar Corporation, created by the Government in 1936 to promote domestic production of beet sugar for reasons of national security; Cable and Wireless, acquired in two stages (1938 and 1946) with a view to extending state ownership in telecommunications activities; Short Brothers and Harland (aircraft and aircraft components), acquired during the Second World War because the company was not being operated efficiently and the Government was not prepared to see it collapse; Rolls-Royce and British Leyland (now the Rover Group), both taken into public ownership in the 1970s to mitigate the consequences of impending bankruptcy.

In addition, the Labour Government of 1974–1979 established the National Enterprise Board (renamed the British Technology Group in 1981) to provide finance for industrial investment and to act as a state holding company for shares either transferred to it by the Government (e.g. the shares of Rolls-Royce and British Leyland) or acquired on its own initiative. The National Enterprise Board subsequently built up investments in several tens of commercial companies, mostly small, but also including larger firms such as Ferranti (electronics), Herbert (machine tools), and International Computers.

Whether measured in terms of assets, employment, or output, however, publicly controlled commercial companies have accounted for only a small fraction of the state sector of U.K. industry, and by far the most important type of state-owned enterprise has been the public corporation. The aim of this institutional innovation was to combine freedom for management from Government supervision of day-to-day operations with public control of the broader policies of the enterprises. In the words of Robson (1960):

"The public corporation is based on the theory that a full measure of accountability can be imposed on a public authority without requiring it to be subject to ministerial control in respect of its managerial decisions and multitudinous routine activities, or liable to comprehensive parliamentary scrutiny of its day-to-day working. The theory assumes that policy, in major matters at least, can be distinguished from management or administration; and that a successful combination of political control and managerial freedom can be achieved by reserving certain powers of decision in matters of major importance to Ministers answerable to Parliament and leaving everything else to the discretion of the public corporation acting within its legal competence. The Government are further endowed with residual powers of direction and appointment which mark their unquestionable authority."

Although there are case-to-case variations, the main distinguishing features of the typical public corporation are as follows.

(i) It is a corporate body, established by statute, with its own legal existence.

(ii) It is free to manage its own affairs without detailed control by Parliament.

(iii) The relevant minister of the Crown has powers to give directions (a) of a general character as to the exercise and performance of the functions of the corporation and (b) in regard to specified matters of special importance (e.g. major capital expenditure programs).

(iv) The relevant minister appoints the whole or majority of the board of management, and such appointments are generally for a fixed number of years.

(v) It is financially independent in the sense that it has powers to maintain its own reserves and, within limits laid down by Parliament, to borrow (unlike some other public bodies, trading surpluses do not automatically revert to the Exchequer).

(vi) Most external finance is obtained from the Exchequer, via the National Loans Fund, at fixed rates of interest, and the relatively small levels of borrowings from the private sector are backed by Treasury guarantees.

Public corporations therefore constitute a category of institution that lies somewhere between direct government trading undertakings and private commercial enterprises. To a first approximation, they can be viewed as trading bodies for which the Government is both the sole shareholder and the sole banker.

In addition to these three types of public enterprise, which each fall within the central-government sector of the economy, a wide range of goods and services are produced and/or supplied by local government authorities. Although of great importance for the economy, since our analysis of privatization policies will largely be restricted to enterprises operating at the national level, they will not be considered in any detail in what follows.

5.3   Accountability and Control

In the postwar period, a principal objective of the legislation that established public corporations was to create an "arm's length" relationship between government and management. Objectives for the various industries were set out in statute, but these were expressed only in the most general of terms. For example, the Central Electricity Generating Board (CEGB) was required to develop and maintain an efficient, coordinated, and economical system of supply of electricity in bulk for all parts of England and Wales. Given this type of vagueness in statutory duties, considerable weight was placed on the assumption that managers would pursue public interest objectives. In 1933, Herbert Morrison, the Labour Minister who had the greatest influence on the direction of the early postwar nationalization program, expressed this position as follows:

"The public corporation must be no mere capitalist business, the be-all and end-all of which is profits and dividends, even though it will, quite properly, be expected to pay its way. It must have a different atmosphere at its board table from that of a shareholders' meeting: its board and its officers must regard themselves as the high custodians of the public interest. In selecting the Board, these considerations must be in the minds of the Minister."

As noted earlier, however, the indirect ministerial influence on enterprise decision making, embodied in the power to make appointments to the boards of directors, was supplemented by powers to give directives of a general character. The chain of accountability was then completed by making ministers answerable to Parliament for such directives. In this way it was hoped that the minister, and ultimately Parliament, would be able to control the broad strategic decision making of the corporations, while leaving managements in full control of operational matters.

In practice, as might have been expected, this framework of control for the nationalized industries has not functioned in the way that its creators had intended. Ministers were left free to adopt their own definition of the public interest, which came to resemble the interests of the political party in power, and there have been frequent political interventions to influence operational decision making. Parliamentary control has been weakened by the fact that, although ministers are answerable to Parliament for actions they have taken in relation to the public corporations (e.g. general directives), they are not so answerable for any informal pressures that they apply to the corporations' managements. In fact, very few formal directives have been given to the corporations; the mere threat of their use, coupled with the threats deriving from ministerial powers of appointment, have been sufficient to enable politicians to exert considerable "unofficial" control over all aspects of the corporations' decision making.

Following the extensive nationalization program of the 1945–1951 Labour Governments, it was not long before the breakdown of the arm's length principle became widely recognized. Partly in response to this new perception, a House of Commons Select Committee on Nationalized Industries (now the Departmental Industry and Trade Committee) was established in 1952 with the purpose of investigating the performance of the various public enterprises. Over time, the scope of the Committee's investigations has broadened, and it has examined a wide range of issues connected with the control of public enterprises.

The House of Commons Select Committee has few formal powers but has, nevertheless, been influential in stimulating debate and discussion about the reform of the structures of governance for nationalized industries. In 1968, for example, it reported that, whereas Parliament's original intention was that ministers should provide general guidance to managements concerning enterprise objectives and should abstain from detailed interventions in operational matters, in practice the opposite had occurred: general guidance was rarely offered, but specific interventions were common (House of Commons, 1968). Developing this line of criticism, the Committee later recommended that the framework of accountability and control should be completely re-examined, a recommendation that led to a major report on the nationalized industries by the National Economic Development Office (NEDO) in 1976.

The NEDO Report concluded that the arm's length principle should be underpinned by the creation of an additional management tier, labelled the Policy Council, interposed between a corporation's board and the sponsoring government department. It was recommended that the Policy Council should include the relevant ministers and the corporation chairman, together with representatives of other interests in the industry (e.g. trade unions, consumers, suppliers, and members of the financial community). The Policy Council would be responsible for the development of long-term objectives and strategies, leaving the main board free to deal with implementation of those strategies and with operational matters. In this way, it was believed that a barrier to operational interventions by ministers could be created. However, in recognition of the ultimate authority of the Government with respect to the control of public enterprises, it was also recommended that, alongside powers to make appointments to the Policy Council, ministers should have the right to issue specific, as well as general, directives to the Council on matters of national importance.

Whilst accepting much of NEDO's analysis of the control problem, the (Labour) Government of the day rejected the Policy Council proposal. The chairmen of the nationalized industries were hostile to the recommendation, and it was generally felt that the creation of a further hierarchical level in the control system would, on balance, impede effective decision making by lengthening the line of communication between the Government and managers. The distinction between strategic and executive/operational decisions is not always clear cut, and there was a well-founded fear that, in practice, all three tiers of the hierarchy (corporation board, policy council, and department of state) would come to be involved in both types of decision.

Thus, despite the weaknesses of the established framework of accountability and control for the nationalized industries, the system remained unreformed. To the extent that there have been changes to it over the past decade, these have generally been in the direction of either increasing ministerial powers (see section 5.4) or strengthening existing procedures. For example, the provisions of the Competition Act 1980 authorize the Secretary of State for Industry to order the Monopolies and Mergers Commission to conduct investigations into the efficiency of the nationalized industries. The terms of reference for such investigations are set by the minister, who also has the authority to decide whether or not to implement any of the resulting recommendations for action.

The fact that, nearly 30 years after deficiencies in the framework of accountability and control were first widely recognized, little progress had been made in resolving substantive issues concerning the respective roles of the management boards, ministers, and Parliament became, in the late 1970s, a major source of dissatisfaction with Government policy towards the public corporations. The effect of the failure was to buttress the case for privatization: given that flaws in the the arrangements had proved so difficult to correct, it could more easily be argued that progress in solving the underlying problems required a radical shift in the relationships between Government and the enterprises concerned, and that transfer of ownership to the private sector was the most direct method of achieving the desired adjustment.

5.4   Objectives and Financial Constraints

In part, the objectives of public corporations are set out in their statutes. As we have already noted, however, statutory duties are frequently couched only in the most general of terms, and the stipulated requirements—to run an efficient service, to break even taking one year with another, to avoid undue preference in the provision of supplies, and the like—offer very little in the way of explicit guidance to managements as to how they should conduct their businesses. Nor is it very satisfactory to exhort corporation managements to act, in Morrison's words, as "high custodians of the public interest." The imprecision here is an open invitation to managers and politicians to pursue their own objectives under the guise of acting in the national interest: wolfish self-interest is all too easily cloaked in the public interest sheepskin.

The policy response to this problem was a series of attempts to give the managements of public corporations objectives that were more specific than those contained in the relevant statutes. This was done in three successive White Papers: *Financial and Economic Obligations of the Nationalised Industries* (HM Treasury, 1961); *Nationalised Industries: A Review of Economic and Financial Objectives* (HM Treasury, 1967); and *The Nationalised Industries* (HM Treasury, 1978). We will comment on each of them in turn, but for more comprehensive evaluations see National Economic Development Office (1976) and Heald (1980).

The principal innovation of the 1961 White Paper was the introduction of financial targets for the public corporations. These were to be determined in the light of each industry's "circumstances and needs," and have typically been expressed in terms of a specified rate of return on capital assets employed. The target rates of return have therefore varied from industry to industry, depending upon factors such as demand and cost conditions and the extent to which the enterprises have been required to operate unprofitable "social" services (e.g. loss-making rural railway lines).

Rate-of-return targets were established in an attempt to correct what was perceived to be the poor financial performance of the nationalized industries during the 1950s. While the targets did constrain managerial actions, it rapidly became clear that a large measure of discretion remained: the 1961 White Paper was silent on the question of how managements should assess the relative merits of alternative means of meeting the financial constraint. Corporations with market power, for example, could meet targets by raising prices, as well as by reducing costs, and there was no policy injunction against cross-subsidization, which was prevalent. Nor was any guidance given to managements on the important issue of investment expenditures. Subject to the financial constraint, corporations were implicitly expected to maximize something, but what that something was was not spelled out, and, until this prior question was settled, the problem of providing incentives for the attainment of social objectives could not even be tackled.

The 1967 White Paper was much clearer about what the underlying objectives of the public corporations should be. Its main points were as follows.

(i) Prices should be set so as to reflect long-run marginal costs, but with some adjustment towards short-run marginal costs when it was apparent that the existing level of capacity was substantially suboptimal.

(ii) As a consequence, where possible, cross-subsidization should be avoided.

(iii) Investment should only take place when the anticipated rate of return exceeded a prescribed test discount rate, intended to reflect yields on low-risk private sector projects and initially set at a real rate of 8 percent (later increased to 10 percent).

(iv) Noncommercial activities should be accounted for separately, with Government deciding whether or not to support such activities on cost–benefit criteria.

(v) Industries would continue to be required to meet a financial target, individually set for each in the light of market conditions and of the industry's pricing and investment objectives.

These guidelines follow fairly naturally from the notion that the objective of the industries should be the maximization of economic efficiency. Thus, the pricing rules were designed to maximize allocative efficiency for given demand and cost/capacity conditions, while the application of the test discount rate criterion was intended to ensure an efficient allocation of investment funds between the public and private sectors of the economy. Similarly, the financial target can be interpreted as a means of incorporating a variety of other efficiency considerations into the decision-making process, including the promotion of cost efficiency and the inclusion of allowances for second-best factors (targets could differ from those implied by first-best pricing and investment rules to reflect, say, the nonzero resource costs of Government finance or externalities arising from deviations from first-best conditions in competing sectors).

The 1967 White Paper therefore rested upon an intellectually coherent approach, derived from welfare economics, to the problem of specifying objectives for public enterprises. It did, however, leave two quite fundamental issues untouched. First, there was no attempt to develop an adequate structure of incentives to encourage managers to act in the desired ways. That is, both aspects of the monitoring problem—measuring performance and allocating rewards and punishments—were largely ignored. As a result, to a first approximation many public corporations simply ignored the pricing and investment guidelines. In some cases (e.g. telecommunications) it was claimed that marginal cost pricing was too ambiguous and/or difficult a policy to apply in practice; in others (e.g. electricity) corporations made use of their considerable discretion in respect of cost definitions and cost allocations to devise tariff structures that could be defended on marginal cost grounds, but which in reality were designed to meet objectives other than allocative efficiency. Similarly, the test discount rate was ineffective either because industries claimed that, in integrated networks, it was impossible to assign a rate of return to individual projects, or because subjective estimates of future cash flows could easily be adjusted to obtain the result that best contributed to managerial objectives (there are very few examples of major projects having been abandoned as a result of failing the discount rate test).

The second unresolved issue concerned the control problem discussed in section 5.3: ministers could, at any stage, use their considerable formal and informal powers to override managerial decisions in respect of pricing and investment and, in the event, they frequently did just that. Thus, at different times, there were ministerial interventions to hold down prices as part of a prices and incomes policy, to force up prices when public sector borrowing became the significant macroeconomic policy objective, to speed up investment programs and slow down plant closures when unemployment was perceived as a major problem, and so on. As a result, even if the managements of the public corporations had seriously wanted to pursue the economic efficiency objectives implicit in the White Paper, their efforts would substantively have been undermined by politicians' behavior.

In summary, then, the 1967 White Paper was largely unsuccessful because, from the perspective of the nationalized industry managements, it embodied an approach that can be described as *recommendation without regulation* in which, because of divergences between efficiency goals and short-run political objectives, the recommendation itself lacked credibility. Thus, the overall system of accountability and control left the way clear for the displacement of economic efficiency objectives by managerial and political goals, and, unsurprisingly, managers and politicians took full advantage of the discretion that was allowed them.

The 1978 White Paper went some way towards reducing *managerial* discretion by strengthening the financial controls exerted by Government on the public corporations. Pride of place was accorded to the financial target, and marginal cost pricing was relegated to a more subordinate role. With respect to investment, the test discount rate for individual projects was replaced by a required rate of return for investment programs as a whole, which was set at a level of 5 percent real (the reduction from the earlier test discount rate of 10 percent was a response to the falling yields on private sector investment in the mid-1970s). In addition, each industry was required to publish a series of performance indicators that could be used by sponsoring departments to assess its internal efficiency. Examples of such measures include a variety of productivity and unit cost indices. Finally, although not an innovation of the White Paper itself, the post-1978 framework of control has relied heavily upon *external financing limits*, otherwise known as cash limits.

External financing limits (EFLs) place constraints upon the annual change in the net indebtedness of public corporations to the Government, and can therefore be regarded as establishing maximum levels for the difference between revenues and the sum of current and capital expenditures. They were originally intended to be instruments for increasing the accountability of managements with respect to their short-term financial management, but have subsequently come to play a much more central role in policy towards the public corporations, largely because they can be used to control the consequences of the activities of the nationalized industries for the aggregate public sector borrowing requirement (PSBR), which fiscal measure has been a key target variable in recent short- and medium-term macroeconomic policy. Thus, for example, the PSBR can be reduced by tightening public corporations' EFLs, thus forcing the enterprises to increase revenues and/or cut current and capital expenditures. Since 1979, preoccupation with PSBR targets has sometimes led to situations where the EFLs have become the only binding constraint on the nationalized industries, displacing both the financial target (usually set for a three- to five-year period) and the required rate of return on new investment.

In part, the 1978 White Paper was motivated by a desire to set goals for public corporations in a way that would facilitate *ex post* metering of their performance. Evaluation of the corporations' use of the test discount rate criterion, for example, had proved extremely difficult, and it was hoped that, since it could be undertaken with less detailed information, assessment of investment performance as a whole would be easier. This explains the introduction of the required rate of return. Similarly, the adoption of performance targets was seen as a way of keeping a closer eye on internal efficiency, and of supplementing the relatively clumsy instrument of financial targets in providing pressures for productivity improvements and reductions in unit costs.

A second important factor explaining the change of emphasis in policy towards the nationalized industries was the increasing emphasis accorded to financial flows in Government macroeconomic objectives. The emergence of large fiscal deficits in the U.K. economy during the 1970s effectively led to the attachment of a greater priority to reducing the "costs" of Exchequer finance to the public corporations. Thus, whereas in the 1967 White Paper, it was implied that financial targets should be set so as to be consistent with "first-best" pricing and investment policies, the later approach can be characterized as giving a much higher weight to second-best considerations associated with the provision of Government finance. Indeed, rather than being *derived* from pricing and investment policies, there has been a tendency for financial targets and EFLs to be accorded the status of independent goals which might, for example, justify substantial deviations from marginal cost pricing.

Roughly speaking, since 1978, public corporations have been exhorted to maximize economic efficiency subject to a generally tighter set of constraints on financial and productivity/cost performance. We will analyze and assess some implications of this shift in more detail in sections 5.5 and 5.7. At this point, however, we simply note that, whereas the 1978 White Paper led to a strengthening of Government control over the behavior of the nationalized industries and therefore went some way to attenuating managerial discretion, the shift of emphasis served to highlight the other unresolved aspect of the control problem which had arisen from the use of ministerial powers to promote sectional political objectives. If anything, the introduction of tighter financial constraints in general, and of short-run (annual) external financing limits in particular, served only further to undermine the arm's length principle.

5.5*   Financial Constraints: Theoretical Analysis

Some of the potential effects of ministerial use of financial targets to influence the behavior of nationalized industries can be explored by extending the simple public enterprise model developed in section 2.4. For this purpose we will modify the model in two ways. First, the noncapital costs of the firm will be assumed to be equal to $C(q,k,x)$, where k is the level of capital input, x is the level of cost-reducing expenditure, $C_q > 0$, $C_k < 0$, and $C_x < 0$. Second, it will be assumed that the firm is required to achieve a given rate of return on capital assets (the financial target), denoted $\theta(k)$, where $\theta_k < 0$. The negative relationship between θ and k captures the dependence of the financial target on the capacity position of the firm in question. Thus, if the firm has excess capacity relative to the long-run equilibrium, it is assumed that the value of the financial target will be reduced to allow some movement in the direction of short-run marginal cost pricing (a principle that is explicitly set out in the 1967 White Paper). By similar reasoning, deficient capacity is taken to lead to a higher financial target. If the first-best long-run equilibrium level of capital input is k^*, it might also be assumed that $\theta(k^*) = r$, where r is the test discount rate or required rate of return (the cost of capital), although the main points we want to make are not dependent upon this condition.

Given these amendments to the model, managers will seek to maximize

$$V(q) - C(q,k,x) - bx - rk$$

subject to

$$p(q)q - C(q,k,x) - x - \theta(k)k \geq 0.$$

If λ denotes the value of the multiplier on the constraint, the first-order conditions for a maximum are as follows:

$$\frac{p - C_q}{p} = \frac{\varepsilon\lambda}{1 + \lambda}, \tag{5.1}$$

$$-C_x = \frac{b}{1 + \lambda} + \frac{\lambda}{1 + \lambda}, \tag{5.2}$$

and

$$-C_k = \frac{r}{1 + \lambda} + \frac{\lambda\theta[1 + \mu(k)]}{1 + \lambda}, \tag{5.3}$$

where $\mu(k)$ (<0) is the elasticity of the financial target with respect to capital employed.

When the financial constraint is not binding ($\lambda = 0$), first-best conditions are satisfied in respect of pricing and investment policies: price equals marginal cost, and capital is employed up to the point where its marginal return is equal to its marginal cost. As in section 2.4, however, for given output and given capital input, the level of cost-reducing expenditure is suboptimally low (efficiency requires that $-C_x = 1 < b$). This is a consequence of managerial preferences for reduced effort coupled with imperfect monitoring.

Tightening (increasing) the financial target causes λ to rise, leading to price being set at a level in excess of marginal cost. As intended by the White Papers, however, it also leads to some increased pressure in the direction of cost reduction. The right-hand side of equation (5.2) is a weighted average of b and 1, with the relative weight on b *falling* as λ increases. Since, by assumption, $b > 1$, this implies that, for given q and k, costs fall as the financial constraint is tightened. It should also be noted, however, that a stricter financial target will tend to reduce the equilibrium output level and hence diminish the marginal payoff from increased effort $(-C_x)$ if, as is likely to be the case, $-C_{xq} > 0$. Hence, the net effect on unit costs of increasing λ will generally be ambiguous.

Equation (5.3) implies that capital will be employed up to the point where its marginal yield is a weighted average of the cost of capital and $\theta(k)[1 + \mu(k)]$. Thus if, at equilibrium, the financial target $\theta(k)$ is equal to or "close" to the cost of capital, the firm will be overcapitalized, for, given q and x, the marginal return on investment is less than the cost of capital. The intuition here is that managers will invest more heavily than is warranted by the investment criterion (the test discount rate or required rate of return) because, by so doing, the resulting excess capacity will induce a reduction in the value of the financial target; as in some of the models of regulation examined in section 4.2, managements can use investment as a *strategic* instrument to influence the behavior of government.

The model therefore serves to illustrate some of the weaknesses inherent in the 1967 White Paper. As a matter of observation, it can be noted that, typically, the financial targets for nationalized industries *were* sensitive to the capacity position ($\mu < 0$) and were set at levels below the test discount rate ($\theta < r$). In these circumstances, it is not surprising that there was concern in policy-making circles about the conduct of investment programs.

In terms of the above framework, policy developments since 1978 can be interpreted as seeking, amongst other things, to achieve two important adjustments. The first was to raise the *level* of the financial target (i.e. to raise θ), thereby increasing the pressures for cost reduction (see equation (5.2)) and reducing the bias towards overinvestment (see equation (5.3)).

For firms with market power, however, such an increase could be expected to lead to increased prices and lower output (see equation (5.1)), which, as well as reducing allocative efficiency, would have indirect (adverse) effects on cost-reduction expenditures. On the other hand, for public corporations operating in competitive environments the option of increasing prices is not available to management and hence the financial target is likely to be a more powerful instrument for the promotion of internal efficiency.

Second, by increasing the status of financial targets and making them *independent* instruments of policy, the 1978 White Paper can be interpreted as seeking to weaken the perceived link between the value of the target and capacity levels in the industries (i.e. to reduce the absolute value of the elasticity μ). Assuming that this is feasible (but see the discussion of credibility problems below), it has the advantage of attenuating the incentives for managements to use investment programs as strategic instruments. Hence, any bias towards overinvestment can be mitigated without forcing the financial targets to levels where the allocative losses from higher prices may become severe. In other words, the trade-off between efficiency in investment and short-run allocative efficiency is improved.

The "cost" of breaking the link between financial targets and the public corporations' capacity position is that, when excess or deficient capacity results from exogenous unanticipated changes in the marketplace, avoidable short-run allocative inefficiencies will emerge. Suppose, for example, that demand growth for an industry's output turns out to be less buoyant than could reasonably have been expected at earlier dates, so that capital employed is higher than its long-run equilibrium level. A financial target that was set on the basis of the earlier demand projections would then lead to allocative inefficiency, in the sense that the deviation of prices from short-run marginal costs would be greater than was desirable *ex post*. Since it is deterministic, our model does not capture this particular trade-off, but it should be clear enough how the analysis can be extended to incorporate the effect.

Another problem with attempts to reduce the sensitivity of financial targets to the level of capital employed is that, given ministerial objectives, they may lack credibility. Thus, for example, applying arguments set forth in section 4.2.3, once capacity imbalances have occurred short-run political goals may be better achieved by making the necessary adjustments to the financial constraint; in particular, when capacity is suboptimally high, there will be a strong temptation to allow public corporations to charge lower prices.

The credibility problem may, in part, provide one justification for the increasing role that has been assigned to external financing limits in recent years. Although it is likely that the enhancement of the role of EFLs has had much more to do with controlling the impact of nationalized industries' activities on the PSBR, they do provide Government with an additional means of influencing the efficiency of the industries' investment programs. Moreover, they allow the Government to exert this influence at the time that capital expenditures are being incurred. Thus, unlike in the case of financial targets, public corporations are not easily able to manipulate later EFLs by earlier overinvestment.

However, the effective use of EFLs may imply that financial targets become redundant (i.e. the EFLs are set at levels such that financial targets are no longer binding constraints), in which case the number of financial instruments available to the Government will have been reduced to one. Even allowing for the introduction of a performance target, which can be represented in the model by a constraint on the firm's unit cost level, the Government will be attempting to control three decision variables (q, x, and k) with two instruments. This may not matter very much in cases where the public corporation operates in a competitive product market—since competition serves to supplement the Government controls—but in cases of monopoly the trade-off between allocative and internal efficiency is less favorable.

In the model that has been developed it is assumed that the managers of public corporations maximize a linear combination of consumers' plus producers' surpluses and cost-reducing expenditures (used as a proxy for effort), but it can be argued that this does not accurately reflect the managerial goals that are pursued in practice. Unfortunately, there is no generally accepted specification of managerial objectives in public corporations. Building upon arguments in the literature on managerial theories of the firm, which stress the importance of goals such as size, status, and prestige, Rees (1984b) has suggested that the level of output is likely to be an important argument in managerial utility functions. Possible implications of this line of reasoning can briefly be examined by assuming that managers maximize some function of output and effort subject to a given financial target.

Suppose, in particular, that the managerial objective function is simply $q - (b-1)x$, where $b > 1$. Then the first-order conditions become

$$\frac{p - C_q}{p} = \varepsilon - \frac{1}{\lambda p} ,$$

(5.4)

$$-C_x = \frac{b-1}{\lambda} + 1,$$

(5.5)

and

$$-C_k = \theta(k)[1 + \mu(k)].$$

(5.6)

As before, a tightening of the financial constraint leads to increases in the multiplier λ. From equation (5.5), this leads to improved incentives for cost-reducing expenditures at *given* levels of output and capital employed. In this case, however, the trade-off with allocative efficiency is potentially more favorable. As can be seen from (5.4), the pursuit of output objectives generates an incentive for managers to underprice: when λ is low, equilibrium price is below marginal cost. Up to a certain point, therefore, tightening the financial constraint may improve *both* cost and allocative efficiency. With respect to investment/capital, for given q and x, there may again be either overinvestment or underinvestment, depending upon whether $\theta(1 + \mu)$ is less than or greater than the cost of capital, and if $\theta(1 + \mu) = r$ we have the first-best condition for the level of capital employed.

To summarize, if the aim of public policy is to promote economic efficiency, it appears that the post-1978 enhancement of the role of financial constraints is likely to make a more substantial contribution to this goal when the managers of public corporations have output, rather than economic welfare, objectives and when the public corporations are operating in competitive product markets. Putting matters in this way, however, serves only to draw attention to questions surrounding the nature of political objectives. While recent developments in the framework of control for the nationalized industries may have gone some way to reducing managerial discretion, the problem of political discretion remains.

5.6   The U.K. Nationalized Industries in 1979

The year 1979 is a decisive breakpoint in the history of public enterprise in Britain. Until that year there was a clear, if erratic, trend in the direction of bringing greater numbers of enterprises under public ownership; since 1979, the privatization program has produced a sharp movement in the opposite direction. In the postwar years, the expansion of the nationalized sector of the economy was most rapid under the Labour administrations that held power between 1945 and 1951, during which period most of the larger public corporations were first created. However, both Labour and Conservative Governments were responsible for further significant nationalizations in the subsequent quarter century, including the steel industry, British Leyland, Rolls-Royce, the shipbuilding industry, and British Aerospace.

A broad indication of the relative importance of the nationalized industries in the U.K. economy in 1979 can be obtained from the figures shown in table 5.1. These relate only to the activities of public corporations, and therefore tend to understate the significance of public sector production as a whole; they do not, for example, include the publicly owned water industry in Scotland (see chapter 11), the multitudinous other activities carried out by local government authorities throughout the country, or the National Health Service. Particularly in respect of net capital stock, the figures are also subject to the usual caveats about measurement errors. Apart from indicating the size of the public corporation sector, they do, however, underline the point that, on average, public enterprises have been more capital intensive than other sectors of the economy; capital assets and investment have accounted for larger fractions of the national totals than has output, whereas the employment share has been lower than the output share. Hence, the average productivity of labor in public corporations has been higher than the national average, while the average productivity of capital has been lower.

Table 5.2 shows a list of the major public corporations in 1979, while table 5.3 gives financial performance and employment statistics for some of the more important enterprises to provide an indication of their relative sizes. The industrial sectors in which public ownership has predominated are fuel and power, transport, communications, water and sewerage, and iron and steel. With the exception of the last of these sectors, this pattern of concentration motivates our organization of the analysis of privatization contained in chapters 8 through 11. Whereas large parts of fuel and power, transport, communications, and the water industry exhibit "network" characteristics and/or lack of effective competition, the iron and steel industry has neither of these features. The possible privatization of British

Table 5.1   The public corporations in 1979

		Percentage of U.K. total
Gross domestic product	£18.043 billion	10.5
Numbers employed	2.065 million	8.1
Net capital stock	£104.100 billion	17.2
Gross domestic capital formation	£5.621 billion	15.2

Source: *National Income and Expenditure* (1984 edn).

Table 5.2   Public corporations in existence as at 31 December 1979

Bank of England	National Freight Corporation
British Aerospace	National Ports Council
British Airports Authority	National Research Development
British Airways Board	Corporation
British Broadcasting Authority	National Water Council
British Gas Corporation	New Town Development
British National Oil Corporation	Corporations and
British Railways Board	Commission
British Shipbuilders	Northern Ireland Development
British Steel Corporation	Agency
British Transport Docks Board	Northern Ireland Housing
British Waterways Board	Executive
Cable and Wireless Ltd.[a]	Northern Ireland Transport
Civil Aviation Authority	Holding Company
Commonwealth Development	Northern Ireland Electricity Service
Corporation	North of Scotland Hydro-Electric
Covent Garden Market Authority	Board
Development Board for Rural Wales	Passenger Transport Executives and
Electricity Council	London Transport Executive
Highlands and Islands Development	Post Office
Board	Property Services Agency
Housing Corporation	Regional and National (Welsh)
Independent Broadcasting Authority	Authorities
Land Authority for Wales	Royal Mint
National Bus Corporation	Royal Ordnance Factories
National Coal Board	Scottish Transport Group
National Dock Labour Board	South of Scotland Electricity Board
National Enterprise Board	Trust Ports
National Film Finance Corporation	Welsh Development Agency

Source: *National Income and Expenditure* (1980 edn).
a. Classed as a public corporation in the national accounts.

Steel will therefore be discussed alongside the sale of other, generally smaller, public enterprises that operate in competitive markets.

5.7   The Performance Record

In sections 5.3 to 5.6, we have drawn attention to some of the weaknesses in the framework of accountability and control that was established for the nationalized industries in the postwar period. However, no control system is perfect, and what is ultimately of importance is the performance of the enterprises concerned. With respect to their past records, the public corporations have certainly been subject to a great deal of hostile criticism and, as already noted, this dissatisfaction has acted as a spur to the development of privatization policies. In this section, therefore, we will examine some of the salient features of the recent performance of the public

Table 5.3 The major public enterprises: financial and employment statistics, 1978–1979

	Turnover (£ million)	Net profit before interest and tax (£ million)	Employment (thousands)
Electricity Council	5,445	862	160
Post Office	4,619	1,281	411
National Enterprise Board	4,158	119	279
British Steel	3,288	−77	190
National Coal Board	2,989	96	300
British Gas	2,972	618	102
British Rail	1,979	58	243
British Airways	1,640	115	58
British Aerospace	894	68	72
British Shipbuilders	731	−102	87
South of Scotland Electricity Board	463	88	14
National Bus	437	28	64
British National Oil Corporation	432	12	1
National Freight	394	16	40
North of Scotland Hydro-Electric Board	173	54	4
British Airports Authority	162	35	7

Source: *The Times 1000* (1979).
All figures are rounded to the nearest integer.

corporations. As well as throwing light on the question of whether or not the criticisms directed at nationalized industries have been well founded, this material also helps to establish a benchmark against which the performance of newly privatized firms can be judged.

In attempting to assess performance, we immediately face a difficult question: what criteria should be used in the evaluations? The original legislation intended that public corporations should act in the public interest, but such an objective is extremely nebulous. Indeed, as argued earlier, the vagueness of this goal, and hence of the operational decision criteria that might flow from it, has been one of the central problems of the control framework. Even if pursuit of the public interest is equated with the maximization of economic efficiency (an equation implicit in the 1967 White Paper), the difficulty is far from having been resolved. Statistics measuring consumers' surplus, for example, are not things that can readily be found in official publications.

In these circumstances, the best that can be done is to examine dimensions of performance that are of relevance to a more general evaluation, whilst recognizing that no single measure is likely to be of decisive importance. Thus, for example, although profitability may be the key measure of success for a firm operating in a competitive market that is free of externalities, it cannot be so regarded in cases where the firm has significant market power: if high profits result from monopolistic abuses, they signal economic *inefficiencies*, not efficiencies.

5.7.1 Financial Performance

Compared with private industry, there is little doubt that the profitability of U.K. nationalized industries has been relatively low. Table 5.4, for example, shows the records of the two sectors between 1970 and 1985, and it can be seen that, on average, the ratio of gross trading profit (before allowance for stock appreciation and depreciation) to net capital stock for privately owned companies has been about three times higher than the nearest equivalent measure for public corporations (the ratio of gross trading surplus to net capital stock). The performance gap would be reduced if depreciation was netted out—capital consumption rates are slightly higher in the private sector, where assets are less durable—and if the highly profitable (in pretax terms) oil extraction business was excluded from the calculations. However, when trading surpluses are adjusted to take account of the substantial subsidies provided to some public

Table 5.4 Profitability of public corporations and of industrial and commercial companies (percentages)

Year	Public corporations A^b	B^c	Industrial and commercial companies[a]
1985	5.1	2.6	21.3
1984	6.3	3.4	20.6
1983	6.8	4.8	19.4
1982	6.6	4.8	16.7
1981	5.6	4.0	16.0
1980	4.7	3.4	16.1
1979	5.0	3.6	18.3
1978	5.7	4.4	17.1
1977	6.2	4.9	17.8
1976	6.2	4.8	15.6
1975	4.9	3.1	14.6
1974	4.9	2.4	17.2
1973	6.2	4.3	18.7
1972	6.2	4.6	18.5
1971	6.0	5.3	16.8
1970	6.4	5.6	16.8

Source: *National Income and Expenditure* (various editions).
a. Gross trading profit as a percentage of net capital stock at replacement cost.
b. Gross trading surplus as a percentage of net capital stock at replacement cost.
c. Gross trading surplus, net of subsidies, as a percentage of net capital stock at replacement cost.

corporations, which are treated in the accounts as an additional source of revenue, the comparison becomes less flattering to the public sector.

In table 5.4, the public corporation figures for 1984 and 1985 should be interpreted with some caution. The year-long coal miners' strike of 1984–1985 had a substantial depressing effect on financial performance during this period, particularly in the coal, electricity, and steel industries. In addition, the privatization of British Telecom (BT) in 1984 led to a significant discontinuity in the figures. Taking these factors into account, the effects of the tighter financial constraints imposed on the nationalized industries since the late 1970s are visible in the upward trend in profitability from 1979–1980 to 1983.

The impact of this tighter financial regime on the public corporations becomes more apparent in the figures for the financial deficit of the sector that are shown in table 5.5. From the mid-1970s onwards, the implications of the nationalized industries' performance for the PSBR have been a highly significant factor in the formulation of macroeconomic policy. Thus, since nationalized industry borrowings contribute towards an increased PSBR, attempts to control the latter have frequently involved measures to reduce the financial deficit of public corporations, most usually by a tightening of Government-imposed constraints designed to raise prices, lower investment, and improve internal efficiency.

As can be seen from table 5.5, judged in their own terms, these measures

Table 5.5   The financial deficit of the public corporations as a percentage of the corporations' contribution to gross domestic product

Year	A^a	B^b
1985	−0.4	14.3
1984	2.5	17.8
1983	0.7	11.3
1982	3.5	13.1
1981	4.9	14.1
1980	12.2	20.2
1979	12.2	20.9
1978	6.3	13.7
1977	9.6	16.7
1976	17.6	25.4
1975	26.7	37.5
1974	19.5	36.2
1973	12.5	22.7
1972	13.2	21.1
1971	22.0	25.6
1970	18.5	22.4

Source: *National Income and Expenditure* (various editions).
a. Financial deficit as a percentage of contribution to GDP.
b. Financial deficit plus subsidies as a percentage of contribution to GDP.

Table 5.6 Public corporations' investment expenditures as a percentage of their contribution to gross domestic product

1985	24.4		1977	32.9
1984	29.1		1976	36.1
1983	28.2		1975	37.1
1982	26.4		1974	35.8
1981	27.8		1973	32.6
1980	30.9		1972	31.6
1979	31.3		1971	37.8
1978	30.0		1970	37.4

Source: *National Income and Expenditure* (various editions).

have met with some success. Despite the effects of the miners' strike, the public corporations showed a financial surplus for the first time in 1985, although, as can be seen from column B, the outcome was largely the result of an increase in subsidies, much of which was specifically induced by the strike. Compared with the period up to 1976, over the last decade financial deficits, whether measured gross or net of subsidies, have been substantially reduced relative to the output of the nationalized industries. Given that the movements in profitability have been less sharp, the data suggest that a significant part of the change has been due to reductions in investment programs, an inference that is supported by an examination of the investment record (see table 5.6).

5.7.2   Allocative efficiency

Interpretation of the financial indicators presented in tables 5.4 and 5.5 is a far from easy exercise. One view of the matter is that the figures simply reflect the pursuit of allocatively efficient pricing and investment policies. Thus, if the nationalized industries set prices to reflect marginal social costs, then, given the importance of factors such as scale economies (e.g. in telecommunications, gas, electricity, and water) and externalities (e.g. in rail transport), this perspective suggests that profitability comparisons with private industry are misleading and irrelevant.

With respect to the financial performance of a number of parts of the public sector, we believe that this argument has some merit. Nevertheless, viewed as a general statement about the performance of the public corporations as a whole, there are at least two reasons for skepticism about its relatively optimistic conclusion. The first concerns the magnitude of the difference between private and public sector profitability. Public sector rates of return have been *substantially* below their private sector counterparts, so that, to justify the discrepancy, it would be necessary to show that efficient pricing and investment policies had very large financial implications. In 1985, for example, a one percentage point increase in the public corporations' rate of return would have led to an increase in gross trading surplus of around £1.4 billion. Taking account of the facts that (a) the utility industries can use multipart tariffs to improve the trade-off between efficient pricing and external financial constraints and (b) Government finance has real resource costs, it is difficult to believe that the lower rates of return in the public sector have resulted solely from the adoption of allocative efficiency objectives.

More important, detailed analysis of the pricing behavior of individual nationalized industries indicates that the policies that have been implemented in practice are often far removed from those that would be suggested by efficiency objectives. Thus, a whole series of empirical studies has uncovered evidence of significant suboptimalities in the price levels and/or price structures of public corporations. We will consider some of these suboptimalities at various points in chapters 8 through 11, and simply note here that the conclusions of recent studies include the following.

(i) The Post Office has limited information on consumer valuation of quality changes, and no information on marginal costs (Monopolies and Mergers Commission, 1984a).

(ii) Prior to privatization, BT significantly overpriced its trunk call and international services, and underpriced its local services (Deutsches Institut für Wirtschaftsforschung, 1984).

(iii) Domestic coal prices have been substantially above marginal opportunity costs, as measured by world coal prices (Monopolies and Mergers Commission, 1983b).

(iv) Gas prices have been below long-run marginal costs and, since British Gas has adopted a uniform tariff structure, do not reflect the relative costs of supplying gas at different times of the year and to different parts of the country (Hammond et al., 1985).

(v) The peak/off-peak differentials charged by National Bus have not always been efficiently related to relative costs, and there has been significant cross-subsidization between routes (Monopolies and Mergers Commission, 1982a).

Similar conclusions have also emerged from studies of investment programs. Cases of overinvestment during the 1970s include British Steel (Pryke, 1981), the National Coal Board (Molyneux and Thompson, 1987), and the Central Electricity Generating Board (Monopolies and Mergers Commission, 1981a).

Hence, on balance, the view that the pursuit of public interest objectives can account for the relatively poor financial performance of the public corporations does not appear to be well supported by the evidence. In their examination of the issue, Molyneux and Thompson (1987) conclude rather that inefficient pricing structures have arisen from policies of offering uniform prices and/or service quality in markets where costs differ substantially, and that, in some cases, these inefficiencies derive from a failure of public corporations to respond to changing technologies or patterns of demand. Moreover, Molyneux and Thompson argue that, where improvements in pricing policy have been observed over the past few years, they tend to be associated with the introduction of greater competition into the marketplace (e.g. in telecommunications and in buses).

As a corollary, therefore, it is likely that the low rates of return and large financial deficits which have been a characteristic of the nationalized industries in the postwar period can, in large part, be attributed to some combination of overinvestment and internal inefficiency, phenomena which have resulted from deficiencies in the overall framework of control.

5.7.3   Productivity Performance

Most attempts to assess the internal efficiency of the U.K. nationalized industries have been based upon the analysis of one or more of a variety of productivity indices. Three principal approaches have been adopted, based respectively on international comparisons with similar industries overseas, on comparisons with other U.K. industries, and on efficiency audits (typified by Monopolies and Mergers Commission studies that attempt to identify opportunities for improved performance that have been missed by the relevant management).

In general, it is the international comparisons that have produced results that are the least favorable to the nationalized industries. Examples of the findings of this type of work include the conclusions of Pryke (1981) that the Post Office's output per man in telecommunications was significantly below that of overseas telecommunications companies, of Aylen (1980) that, in the 1970s, the British Steel Corporation's labor productivity was only one-third to one-half of that achieved in comparable plants in Western Europe, of Findlay and Forsyth (1984) that the productivity of British Airways was lower than that of many other international airlines, and of Henney (1987) that labor productivity on new vintages of plant in electricity generation was significantly lower than in most other countries.

The major problem with these international comparisons, however, is that it is not clear to what extent the observed productivity variations can be attributed to the effects of different types of ownership. Over the relevant periods, most studies of international productivity differentials have shown the U.K. lagging behind its principal competitors *irrespective of whether the industry concerned was privately or publicly owned.* The question of interest is whether or not the U.K.'s relative performance is worse when the British industry is nationalized, and most investigators have simply failed to address this more fundamental issue. One exception is the Findlay and Forsyth paper, which argues that the performance of British Airways was bettered by (the privately owned) British Caledonian, as well as by international competitors. For the most part, however, the available evidence is extremely limited and uninformative.

With respect to comparisons with privately owned domestic industries, because of variations in markets and technologies it is clearly difficult to make efficiency judgments on the basis of observed productivity *levels.* Attention has therefore been focused on the more limited objective of assessing *changes* in productivity over time, and table 5.7, derived from figures presented by Pryke (1981) and by Molyneux and Thompson (1987), typifies the sorts of results that have been obtained. As can be seen from the statistics, there are considerable variations among the productivity records of the industries quoted. From 1968 to 1978, four of the nine corporations exhibited declines in labor productivity and/or total factor productivity (the rate of growth of output minus a weighted average of input growth rates), while others showed productivity improvements well in excess of those of the U.K. manufacturing sector as a whole.

The most striking feature of table 5.7 is the improvement in labor productivity growth from 1978 onwards for those public corporations that

Table 5.7   Productivity trends in selected nationalized industries, 1968–1985

	Output per head (percent per annum)		Total factor productivity (percent per annum)	
	1968–1978	1978–1985	1968–1978	1978–1985
British Rail	0.8	3.9	n.a.	2.8
British Steel	–0.2	12.6	–2.5	2.9
Post Office	–1.3	2.3	n.a.	1.9
British Telecom	8.2	5.8	5.2	0.5
British Coal	–0.7	4.4	–1.4	0.0
Electricity	5.3	3.9	0.7	1.4
British Gas	8.5	3.8	n.a.	1.2
National Bus	–0.5	2.1	–1.4	0.1
British Airways	6.4	6.6	5.5	4.8
U.K. manufacturing	2.7	3.0	1.7	n.a.

Source: Molyneux and Thompson (1987).

did relatively badly in the earlier period, with British Steel being the outstanding example. In these cases, there is evidence that the tighter financial disciplines imposed on public corporations over the past decade have had a material effect on internal efficiency. It is worth noting, however, that the productivity performances of industries such as telecommunications, gas, and electricity either deteriorated or showed little sign of change. While many factors could have contributed to this outcome, one obvious common feature of these sectors is the monopoly power of their public corporations. Thus, where the corporations can easily meet more stringent financial targets by raising prices to customers, the evidence is at least consistent with the view that tighter financial controls are a weak instrument for promoting improvements in internal efficiency (cf. the models in section 5.5).

Table 5.8   Summary of the efficiency findings of the Monopolies and Mergers Commission

Case	Management structure	Financial control	Use of manpower	Use of performance indicators
British Rail	2	4	2	3
Severn Trent Water Authority	1	2	2	2
Central Electricity Generating Board	–	4	3	4
Anglian Water Authority + North West Water Authority	–	2	4	3
National Coal Board	2	2	–	2
Yorkshire Electricity Board	2	3	3	3
Various bus companies	2	3	2	3
Civil Aviation Authority	2	2	2	2
London Transport Executive	3	2	1	3
South Wales Electricity Board	2	3	3	3
Average score	2.0	2.7	2.4	2.8

Source: Collins and Wharton (1984).
1 Severe criticisms.
2 Critical comments.
3 Suggestions for improvement.
4 Generally satisfactory.
– Inconclusive or not covered.

Turning to the "efficiency audit" method of evaluating the internal efficiency of nationalized industries, since the passing of the 1980 Competition Act the Monopolies and Mergers Commission has been asked to conduct a sizeable number of investigations into the performance of public corporations. These have covered a wide range of questions, including costs, productivity, service quality, pricing, and investment policies. Findings from some of these investigations have been quoted in section 5.7.2 above, and table 5.8 sets out a more systematic judgmental summary, due to Collins and Wharton (1984), of the conclusions of a number of the Commission's reports that appeared between 1980 and 1984.

Although the reports of the Monopolies and Mergers Commission have consistently identified weaknesses in the conduct and performance of public corporations, particularly with respect to management structures and the use of manpower, there are no immediate benchmarks against which the significance of these findings can be assessed. In the course of its wider activities the Commission has frequently uncovered performance deficiencies in the private sector, but investigations are made on a case-by-case basis and are not designed for purposes of interindustry comparison. Thus, the findings of the Commission can make only a limited contribution to a more general evaluation of the relative performance of publicly owned industry. Nevertheless, the very fact that the investigations have taken place can be interpreted as a positive sign that, since 1980, the Government has placed a greater emphasis on the desirability of closer monitoring of the public corporations.

5.8   Assessment and Conclusions

The development of the framework of accountability and control for the nationalized industries in postwar Britain can be viewed as an attempt to implement the public interest model of state-owned enterprise that we outlined in section 2.3.1. In this exercise, the key roles were allocated to the managements of the corporations and to the relevant departmental ministers: managers and ministers alike were to be the custodians of the public interest. However, too little attention was devoted to the obvious question: *quis custodiet ipsos custodes?*

In general terms, the answer to this question that was implicit in the evolution of public policy was that ministers, assisted by their permanent civil servants, would monitor managements, Parliament would monitor ministers and civil servants, and, ultimately, voters would monitor Parliament. That there were likely to be substantial imperfections in this chain of principal–agent relationships could hardly be doubted by even the strongest supporters of public ownership. For many of the latter, however, including Morrison, these defects were considered to be of second-order importance, largely as a result of an underlying belief that managers and ministers could be relied upon to promote the public interest. That is, if the agents lower down the monitoring hierarchy had objectives that differed little from those of the ultimate principals (the general public), it would not matter very much that the actions of such agents were only loosely constrained by the political system.

The history of the nationalized industries has shown that this optimistic view of managerial and ministerial behavior was seriously flawed, and that, in the British context at least, a system of control that relies heavily upon agents' internalization of public interest objectives is unlikely to produce good performance. In the event, as we have described above, the results of the policy failure have included widespread goal displacement, lack of clarity in corporate objectives, overlapping responsibilities, and excessive ministerial intervention in operational decisions. These, in turn, have had detrimental effects on the pricing, investment, and internal efficiency performance of the nationalized industries.

The crucial question, however, is whether or not significant improvements in performance could feasibly have been obtained whilst preserving public ownership of the industries concerned. As we have argued, the tighter financial controls that were developed in the late 1970s and 1980s do appear to have had some beneficial effects on certain aspects of performance and are indicative of the fact that ownership is far from being the sole determinant of behavior. However, while the reforms of the last decade have tended to strengthen the hand of Governments in their dealings with managements, they have done little to alter the relationships between ministers, Parliament, and the general public. Fundamental issues of accountability and control have therefore remained unresolved.

Our own view of the matter is that substantial improvements in the control system were (and still are) feasible, including reforms designed (a) to establish arrangements capable of sustaining an arm's length relationship between ministers and managements and (b) to improve the incentives for internal efficiency. In particular, four developments in public policy could have contributed to enhanced performance:

(i) the introduction of greater competitive pressures on those public corporations that have enjoyed protected market positions;

(ii) the creation of specialized regulatory agencies entrusted by Government with duties in respect of price controls and the promotion of competition similar to, but stronger than, those afforded to the regulatory bodies that were later established as part of the privatization program (see chapters 8 and 9);

(iii) the creation of a specialized agency (Audit Office) for the sole purpose of conducting efficiency audits on the nationalized industries and responsible directly to Parliament rather than to the Government;

(iv) the more widespread use of performance-related incentive schemes for the managements of public corporations.

The type of monitoring hierarchy that would have resulted from these changes is shown schematically in figure 5.1.

With respect to the potential impact of such reforms, the beneficial effects of increased competition have been analyzed in chapter 3, and it is sufficient here to refer back to those earlier discussions. The introduction of regulatory bodies that are independent of existing government departments permits greater specialization at the regulatory stage of the monitoring hierarchy (stewardship of public corporations is but one of the many responsibilities of departmental ministers), facilitates Parliamentary control, and, assuming fixed-term appointments, tends to impede

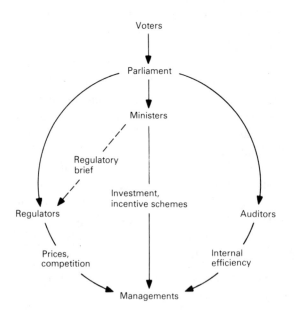

Figure 5.1   A possible public sector monitoring hierarchy

intervention in operational decisions by governments seeking short-term political advantages (government attention would be focused instead on laying down the broad principles of policy within which regulators would be required to work). Similarly, potential benefits from specialization and increased Parliamentary control are also associated with the creation of an independent Audit Office. Auditing functions are currently carried out by the Monopolies and Mergers Commission but, as Curwen (1986) notes, the Commission's role is limited by (a) its inability to investigate other than when instructed by the Government, (b) its lack of unrestricted access to persons, papers, and premises, and (c) its inability to advise all-party Parliamentary Select Committees. Thus there exists scope for introducing greater pressures toward internal efficiency by strengthening the powers of independent investigators. Finally, the more explicit use of formal performance-related incentive structures helps to attenuate managerial and (by forcing the revelation of objectives) ministerial goal displacement.

In fact, none of proposals (i)–(iv) is novel. In telecommunications, energy, and transport, a number of measures to increase competitive pressures on public corporations were implemented by the Government prior to privatization, and we will describe some of these developments in the chapters that follow. Proposals to create a specialized regulatory body for the electricity supply industry were considered in the mid-1950s (see section 9.3.1). In 1982, a Private Member's Bill was introduced in Parliament which proposed that the Comptroller and Auditor General should have access to the accounts of the nationalized industries and, in carrying out his monitoring duties, should be made responsible to the House of Commons. Also, the 1979–1983 Conservative Government experimented with performance-related incentive schemes, most notably in the case of British Steel where the salary of the chairman was linked directly to changes in the Corporation's trading deficit.

In each case, however, either the initial proposals were rejected—with respect to the creation of independent regulators and auditors, for example—or the policies were not pursued with great vigor; some of the measures to increase competition have had little practical effect, and only extremely limited use has been made of performance-related incentive schemes. This leaves us with a major difficulty when evaluating the impact of privatization on economic performance. For comparative purposes, the simplest benchmarks to use in the evaluations are those based on actual behavior in the state sector during the period immediately preceding the transfer of ownership. However, since privatization, coupled with its associated measures (e.g. regulatory reforms), was only one of the possible policy responses to the perceived performance deficiencies of the public corporations, the more appropriate way to proceed is to compare the Government's policies with other feasible options. As well as alternative methods of privatization, the latter include options consistent with the retention of either complete or partial public ownership. Therefore, although it necessarily complicates the analysis, this is the approach that we will adopt in the chapters that follow.

The Privatization Program—an Overview

6.1 Introduction

The importance that privatization would come to have in the economic policies of Mrs Thatcher's Government could not have been foreseen at the time of her election victory in May 1979. The Conservative election manifesto had relatively little to say about privatization, although the party's dissatisfaction with the performance of nationalized industries and its desire to "roll back the frontiers of the state" were prominent Conservative themes. During the Government's first term in office, the proceeds from the sale of state assets were below £500 million per annum, but after Mrs Thatcher's re-election in June 1983 the privatization program accelerated dramatically (see table 6.1). By the time of the 1987 election the annual proceeds from asset sales were approaching £5 billion, i.e. ten times the earlier level.

The expansion in the scale of the program accorded with a fundamental change in its nature. Before 1984 the firms that were privatized mostly operated in reasonably competitive industries. Firms like British Aerospace, Britoil, Cable and Wireless, and Enterprise Oil are important and sizeable companies, but they do not enjoy such market power as to pose major regulatory problems. The privatization of British Telecom (BT)—the first in a series of utility companies with great market power—therefore represented a radical shift in policy. Regulated private

Table 6.1 Privatization proceeds

Financial year	£ million
1979–1980	377
1980–1981	405
1981–1982	493
1982–1983	488
1983–1984	1,142
1984–1985	2,132
1985–1986	2,702
1986–1987	4,750*
1987–1988 to 1989–1990	5,000* annually

Source: HM Treasury (1985, Table 2.14; 1986, Table 2.23; 1987, Table 2.21 and p. 30).
Figures shown are net proceeds. * Expected receipts.

enterprise was now regarded as superior to nationalization (see Moore, 1985) even in natural monopolies, where competition was impractical. With this extension of Government philosophy, privatization policies appear to have virtually unlimited scope in their application to state ownership of industry. Following the Conservative victory at the election in June 1987, the British Airports Authority (BAA) was sold, and the water authorities and the electricity supply industry are set to join BT, British Gas, British Airways (BA), and other privatized firms in the private sector.

The sale of public enterprises has been one of several components of policy designed to reduce state involvement and enhance private enterprise and ownership. Another important element has been *contracting out*—the private supply of publicly financed services. Instead of relying on internal supply, numerous Government bodies have been encouraged to introduce competitive tendering between rival contractors. Local authorities have contracted out rubbish collection, catering, cleaning, and construction and maintenance work. Public employees, who often enjoyed a quasi-monopoly position previously, were faced with competition from the private sector, and the evidence to date shows important gains in cost efficiency. Likewise, the Department of Health and Social Security and the Ministry of Defence are introducing competitive tendering for catering, cleaning, and a wide range of other services. We do not discuss contracting out at any length in this book (see Hartley and Huby, 1985), but we do touch on several of the relevant economic principles, notably in section 4.6.1 on franchising where some of the strengths and weaknesses of contracting out are surveyed.

The sale of public sector *housing* after 1979 was another major policy measure to enhance private ownership in Britain. Nearly 600,000 housing units were sold by local authorities between 1979 and 1983, more than in the entire postwar period before that time. Receipts amounted to almost £2 billion in 1982. Private purchase was encouraged by the policy of selling property to tenants (of some years' standing) at substantial discounts to market value. However, the rents under public ownership were often below commercial levels, and local authorities were relieved of maintenance burdens and saved significant administrative costs. Just as the privatization program was used to promote wider share ownership, public sector housing sales were used to extend private property ownership. Both measures were at the center of the Conservatives' desire to enhance "property-owning democracy" in Britain as strongly as possible.

Alongside policies to promote private enterprise and ownership, the Government introduced measures to stimulate *competition* in several public sector activities. The use of contracting out and competitive tendering by local authorities and Government departments has already been mentioned. There were also major pieces of legislation designed to remove some barriers to competition in some nationalized (and often soon to be privatized) industries. The 1981 British Telecommunications Act, the 1982 Oil and Gas (Enterprise) Act, and the 1983 Energy Act sought to introduce some competition into parts of the telecommunications, gas, and electricity supply industries, and the Transport Acts of 1980 and 1985 radically deregulated the markets for coach and bus services. However, as we shall see in the chapters that follow, these liberalizing measures have often had limited practical effect, and policies to encourage private ownership have generally taken precedence over measures to promote effective competition in the frequent cases of tension between the two.

The purpose of this chapter is twofold. First, we discuss the principal aims and objectives behind the British privatization program. Secondly, we give an outline history of the main asset sales to date. Subsequent chapters will examine the economics of competition and regulation in four key industries—telecommunications, energy, transport, and water—in greater detail. Other discussions of the privatization program are given by Beesley and Littlechild (1983), Kay and Silberston (1984), Vickers and Yarrow (1985), Kay et al. (1986), Kay and Thompson (1986), Yarrow (1986), and Veljanovski (1987).

6.2   Objectives of Privatization

In the British privatization program no one has defined a comprehensive list of goals ranked by priority or weight. Indeed, objectives are likely to differ between Government ministers and to change over time as opportunities, constraints, and perceptions develop. However, the following list summarizes what appear to have been the principal aims:

(i) improving efficiency;

(ii) reducing the public sector borrowing requirement (PSBR);

(iii) reducing government involvement in enterprise decision making;

(iv) easing problems of public sector pay determination;

(v) widening share ownership;

(vi) encouraging employee share ownership;

(vii) gaining political advantage.

The last of these objectives has only been implicit, but it has shaped a number of key policy decisions.

Privatization enhances economic efficiency if it sharpens corporate incentives to cut costs and set prices in line with costs. But we saw in chapter 2 that the achievement of efficiency improvements depends crucially upon the framework of competition and regulation in which the privatized firm is to operate. In the first phase of privatization, in the period up to 1984, there was relatively little concern in this regard, because the industries in question were reasonably competitive. But when utility companies like BT were sold to the private sector, measures were needed to reduce and contain market power, and a central stated objective of policy was to improve efficiency by unleashing competitive forces.

When the intention to privatize BT was announced in July 1982, much emphasis was also placed on another source of efficiency improvement—allowing BT to borrow freely from the capital markets without having to obey the borrowing constraints faced in the public sector. In short, privatization would facilitate more efficient capital allocation. Of course privatization is not necessary to achieve this end, because the borrowing constraints could be relaxed without transferring ownership, but there is a difference (at least in legal terms) insofar as the borrowings of a private sector company are not backed by Government guarantee.

A more important difference arose from the Government's objective of reducing the PSBR, because the borrowings of a formerly nationalized firm are no longer part of the PSBR once the firm has entered the private sector. Moreover, as a result of a curious accounting definition, the proceeds from the sale of state assets directly reduce the PSBR because they are treated as "negative public expenditure"! Unlike sales of gilts (i.e. U.K. Government bonds), sales of shares in privatized companies (i.e. Government equities) are deemed technically not to be borrowings, although in reality there is little difference between the two methods of Government finance. Privatization therefore accorded well with the objective of reducing the PSBR so as to meet the targets that the Government had set itself as part of its medium-term financial strategy for anti-inflationary monetary control.

Privatization also offered a direct way of furthering the aim of reducing state involvement in enterprise decision making, part of Mrs Thatcher's general philosophy of pushing back the frontiers of the state. A major weakness in the administration of nationalized industries was their vulnerability to short-term political intervention by ministers, and privatization provided a credible way of giving industry managements the independence to develop their business strategies free from interference. However, once again we would note that it is not the only way to achieve the desired result.

Privatization was also seen as a way of promoting Government objectives regarding the labor market. The labor relations record of many nationalized industries was bad, and public ownership was held partly responsible. Nationalization can increase the monopoly power of unions if public sector managers and their supervising ministries have weak incentives to reduce labor costs and a virtually unlimited purse with which to finance high wage settlements. However, privatization may do little by itself to reduce union power. It does not diminish the cost and damage that strikes could inflict, and if monopoly power persists, the company's purse is likely to remain effectively bottomless. Indeed, it can be argued that Government can resist union pressure better than private employers. It has greater resources with which to withstand union pressure, and, by virtue of its involvement with numerous groups of public sector workers, the Government has reputation reasons for not wanting to concede an unduly generous settlement to any one group. Both these effects were at work in the year-long coal strike in 1984–1985. The Government was content to incur massive financial losses to secure victory, and its resolve to defeat the National Union of Mineworkers was inspired in large part by the demonstration (or signaling) effect on other wage bargains in the economy—a factor that would not have entered the calculations of private sector negotiators.

In the labor market, as elsewhere, it is competition rather than ownership that matters most. Union power in the coal industry derives chiefly from the monopoly power of British Coal, which is sustained by restrictions on entry, and not from public ownership. Privatization did not prevent the strike by BT engineers early in 1987, in which the telecommunications unions had a strong hand because of the limited extent of competitive alternatives to BT. Nevertheless, the impending arrival of privatization was a time of major reductions in staff numbers at BT, and the same thing happened at British Airways.

The encouragement of wider share ownership, especially by company employees, was another major goal of the program, though it must again be said that privatization by itself does not further the objective. Rather, it provided an excellent vehicle for rapidly expanding share ownership, because it gave a rare opportunity to offer shares to the general public at a discount and with additional bonuses for the small shareholder. Chapter 7 explains the size and scope of these incentives, and the massive public response that they brought forth. The chapter also quantifies their cost, and asks whether there are more efficient and less distortionary ways of widening share ownership than by selling state assets at discount prices.

That policy has nevertheless yielded important political benefit to the Conservatives. Millions of new small shareholders have portfolios that typically consist entirely of "privatization stocks" such as BT and British Gas. Share price movements before and during the 1987 election campaign showed that privatization stocks were highly sensitive to assessments of Mrs Thatcher's likely electoral fortunes. A visible financial interest of millions of people in Conservative victory was plain, and the party underlined that interest by writing to the shareholders concerned. Moreover, the windfall profits to successful applicants for shares in privatization issues had made the program politically popular. In contrast, the relative loss borne by taxpayers and consumers of public services as a result of underpricing was imperceptible, though nonetheless real. Politically, privatization was a winner, at least in the short term.

6.3   The Main Asset Sales 1979–1987

In this section we briefly describe the main asset sales in the eight years up to the middle of 1987. We list the companies in alphabetical order for ease of reference, and because some asset sales occurred in stages. In most cases our treatment is extremely brief; we comment at greater length only where there are points to make that are not covered in other chapters. For a summary of information relating to the pricing of the share issues, the reader is referred to table 7.1 in the next chapter.

Amersham International   Amersham's main business is the development, manufacture, and sale of radioactive materials for medical, research, and industrial uses. In February 1982, £63 million was raised from Amersham's offer for sale. The offer was heavily oversubscribed, and the shares went to a hefty premium when dealings began. A political storm resulted, partly because the important and controversial sale of the British National Oil Corporation (in the shape of Britoil) was soon to take place. In the year to 31 March 1987 Amersham made pretax profits of £22 million on turnover of £148 million.

Associated British Ports (ABP)   As well as its port operations, ABP has interests in property development and investment. It was privatized in two stages. Part of the company's equity was offered for sale in February 1983, and the remainder was sold by tender offer in April 1984. In total about £100 million was raised from the sales. In 1985 the company made pretax profits of £21 million on turnover of £138 million.

British Aerospace   British Aerospace manufactures military and civil aircraft and weapon systems. The Conservatives were committed to the denationalization of the aircraft and shipbuilding industries when they came into power in 1979, and the Government sold approximately half of its stake in the company for £149 million in February 1981. Its remaining shareholding was offered for sale in May 1985 along with some new shares issued by the company, and a further £550 million was raised. In 1986 British Aerospace made pretax profits of £182 million on turnover of £3.14 billion. In early 1987 British Aerospace paid £190 million to acquire the **Royal Ordnance** munitions factories from the Government.

British Aerospace is a member of the European Airbus civil aircraft consortium: it makes the wings. Large amounts of Government finance have been committed to the Airbus project notwithstanding the privatization of British Aerospace. Thus £450 million of British launch aid for the A330/340 aircraft was announced in May 1987. The aid is mostly repayable as a levy on future sales. (In this respect it is perhaps closer to equity finance than debt finance.) Whatever its motivation may have been, this aid shows that privatization does not rule out public financing (which the private sector was unwilling to provide) for risky commercial ventures. The Government has sold its shareholding, but it continues to shield the company and its shareholders from important market disciplines. Even after privatization, it is taxpayers who are bearing some of the risk.

British Airports Authority   BAA operates seven of the principal airports in Britain, including Heathrow, the busiest airport in the world, and Gatwick. £1.28 billion was raised when the company was offered for sale in July 1987. For a fuller discussion of BAA's privatization see section 10.3 below.

British Airways   British Airways, one of the leading airlines in the world, was a prime candidate for privatization for several years. It was finally offered for sale in January 1987, and £900 million was raised. Section 10.2 is concerned with British Airways.

British Gas   In terms of sales proceeds, British Gas is the largest privatization in Britain so far, apart from the offering of the tranche of BP shares in October 1987 (see below), and was sold as a single entity in December 1986 for £5.6 billion. The company is the subject of section 9.2.

British Petroleum (BP)   The British Government's initial stake in BP, one of the giant "seven sisters" of the oil industry, was acquired just before the

First World War. In general Governments have not participated actively in the running of the company, and BP has enjoyed about as much commercial freedom as privately owned companies such as Shell. Since the mid-1970s the public shareholding in BP has progressively been reduced by sales of tranches of shares by both Labour and Conservative Governments. The last tranche (31.5 percent of the company) was offered for sale (together with a rights issue) in October 1987 and raised £7.2 billion, to become the largest ever share offering. The stock market crashed before the share offer closed, and virtually all the new shares were left with the underwriters (see section 7.2 below). BP is discussed further in section 9.4.

British Telecom   BT was the first major utility company in Britain to be privatized. Approximately half its shares were offered for sale in November 1984, and £3.9 billion was raised. The government continues to own fractionally less than half of BT's shares, but BT's management has complete commercial freedom. Chapter 8 below is devoted to the privatization of BT.

Britoil   Britoil is the successor company to the British National Oil Corporation (BNOC), the nationalized North Sea oil exploration and production company set up by the Wilson Government in 1975. The offer for sale by tender of Britoil shares in November 1982 was the worst flop of the privatization program before the BP offer in 1987. Seventy percent of the shares were left with the underwriters amid gloomy reports of the company's profit prospects and signs of weakness in the oil price. The rest of Britoil's shares were sold in the summer of 1985, and the privatization of the company raised £1 billion in total. BP made a bid for Britoil in December 1987. Britoil is discussed further in section 9.4.

Cable and Wireless   Cable and Wireless provides telecommunications services, mostly under franchise agreements with governments, in numerous countries. Its subsidiary, Mercury Communications, is the only public network operator licensed to compete with BT (see chapter 8, especially sections 8.2.2 and 8.4.4). Cable and Wireless was privatized in three phases. After the passage of the British Telecommunications Act 1981, the Government sold 49 percent of the shares in Cable and Wireless. Its stake was reduced further by dilution due to the company's rights issue in 1983 in connection with the acquisition of Hong Kong Telephone, and the Government sold a further tranche of its shares by tender offer in December of that year. The issue was not fully subscribed, and a portion of the shares was left with the underwriters. The final 23 percent Government holding was sold in December 1985 along with some newly issued shares. The three sales together raised about £1.1 billion for the Exchequer. In the year to 31 March 1987 the company made pretax profits of £340.5 million on turnover of £913 million.

Enterprise Oil   Enterprise Oil was formed after the 1982 Oil and Gas (Enterprise) Act to take over the offshore oil interests of British Gas. The company is engaged in oil and gas exploration and production. It has interests in more than a hundred U.K. Continental Shelf blocks, the bulk of which have yet to be developed. (British Gas sold its 50 percent stake in the Wytch Farm onshore oilfield in May 1984 after three years of wrangling between British Gas, potential bidders, and ministers. The buyer was the Dorset Bidding Group consortium, who agreed to pay £215 million to the Government over five years and a profit share to British Gas.) See further section 9.4.

Jaguar   Jaguar, the luxury car maker, became a subsidiary of British Leyland (BL) in the industrial reorganization of the car industry in the 1960s. BL went bankrupt in 1974, and was rescued by large injections of public money. There followed years of further heavy losses, labor relations problems, and declining market shares, despite successive attempts to rationalize the company's operations. Conservative policy has been to sell off the more profitable parts of the business. Thus Jaguar was offered for sale for £294 million in July 1984. Since returning to the private sector, the company's performance has been strong, especially in the United States, although the recent weakness of the dollar may restrain progress. In 1986 Jaguar made pretax profits of £121 million on turnover of £830 million. The XJ6 model was well received when it was launched in the spring of 1986, and Jaguar's car production is growing at around 15 percent annually.

National Freight   National Freight, the road haulage operator, was sold for £53 million to a consortium of managers, employees, and company pensioners in 1982. However, the Government paid £47 million back to the company's pension fund to remedy previous underfunding. Its shares have not been quoted on the Stock Exchange, although plans to float the company were announced in May 1987. The interests of managers and employees have been safeguarded by the restriction on the transferability of National Freight's shares—investors have only been able to buy and sell equity from and to the company at a price periodically fixed by accountants. The sale of National Freight yielded little net revenue to the Exchequer, but it has been one of the greatest successes of the privatization program. Its pretax profits rose ninefold from £4.3 million in 1981 (before privatization) to £37 million in 1986. The fact that National Freight has become such a thriving business underlines the importance of good incentive structures—achieved in this case by the employee buyout—in determining the success of privatization.

Rolls-Royce We comment on Rolls-Royce (R-R) at greater length because to date it is the largest privatization not covered in other chapters, and because the company has been at the heart of British industrial policy for some two decades. The company was formed in 1906 by the merger of the Rolls and Royce motor car companies. In the First World War R-R began to design and manufacture aero-engines in addition to its car business. In the 1940s R-R was the leading firm in jet engine technology, and for a while it enjoyed considerable commercial success in both civil and military markets. Competition from Pratt & Whitney, helped by the American dominance of the civil airframe industry by Boeing and McDonnell Douglas (M-D), posed growing problems for R-R in the 1960s. The company embarked on the major RB-211 project to develop its own new large jet engine to compete with the American rivals. But by 1971 it became apparent that R-R did not have the financial, technological, and organizational strength needed to accomplish the project on time.

The company went into liquidation in February of that year. The Government bought the aero-engine business, and the Rolls-Royce motor car business was put into a separate company which is now a subsidiary of Vickers. In the 1970s R-R's aero-engine business recovered. The RB-211 engine was successfully developed, and was bought in large numbers by Boeing and Lockheed for aircraft sold to airline companies throughout the world. But the civil aircraft industry entered a period of recession in 1980 as oil prices rose, before demand strengthened in the mid-1980s. (The fortunes of British Airways followed a similar pattern—see section 10.2.) Employee numbers were cut by more than a third in the recession, and efficiency improvements were reflected in profitability. Operating profits (before net R&D) increased from £74 million in 1983 to £273 million (on a turnover of £1.8 billion) in 1986, largely thanks to a recovery in the civil aero-engine business. Over the same period a pretax loss of £115 million was converted into a pretax profit of £120 million.

This improvement in R-R's performance made privatization attractive.

In May 1987, 801 million shares were offered for sale at 170 pence each, payable in two equal instalments, to raise £1.36 billion for the Government. Two million people applied for shares, and the public offering was 9.4 times oversubscribed. When dealings began on 20 May, the shares went to an immediate premium of 62 pence, or 73 percent over the partly paid share price.

The company's future prospects depend heavily upon continued growth in world airline demand, exchange rate movements (especially the sterling/dollar rate), and technological developments. R-R is collaborating with Pratt & Whitney on propfan engine technology, which may be used in future generations of long-range airliners being developed by Boeing, M-D, and the European Airbus consortium (of which British Aerospace is a member). On the military side, R-R can anticipate substantial business in the 1990s if the European Fighter Aircraft goes ahead.

Although the future is full of uncertainties, R-R faces it as a soundly based private sector company. The Government rescue of the company in 1971 has turned out to be comparatively successful, though perhaps the main strides towards commercial viability were made in R-R's latter years in the public sector. In the 16 years under public ownership the Government acted essentially as R-R's investment banker, in circumstances where private finance was not forthcoming. When R-R's prospects were improved, that task was done and privatization became appropriate. Together with the social benefits of saving such a company the successful flotation of R-R in 1987 is evidence that, at least on this occasion, the public investment paid off.

Trustee Savings Bank (TSB)   It was the Government that decided to "privatize" the TSB, but strictly speaking the sale of the TSB Group was not a privatization because it emerged that the Government did not after all own the assets in question. In fact it was ruled that no one, not even the bank's depositors, owned the TSB, and the proceeds of the sale were retained by the bank itself. This posed peculiar problems for pricing the issue because, whatever the issue price, the shareholders would end up owning not only the assets of the bank, but also the money that they paid for those assets! Thus the TSB was almost literally given away. Ignoring transactions costs, there could be no finite equilibrium price (unless the TSB's management was thought to be worse than the shareholders at looking after their money).

Strong demand for the issue was therefore guaranteed. In September 1986 the offer for sale by the TSB Central Board of 1.5 billion shares at 100 pence was heavily oversubscribed, and large profits were immediately gained by lucky applicants. Priority was given to TSB customers and to employees and pensioners of the company. A one-for-ten share bonus was offered to shareholders prepared to keep their shares for three years (rather than just take their short-term profits), and 135 million of the shares were retained for this purpose. The Group raised further capital in November 1986 when it offered for sale 49 percent of the equity in its Channel Islands subsidiary.

Personal banking services constitute the TSB's main business. The bank has 1,600 branches throughout the U.K., and services 14 million accounts for its massive base of 7 million customers. The Group also provides investment management services, insurance and unit trusts, credit card operations (via its Trustcard), and vehicle rental services (through its Swan National subsidiary). In 1986 the TSB's pretax profit exceeded £200 million. The Group is now facing the challenges presented by the growth of competition throughout the financial services industry. With its large and relatively underexploited customer base, the TSB has an opportunity to grow rapidly in the years to come. The question is whether it has the management expertise to do so.

Other Asset Sales   The companies above do not by any means constitute an exhaustive list. Denationalization of state-owned **shipbuilding** industries has been on the Conservative agenda ever since 1979, but progress here has not been easy, especially because of the loss-making state of parts of the industry. Nine subsidiary companies were sold in 1983, and the following year the Government announced its plan to sell off **British Shipbuilders'** warship yards (which happen to include Vickers and Yarrow). Yards have been sold piecemeal to British companies (such as GEC and Trafalgar House), but relatively little net revenue has been raised because of the unprofitability of the industry. Indeed, it may be impossible to sell some yards except perhaps at negative prices.

Some of **British Rail**'s (BR's) assets have been sold to the private sector, for example BR hotels, and in July 1984 the Sealink ferry subsidiary was sold by tender to British Ferries Ltd, a subsidiary of Sea Containers Ltd. Three companies submitted proposals to buy Sealink, but there was only one firm bid which was accepted. The £66 million realized from the sale fell far short of the £108 million book value of the company, and it is questionable whether the method and timing of sale were entirely appropriate. Other nonrail interests of BR have been grouped into British Rail Investments Ltd, and are being sold piecemeal to the private sector.

The prospects for privatizing parts of BR's core railway business are briefly discussed in section 10.5.

The Government's 24 percent holding in **British Sugar** was sold in 1982. The public shareholding dated back to the company's formation as a result of amalgamations in 1936. Before the U.K. joined the EEC in 1973 the Government provided support for the sugar beet industry, but the EEC then took over that function. In May 1980 a bid for British Sugar was made by **S&W Berisford**, and this was approved after a reference to the Monopolies and Mergers Commission. Berisford completed its purchase of British Sugar's shares in 1982. There have since been further unsuccessful attempts to acquire British Sugar from Berisford.

The electronics companies **ICL** and **Ferranti** were amongst those that received public support under the auspices of the National Enterprise Board (NEB) set up by the Wilson Government in the 1970s. The Government had taken a 10 percent stake in ICL at the time of the company's formation by merger in 1968, and its shareholding was increased to more than 24 percent in 1976. The Conservative Government sold its shareholding at the end of 1979 for £37 million. ICL hit serious problems in the recession shortly afterwards, and further public aid was provided in 1981. However, a turnaround was then achieved, and the company was acquired by STC in 1984. The Government's rescue of Ferranti also turned out to be successful. After the company's transformation in 1974–1979 the NEB's 50 percent holding was sold for £55 million. In 1980–1981, under the Conservative policy of reducing state involvement, the NEB disposed of numerous other shareholdings, including Fairey, and pulled out of other companies (e.g. Sinclair, Cambridge Instruments, and Alfred Herbert, the machine tool company). Its two largest interests (BL and R-R) were transferred to direct Government control. In general the NEB had a mixed record; on commercial criteria, NEB investments performed badly on average. Some companies were rescued successfully, but others were a constant drain on public funds. (For a critical view of Government involvement in industry over this period see Redwood (1984).)

6.4   The Future of the Program

The Conservative Election Manifesto in 1987 set out the party's future plans for privatization:

"We will continue the successful programme of privatisation. In particular, after the privatisation of the British Airports Authority we will return to the public the

Water Authorities, leaving certain functions to a new National Rivers Authority.

Following the success of gas privatisation, with the benefits it brought to employees and millions of customers, we will bring forward proposals for privatising the electricity industry subject to proper regulation."

The Liberal–SDP Alliance Manifesto opposed the privatization of the water and electricity industries on grounds of concern for safety and the environment. The party stated that, despite its opposition at the time of privatization, it would not return BT or British Gas to the public sector, but would focus instead on competition and efficiency in those industries. The Alliance said that it would consider the privatization of British Steel.

The Labour Party announced plans to extend social ownership. Its manifesto stressed the importance that the party attached to social ownership of basic utilities like gas and water. Labour stated that it would

". . . start by using the existing 49 per cent holding in British Telecom to ensure proper influence in their decisions. Private shares in BT and British Gas will be converted into special new securities. These will be bought and sold in the market in the usual way and will carry either a guaranteed return, or dividends linked to the company's growth."

Labour also proposed to set up British Enterprise, a socially owned holding company, to invest public funds in, for example, high technology industries.

Following the Conservative election victory in June 1987, the BAA was offered for sale the following month (see section 10.3). The water industry is expected to be privatized in 1989 (see chapter 11) and plans are being developed to sell parts of the electricity supply industry (see section 9.3). It is not clear how the latter sale will be structured, but senior management has declared its opposition to splitting up the Central Electricity Generating Board into competing private companies.

Other industries are likely to be on the agenda for privatization before long. After years of heavy losses, **British Steel** has returned to profitability (£178 million net profit in 1986–1987) following a radical efficiency drive involving manpower reductions and plant closures. The company has therefore become a natural candidate for privatization.

The Government has also asked the **Rover Group** (formerly **British Leyland**) to prepare plans for its privatization, preferably to individual shareholders, by 1992. As well as Jaguar (see above), parts of the group have already been sold, including Leyland Bus, Leyland Trucks, and the spares business Unipart. Political controversy arose in 1986 when it emerged that Austin Rover cars and Land Rover might be taken over by the American companies Ford and General Motors. The plans were dropped, but the episode highlights the central difficulty in privatizing the Rover Group. The company's past record of financial losses and declining market share is so poor that it is unlikely to appeal to individual investors except at a very low offer price. The alternative of selling the group to a foreign competitor would raise more revenue, but is fraught with political difficulty for the Government.

The **Post Office** has often been regarded as a possible candidate for privatization, but the sale of the Royal Mail was ruled out by Mrs Thatcher during the 1987 election campaign. The Post Office monopoly on time-sensitive mail has already been relaxed, and the question arises of whether its monopoly of the letter post should cease, whether or not privatization occurs. The Chairman of the Post Office has argued against such liberalization on the grounds that "cream skimming" by entrants into profitable business segments and cut-price intra-urban mail services would cause price increases in rural areas and would jeopardize efficiency. These points are debatable, but once again we have the familiar picture of senior management opposing liberalization.

The list of possible future privatizations does not end there. In the 1987 election campaign Mr Peter Walker, then the Energy Secretary, said that **British Coal** (see section 9.5) would not be privatized during the next Parliament, but its sale may be contemplated eventually. Privatization would be fiercely opposed by mining unions, but with a comfortable majority and the earlier victory in the 1984–1985 coal strike the Government might not be deterred from returning the company to private ownership. The privatization of **British Rail** (see section 10.5) is perhaps a more remote prospect, though Conservative philosophy is now such that little can be ruled out. Between 1979 and 1987 more than a third of state-owned businesses were privatized, the bulk of which were sold from 1984 onwards. Privatization is set to go much further in the next few years.

Chapter 7

Selling State Assets and the Stock Market

7.1 Introduction

One of the most controversial aspects of the privatization program has been the pricing of the shares of the companies offered for sale. In a number of cases, including British Telecom (BT), the Trustee Savings Bank (TSB), and British Airways, large and immediate profits have gone to the individuals and institutions fortunate enough to be allocated shares. The proceeds to the Government have been correspondingly lower than they might have been, to the tune of hundreds of millions of pounds, a loss which ultimately falls upon individuals generally who have to pay higher taxes or who receive poorer public services and benefits than they otherwise would. This has occurred despite the fact that the Government has spent large sums of taxpayers' money on underwriting fees and on advertising new share issues.

Need this have happened? Immediately it must be said that the Government and its financial advisers have to strike a difficult balance when they price a new issue. Underpricing leads to revenue loss, windfall profits, and arbitrary redistributions of wealth, but overpricing means that the Government (or its underwriters) are left with shares on their hands, applicants for shares face losses, and there is general embarrassment for the Government. It is also true that new issues of the shares of private companies often go to a premium on their first day of trading. Similarly, governments privatizing companies in other countries have tended to underprice their share issues. Premiums immediately arose when trading in the shares of St Gobain and Paribas began in France, and there were prodigious rises in the share price of NTT, the Japanese telephone company, despite the fact that its offer price was already astronomical by world standards. Finally, selling the shares of privatized companies at a discount to their true value is a way of promoting the objective of wider share ownership, though it is arguable whether it is the best way.

Nonetheless we believe that there have been serious and very expensive flaws in U.K. Government policy for selling state assets. In particular, the extent of underpricing, especially in the larger privatizations, has been much greater than in typical private issues. One of many criticisms of its techniques of sale is that it was quite unnecessary to sell off such large chunks of the equity of firms such as BT, British Gas, or British Airways. If a company's equity is sold in several tranches there is still the difficulty of pricing the first tranche of shares—especially if there are few comparable companies already quoted on the market—but the pricing of subsequent tranches is made easier by the fact that the market has already been able to determine the value of the shares. Government policy on the underwriting of new issues has also been strange, especially in view of its generous pricing strategies and its ability to bear risk better than underwriters. Above all the pricing of new issues has erred very much on the low side, as we will detail below. Perhaps this is not so surprising in view of the costs and benefits to politicians and their financial advisers of overpricing and underpricing.

The plan of the chapter is as follows. In section 7.2 we set out the evidence on the pricing of shares in privatized companies, in particular the size of the discounts or premiums at which they were sold. This is seen to depend on the method of sale (tender offer or offer for sale) and on whether shares in the company were already traded on the stock market. We describe the implications for wealth distribution of the windfall profits that have typically arisen in large share issues. We then look at the costs of sale, including underwriting and advertising costs, which have been quite high, and we ask what alternative methods of sale might have been employed by the Government.

Section 7.3 is concerned with the net effect of privatization on the Government's financial position. Along with the huge proceeds from the sale of shares, account must also be taken of the loss to Government of the profits of the firms, the removal of the need to pay for their capital expenditure programs, and tax considerations. Section 7.4 contains evidence on the role of privatization in encouraging the objective of wider share ownership in the U.K., and we ask whether privatization is a sensible way of promoting that objective. In section 7.5 we conclude by offering our assessment of the Government's record in selling state assets, and we consider the political and financial motives that may have influenced policy.

The chapter relies heavily on the work of Mayer and Meadowcroft (1985), Yarrow (1986, sections 7–10), and Jenkinson and Mayer (1987). The interested reader is also referred to the entertaining and informative account of the selling of BT in the book by Newman (1986).

7.2   The Sale of State Assets

7.2.1   The Pricing of Shares

Table 7.1 summarizes information regarding the pricing of shares in the main companies in the U.K. Government's privatization program up to mid-1987. We also include the TSB, the sale of which was essentially equivalent to privatization, although the proceeds of the sale were retained by the bank itself and not the Government (see section 6.3 for further details). The companies are listed alphabetically in two groups. First come the companies that were sold to the public by an "offer for sale." That is to say, the Government invited applications for shares at a set price. For example, in November 1984 the Government issued a prospectus offering shares in BT for sale at 130 pence (payable in three instalments), and individuals and institutions duly applied for shares. The issue was oversubscribed—five times as many shares were applied for as were available, and they were allocated according to a rationing scheme of the Government's choosing. The second group of companies were sold by "tender offer." The Government invited bids for shares above a given minimum tender price. With the exception of the British Airports Authority (BAA) (see below), in the event of oversubscription shares were allocated to those who entered the highest bids, and the share price became the "striking price" at which demand equals supply. Thus excess demand is rationed by the price mechanism. If a tender offer is undersubscribed, bidders' demands are satisfied at the minimum tender price previously set by the Government. The underwriters—financial institutions which in return for a fee agree to accept shares if demand from the public is inadequate—then have to take up the remaining shares at the minimum tender price. The Government has also used underwriters when selling shares by an offer for sale, but there is no necessary reason why it has to do so (see section 7.2.4 below).

The privatization of BAA (formerly the British Airports Authority) needs separate comment, since it was a novel combination of an offer for sale and a tender offer. Three-quarters of its 500 million shares were offered for sale to the general public and placed with institutions in the normal way, but the remaining 25 percent were sold by tender. Most tender offers are operated as described in the previous paragraph—successful bidders pay the striking price at which supply equals demand—but the BAA tender was different. Tenderers were committed to pay the price that they offered, and some therefore acquired their shares more cheaply than others. Because of the two elements in the share offer, BAA appears twice in table 7.1. The

Table 7.1 The pricing of shares in privatized companies

(1) Company	(2) Gross proceeds of sale (£ million)	(3) Offer/tender price (p)	(4) First trading day	(5) Price at end of first trading day (p)	(6) Percentage rise (fall) in price relative to offer/tender price	(7) Application multiple	(8) Under (over) valuation (£ million)
Offers for sale							
Amersham International	63	142	25 Feb 82	188	32	25.6	20
Associated British Ports (1983)	22	112	16 Feb 83	138	23	35	5
British Aerospace (1981)	149	150	20 Feb 81	171	14	3.5	21
British Aerospace (1985)	550	375	14 May 85	420	12	5.4	66
BAA (British Airports)[a]	919	245	28 Jul 87	291	19	8	173
British Airways	900	125	11 Feb 87	169	35	32	315
British Gas	5603	135	8 Dec 86	147.5	9	4	519
British Petroleum (1979)	290	363	12 Nov 79	367	1	1.5	3
British Telecom	3916	130	3 Dec 84	173	33	5	1295
Britoil (1985)	450	185	12 Aug 85	207	12	10	54
Cable and Wireless (1981)	224	168	6 Nov 81	197	17	5.6	39
Cable and Wireless (1985)	602	587	13 Dec 85	590	0.5	2	3
Jaguar	294	165	10 Aug 84	179	8	8.3	25
Rolls-Royce	1360	170	20 May 87	232	36	9.4	496
TSB	1360	100	10 Oct 86	135.5	35.5	8	483
Tender offers							
Associated British Ports (1984)	52	270	19 Apr 84	272	0.7	n/a	0.3
BAA[a]	362	290	29 Jul 87	291	0.3	6	1
British Petroleum (1983)	565	435	26 Sep 83	441	1	2.7	8
Britoil (1982)	548	215	23 Nov 82	196	-9	0.3	-49
Cable and Wireless (1983)	275	275	5 Dec 83	273	-1	0.7	-2
Enterprise Oil	393	185	2 Jul 84	185	0	0.7	0

Sources: National Audit Office (1985, 1987a, 1987b), Mayer and Meadowcroft (1985), *The Financial Times*.
a. Shares in BAA were sold by a combination of an offer for sale and a tender offer (see text).

entry in the first part of the table concerns the 75 percent of shares offered for sale. The second entry concerns the 25 percent of shares offered by tender, and the calculation of the premium is based on the average tender price accepted (290 pence).

The shares of some of the companies in the table were sold in two or more tranches. In those cases the years in which the tranches were sold are indicated in parentheses. For example, there was a tender offer for a portion of Britoil's equity in 1982, and an offer for sale of the remainder of its shares in 1985. The absence of a year after the name of a company does not necessarily imply that all its shares were sold at once. For example, approximately half of BT's equity has so far been sold to private hands.

The gross proceeds of the sale of shares are indicated in column 2 of the table. We have not deducted costs such as advisory fees, promotion costs, underwriters' fees, and the cost of the discounts on shares sold to employees of the companies in question. In column 3 we state the offer price of each issue in the case of offers for sale, and the equilibrium tender price in the case of tender offers. We state full offer prices, although their payment often occurs in two or more stages. For example, payment of the 130 pence price for BT shares occurred in three instalments—of 50, 40, and 40 pence—spread over a period of approximately 18 months.

Column 4 states the first day on which the newly issued shares were traded. We use the price at the close of trading on that day (see column 5) as the basis for calculating the percentage appreciation or depreciation of the shares relative to their offer price. This is not the only date that could be used for measuring undervaluation or overvaluation, and the profits or losses accruing to successful subscribers for shares. There is often considerable volatility in the share price as soon as trading opens, and this tends to settle down after a few days. However, the price at the end of the first day of trading is rarely very different from the price several days later, and it has the merits of simplicity and immediacy as a basis for comparison. A case in point is the TSB, whose shares opened at 100 pence for the 50 pence partly paid shares, but closed on the first day of trading at around 85 pence, which is roughly where they stayed for some days afterwards. The high volatility was in the first few hours.

Another reason for using a price soon after trading began is that there is less time for news to affect the price. Since that news could not have been taken into account at the time when the shares were originally priced, the use of a later price might introduce some distortions into the comparison. One way of allowing for part of such distortions is to adjust the price of the shares by the percentage movement in the share index for the U.K. market as a whole, or for the relevant sector of the market, for the period in question (see Mayer and Meadowcroft, 1985). Indeed, there is a case for making an adjustment of this kind even when the price at the end of the first day of trading is used for the comparison, because some time (perhaps as much as a fortnight) will have elapsed between the pricing of the issue and the commencement of trading. However, we have not made any adjustments, preferring instead to base our comparisons on the raw data. We do not believe that this is unjustified. First, for the cases shown, movements in the market were on average close to zero in a period as short as a couple of weeks. Secondly, relative movements of even several percentage points would not have had a large influence on the proportionate disparities between offer prices and trading prices of shares in these privatizations.

Some authors have measured the relative performance of shares in privatized companies over several years (see Mayer and Meadowcroft, 1985; Yarrow, 1986). We do not do so here, because our present concern is with the degree to which shares were undervalued or overvalued. The level of a share price two years after privatization, even relative to the market, is influenced by so many factors unknown at the time of sale that we would not wish to attach too much weight to longer-term comparisons in judging the pricing of the offers. They are perhaps more useful for appraising company performance over time, but even here there are shortcomings. The price of BT shares in 1986 was affected by many other things, such as politics.

Column 6 gives the percentage appreciation or depreciation of the share price when trading opened relative to its offer price, i.e. the percentage difference between the numbers in columns 5 and 3. Note that we are using the full offer price rather than the first instalment of payments. (Strictly speaking, we should revise downward the full offer price to reflect the interest that accrues on later instalments, but since we do not do this, we underestimate the true gains somewhat.) It is the increase relative to the first instalment that represents the percentage profit (or loss) to the successful applicants for shares. Table 7.2 shows that these profits have been enormous in major privatizations.

Moreover, individuals applying for shares are often entitled to substantial additional benefits if they hold the shares for long enough. Customer shareholders of BT and British Gas could apply for free vouchers to set against their telephone or gas bills. In the case of British Gas a customer could in time receive a voucher worth £40 (tax free) for every 400 shares held. This and the dividend would have made the post-tax annual rate of return on the shares more than 20 percent in the first six months or

Table 7.2 Immediate profits

Company	First instalment (p)	Opening price (p)	Percentage gain
BT	50	93	86
TSB	50	85.5	71
British Gas	50	62.5	25
British Airways	65	109	68
Rolls-Royce	85	147	73
BAA	100	146	46

so even if the share price had not appreciated at all. Another form of benefit for small shareholders has been the issue of free bonus shares, typically 10 percent after three years. As well as BT and British Gas, other companies such as the TSB and British Airways offered this benefit. In section 7.2.3 we will consider the effective cost of these benefits to shareholders, which further inflate the gains reaped by successful applicants for shares. In section 7.4 we will discuss the role of these shareholder "loyalty bonuses" in inducing investors not to sell their shares, and the resulting effect on the distribution of share ownership.

Column 7 gives the application multiple, i.e. the number of shares subscribed for divided by the number available. (An application multiple of less than unity indicates undersubscription.) Broadly speaking there are three classes of applicant for shares—individual investors, U.K. institutions, and overseas institutions. A proportion of the shares is usually placed with institutional investors in advance, who are typically clients of the stockbrokers and merchant bankers handling the issue for the Government. When British Gas was privatized, 40 percent of the shares were placed with U.K. institutions and 20 percent with overseas institutions, leaving 40 percent for the general public. Applications from the latter group were so numerous that "clawback" provisions were triggered, and 64 percent were eventually allocated to the public. Institutional holdings were scaled down correspondingly. Overall the issue was four times oversubscribed. This application multiple happens to lie between some of the extremes that have occurred in the privatization program. For example, British Airways was oversubscribed 32 times, whereas 70 percent of the Britoil shares offered for tender in 1982 were left with the underwriters.

What are the main lessons to be drawn from table 7.1? First, and most obvious, is the underpricing of shares in most privatizations, and especially the major ones. The figures in column 8 state the difference between the value ascribed to the shares when they were offered for sale and their value on the first day of trading, i.e. the sum in column 2 multiplied by the percentage in column 6. The figures in column 8 sum to about £3 billion (even excluding TSB). It could not be expected that the Government would fine tune the pricing of each issue so that the average premium would be zero, but the windfall profits to lucky applicants for shares have been far greater in both relative and absolute terms than the average profits to those who "stag" private issues. The weighted average of the immediate price changes in column 6 is 18.4 percent of gross proceeds (i.e. in relation to fully paid share prices), and well over 30 percent in relation to partly paid share prices. That is far greater than the degree of underpricing typical in private issues. Buckland et al. (1981) estimated that, in times of rising equity markets, premiums on private offers for sale averaged 12 percent. In a more recent study of new equity issues on the London stock market between 1983 and 1986, Jackson (1986) found that the average degree of underpricing of larger issues was 5.3 percent in offers for sale and 7.3 percent in tender offers. In addition private issues rarely have the additional shareholder benefits of vouchers and bonuses that have been a feature of the major privatizations. Moreover, there is good reason to believe that the Government could and should have sold the shares in a way that led to smaller initial price rises than those that occur in private issues.

The second point to note is that the size of undervaluation varies according to how the issue is sold. The average price change for offers for sale is 21.1 percent of gross proceeds (and over 40 percent in relation to partly paid prices), but for tender offers it is −1.9 percent (cf. Jackson's (1986) findings reported above). This difference is not altogether surprising. We would expect tender offers to lead to reasonably accurate pricing, because price is set by the forces of supply and demand, and circumstances make it impossible for bidders for shares to collude. In contrast, with offers for sale there are numerous reasons why members of Government and their financial advisers have an incentive to set prices lower than their equilibrium values. Underpricing is a way of encouraging wider share ownership, it avoids political embarrassment, and it minimizes the chances that individual investors (who have votes) will sustain capital losses. Underpricing is also greatly to the benefit of City institutions. Some degree of underpricing on average is probably inevitable once the Government has decided to sell such large portions of equity at a time (e.g. 100 percent of British Gas) by offers for sale. But there was nothing inevitable about its extent in the major privatizations, and nor did the Government have to sell shares in that fashion.

This leads on to a third point that emerges from table 7.1. The most glaring examples of underpricing occurred where a company was entirely new to the market, as were BT, British Gas, and British Airways. Moreover, there were no companies already quoted on the U.K. Stock Exchange that were comparable with these firms—a fact which makes pricing especially difficult because, apart from the limited availability of international comparisons, price has to be set somewhat in the dark. Essentially the same problem can be faced in the private sector. For example when shares in Wellcome, the pharmaceutical company, were offered for sale early in 1986, comparisons were made with Glaxo, but there are important differences between the two companies and Wellcome shares opened with a large premium of around 30 percent. But the crucial difference between the offer of Wellcome's shares and the offer of shares in (say) British Airways is that Wellcome offered only 25 percent of its equity and not 100 percent. If and when more of Wellcome's equity is offered for sale, there will exist a well-established market in Wellcome's shares, and the market will provide an accurate guide to the appropriate price.

This point is reflected in the smaller than average premiums in the offers for sale of the tranches of shares in British Aerospace (1985), BP (1979), Britoil (1985), and Cable and Wireless (1985). When the Government offers for sale all or part of its remaining holding in BT, it will again have the benefit of an existing market in the shares as a guide to relative pricing.

The Government's final 31.6 percent holding in BP was offered for sale in October 1987. (The event occurred too late to be included in table 7.1.) The offering was valued at £7.2 billion, making it the largest ever share offering in Britain. The shares were priced at 330 pence, which was about 6 percent below the then prevailing price of existing BP shares. In fact the discount relative to the price of the existing shares was greater, by perhaps another 6 percent, because the new shares were payable in three instalments and account should be taken of the interest on the second and third instalments. The prospectus for the new BP shares was issued on 15 October and the closing date for the offer for sale was 28 October. The crash in world equity markets began on 19 October, and by the close of the BP offer, the London market had lost 28 percent of its value two weeks previously. BP shares fell headlong with the market, and it soon became clear that the overwhelming majority of new shares would be left with the underwriters. They urged the Chancellor of the Exchequer to withdraw the issue in order to help the ailing equity market, but he turned down their rather surprising request. After all, underwriters are underwriters. Instead the Goverment put a floor under the price of the new shares by the Bank of England offering to buy them back at 70 pence per partly-paid share, which was 50 pence below the offer price. This scheme was a reasonable compromise in the circumstances, though ironically it involved giving private investors the option to renationalize the BP shares. At the end of this chapter we offer some thoughts on the possible consequences of the equity market slump for privatization policies generally.

7.2.2   Consequences for Wealth Distribution

The extent of underpricing shown in column 8 of table 7.1 shows that the sale of state assets has resulted in substantial shifts in the distribution of wealth. The gainers have been the successful applicants for shares, and the losers have been those who would have enjoyed lower (direct or indirect) taxes and/or better public services if the extent of underpricing had not been so large. Privatization also affects the distribution of income and wealth in other ways—by changing the pricing, output, and employment decisions of firms, and by enhancing the income of the financial services industry—but its most obvious impact on distribution has occurred in the capital market.

An important feature of the process is that the gainers know that they have gained, but the losers are less aware that they have lost. A windfall profit of £200 on BT shares is much more obvious than the effective loss of £20 to each of ten who failed to apply. John Kenneth Galbraith once remarked that few things enhance the overall feeling of wealth better than undiscovered theft. Without wishing to push the analogy too far, we would suggest that there is a common element in the two cases.

Why is the redistribution of wealth undesirable? We believe that there are several reasons. First, it is arbitrary in the sense that the gainers have performed no socially useful function other than the bearing of (negligible) risk. Secondly, the prospective transfer of wealth to successful applicants encourages a great deal of directly unproductive wealth-seeking activity— the transactions costs incurred by potential buyers are far from negligible. Thirdly, many of the windfall profits have gone overseas, because a substantial fraction of the shares have been allocated to foreign investors. From the point of view of national welfare, the profits on those shares are a direct loss. Fourthly, the cost to the economy of raising an amount of tax revenue equal to the extent of underpricing is far greater than that extent. That is because it costs the economy more than £1 to raise £1 of tax revenue. There are costs of tax collection, and, more importantly, there is an additional distortion to efficient resource allocation caused by the extra taxation. In a nutshell, higher proceeds from a given share sale have all the advantages of lump-sum taxation plus the virtue of being fairer.

Finally we must consider the effect on wealth distribution if the process of privatization were put into reverse. If investors were given "fair" compensation (whatever that may be) when a company was renationalized, then there would be no further redistributive impact. But if shares were taken back at (say) the original offer price, then existing shareholders would sustain a capital loss or gain equal to the difference between that price and the previously prevailing market price. Of course the latter price might itself be influenced by the prospect of renationalization. Politically it would be very difficult for a government to cause shareholders to incur large capital losses, especially because many current shareholders would not have been the shareholders that reaped the initial windfall profits. Moreover, renationalization on less than fair terms would be a process in which the losers would know that they had lost but the gainers would not know that they had gained in relative terms. The Chairman of the Conservative Party, Mr Norman Tebbit, probably had these considerations in mind when writing to BT shareholders in 1986 asking them to think how much a Labour Government could cost them. This suggests that a side effect of the privatization program has been to make more visible some consequences of various electoral outcomes for the distribution of wealth in the U.K.

7.2.3   Costs of Sale
We have already discussed the largest component of the cost of selling state assets—the revenue foregone due to underpricing. The other main items of expenditure are costs of promotion, professional and advisory fees, and underwriting fees. Table 7.3 gives the costs associated with the sale of the major privatized companies. The figures exclude costs borne by the

Table 7.3   Cost of major asset sales

Company	Date of sale	Expenses (£ million)	Expenses as percentage of proceeds
Cable and Wireless	1981	7	3.1
British Aerospace	1981	6	3.8
Amersham	1982	3	4.6
Britoil	1982	17	3.2
Associated British Ports	1983	2	11.2
Enterprise Oil	1984	11	2.8
BT	1984	263	6.8
British Gas	1986	360	6.4
BA	1987	42	4.7

Source: National Audit Office (1987b).

Table 7.4   Receipts and costs of BT and British Gas privatizations (in £ million)

	BT	British Gas
Value of shares at offer price	3,916	5,603
Less: Employee discounts and free shares	(56)	(37)
Premium from sale of retained shares	3	4
Estimated premium from further bonus share sale	–	21
Sales proceeds	3,863	5,591
Direct U.K. sale costs		
Underwriting and commissions	87	69
Bank and registration costs	20	45
Marketing	14	40
Advisers' fees	6	5
Less: Interest on application money	(4)	(7)
Contribution from BT sale	(1)	–
Total U.K. sale costs	122	152
Overseas sale costs	30	23
Small-shareholder incentives		
Bill vouchers	23	63
Bonus shares	88	122
Net costs	263	360
Net proceeds	3,600	5,231

Source: National Audit Office (1985, 1987a).
In addition to the sale of its shares, another £2,500 million was raised from the sale of British Gas debt.

companies themselves, which include the value of managerial time and effort, and other advisory and promotion expenses. For example, BT is estimated to have paid more than £8 million to its own advisers, and to have spent some £25 million on its own preflotation advertising campaign.

The most expensive asset sales have been those of BT and British Gas. Table 7.4 gives a breakdown of the expenses involved. The two largest components of the expenses on selling BT were small-shareholder incentives (£111 million) and fees and commissions associated with underwriting and placing shares (£87 million). In addition, many millions of pounds were spent on professional and advisory fees.

Aside from the sale of BT, in which expenses came to 6.8 percent of proceeds, costs have generally been in line with expenses on large private issues, which Dimson (1983) estimates to be approximately 4.5 percent in the U.K. However, there are several reasons why the Government could and should have privatized at a lower cost than a private issue of shares. Mayer and Meadowcroft (1985) point out several important differences between the position of a Government selling state assets and that of a private company raising funds on the equity market. First, the Government does not face the cash flow constraint of a private firm. The operations of a private firm raising funds often depend critically upon it selling all the shares being offered to investors. Failure to do so might mean that the firm became indebted to a perilous extent, or that it would have to shelve its real investment plans. In the face of these dangers, it makes good sense for private companies to underwrite their issues and to err on the side of generosity in pricing. The Government has no such cash flow constraint. Its borrowing powers mean that it could make up any shortfall in share proceeds with relative ease and without undue jeopardy to its real expenditure plans.

Secondly, the Government's capacity to bear risk is vastly greater than that of any private firm and, more to the point, that of any underwriter. The function of underwriters is to bear the risk of the issuer by agreeing in return for a fee to buy unsold shares at the offer price. The issuer is then guaranteed to receive the funds being sought. Underwriting makes sense only if the underwriting institutions are less risk-averse than the issuer. But no institution can be less risk-averse than the Government, because the economy as a whole bears the cost (in terms of debt or tax burden) that arises from incorrectly pricing the shares in privatized companies. Further risk-spreading is impossible, and it is therefore curious that the Government should have spent so much on underwriting fees. Mayer and Meadowcroft (1985) report that underwriting costs of £0.7 million, £0.4 million, £4.6 million, £22.4 million, £9.8 million, and £4.5 million were incurred in the privatizations of Amersham, Associated British Ports, BP, BT, Britoil, and Cable and Wireless respectively. Underwriting is all the more mysterious in view of the evident generosity with which the major privatized issues were priced.

7.2.4 Alternatives

Notwithstanding the delight of successful applicants for shares and of the

City, the techniques of sale used by the Government in the privatization program have been seriously flawed. Massive transfers of wealth have occurred both within and away from the U.K. economy, and huge transactions costs have been incurred. Yet superior alternatives were available.

First, market forces could have been used to a far greater extent in the setting of prices. Tender offers lead to much more accurate pricing than offers for sale, and an element of tendering can be employed even when an offer for sale is the chosen method. In the United States it is common for syndicates to be required to make firm bids stating prices and quantities in advance of the pricing of offers for sale. This enables the issuer to exploit the information of participants in the marketplace. In contrast, in the U.K. it is typical practice for soundings to be taken among a few institutions regarding an appropriate offer price. Such a system hardly creates incentives for accurate pricing, and in the words of the *Financial Times* Lex Column (16 February 1987) "Naturally the funds name the lowest price that does not beggar belief and frequently they get away with it."

Secondly, it is manifestly sensible to sell portions of equity over time rather than all at one go. Once the first tranche is sold, a well-established market exists and further tranches can be priced with some accuracy. This practice has been followed most notably in the case of BP, and several other privatized companies (including BT) were or will be sold in stages. But massive companies like British Gas and British Airways (and the TSB) were sold in one chunk, and it was not necessary to sell as much as half of BT at once. In contrast the Japanese Government began by selling just 10 percent of NTT. Selling in stages need not even affect the cash flows to the Government. For example, three tranches, each of one-sixth of BT's shares, could have been sold at the times when the three instalments of the half of BT's equity offered for sale in November 1984 were due for payment.

Thirdly, the expenses associated with sale could have been substantially reduced. As we argued above, the elementary logic of risk-bearing implies that it was inappropriate for the Government to underwrite many privatizations, especially in view of its pricing strategy.

Finally, a simple alternative would have been to *give* to each adult member of the population an equal number of shares in massive companies like BT and British Gas. Commentators such as Samuel Brittan in the *Financial Times* argued forcefully for this way of cutting out the financial middlemen. It has three major advantages. First, it is a manifestly fair method of asset disposal. Each member of the population would own exactly as much of the company immediately after privatization as he or she did (in effect) under public ownership. Privatization would merely provide freedom to vary one's share of the company. There would be no arbitrary redistributions of wealth, and no windfall profits would accrue to overseas institutions. Secondly, there would be no need to worry about such matters as pricing and underwriting. Price would be set by the market when trading begins. Thirdly, there is no more direct method of promoting wider share ownership.

Shareholdings would not be unreasonably small if this method were adopted. BT was valued at well over £10 billion when trading in its shares began. The shareholding of each (adult) individual would have been worth more than £250, and multi-member households would have received two or more holdings of that size. Transactions costs would compare favorably with the method of sale actually chosen. Sending each member of (say) the electoral register the same documents is a simpler operation than promoting, underwriting, and dealing with varied applications for a new issue.

However, there is an objection to giving shares away free. Such a policy would increase the need to raise finance from other sources, and hence would tend to increase distortions throughout the economy caused by tax and debt burdens. In short, £1 in receipts from privatization costs the economic system less than £1 raised by extra debt or taxes. But perhaps this is not a decisive argument against the alternative of simply giving shares away, especially in view of the costs and unfairness of the methods that have been employed. Unless those methods are improved—as we believe they certainly can be—the option of cutting out the middlemen may appear to be rather attractive if and when the time comes to privatize all or part of the massive electricity supply industry.

7.3   Effect on Government Finances

In considering the effect of privatization upon the financial position of the Government it is important to distinguish between the short-term impact on the Government's accounts and the effect on its real economic position in the longer term. A major short-term attraction for the Government of selling state assets is that the sales proceeds are deducted from the "public sector borrowing requirement" (PSBR). Indeed, according to a curious accounting practice, the sales proceeds are treated as negative public expenditure! Mrs Thatcher's Government always attached great import-ance to reducing the PSBR, and, thanks to accounting definitions, privatization offered a very convenient way of doing so without further cutting public expenditure or raising taxes. The 1982 White Paper that announced the intention to privatize BT is a clear illustration of the importance of the PSBR motive. But privatization is simply the sale by Government of equities in place of bonds. They are simply alternative methods of financing.

The short-term impact of privatization on the PSBR has several components (see Mayer and Meadowcroft, 1985, section III). The PSBR is reduced by the extent of the sales proceeds, the capital expenditure program of the company being privatized, and the company's payments of interest and dividends. However, the gross profits of the company move out of the public sector accounts and hence increase the PSBR. The net effect will depend primarily upon the relative sizes of the investment expenditures and the gross profits of the company, as well as the sales proceeds. Mayer and Meadowcroft (1985, table 4) show that the proceeds from the sale of BT in 1985–1986 were reduced somewhat by these other factors, largely because of the loss of BT's gross profit of approximately £3 billion, but the net effect was nevertheless to reduce the PSBR in that year substantially.

For BT 1985–1986 was the first full year after privatization—"year 1" so to speak. What will be the effect of its privatization upon the PSBR in years 2, 3, 4, and so on? Most importantly, what will be the effect on the Government's net worth overall, i.e. the discounted value of effects on all future PSBRs? That is the question of significance for the macroeconomic consequences of privatization (see Buiter, 1985). Let us begin by assuming that the privatization of a company does not alter its behavior. Then the Government simply sells the dividend stream of the company when privatization occurs. The net worth of the Government does not change at all provided that (i) the issue is correctly priced and (ii) there are no transactions costs. Unfortunately neither of these conditions is met in practice. We saw above that privatization issues have generally been seriously underpriced, and transactions costs—expenditures on promotion, professional fees, underwriting, etc.—have been large. Bond financing clearly has advantages over equity financing insofar as conditions (i) and (ii) are close to being fulfilled. The Government's privatization program therefore *impoverishes* its net worth by an amount equal to the extent of underpricing and transactions costs in these circumstances. Privatization actually *worsens* its long-term financial position.

Now let us relax the assumption made in the last paragraph by supposing that privatization increases the profitability of the company being sold to the private sector. The Government is then able to sell a more valuable income stream than it would have received itself under continued public ownership. The overall effect on Government net worth becomes ambiguous. The cost of underpricing and transactions costs (relative to sales of government bonds) must be set against the increase in value of the income stream. As regards the latter, it is not the transfer of ownership but rather the associated change in the operation of these enterprises which has the potential to make substantial contributions to the public finances, the point so lucidly made in the quote from Adam Smith at the start of chapter 1. Here two cases have to be distinguished.

First, consider the case in which privatization induces an improvement in the internal efficiency of the enterprise and where there are no offsetting market failures. Since the assets are more productive under private than public operation, privatization will raise more revenue than the income stream which would have been earned had the assets remained under public ownership. Privatization improves both economic efficiency and the public finances.

However, a critical policy trade-off emerges if the superior financial performance of the private firm is the result only of greater exploitation of market power. Efficiency and financial objectives are now in conflict. Sale proceeds will be higher if the enterprise is privatized against a background of light regulation and a sheltered market environment, but economic efficiency is then likely to be damaged. Alternatively, stricter regulation, coupled with other measures to open up the firm to greater competitive pressures, promotes efficiency but reduces the revenue which is likely to be raised from the initial asset sale.

Finally, we turn to the financial effect of privatization on existing firms in the private sector. Other things being equal, the main result of the Government's selling equity instead of bonds is slightly to depress equity prices relative to bond prices. This in turn makes bond finance slightly more attractive to firms, relative to equity finance. However, there is no reason why the method of financing chosen by the Government should affect the overall cost of capital to firms. That depends, among other things, on the total financing requirement of the Government and not on whether that requirement is met by bond or equity issues. This is yet another illustration of why the accounting definition of the PSBR is misleading because it makes an artificial and irrelevant distinction between essentially similar methods of finance.

In sum, the merits of privatization from a financial viewpoint depend primarily upon three factors:

(i) whether a short- or longer-term perspective is adopted;

(ii) the costs (including underpricing) of selling equity as opposed to bonds;

(iii) whether privatization increases the earnings stream of the firm.

In section 7.5 we will consider the role of these factors—especially the first of them—in shaping the events that took place.

7.4 Wider Share Ownership

An important objective of Mrs Thatcher's Government has been to promote wider share ownership, and especially share ownership by employees of companies, as part of the desire to extend "property-owning democracy" in Britain. In this section we focus on two questions:

(1)   How far does privatization promote wider share ownership?

(2)   Is privatization one of the best ways of achieving this goal?

We do not consider the broader question of whether wider share ownership is a desirable objective in the first place. A discussion of this point would take us too far from the main concerns of this book (for an excellent assessment of profit sharing and employee share ownership, see Estrin *et al.* (1987)).

7.4.1 The Ownership of Shares in Privatized Firms

In answer to question (1) above, the first point to note is that by itself privatization does little or nothing to promote wider share ownership. Individuals' investment decisions depend upon the information that they have and their incentives. Privatizations have often been accompanied by measures that have made the information about, and incentives to buy, the shares in privatized companies very different from information and incentives relating to other share issues, but it is those measures, rather than the privatizations, that stimulate wider share ownership. The main informative measures have been massive advertising campaigns, such as the very successful (albeit somewhat condescending) "Tell Sid" campaign to create wide awareness of the opportunity to buy shares in British Gas. The principal incentives have been the prospects of immediate capital gain due to generous pricing, and rewards in the form of vouchers and bonus shares for shareholders who keep their shares for some time.

These measures have had a large impact on the pattern of shareholding in Britain. Before the privatization program began there were approximately two million individual shareholders—about 5 percent of the adult population. The tax system encouraged, and continues to encourage, investment via large financial institutions such as pension funds and life assurance companies, and, above all else, investment in home ownership. The privatization of BT in 1984 gave the first major boost to individual share ownership and further impetus came from the sales of the TSB and British Gas in 1986.

Several surveys of the growth in share ownership have been commissioned by newspapers, the Treasury, and the Stock Exchange. A large NOP survey of 7,200 people in April 1986 suggested that as many as 14 percent of the adult population (i.e. almost six million individuals) owned shares directly, but other surveys produced lower figures more in the region of 10 percent. An interesting finding of these surveys was the broad spread of share ownership among socioeconomic groups. Early in 1987, after the TSB and British Gas had been privatized, a survey of 954 adults carried out for the *Observer* (16 January 1987) suggested that 23 percent of adults in Britain—some 9.2 million individuals—owned shares. It was estimated that 0.8 million people owned BT shares only, that 2.4 million owned shares in British Gas only, and that 1.6 million owned TSB shares only. The survey found that about 1.6 million individuals owned shares in the company for which they worked. Only 2.8 million adults were found to be in none of the above categories. Other surveys (see Grout, 1987) also suggest that around 20 percent of British adults own shares. They all show the overriding importance of privatization in promoting wider share ownership.

Further information is provided by figures on the ownership of shares in individual companies. The evidence is that the privatizations early on in the Government's program did relatively little to extend share ownership. A number of enterprises—including International Aeradio, British Rail Hotels, Wytch Farm, and Sealink—were sold to other companies and therefore made no direct contribution to spreading ownership. In other cases, while the flotations were designed to favor small investors, most of those subscribing to the share issues quickly sold their holdings. That is, individual investors typically regarded the flotations as an opportunity to make a quick killing, rather than as a chance to acquire a longer-term asset. Within one month of flotation, the number of shareholders in Amersham had fallen from 62,000 to 10,000; within one year of flotation, the number had fallen from 150,000 to 26,000 in Cable and Wireless (first tranche) and from 158,000 to 27,000 in British Aerospace. Britoil (first tranche) and Enterprise Oil showed less dramatic drops in the number of shareholders since the initial offers were pitched at levels that did not produce anticipation of large short-term capital gains. Hence fewer small investors applied for shares in the first place.

However, some subsequent privatizations did much to increase the number of shareholders, because the shares were sold cheaply and incentives to retain shares were significant. There were 2.3 million shareholders in BT immediately after it was privatized. This number fell by just over a quarter in the year after privatization, and at 31 March 1987 there remained 1.4 million shareholders. Thus the erosion of the number of shareholders has been much less than in the earlier privatizations. A similar picture emerges for the TSB and British Gas, although massive quantities of shares changed hands at the opening of trading in these issues. More than a million applicants received shares in British Airways, but the number of shareholders fell to 420,000 in May 1987, only three months after the sale. The common feature of these cases is the presence of incentives to retain shares, at least for a few years. It will be interesting to see what happens to share ownership in these companies after the vouchers and share bonuses for loyalty expire.

Finally, it must be noted that the pattern of wider share ownership associated with privatization in Britain is of a very specific form (see Grout, 1987). Although the number of shareholders has risen sharply, the new shareholders typically own very few shares. Most own shares in only one firm, and most have shareholdings worth less than £1,000. Thus the ownership of shares has become wider, but is spread very thinly. The proportion of shares owned by individuals has therefore not risen in line with the growth in the number of shareholders. Indeed, according to Grout (1987, p. 60), the proportion of the stock market owned by individuals in Britain is continuing its long-term decline. Although privatization has increased the number of shareholders, it will require other measures to deepen share ownership.

The simple lesson to be drawn from the evidence on privatization and share ownership is that large numbers of the British public know a bargain when they seen one, and make decisions on buying and holding shares according to monetary incentives. Privatization has provided a vehicle for extending share ownership by enabling price incentives to be attached to huge blocks of new shares. Such opportunities occur less frequently in private issues because private issuers have no incentive to underprice (except insofar as they rationally avoid the large risks to them that are often associated with new issues). We now turn to the question of whether sensible methods have been used to extend share ownership.

7.4.2   How to Encourage Wider Share Ownership
There are two main arguments against encouraging wider share ownership

by the methods used in the privatization program. The first is that they have been an inordinately expensive way of promoting the objective. Many hundreds of millions of pounds have been lost to the Government because of the underpricing of shares in companies unnecessarily sold in large blocks. The second objection is that the methods have been distortionary in the sense that share ownership has been strongly encouraged only in relatively few privatized companies. More general incentives would have led to unbiased choice and more balanced portfolios.

What alternative methods could be used to encourage wider share ownership? The most obvious answer to this question is the removal of the incentives that exist for other forms of personal saving in the U.K. Tax relief on mortgage interest payments (up to a limit of £30,000) and the absence of taxation on imputed income from owner occupation together create strong incentives for individuals to invest heavily in home ownership. This tendency has been further strengthened by the sale at less than market prices of housing owned by local authorities, and perhaps by controls relating to rented accommodation. Tax incentives exist also for indirect investment via institutions—pension funds and (until the 1984 budget) life assurance companies. In view of all these encouragements to other forms of saving and investment, it is hardly surprising that a relatively small proportion of the population engaged in direct share ownership until recently.

The bias can be rectified either by removing privileges afforded to other forms of saving and investment or by extending them to direct share ownership. The political constituency against removing the tax privileges of home ownership is very powerful, and radical reform on that front is therefore unlikely. However, steps are being taken to extend tax advantages to investment in shares. Estrin et al. (1987, section 2) describe the encouragement that governments in the U.K. and elsewhere are extending to employee share ownership and profit-related pay. Measures are also being taken to promote personal pension plans and personal equity plans (PEPs). The former are intended to enhance labor mobility by increasing the "portability" of pensions, a feature lacked by many company pension schemes. PEPs allow individuals to invest up to £2,400 per annum in a personal pool of equities which escapes tax on dividends and capital gains. A difficulty is that the management and administration fees charged by financial intermediaries more or less outweigh the tax advantages of PEPs for basic rate taxpayers. The schemes are more advantageous for wealthy individuals, but they are more likely to be share owners in the first place. Moreover, it is a feature of all schemes giving tax-free allowances that they offer greater encouragement to the rich than the poor. Selling state assets too cheaply partly avoids this aspect of unfairness, although it does favor those with available liquidity.

Nonetheless the basic point remains. Promoting share ownership by underpricing the share issues of privatized companies, and by providing incentives to retain shares for a few years, is both expensive and selective in its impact. Cheaper and more neutral methods—including the reduction of privileges to other forms of investment—are available and desirable. For one thing, they would encourage longer-term ownership of shares generally, rather than the seizing of virtually sure prospects of quick profits in just a few companies.

7.5 Assessment

The sale of state assets on the stock market has been widely acclaimed by Government and much of the media as a resounding "success." Massive offerings of shares have been taken up by willing investors, the Government has raised billions of pounds, and share ownership has been extended to millions of new households in the process. But success must be judged relative to given objectives and opportunities. The principal stated objectives of the Government have been to maximize sales proceeds and to widen share ownership. The underpricing of major share issues has meant that the first of these aims has not been achieved at all successfully, and the second has been met in a highly expensive and rather distorted way.

There can be little doubt that the extent of underpricing in privatizations has been unnecessarily large. It has been higher than the average degree of underpricing of new private share issues despite the fact that private firms have more reason than Government to be risk-averse.

A less hasty program of share sales would have enabled the Government to sell smaller tranches sequentially, and to have priced all but the first tranches more accurately in the light of information provided by the market. Moreover, the costs associated with selling shares in privatized companies have been great: the case for underwriting was particularly questionable.

A judgment of Government policy for selling state assets—especially pricing policy—depends critically upon three factors:

(i) attitude towards the transfers of wealth from taxpayers generally to successful applicants for shares;

(ii) attitude to the risk of share issues being undersubscribed;

(iii) urgency of transferring ownership of state assets.

Our assessment of the public interest in relation to these factors will be apparent from what has gone before in this chapter. Briefly, the transfers of wealth are undesirable. In part they go abroad, and are therefore a real loss to the U.K. economy, and in general they entail higher taxation—and hence distortion of choice—than would be the case if pricing were more accurate. The Government has reason to be more tolerant of risk than any other participants in the economy, and the urgency of transferring ownership is not so great that firms the size of British Gas and British Airways have to be sold at one go.

However, the incentives of Government ministers and their financial advisers may be rather different. In political terms, the transfer of wealth to successful applicants for shares even has some advantages. First, the gainers know that they have gained but the (relative) losers do not feel their loss. Secondly, the larger is the extent of underpricing, the lower is the probability that share owners will suffer an unpleasant capital loss before the next election occurs. Thirdly, the prospect of a Labour Government renationalizing on the basis of "no speculative gain" becomes nastier the more that shares in privatized companies are underpriced, because the possible capital loss is greater. Thus privatizing by selling state assets to individuals cheaply creates a vested interest in the status quo—a point not lost on Mr Norman Tebbit, Chairman of the Conservative Party, when he wrote to shareholders in BT in 1986. Finally, the Government's City advisers have a clear financial incentive in low pricing, because they and their clients receive part of the resulting transfer of wealth.

Politicians and financial advisers are likely to be much more risk-averse than the state ought to be. The burden of embarrassment would fall largely upon them, and it is not surprising that they should seek to avoid it. They are also likely to be rather impatient to carry the program through. The electoral fortunes of politicians may suffer reversals, and it is hardly in the interests of merchant bankers to recommend partial sale when the Government is prepared to sell all of a company at once.

Whatever the underlying motives of policy makers may have been, it is hard to see how their methods of selling state assets can be judged other than a failure in terms of the general public interest and in view of the opportunities available. Their short-run success in political terms is another matter.

This chapter would not be complete without some comments on the possible consequences for privatization policies of the stock market crash of October 1987. (These remarks take the form of a postscript because publication deadlines required our text to be essentially complete some weeks previously.) In Britain the most immediate impact concerned the massive BP share offer, which was described above. The underwriters were left with huge losses as a result of the market's fall, although they may have hedged some of the risk, and they obtained some respite through the Bank of England's offer to buy back shares at 50 pence below the offer price. From the Government's point of view, underwriting had the advantage of securing the full proceeds from the sale, but the disadvantage of adding to the downward pressure on the market when the authorities least wanted it.

Most privatization stocks remained well above their original offer prices even after the initial crash, but it seems likely that the fall will affect the attitude of individual investors towards privatization issues in the future, irrespective of whether the market recovers its earlier levels. In particular, the sharp fall in share prices made investors acutely aware of the downside risk of holding on to their shareholdings. This may encourage more stagging (i.e. immediately selling share allocations at a profit) at the expense of longer-term investment by individuals in privatization issues, which would be damaging to the Government's objective of promoting wider share ownership. To counteract this tendency, the Government may have to offer yet greater inducements to encourage individuals to hold future privatization issues.

Until the BP share offer in 1987, the Government was fortunate to be privatizing in a rising stock market. The privatizations of the electricity and water industries are set to go ahead in any event, but it is interesting to ask what would happen to the privatization program in the longer term if a bear market sets in. If the Government continued to aim at a given level of privatization proceeds, then lower share values would imply that the pace of privatization would have to increase. On the other hand, a downward move in share values relative to bond prices would tend to make bond finance (i.e. selling gilts) relatively more attractive than share sales as a way of raising Government revenue. Lastly, the fear of a continuing slide in share prices, and its possible political consequences for a party that is so much identified with promoting wider share ownership, might deter Mrs Thatcher's Government from privatizing as rapidly in the future as it has done in the recent past.

8.1 Introduction

British Telecommunications plc (BT) became the first public utility company to be privatized by the Conservative Government when its shares were offered for sale in November 1984. More than three billion shares, representing 50.2 percent of BT's equity, were offered at 130 pence per share payable in three instalments. When applications closed on 28 November, the offer was heavily oversubscribed, and after dealings began on 3 December the share price soon rose further. In chapter 7 we discussed the techniques used to sell shares in BT and other privatized companies, and we examined the consequences for wider share ownership. The purpose of the present chapter is to examine the framework of competition and regulation devised for the privatized BT.

The chapter has five sections. The rest of this Introduction contains an outline of some elements of telecommunications economics—the principal products and services supplied by the industry, new technologies, the nature of demand, and cost conditions. Section 8.2 briefly describes the main firms operating in the industry today, notably BT and Mercury. The following section then explains the rapid evolution of the framework of competition and regulation within which those firms operate, in particular the 1981 and 1984 Acts of Parliament, which respectively introduced measures of liberalization and privatization. Section 8.4 describes some of the main events after privatization, including the ruling by Oftel on interconnection, BT's takeover of the equipment manufacturer Mitel, and BT's pricing policies in the face of competition from Mercury. The final section then offers an economic assessment of the competitive and regulatory mechanisms that have been introduced, and discusses some of the key issues that will arise for future policy towards the industry.

8.1.1 Some Basic Elements of Telecommunications Economics

The numerous elements of a telecommunications system can be broadly classified as follows. First, there is the physical *equipment* in the system. This includes customer premises equipment (telephone handsets, facsimile machines, private automatic branch exchanges (PABXs), etc.), public switching systems or exchanges (which establish links between users of the network), and transmission media (cable, satellite, etc.). Secondly, there is *network operation*. Telecommunication networks are typically operated in a tiered manner, with users connected to a local exchange which is connected by trunk or long-distance links to other local exchanges and to the international network. Thirdly, there are the *services* provided by the system. The basic service is the conveyance of voice, which still accounts for the bulk of traffic, but the number and variety of services is increasing very rapidly. Visual images, data, and signals of all kinds are being transmitted through telecommunications systems as the application of information technology expands. There is particular growth in value-added network services (VANS), which are services that do more than the simple conveyancing of messages, for example by storing and forwarding messages, accessing databases, or providing electronic mail facilities.

Rapid technological advance is taking place throughout the industry, partly because of the convergence with data processing technologies. Electronic switching systems are replacing the old electromechanical "Strowger" technology. Developments in software are greatly enhancing the functional capability of telecommunications apparatus. Optical fiber technology is being introduced instead of coaxial cable for long-distance transmission because of its excellent high capacity properties. Microwave radio technology is being developed and applied in satellite networks and mobile radio (including "cellular" radio systems, in which an area is divided into interconnected cells, each of which can use the same radio channels). Cabling for TV and home entertainment also offers opportunities for the potential provision of telecommunications services. These technological advances greatly expand the potential uses for telecommunications systems, and they open numerous opportunities to bypass the traditional public network.

It is worth noting some features of the demand for telecommunications services. There is an externality effect between users because the desire of any individual to subscribe to a network depends on who else subscribes to it. This externality is sometimes claimed as a justification for the subsidy of telephone rentals. It is also at the heart of the question of the interconnection of rival networks. Another externality arises from the fact that the cost of a call is generally borne by the caller, although the call usually (but not always) also benefits its recipient. In principle, this externality might influence the optimal pricing of calls. Social benefits may also justify special measures to ensure the provision of emergency services, widespread call boxes, and services in rural areas for example.

On the cost side we are particularly interested in whether natural monopoly conditions exist (i.e. whether single-firm production is most efficient). This question is complicated by the fact that the outputs of the industry are many and varied. Equipment supply and the provision of VANS are evidently not naturally monopolistic, but the question is not quite so clear cut in relation to network operation, especially at the local level, although competition is more likely to be efficient on long-distance and international services. There are some scale economies in switching and transmission, and the network as a whole must be planned in an integrated fashion. An excellent account of these matters, and the econometric evidence, is given by Sharkey (1982, chapter 9) who concludes (p. 213) that:

"Quite clearly the industry has many of the characteristics of a natural monopoly. At the same time, changing technology is expanding the boundaries of the industry and blurring the distinctions between communications and information processing. Certainly under the broadest definition this evolving industry is not a natural monopoly."

(More recent econometric studies include those of Evans and Heckman (1984) and Charnes *et al.* (1985).) As demand grows and technology advances, the case for competitive mechanisms strengthens. What used to be a natural monopoly may cease to be so, and we saw in chapter 3 that, even where natural monopoly elements possibly remain, the benefits of competitive pressure may nevertheless be considerable.

8.2   The Telecommunications Industry in Britain

Before examining the regulatory and competitive regime in which they operate, we now describe the principal firms in the telecommunications industry in Britain—BT, Mercury, equipment suppliers (including GEC and Plessey), and competitors in other areas including cellular radio, cable, and VANS.

8.2.1   British Telecom

From 1912 until the 1981 British Telecommunications Act, telecommunications in Britain were the responsibility of the Post Office, a state-owned monopoly. That Act separated telecommunications from postal services and established BT. The company became a public limited company in April 1984 and was privatized in November of that year.

BT is required by its license to comply with the RPI − 3 price control formula (see below), and to meet various service obligations (e.g. regarding universal service and special community needs) and fair trading obligations. Otherwise it has normal commercial freedoms in domestic and export markets. BT's internal organization has recently been reformed in response to privatization, competition, and regulation. Its operating divisions (see BT's 1987 Annual Report) are as follows.

(a) U.K. Communications, which operates BT's local and long-distance networks, and is responsible for the supply and maintenance of customer premises equipment. This division was recently formed by amalgamating BT's previously separate local communications and national networks divisions.

(b) BT International, which is responsible for international communications and business services.

(c) Overseas Division, which sells BT's knowledge and expertise abroad.

(d) International Products Division, which develops, produces, and markets BT's telecommunications and information technology products internationally. This division also manages BT's majority interest in Mitel (see section 8.4.2 below).

(e) BT Enterprises, which is responsible for developing, procuring, and selling apparatus to consumers and businesses (telephones, PABXs, etc.), for BT's interests in mobile communications, and for value-added systems and services such as Yellow Pages and Prestel.

(f) Engineering and Procurement, whose responsibilities include R&D and the purchase of major systems such as System X.

Table 8.1 shows BT's revenues and profits for its main services in the year to 31 March 1987, with Mitel consolidated. Operating profit (£2,349 million) as a percentage of sales revenue was 25 percent, and the return on capital employed, measured in historic cost terms, was 21.1 percent. On 31 March 1987 BT's stock market capitalization was about £15,000 million (compared with £7,800 million at the time of flotation). Demand has been growing rapidly in recent years, with inland call volume increasing annually at about 7 percent and international volume at around 11 percent. BT has made major investments in new technology, notably digital public switches, and in the year to 31 March 1987 its capital expenditure was £2,107 million. The company employs approximately 235,000 people; staff numbers have been cut in recent years.

In summary, notwithstanding the introduction of the competitive and regulatory framework after privatization, BT is a highly profitable

Table 8.1   Financial information on British Telecom for the year to 31 March 1987

	Turnover (£ million)	Profit (loss) (£ million)
Public telephone service		
Rentals		
Business	456	
Residential	1,030	
Customers' calls	3,536	
Apparatus	1,164	
	6,186	1,697
Public payphones	145	(39)
Private circuits, telex	1,062	124
Total inland services	7,393	1,782
International services	1,713	603
Overseas activities	318	(36)
Total	9,424	2,349
Net interest payable		(282)
Profit on ordinary activities before taxation		2,067
Capital employed (total net assets less current liabilities)		11,112

Source: *BT Annual Report* (1987).

enterprise that dominates more or less every aspect of the telecommunications industry in Britain.

8.2.2   Mercury

Mercury Communications Ltd is the only national telecommunications network operator in competition with BT, and the Government has announced an intention not to license further competitors at least until 1990. (There is a third public telecommunications operator, the Kingston upon Hull City Council which runs its local network, but we shall not refer to it further.) Mercury is a subsidiary of Cable and Wireless, which was itself part of the Government's privatization program. Originally Mercury was owned by a consortium to which British Petroleum (BP) and Barclays Bank also belonged, but they withdrew to leave Cable and Wireless as sole owner. Mercury obtained its first license in 1982 and now operates under a new license granted under the 1984 Act.

Mercury's strategy in the U.K. is to establish a new digital telecommunications network linking major business centers. Its "figure of eight" optical fiber network links cities such as Manchester, Leeds, Birmingham, Bristol, and London. This network is being extended to major centers on the south coast, and there are microwave links to Scotland. Mercury also has an extensive network in the City of London. Mercury's service was launched in May 1986, and its aim is to have 5 percent of the U.K. market by 1990. The main target is the business market, especially in the City, but Mercury is also making limited progress in the residential market. Mercury is attacking the lucrative international market as well. It has two satellite earth stations in Oxfordshire and London and it has been actively seeking to negotiate agreements and joint ventures with overseas operators, especially in North America and Japan.

Mercury launched its public telephone service in May 1986 following the pro-competitive ruling on interconnection by Oftel in October 1985, which we shall describe in section 8.4.1. We shall look at the nature of competition between BT and Mercury in section 8.4.4.

8.2.3 Equipment Suppliers

The largest U.K. suppliers of telecommunications equipment are GEC and Plessey. They lie approximately tenth and twelfth in world telecommunications sales rankings, being much smaller in size than such companies as AT&T (whose manufacturing subsidiary is Western Electric), ITT (who formed a joint venture with the French company CGE at the end of 1986), Siemens, Northern Telecom, Ericsson, and NEC. Nevertheless GEC and Plessey supplied about half of the £1,600 million U.K. market in 1984–1985, according to the Monopolies and Mergers Commission (1986b, p. 28). Another major U.K. supplier is STC. However, BT, the main purchaser of telecommunications equipment, is increasingly looking to overseas sources of supply, and domestic sourcing is likely to fall further in proportionate terms. This trend is illustrated by BT's policy for the procurement of public switching equipment.

In the late 1970s agreement was reached between the Post Office, GEC, Plessey, and STC (who later withdrew) to collaborate on the development of the System X digital public switch. After disappointing difficulties and delays with System X, BT placed an order in 1985 for the rival System Y, which is produced in the U.K. by Thorn Ericsson using Swedish technology developed by its parent. Oftel intervened to try to limit for three years BT's purchases from sources other than System X in order to give GEC and Plessey some time to adjust to the more competitive market situation. In the future BT will use competitive tendering in procurement. GEC made a bid for Plessey in 1986, but the Monopolies and Mergers Commission recommended that the proposed merger was against the public interest, mainly because of concerns relating to defense electronics. However, GEC and Plessey are to merge their telecommunications equipment businesses.

Suppliers of customer premises equipment include the major international companies mentioned above, and BT itself as a result of the acquisition of Mitel. We will consider competition in apparatus supply later in the chapter.

8.2.4   Competitors in Other Areas

Under this heading come competitors in cable, cellular radio, and value-added services. Government policy on cabling is contained in the Cable and Broadcasting Act 1984, which followed the Report of the Hunt Committee (1982). The Cable Authority is responsible for licensing, and for safeguarding standards and compatibility. As well as its potential to transform information and home entertainment services generally, cabling is important for competition in telecommunications because it offers the future prospect of rivalry between local network operators. However, at present cable companies are allowed to offer voice telephony services only if they do so in conjunction with BT or Mercury, the network duopolists. The extent of cabling in Britain has so far been limited. By the end of 1986 the Cable Authority had awarded cable franchises in 22 towns and cities. Nine of these were licensed as public telecommunications operators and are planning the introduction of telephone services. The cable companies in Coventry and Swindon are BT subsidiaries, and BT also has a stake in the Aberdeen and Westminster cable companies.

There are two organizations licensed to operate cellular radio networks—Cellnet (owned by BT and Securicor) and Racal-Vodaphone. Both began operations in January 1985 on roughly level terms, and the. market has been characterized by fierce competition and spectacular growth. Several firms, including Mercury and Racal, have also been licensed to run nationwide radiopaging services.

In October 1982 the Government issued a General Licence for VANS, and licensing became the responsiblity of the Department of Trade and Industry. A new 12-year class license for value-added and data services (the VADS Licence) was signed in May 1987 (see section 8.4.6). Since the liberalization of value-added services several hundred suppliers providing a wide range of specialized services have entered the market. Entry barriers are now fairly low, and there is little or no regulatory impediment to entry.

8.3   The Framework of Competition and Regulation

The regime of competition and regulation established for the British telecommunications industry in the 1980s represents a radical departure from long-standing earlier practice. Although competition to supply telegraph services existed for a brief period in the mid-nineteenth century, in 1869 the Post Office (a government department) was given a statutory monopoly of inland business. In 1880, four years after Bell patented the telephone, this monopoly was extended to telephone services. The chosen approach was therefore to limit competition and for Government to run the industry according to public interest objectives broader than the pursuit of profit. For a period of about 40 years the Post Office granted licenses to private companies and municipal authorities, but the regime of competition and regulation did not work satisfactorily (see Hazlewood, 1953), and by 1912 the Post Office had taken over all telecommunications suppliers (except for the municipal authority in Hull). The Post Office remained a government department until 1969 when it became a public corporation. It had the monopoly, or "exclusive privilege," of running the networks and of approving, supplying, installing, and maintaining customer premises equipment. Before describing how the regulatory system in Britain was reformed in the 1980s, it is worth briefly reviewing parallel developments in the United States (see Brock, 1981).

8.3.1   Policy Developments in the United States
Bell's invention in 1876 was a major threat to the telegraph patent of Western Union, and in 1879 patent litigation between the two firms was settled by an agreement which gave Bell a monopoly in local services and Western Union a monopoly of long-distance telegraph services. Bell's main patents ran out in 1894, and numerous competitors entered the industry. Bell responded by bringing patent suits, by cutting prices, by acquisitions, and by using its control over the long-distance network. Bell (now AT&T) restored its market dominance by mergers and by the advent of regulation at state level, which afforded it welcome protection from competition. The passage of the Communications Act in 1934 marked the beginning of federal regulation. Subsequent rulings by the Federal Communication Commission (FCC) had the effect of inhibiting entrants, for example those seeking to use microwave technology. A government antitrust challenge to AT&T was met by the 1956 Consent Decree, which confined AT&T to its regulated businesses but did not greatly affect its operations there. Changing technologies brought new competitive threats from long-distance

carriers such as MCI and terminal equipment suppliers. AT&T delayed entry by using lengthy regulatory procedures, by restricting interconnection, and then by price-cutting. The FCC did eventually remove regulatory barriers to entry, but its approach was not vigorously pro-competitive and its net effect was to delay entry (see Brock, 1981, chapters 8 and 9). The historical record for this period shows the importance of vertical integration, the terms of interconnection, the pricing strategies of the dominant firm, and the role of regulation in inhibiting competition.

However, by the early 1970s a number of competitors had entered the industry, or were threatening to enter. Many of them brought antitrust suits against AT&T (such private actions are not possible under U.K. law), and in 1974 the Justice Department began another major action against the company. When the case ended in January 1982, AT&T was required to divest itself of its local network operations, which are now run by separate regional Bell companies (the so-called "Baby Bells"). AT&T retained its long-distance division, Bell Laboratories, and Western Electric, the communications equipment manufacturer. The settlement gave AT&T greater freedom to compete in data processing and information systems. The Baby Bells were barred from the long-distance market and from apparatus production, but they were permitted to market equipment. American policy to combat the danger of anticompetitive behavior by an integrated dominant firm has therefore been one of vertical separation. Being under separate ownership, the local network operators have less incentive to favor any particular long-distance carrier. AT&T and the Baby Bells are confined to separate spheres—long-distance services and equipment manufacturing on the one hand, and local networks on the other—and incentives to distort competition are lessened.

Since the break-up, AT&T's long-distance business has prospered. Its market share has remained at around 80 percent, and its main rivals—MCI and GTE Sprint—have incurred large losses. A major network modernization program is cutting AT&T's costs, and long-distance tariffs have fallen substantially. AT&T Network Systems (the successor to Western Electric) has also done well supplying equipment to the Baby Bells, but AT&T's business supplying telephone and computer equipment to users has not been profitable. Pressure is mounting to relax some of the restrictions imposed on the Baby Bells by the 1982 settlement. The Justice Department has recommended that they should be allowed to compete in long-distance services outside the regions where they operate local networks. They may also be allowed to enter apparatus production. It is too soon to judge what would be the result of these policies of regulatory reform, but the emergence of head-to-head competition between former parts of the AT&T empire is a distinct possibility. As we shall see in the rest of this chapter, British telecommunications policy has been very different from the American approach of radical structural reform.

The regulation of AT&T's pricing is also undergoing reform. The Federal Communications Commission proposed in the summer of 1987 that rate-of-return regulation should be replaced by price caps on AT&T's long-distance services. In similar spirit to British $RPI - X$ regulation, price caps are intended to sharpen AT&T's incentive to secure efficiency gains. We will argue below that the effectiveness of such a method of price control depends critically upon the information available to the authorities at times of regulatory review.

8.3.2   Liberalization and the 1981 British Telecommunications Act

In July 1980 the Secretary of State for Industry, Sir Keith Joseph, announced to Parliament the Government's proposals to end the state telecommunications monopoly by introducing some measures of liberalization. The resulting British Telecommunications Act, which received Royal Assent in July 1981, established BT as a public corporation separate from the Post Office and opened the way to some competition in equipment markets, network operation, and the provision of services.

As regards customer premises equipment, the Act did two things. First, it abolished BT's exclusive privilege to supply customer apparatus, with the exception of BT's right to supply a customer's first telephone ("the prime instrument") which did continue for a while. Secondly, it established independent machinery to set standards and approve equipment. Approval either from the British Approvals Board for Telecommunications (BABT) or from the Secretary of State became necessary for equipment to be supplied for attachment to BT's network. The Act made competition from network operators possible by giving the Secretary of State powers to license firms other than BT to run telecommunications systems. Those powers were exercised when Mercury was granted its license. The Act also liberalized the use of BT's network by allowing competition in value-added network services.

An economic assessment of the liberalization of VANS was commissioned in 1980 from Professor Michael Beesley of the London Business School. The Beesley Report (1981) on *Liberalisation of the Use of British Telecommunications Network* was duly published in January 1981. Beesley argued that the study should not be confined to "value-added" services, and that the central questions involved the general principle of reselling BT's capacity. He concluded that unrestricted resale should be allowed: "In the home market there should be no restriction on the freedom to offer services to third parties" (Beesley, 1981, p. ix). Beesley was impressed by the potential for competition and innovation using leased lines, including the use of concentrators to economize on the number of lines required in applications, and the sharing of lines by several firms. Against liberalization, BT argued that it would lose revenue and profit as business was transferred to leased lines, that cross-subsidization would be made more difficult, that concerns would arise over standards and compatibility, and that the cost-efficiency advantages of natural monopoly would be lost.

Beesley nevertheless concluded that the public interest was best served by permitting unrestricted resale. He also recommended that BT should be free to compete in non-voice markets, subject to regulatory and antitrust requirements to safeguard against entry-deterring and predatory behavior by BT. In the event the Government chose not to allow unrestricted resale for the time being and to liberalize VANS only, although it has proved to be far from easy to define what exactly is a "value-added" service.

The 1981 Act therefore opened the way to competition to a limited degree. The true extent of liberalization depends, however, not only on the legal form of the legislation. First, there is the question of how far the Secretary of State exercises his powers to license further competitors. Secondly, there is the issue of whether the dominant firm can thwart or inhibit forces of potential competition by anticompetitive measures. This depends upon the effectiveness of the framework of competition and regulation, which we shall consider further below.

8.3.3 The Question of Price and Profit Regulation

The Government's plan to privatize BT was announced to Parliament in July 1982 in the White Paper on *The Future of Telecommunications in Britain* (Department of Trade and Industry, 1982). As well as stating the Government's desire to promote consumer choice and market forces, the White Paper gave particular emphasis to the financial motive allowing BT access to capital markets without increasing the public sector borrowing requirement (PSBR) (indeed the proceeds from privatization are deemed to reduce the PSBR, as we discussed in chapter 7).

Given BT's dominant position throughout the industry, the prospect of privatization clearly required the development of a framework of regulation to contain BT's market power. Officials in Government initially proposed a maximum rate of return for BT as a whole, but Professor Alan

Walters, the Prime Minister's Economic Adviser at the time, argued against rate-of-return regulation. He said that it was akin to 100 percent taxation, that it created poor incentives for innovation and efficiency, and that American experience showed it to be wasteful, bureaucratic, and inefficient (we reviewed these arguments in chapter 4). Walters proposed instead an output-related profits levy (ORPL), according to which BT would be taxed less the more it expanded output. The idea of this scheme was to deter monopolistic behavior by imposing tax penalties and incentives. A Working Group of officials examined both suggestions and proposed yet another scheme. They proposed that a maximum rate of return (MMR) be set for each of the local, long-distance, and international businesses of BT, and that a partial rebate (i.e. less than 100 percent) should be made to consumers in the event of BT exceeding the allowed rate in any business segment. As to the appropriate level of the maximum rate, they seem to have envisaged 5–7 percent in real terms (see Littlechild, 1983, section 7).

With this increasing number of regulatory options under debate, a study was commissioned from Professor Stephen Littlechild of Birmingham University at the end of October 1982. His report on *Regulation of British Telecommunications' Profitability* was presented in February 1983. Littlechild considered none of the above schemes satisfactory, and instead he recommended a local tariff reduction (LTR) scheme, better known as the RPI − X proposal. The scheme requires BT to set tariffs such that the price index for a basket of its services increases by no more than the rate of general price inflation minus X percent annually. In other words, the prices of the regulated telecommunications services must fall in real terms by X percent per annum. A version of this proposal was adopted, with X set at 3, although the version implemented differs from Littlechild's proposal in important respects that we will discuss later. A review of the pricing formula will occur by 1989.

Littlechild arrived at his decision after comparing five schemes (MRR, ORPL, LTR, a profit ceiling, and a regime of no explicit constraints) against the following five objectives (Littlechild, 1983, p. 10):

(1) protection against monopoly;

(2) encouragement of efficiency and innovation;

(3) minimization of the burden of regulation;

(4) promotion of competition;

(5) maximization of net proceeds from privatizing BT and enhancement of its commercial prospects.

Clearly there is some degree of conflict between these criteria—for example

Table 8.2   Ranking of schemes for regulating British Telecom's profitability

Criteria	No explicit constraints	Working group MRR	ORPL	Profit ceiling	LTR
Protection against monopoly	5	3	2	4	1
Efficiency and innovation	1 =	4 =	4 =	3	1 =
Burden of regulation	1	5	4	3	2
Promotion of competition	1	5	4	2 =	2 =
Proceeds and prospects	1 =	4	5	3	1 =

Source: Littlechild (1983, p. 2).
Ranking of options by criteria: 1, best option; etc.

between (1) and (5), and between (4) and (5). Table 8.2 shows Littlechild's final ranking of the schemes. Although we do not agree completely with all aspects of this ranking of alternatives, it does reflect some of the points made about regulation in chapter 4. Forms of rate-of-return regulation, including MRR and profit ceiling, do not have good incentives for internal efficiency and innovation is discouraged. Moreover, it imposes a greater burden on the regulatory agency—to administer tariffs and so on—than does the RPI − X system, which (at least on the face of it) requires the regulator only to check that the price formula is being met. Being less discretionary, the RPI − X scheme also has less danger of regulatory capture. Finally, the RPI − X method can be easily targeted on those aspects of the business where regulation is most needed. In principle rate-of-return regulation can be targeted similarly, but the practical difficulties of disaggregated rate-of-return measurement would impose a considerable burden.

We agree that the RPI − X method of fixing a maximum price path for an interval of time has attractive features, but we believe that it is perhaps not so different from rate-of-return regulation as first appearances might suggest. Indeed, rate-of-return regulation in practice itself involves setting prices until the next regulatory review. The main question is how prices (or price paths) are set and reset when regulatory review occurs. If rate of return on capital is the criterion, which seems very probable, then RPI − X is just another form of rate-of-return regulation. RPI − X might involve deliberately longer periods of regulatory lag than U.S.-style regulation, and review might occur at given fixed points rather than stochastically or endogenously, but these differences concern *timing*, not the fundamental basis for profit regulation (price or cost). In order to avoid the inefficiencies and strategic behavior associated with rate-of-return regulation it is necessary for reviews of pricing to be based on criteria other than the cost or profit level of the firm being regulated. The RPI – X formula is not directed to this question, however. We will discuss this matter further in section 8.5.3 on the future prospects for price regulation in the industry. We consider the appropriate determination of X in section 8.3.5.

8.3.4   The 1984 Telecommunications Act
A Bill to privatize BT and to establish a regulatory framework was presented in November 1982. This Bill did not clear Parliament before the General Election in June 1983, after which a similar Bill was presented to the new Parliament. After very lengthy debates in the Commons, the Lords, and parliamentary committees, the Telecommunications Act received Royal Assent on 12 April 1984.

Section 1 of the Act requires the Secretary of State for Trade and Industry to appoint a Director General of Telecommunications (DGT) and gives the DGT powers to appoint a staff. We will consider the role of the Office of Telecommunications (Oftel) in more detail in section 8.3.6. Section 2 abolishes BT's exclusive privilege of running telecommunication systems. Section 3 imposes upon the Secretary of State and the DGT duties to act

"in the manner which he considers best calculated—

(a)   to secure that there are provided throughout the United Kingdom, save in so far as the provision thereof is impracticable or not reasonably practicable, such telecommunications services as satisfy all reasonable demands for them including, in particular, emergency services, public call box services, directory information services, maritime services and services in rural areas; and

(b)   . . . to secure that any person by whom any such services fall to be provided is able to finance the provision of those services."

There are eight additional guidelines regarding the exercise of those general duties. They call for the promotion of the following:

(a)   the interests of consumers, purchasers, and other users in the U.K.;

(b)   effective competition;

(c)   efficiency and economy;

(d)   research and development;

(e)   the establishment of businesses in the U.K. by overseas telecommunications firms;

(f)   the provision of internal transit services;

(g) and (h)   the international competitiveness of U.K. firms supplying telecommunications services and apparatus.

These criteria offer some guidance about the implementation of policy, but the discretion of the Secetary of State and the DGT remains wide. The phrase "which he considers best calculated," and the multiplicity and generality of the criteria, would make it hard for anyone to challenge an executive decision. However, guideline (b) does strengthen the hand of a regulator inclined to be pro-competitive.

Section 5 of the Act prohibits the running of unlicensed systems. Under section 7, licenses can be granted by the Secretary of State after consultation with the DGT or by the DGT with the consent of, or in accordance with a general authorization given by, the Secretary of State. Any license for a system designated by the Secretary of State as a "public telecommunications system" (section 9) is governed by important provisions set out in section 8. These require the operator of such a system to permit interconnection with other systems, not to show undue preference or to exercise discrimination, and to publish charges and other terms and conditions for services and connections.

Section 12 gives the DGT power to modify license conditions by agreement, and section 13 gives him power to make references to the Monopolies and Mergers Commission (MMC). In making such a reference, the DGT asks the MMC to report on the questions (a) whether the matters referred to operate, or may be expected to operate, against the public interest, and (b) whether modification of license conditions could remedy or prevent those adverse effects. If an MMC report finds adverse effects on the public interest and specifies modifications of license conditions, the DGT can make such modifications as he thinks appropriate, unless the Secretary of State directs him not to do so on grounds of national security or foreign relations (section 15).

The DGT has powers to secure compliance with license conditions. If he believes that a license condition is being broken by a licensee, and if the licensee does not respond to a request by the DGT to comply with the condition, then the DGT must make an order requiring compliance. A licensee who failed to obey such an order would be in violation of a statutory duty and liable to action in the Courts brought by an aggrieved party or the DGT. In the end the license could even be revoked. If the DGT failed to make an order in circumstances such as those just described, he could be taken to Court by a party affected by the license violation. The Act (sections 20–24) gives power to make approvals (e.g. of apparatus) to the Secretary of State or, with his consent or authorization, to the DGT. The DGT is also required to collect information, to advise and assist the Secretary of State, to publish information and advice, and to investigate complaints.

Section 50 gives the DGT functions and powers relating to competition in telecommunications parallel to those of the Director General for Fair Trading (DGFT). Thus the provisions of the Fair Trading Act 1973 and the Competition Act 1980 are brought to bear on the industry, with the two Directors having joint powers to make competition references to the MMC and so on. However, the DGFT has sole authority on telecommunications merger references.

Part V of the Act provided for the privatization of BT. The Secretary of State was given powers to vest the property of the nationalized BT in a "successor company" whose securities were allotted to him. With Treasury consent the Secretary of State was empowered to dispose of securities. The Act also dealt with financial structure. The writing off of debts was important for a successful flotation.

In summary, the Act gives regulatory powers to three bodies—the Secretary of State, the DGT, and the MMC. The functions, powers, and duties accorded to these bodies are defined in very broad terms, but the criteria listed in section 3 at least give some guidance (though not a great deal). The Secretary of State and the DGT have wide discretion, and the effectiveness of the regime of competition and regulation therefore critically depends upon how they choose to perform their duties. Judicial review of their behavior is unlikely to be effective because the Act gives such loosely defined discretion.

BT and its senior management had a strong interest in the Act and in license provisions, and throughout they maintained close links with Parliament, politicians, and civil servants. Their main interests were (i) to avoid a break-up of BT (such as happened to AT&T in America), (ii) to minimize the competitive threats facing the company, and (iii) to secure a light-handed regulatory regime so as to have as much discretion as possible. Policy measures meeting these managerial objectives would also satisfy those in Government most interested in maximizing the proceeds from selling BT's shares, a matter which was also of concern to merchant bankers advising on the flotation.

Newman (1986, pp. 12–13) describes how BT acted during debates on the Bill to attempt to obtain a favorable regulatory regime. The company's Corporate Affairs Department conducted numerous programs to brief MPs. Representatives were always present at debates in the Commons and in Standing Committees, and BT even had the ability to put forward its own amendments to the legislation. Very close links were maintained with officials at the Department of Trade and Industry, and license conditions were negotiated with BT. For example, Parliament did not have an opportunity properly to consider some central elements of BT's license, which were not disclosed until after the 1984 Act was passed (see section 8.3.5). As economists it is not for us to examine in detail the political events surrounding the formulation of the legislation, but they provide an interesting case for students of Whitehall and Westminster, and they must form part of the explanation of why policy took the form it did.

8.3.5   BT's License

The 25-year license granted to BT by the Secretary of State (Department of Trade and Industry, 1984) under section 7 of the Act came into effect on 5 August 1984. The license is a lengthy document, but Appendix 6.1 of the MMC report on the merger between BT and Mitel summarizes its conditions (see Gist and Meadowcroft (1986, especially pp. 48–52) for a discussion of provisions in the license against anticompetitive conduct).

The license authorizes BT to run its public telecommunications systems. (Mobile radio services require a separate license, as do private branch systems. Smaller private branch systems are authorized as for other suppliers under the Branch Systems General Licence, but larger ones require special licenses.) The license has four schedules, of which the first is the most important. It deals with BT's public service obligations (emergency services, call boxes, directory information, rural services, etc.), competition matters, and price control.

Anticompetitive Practices   Some of the main measures designed to combat anticompetitive behavior by BT are as follows. Conditions 13 and 14 require BT to connect licensed systems and apparatus to its public network. The conditions are vague as to the all-important terms of interconnection, but the DGT is given powers to determine interconnection arrangements in the event of dispute, as he did in the case of Mercury's network (see section 8.4.1). Condition 17 prohibits undue preference and undue discrimination—BT must not favor its own businesses unfairly to the detriment of competitors. It is up to the DGT to interpret and decide how to enforce provisions of this kind. Condition 18 requires BT not to cross-subsidize apparatus, VANS, etc. from other parts of the business. Condition 20 requires BT to provide by April 1987 separate accounting and reporting systems for its network and apparatus supply businesses. Without such information, the effectiveness of the regulations is seriously diminished, as we argued at length in chapter 4. For example, it is unclear how a charge of cross-subsidization could be substantiated without separate cost information. Condition 21 is concerned with apparatus production—BT must establish a separate subsidiary for apparatus production, and must purchase equipment by open tender. We return to these issues in relation to the Mitel acquisition (in section 8.4.2). Condition 22 prohibits discrimination in BT's supply of services in favor of customers using apparatus supplied by BT. Other conditions prohibit tie-ins, aggregated rebates, and the anticompetitive use of intellectual property rights (patents, etc.).

The long list of prohibited anticompetitive practices is an indication of the numerous devices that a company in BT's position could use to prevent or distort competition if it were left unchecked. Many of the concerns arise from the integrated nature of BT's operations as the main network operator (local, long-distance, and international), a major supplier (and now manufacturer) of apparatus, a powerful purchaser of equipment, and an important provider of VANS, mobile radio, and so on.

In contrast with the American telecommunications policy of employing a *structural* remedy to reduce the danger of anticompetitive behavior, British policy has taken the very different route of a *regulatory* remedy. Instead of changing incentives in the firm by structural break-up, a regulatory agency is given the job of monitoring the conduct of the firm. The effectiveness of this approach depends very much upon the pro-competitive energy of the regulator, and upon the information (especially regarding costs) that is available to him. There is little in the legislation to compel the DGT to be a vigorous protector of effective competition. The promotion of competition is just one of several criteria to which he must give regard, and his subjective view of what promotes these criteria is all that matters.

Gist and Meadowcroft (1986, p. 49) make two specific criticisms of the nature of the license conditions. The first is that the listing of *specific* prohibited actions is a weak safeguard against anticompetitive behavior because such behavior often takes the form of a combination of acts, none of which may be objectionable in isolation. They argue that the regulator would be more effective if he had power to attack a *course of conduct* (in the words of the Competition Act 1980) with the likely or intended effect of preventing, restricting, or distorting competition. Secondly, Gist and Meadowcroft say that the license conditions place the regulator in a difficult investigative role, but that he has limited cost information with which to carry out that role. If the burden of proof in cases of, for example, discrimination, lay more squarely with BT, the effectiveness of regulation might be enhanced.

Price Control   Condition 24 of the license deals with the price controls on certain of BT's services. For a five-year period the price of an index of BT's services must not increase in any year by more than the rate of retail price inflation minus 3 percent. The license is silent as to what will happen at the end of the five-year period (i.e. after 31 July 1989), but it can be presumed that price control will operate by a license modification that is either agreed with BT or imposed on BT after an MMC recommendation on public interest grounds. We discussed the RPI – X formula in section 8.3.3, but the price control mechanism put into effect differs from Littlechild's LTR scheme in several important respects. Two basic questions concerning the RPI – X price formula are as follows.

(i)   To what services should the formula apply?

(ii)   What should X be?

In Littlechild's LTR scheme it was proposed that the formula should cover rentals and the prices of local calls (including call boxes). He argued that trunk calls should be excluded from the scheme, in view of imminent competition from Mercury. In the event, however, national trunk calls were *included*, along with local calls and business and residential rentals. The weights accorded to each regulated service in calculating the price index in any year are proportional to their respective contributions to turnover in the previous year. The prices of international calls, leased lines, customer premises equipment, VANS, mobile radio, telex services, etc. are outside the price control formula. Call box charges are also excluded from control. In terms of revenues, about half of BT's services are subject to price control.

Although the inclusion of long-distance calls within the basket of services subject to RPI – X may appear to strengthen the regulatory constraint, the effect is actually to weaken price regulation of local calls. This is because BT can increase charges for local calls in real terms without breaching RPI – 3 on average. Since technological advance and competitive pressures are greatest in relation to long-distance calls, prices there should fall sharply in any case. This gives substantial scope for increasing local call charges within the pricing formula. Another effect of including local and long-distance call charges within the same price control formula is to make aggressive pricing of long-distance calls less costly to BT, because it can recoup revenue losses by raising local charges. This fact has implications for incentives for predatory pricing (see section 3.5.2).

In addition to the RPI – 3 average price constraint, BT gave an undertaking that it would not increase domestic rental charges by more than RPI + 2 percent in any year. No such undertaking was given in relation to local call charges, and controversy arose when BT announced price increases in October 1985 and October 1986. We discuss this below in section 8.5.3. As a more general point, the weights in the index are based on BT's revenues rather than on the demand pattern of a typical domestic user.

We now come to the question of what X should be, and the related question of the price *levels* at which the constraint (expressed in rates of change) should be based. In principle, the potential for cost reduction should determine the prices that the firm is allowed to charge. In addition, account must be taken of changes in the level of demand if unit costs depend on the firm's output. There are scale economies in some of BT's businesses (e.g. local networks): marginal cost is lower than average cost, because average cost includes fixed costs that do not depend on volume. If we began from a position where that business was breaking even and if demand then grew, the business would earn supernormal profits even if its costs did not fall. A price reduction would then be needed to remove the supernormal profits. Similarly, if demand is growing *and* costs are falling, the price reduction should be greater than the rate at which costs are falling.

To see this in more detail, consider the following illustrative example. Let $A[Q(t), t]$ be the average cost level of a regulated single-product firm at time t if its output then is $Q(t)$ and if it achieves the maximum potential for cost reduction. Let demand at time t be $Q[P(t), t]$, where $P(t)$ is the price at t. The government must choose the permitted price path $P(t)$. If the government seeks to maximize welfare (as it is usually defined) subject to the firm's being able to finance its operation in the sense of breaking even, then the government will want the equality $P = A$ to hold at all times. Noting the functional dependence of these terms upon t we have

$$P(t) = A\{Q[P(t), t], t\} \tag{8.1}$$

Total differentiation of (8.1), and some manipulation, yields the result

$$\hat{P} = \frac{\hat{A} + \alpha\hat{Q}}{1 + \alpha\eta}, \tag{8.2}$$

where

$$\hat{P} = \frac{1}{P}\frac{dP}{dt}$$

is the rate of change of price,

$$\hat{Q} = \frac{1}{Q}\frac{\partial Q}{\partial t}$$

is the rate of change of demand,

$$\hat{A} = \frac{1}{A} \frac{\partial A}{\partial t}$$

is the rate of change of average cost,

$$\alpha = \frac{\partial A}{\partial Q} \frac{Q}{A}$$

is the elasticity of average cost with respect to output, and

$$\eta = \frac{-\partial Q}{\partial P} \frac{P}{Q}$$

is the price elasticity of demand.

If average cost is invariant to output, then $\alpha = 0$ and the formula recommends $\hat{P} = \hat{A}$. The rate of change of price should equal the rate of change of unit costs. But if there are scale economies ($\alpha < 0$) and demand growth ($\hat{Q} > 0$), then price should fall even if technology is not advancing at all. As the demand curve moves to the right, its intersection with the average cost curve occurs at a lower level of price.

Figure 8.1 depicts what happens when demand grows (from D1 to D2) and the average cost curve falls (from A1 to A2). Price should fall from P1 to P2, a reduction that is greater than the fall in average costs for two reasons. In the diagram the average cost level falls by P1 – P4. However, even if the demand curve stayed at D1, price should fall by the larger

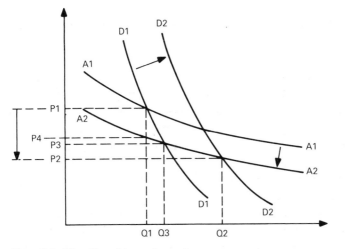

Figure 8.1   The effect of demand growth on average cost

amount P1 – P3 because of the greater demand due to a lower price and the downward slope of the average cost curve. The outward shift in the demand curve from D1 to D2 reduces price by another P3 – P2 to give the overall reduction from P1 to P2.

It follows from these considerations that if scale economies exist (as they surely do in local networks for example) then the X in the RPI – X formula should be *greater than* the expected extent of cost reduction for a given level of output. This is especially so if demand is growing (as it is for BT—inland call volume is growing by 7 percent per annum).

The level of X was negotiated between BT and the Department of Trade and Industry, and $X = 3$ was the chosen solution. In addition there is BT's informal undertaking to keep the increase in domestic rentals within RPI + 2, but otherwise there is wide scope for BT to vary relative prices within the basket of regulated services. The RPI – 3 constraint is not very demanding, especially in view of the rapid rate of technological advance in the industry generally and the growth of demand. The cost of long-distance calls—a major component of the regulated basket—is estimated to have fallen by $2\frac{1}{2}$ percent per annum on average in the ten years to 1983. In addition, the scale of BT's profits, which was becoming apparent by 1984, does not suggest that the constraint is tight. Furthermore, the potential for cost reduction is a major advantage of privatization according to its advocates, who often criticize state ownership primarily on the grounds of internal inefficiencies. If such scope for efficiency gains does indeed exist, little account was taken of it in the framing of BT's price control formula.

8.3.6   Oftel

The first DGT is Bryan Carsberg, a professor of accountancy at the London School of Economics. His Office of Telecommunications (Oftel) is is a nonministerial government department with a staff of approximately 120, which is small relative to regulatory agencies in the United States. Parliament finances Oftel's operations, but their cost is almost all covered by license fees. The institutional position of Oftel, including its relationships with the Department of Trade and Industry and the MMC, is modeled on that of the Office of Fair Trading. The regulatory authority for gas follows the same pattern.

In describing the main provisions of the 1984 Telecommunications Act we have already covered the principal functions of the DGT and the objectives that he must seek (i.e. to secure the provision of telecommunications services to meet all reasonable demands in the U.K. and to ensure the ability of suppliers to finance their operations, plus the eight subsidiary objectives of promoting consumer interest, competition, and so on). We noted in particular the wide range of discretion delegated to the DGT (and even more so to the Secretary of State), which is wider still because of the fuzziness and sometimes the inconsistency of the several criteria to which he must have regard. This degree of discretion increases the risk of regulatory "capture" (see section 4.5), despite the views of Littlechild and others that the danger of capture should be minimized.

It follows that a very geat deal depends on the individual appointed as DGT. A DGT might opt to be passive rather than active, and he can choose to give weight to any one of a number of objectives. Professor Carsberg, however, decided upon an active pro-competitive stance right from the start. In his first annual Report to the Secretary of State, Carsberg wrote: "I attach a high priority to my duty to promote effective competition and I have quickly come to believe that this is one of the most important and urgent of the duties laid upon me by the Act" (Oftel, 1985a, p. 8). It will be clear from the rest of this chapter that Oftel's behavior has lived up to these words. It is perhaps regrettable that the Government did not have Professor Carsberg's pro-competitive vigor when it established the framework of competition and regulation for the industry.

8.4   Events Since BT's Privatization

In this section we focus on six of the main issues that have arisen in the industry since BT was privatized in November 1984:

(1) the interconnection of BT's and Mercury's networks;

(2) BT's acquisition of Mitel;

(3) BT's pricing and profitability;

(4) competition between BT and Mercury;

(5) competition in apparatus supply and services;

(6) the Labour Party's plans for the industry.

8.4.1   The Ruling on Interconnection

The effectiveness with which Mercury could compete with BT depended crucially upon the terms of interconnection between the networks. Mercury's strategy is primarily to compete with BT for long-distance business, but BT has a virtual monopoly on local networks. Without access to these local networks, Mercury's strategy would collapse because it could then only provide telecommunications services between very few subscribers. Users want access to the general network, especially in view of network externalities, and for Mercury this depends on interconnection. The terms on which interconnection is allowed are all important, since they determine the geographical scope of Mercury's services, the ease with which customers can use its network, and Mercury's cost level.

We showed in section 3.5 that a company in BT's position has every incentive to exclude competition by refusing interconnection or, failing that, to minimize the effectiveness of competition by fixing interconnection charges as high as possible. The determination of the terms of interconnection therefore cannot be left to BT. One option for public policy makers would be to set interconnection charges equal to BT's normal charges for the use of its lines. But those charges contain an element of profit for BT, and a more efficient solution is achieved by setting interconnection charges equal to BT's marginal cost of providing the use of the relevant parts of its network. In fact there is a case for setting those charges below marginal cost when there is imperfect competition in order to intensify the degree of competition between the duopolists (see section 3.5.2). Moreover, the ruling must go beyond a stipulation of access charges. The freedom of access and routing is also at stake. Furthermore, account must be taken of the fact that the investment policies of both firms are much influenced by the terms of interconnection.

The background to Oftel's ruling is as follows. Condition 13.1 of BT's license requires BT to enter into a connection agreement with any operator licensed to run a connectable system who needs connection to BT's network. Condition 13.5 gives the DGT powers to determine the terms and conditions of the connection agreement if the parties themselves fail to agree them within a reasonable period of time. In exercising this power the DGT has a duty to secure that the other operator pays BT's costs (including relevant overheads and a reasonable rate of return), that quality is maintained, and various other matters. Condition 13.6 states that the DGT should also have regard to the need to ensure freedom of choice in routing and conveying calls, and the requirement of fair competition.

Mercury did require BT to enter into a connection agreement, but they failed to agree terms. Early in 1985 Mercury applied to the DGT to make a ruling under conditions 13.5 and 13.6. There followed a delay because BT challenged in the courts whether the DGT did indeed have power to make a ruling. At issue was a "Heads of Agreement" document signed by BT and Mercury the previous year. The Court found that the document was not legally binding, and it followed that the DGT could make his ruling on interconnection, which he did in October 1985. In our view it is remarkable that the question was not resolved until this late date. The DGT acted with all due speed once his legal position was established, but it is a serious criticism of the regulatory framework established by Government that the matter could not be settled sooner. Many of Mercury's investment plans depended on the terms of interconnection, and the delays in arriving at the establishment of these terms held up the arrival of effective competition from Mercury in important respects.

Oftel ruled that the two networks must have full interconnection for both domestic and international calls. This means that any subscriber to either network can call any other subscriber to either network, and can choose which network will convey the call. Thus Mercury can provide a nationwide service despite having a geographically limited network. Typically a long-distance call on Mercury's network will be carried on BT's local networks at each end. BT is also required to provide international connections for calls to or from Mercury subscribers.

The interconnection charges are based on BT's costs, and as a result Mercury pays substantially less than BT's normal charges for the use of its lines. The interconnection determination contains tables that set out the amounts that Mercury must pay BT for carrying its subscribers' calls. For the future the charges are linked to an index of the costs of providing voice telephony (switching, transmission, etc.). The charges depend on the time of day and on whether they are local or national. The pricing structure gives Mercury an incentive to extend its own network in order to save on payments to BT for carrying its calls. The ruling also stipulates that Mercury should pay 50 percent of the cost of the extra capacity that it will need.

The ruling set a timetable for achieving the physical connection of the two networks. By 30 March 1986 the networks had to be linked at 36 exchanges. The ruling called for billing procedures such that customers would receive one bill from their chosen operator, and for cooperation in the provision of telephone directories on a cost-sharing basis. BT and Mercury are also encouraged to cooperate on numbering, notwithstanding BT's view that telephone numbers are its private asset rather than a public asset.

Oftel's ruling was a major pro-competitive step which indicates the weight given by the DGT to promoting effective competition. Full interconnection was an essential prerequisite for the possibility of fair competition between the two network operators, and it is regrettable that the final terms and conditions were left uncertain for so long. A lengthy delay could have been avoided if it had been established at the outset that the DGT was to determine conditions of interconnection, and uncertainty could have been diminished generally by the early announcement of clear pro-competitive guidelines for the interconnection decision. Oftel's decisions at last established the ground rules for competition between Mercury and BT. We shall discuss how competition is taking shape later in this chapter.

8.4.2   BT's Acquisition of Mitel

In 1985 BT announced its intention to acquire a controlling interest in Mitel Corporation, the Canadian manufacturer of private automatic branch exchange (PABX) equipment, at a cost of some 320 million Canadian dollars (about £160 million). This move of vertical integration proposed by BT raised concerns about the effect upon competition between manufacturers and between distributors in a major part of the apparatus market. Following the advice of the DGT and the DGFT, the Secretary of State for Trade and Industry duly referred the matter to the MMC in June 1985. The reference was made under general competition law (the Fair Trading Act 1973), but it is an important episode in policy regarding competition and regulation in the telecommunications industry. Moreover, the main participants—the MMC, the DGT, the Secretary of State, and BT—would all be involved again if, for example, the DGT were ever to seek a modification of BT's license. The Mitel merger reference gives an opportunity to see how they might fulfill their respective roles in such circumstances.

The main facts relating to the merger are as follows (see Monopolies and Mergers Commission (1986a) for a detailed account, and Gist and Meadowcroft (1986) for an analysis of the case). Before 1981 the Post Office (which then had responsibility for telecommunications) chose not to exercise its monopoly powers in relation to the supply of large PABXs, i.e. those with more than 120 extensions, but it dominated the supply of other PABXs. In 1981 BT's shares of U.K. sales of small and medium PABXs were approximately 100 percent and 90 percent respectively. In 1984 those figures had fallen slightly to 91 percent and 84.4 percent, and BT had established a 13.2 percent share of the large PABX market. The MMC estimates that the total value of PABX equipment supplied in the U.K. in 1984 was £407 million, and the market was growing quite rapidly.

Since BT did not itself manufacture PABXs, it was the dominant U.K. buyer of such equipment from manufacturers, of whom four—GEC, Plessey, TMC, and Mitel—accounted for more than 80 percent of U.K. deliveries. In 1984 Mitel's volume share of PABX deliveries in the U.K. was 18 percent. An increasing proportion (28 percent by 1984) of Mitel's deliveries were to independent distributors and end-users, and not to BT. Indeed, Mitel accounted for about half of all deliveries to independent distributors in that year.

The proposed merger therefore posed a considerable threat to competition between distributors of PABX equipment, because Mitel was the major supplier to the independent distributors competing with BT. Moreover, the proposal raised concerns about competition between manufacturers, because the dominant buyer (BT) might be tempted to favor its manufacturing subsidiary unfairly to the detriment of other manufacturers, despite regulatory measures designed to combat such discrimination.

In defense of the proposed merger BT argued that the competitiveness of its product range in the U.K. required the ownership and control of an integrated unit responsible for the R&D, manufacture, and distribution of some major products. BT contended that the acquisition would give it a substantial presence in overseas markets—an important step towards its ambitions of expansion in export markets. BT gave assurances that it would treat Mitel on an arm's length basis regarding procurement, and that it would continue to distribute the products of numerous small manufacturers. BT dismissed suggestions that major companies such as GEC and Plessey would be unfairly disadvantaged by the merger, and the idea that competing manufacturers of innovative products would be inhibited from approaching BT as a distributor.

Professor Carsberg, the DGT, gave evidence to the MMC. He expressed Oftel's concern about the effect of the proposed merger upon competition in apparatus supply. He said that BT had many natural advantages over competitors, including its past monopoly of supply of smaller PABXs, its huge customer base, its extensive sales and service network, its dominance of maintenance, and its ownership of much of the relevant wiring. Although measures were in hand to deal with the last two factors, BT undoubtedly enjoyed many advantages from its established dominant position as a supplier of apparatus. Further benefits to BT came from its dominance as network operator. Some customers feared that, despite regulatory safeguards, BT employees might discriminate against them in the provision of network services unless they obtained their apparatus from BT.

Since competition had not developed fully enough to contain BT's market power as the integrated dominant supplier and since existing regulation was not comprehensive in limiting BT's advantages, Carsberg recommended that the merger should not be allowed unchecked. It should either be stopped or it should be allowed with appropriate strengthening of the regulatory regime to contain the adverse effects of the merger and to safeguard competition.

The MMC concluded from its investigation that the merger could be expected to operate against the public interest particularly because of the following:

(i) distortion of competition between equipment manufacturers resulting from undue preference by BT for Mitel products;

(ii) adverse effect on competition between equipment distributors resulting from reinforcement of BT's market power as a distributor of PABXs.

However, a majority of the MMC did not recommend stopping the merger, although one member did. The majority recommended that the merger should be allowed only if BT gave the following undertakings:

(a) not to acquire from Mitel apparatus for use in BT's own public network in the U.K., or for supply to end-users in the U.K., at least until the end of 1990;

(b) not to cross-subsidize Mitel's production of apparatus for supply in the U.K.;

(c) not to prevent Mitel from providing spares and enhancements for Mitel equipment supplied in the U.K.;

(d) to renegotiate a contract with Mitel for a particular PABX so that BT did not have the exclusive right of supply;

(e) to keep the U.K. marketing, sales, supply, and maintenance organizations of BT and Mitel entirely separate;

(f) not to require other manufacturers to distribute their products through Mitel.

The MMC's decision to recommend the merger subject to conditions allows BT's international expansion, but reflects a high degree of optimism about the effectiveness of regulation in coping with the dangers to competition that the MMC recognized. The dissenting member of the Commission, Mr D.P. Thomson, was not convinced that the conditions gave a practical and enforceable safeguard against the extension of BT's market power. In his view they did not remove the unfair advantage to Mitel's products whoever distributed them, and he had doubts about the effectiveness of monitoring and enforcing the conditions (even if they had been incorporated as modifications to BT's license rather than being mere undertakings).

We share Mr Thomson's doubts, as do Gist and Meadowcroft (1986).

Where competition is not fully effective, vertical integration alters *incentives* in a way that further jeopardizes the competitive process. In this case the MMC recognized that danger, but advocated regulation of *conduct* to contain the anticompetitive results of the adverse change in incentives. That would be fine if regulators were fully informed about industry behavior, and if they were willing and able to penalize anticompetitive conduct. But the difficulties of identifying cross-subsidy (for example) are notorious. A much more economical method of containing the danger would be to prevent the undesirable change in incentives by stopping the merger.

On 27 January 1986 the Secretary of State, Mr Leon Brittan, announced his decision to allow the merger. He imposed conditions less restrictive than those recommended by the MMC. Undertaking (a) above was relaxed to allow BT to acquire Mitel apparatus for use or supply in the U.K. up to the amount that it acquired in 1985. BT was permitted to acquire new products from Mitel if no comparable products were available in the U.K., and a ceiling was placed on BT's sales of new Mitel products in the U.K. The logic behind these concessions by the Secretary of State to BT is not clear, especially in view of the concerns expressed by all the members of the MMC panel. The majority of that panel had suggested a compromise rather than recommend that the merger should be stopped. In the event the Secretary of State compromised the compromise, and the danger to competition in the U.K. apparatus supply market is all the greater.

8.4.3   BT's Pricing and Profitability

BT's pricing policies since privatization have aroused considerable controversy. We will begin by describing changes in the prices of services within the RPI − 3 price control mechanism.

BT announced a series of price changes with effect from November 1985, a year after privatization. Inflation was then running at 7 percent, and so the RPI − 3 formula permitted an average price increase of no more than 4 percent. BT increased rental charges by 8.5 percent, which was within the 9 percent limit implied by the RPI + 2 undertaking about domestic rental charges. Local call charges were increased by 6.4 percent and charges for long-distance calls under 35 miles rose by a similar extent, but the prices of calls over 35 miles were substantially reduced. The weighted average price increase was 3.7 percent. Oftel (1985b) estimated that the bills of typical domestic users would rise by 7.1 percent for a low user, 6.3 percent for a moderate user, and 5.7 percent for a high user. Public reaction to the 1985 price changes suggests that many people were surprised that the RPI − 3 formula allowed such increases in the prices of domestic services. In this regard it is interesting that Littlechild (1986, para. 11.15) himself says that

"In retrospect, it is apparent that domestic customers were not aware of the extent to which BT wished to rebalance its tariffs, nor of the extent to which the RPI – X constraint allowed this; had they been better informed they might have wished the undertaking to have been framed differently (e.g. to cover local calls as well as domestic rentals)."

Another round of price changes was announced by BT with effect from November 1986. They followed a similar pattern. Inflation was then at 2.5 percent, but BT had not increased prices as much as it could have done the year before and so it had to reduce average prices by at least 0.14 percent (rather than by at least 0.5 percent, as RPI – 3 would have implied if BT had not retained some slack from the previous year). In the event BT reduced average prices by 0.3 percent. Domestic rentals rose by 3.7 percent (well within the 4.5 percent allowed under the RPI + 2 undertaking) and business rentals rose by 3.9 percent. Local calls at peak, standard, and cheap times of day were changed by +18.9 percent, +6.4 percent, and –3.6 percent. The charges for long-distance calls of less than 35 miles rose slightly, and those for calls of over 35 miles were reduced sharply by around 12 percent.

BT announced in August 1987 that it would not alter charges for its main inland services that year, despite being allowed under the price control formula to raise average charges by 1.2 percent. The decision to freeze charges, which is estimated to cost £58 million in the year in lost revenues, was widely regarded as a response to the criticism of BT's quality of service at the time (see below). BT attributed the decision to its sound trading performance and financial position. International calls and rental and connection charges for some equipment were increased.

Rebalancing   In making these changes, BT took the opportunity to alter the *relative* prices of local and long-distance calls to a considerable extent, as it was perfectly entitled to do under the RPI – 3 formula. This "rebalancing" of charges can be justified by the fact that prices in the past had moved out of line with costs so that users of long-distance services were being overcharged relative to users of local services. Rebalancing to bring prices more closely into line with the costs of providing the different services is desirable on grounds of economic efficiency (although there is a theoretical justification for some subsidy to rentals because of the network externality described in section 8.1.1). However, it is also true that BT's relative price changes involved cutting prices where competition from

Mercury was present, and raising them where competition was absent. If there were no check on the degree of rebalancing, the regulatory framework would become somewhat farcical inasmuch as BT could recoup any losses from competition (or predatory pricing) by wielding its monopoly power in local networks. This would not have been possible if—as Littlechild originally recommended—the $RPI - X$ constraint applied only to local services (although we believe that an additional control on long-distance services would then have been needed), or if an undertaking had been made by BT in relation to those services.

Oftel carries out detailed investigations of BT's price changes and publishes reports on them—see Oftel (1985b, 1986b), the DGT's annual reports (Oftel, 1985a, 1986a, 1987), and the Oftel working paper on optimal pricing structure (Culham, 1987). As well as confirming that the changes comply with BT's license, the DGT has commented on other matters such as rebalancing and BT's profit rate. On the basis of accounting evidence the DGT concluded after the changes in 1986 that rebalancing between local and long-distance calls had not been carried beyond the point justified by costs. However, he added that he did not expect substantial increases in charges for local calls in the future. Other relative prices are under review by Oftel, including charges for rentals, differentials related to time of day, and the discount offered on certain long-distance routes. A major difficulty in assessing these questions is the quality of the accounting information available, and Oftel is working with BT to improve information flows. There are also conceptual problems concerning, for example, the allocation of joint costs in a multiproduct enterprise such as BT.

Prices of Services Outside the Basket   BT is free to set prices outside the basket of services subject to $RPI - 3$ as it wishes, but the DGT could in principle take action regarding those prices, for example by seeking a modification of BT's license so as to bring them under control. Some of the strongest complaints about pricing outside the regulated basket have concerned access lines and private leased lines. In some cases BT more than doubled its rental charges for these dedicated lines over two years. The DGT investigated these complaints, and his preliminary finding was that the price increases remedied a previous loss on the services in question, and that BT was not making an excessive return on them.

Other complaints have concerned telex services, maintenance, payphone rentals, and operator-assisted calls. BT has to notify the DGT of prices and price changes, but (apart from license conditions requiring separate accounts for BT's apparatus supply business etc.) does not have to give him financial information about specific services unless he requests it. This makes it harder for Oftel to investigate complaints. Here again we see that information flows to the regulatory body are crucial. In this regard, the DGT wrote in his report for 1985:

"I believe that a strong case exists for BT's submitting to me, on a regular basis, accounting information about the results of all aspects of its business ... I understand that its accounting systems have not yet been developed to the point at which it can provide the information that I require on a routine basis. I shall therefore have to continue to seek the information needed to deal with specific enquiries as they arise and I shall do this energetically. I shall also continue to press BT for agreement to the provision of regular flows of information, conscious that the information I require is no more than is required by management for the effective running of a private sector business—or indeed a public sector business." (Oftel, 1986a, para. 1.15.)

This quotation from a practitioner of regulation underlines the importance of information for effective regulation which we emphasized in section 4.3 above.

BT's rate of profit   As regards profit rates, Oftel has estimated what would be an "acceptable" rate of return and compared it with BT's actual rate of return on capital, which on a historic cost basis was 18.4 percent in 1984–1985, 19.2 percent in 1985–1986, and 21.1 percent in 1986–1987, with similar rates of return from the business segments subject to regulation. In December 1986 Oftel (1986b, p. 3) calculated that an acceptable rate of return might be around 19 percent. Government bond yields were then around 11 percent, and 8 percent was added to reflect the differential over bond yields that the market was said to expect from the equity of a company of average risk. BT's share price has been volatile—partly because of perceived political risks—but the economic risks that it currently faces are rather low. Competition will be limited for the foreseeable future, technological advance is reducing its input costs, its output prices are index linked to some degree, and demand growth is steady. In 1984–1985 BT estimated its rate of return on a current cost basis to be about 11 percent, but it has not published current cost figures since then. However, BT made current cost figures for 1985–1986 available to Oftel, and it is clear (Oftel, 1986b, p. 4) that BT's current cost rate of return was higher in that year. Over the period in question, the real yield on index-linked government bonds was about 3.5 percent. We believe that the yield gap is large in relation to the relatively low level of economic risk faced by BT.

In any event, the DGT has so far decided not to seek any modification of the price control formula so soon after privatization and the passage of the regulatory legislation. However, he has made it quite clear that he would seriously consider exercising his powers to seek such a modification if he found BT's rate of return on capital to be significantly above the minimum acceptable level in competitive capital markets (see Oftel, 1986a, p. 9). In doing so he would take account of the extent to which high profits appeared to be due to improvements in BT's efficiency, although this would be a difficult judgment to make in practice.

Statements of this kind by the DGT accord with the point made above that RPI $-$ X price control is closer to rate-of-return regulation than it might appear at first sight. If the DGT intervened because BT's rate of return was becoming excessive, he would be acting in a manner very similar to how regulatory bodies in the United States often behave. If he does not intervene before the price control formula expires in 1989, it would also seem likely that the review at that time will be based largely upon BT's prospective rate of return, because BT has a near monopoly of information about the provision of most of the relevant telecommunications services in the U.K. The DGT rightly says that account should be taken of the extent to which BT's profits are due to gains in efficiency, but what really matters is how much of the *potential* for efficiency gains has been exploited by BT. This cannot be observed with any accuracy, since it involves comparison with a counterfactual.

Political factors in Britain complicate the assessment of what is a fair rate of return for BT. If investors believe that there is some chance that a future government would renationalize BT on terms unfavorable to investors, then BT's cost of capital is increased to reflect the political risk perceived by the stock market. In section 4.2.3 we discussed the consequences of this for investment policies, and in section 8.4.6 below we describe the Labour Party's plans for BT.

Quality of Service   A discussion of pricing behavior would not be complete without reference to quality of service, because a reduction in quality of service would be tantamount to an increase in price. Widespread dissatisfaction with BT's quality of service since privatization has been expressed by consumer groups, and was reported in a survey published by the National Consumer Council (NCC) in July 1987. According to the survey, BT's record on servicing faults, making installations, and dealing with complaints was worse than that of other public services in Britain, and a majority of users regarded its prices as being unreasonably high. Not all the NCC's findings were based on objective scientific evidence, but BT stopped publishing quality-of-service statistics just before it was privatized. The controversy that arose from the NCC survey, and claims that the regulatory regime for BT was lax and ineffective, caused Oftel to publish BT's previously confidential quality-of-service indicators (Oftel is also collecting its own statistics). The statistics showed how percentages of failed calls, operator and directory calls answered in 15 seconds, service faults, and exchange faults had moved over the five years to March 1986. The overall conclusion was that BT's quality of service had not deteriorated since privatization, but that it had not improved much either. Given the rate of advance of telecommunications technology, this record is poor and does not square with the view that privatization by itself enhances efficiency and responsiveness to consumer demands.

Since competition is at present so limited in the telecommunications market, there is a strong case for incorporating quality-of-service targets into BT's regulatory framework (see Oftel, 1987, p. 7). One method would be to include a quality factor explicitly in the $RPI - X$ formula. If BT failed to meet targets for quality of service, then its maximum permitted price increase would be reduced correspondingly. Such a method would require the definition of a quality index or indices, and a judgment as to the appropriate relationship between price and quality in the regulatory formula. In addition there would be a need for independent measurement of BT's quality of service. None of these questions would be straightforward or without controversy.

An alternative way of sharpening BT's financial incentive to improve quality, which Oftel is considering, is to make BT liable for losses to users caused by faults in the service and undue delays in providing or repairing services. Enforcement of such a system would be decentralized: users claiming damages would take action on a case-by-case basis. This might be more costly to enforce than the method described in the previous paragraph, and might fail to be of effective help to smaller customers who lack the resources to pursue their claims against BT vigorously. Moreover, as Oftel (1987, p. 7) observes, BT's service cannot reasonably be expected to be totally free from fault, and the liability proposal would be tantamount to making BT provide an insurance scheme to all customers. Ultimately the customers would have to pay for the insurance in higher charges, but some might prefer to bear the risk of breakdown rather than pay the implicit insurance premium. However, an optional insurance scheme might be vulnerable either to discrimination by BT in favor of those insured (and against the uninsured) or to free-riding by the uninsured on the general benefits resulting from the insurance taken out by others. All in all, it would seem to be simpler and more effective to incorporate a quality factor into the RPI − X price control formula. Implicitly, quality of service will be taken into account when the price formula comes up for periodic review, but there is a good case for incorporating it explicitly and continuously.

8.4.4 Competition from Mercury

The Government's decision not to license any more network competitors at least until 1990 and the dominant position inherited by BT mean that Mercury and BT operate in a highly asymmetric duopoly that is immune to entry for the time being. In section 8.2.2 above we outlined Mercury's strategy of competing with its modern digital network in the long-distance and international markets for big business customers. We also mentioned its complementary challenge in the London area. In section 8.4.1 we described Oftel's long-awaited ruling on the terms of interconnection between the BT and Mercury networks, which was admirably pro-competitive and hence favorable to Mercury. We now describe Mercury's initial competitive responses to the opportunities that have been opened up.

In return for its £200 million investment program (which compares with BT's more than £10 billion of fixed assets), Mercury hopes to achieve a 5 percent share of the market by 1990, but BT will clearly retain an overwhelming market share. However, Mercury's strategy is targeted on the big business customers that have in the past accounted for a large proportion of BT's profits. Mercury's public telephone service began in May 1986, about six months after the ruling on interconnection. (Previously Mercury had only been able to supply leased lines to customers wishing to communicate on their own private networks.) Mercury set its prices for long-distance calls 15 to 20 percent below those of BT, and claimed superior quality of service due to its digital and optical fiber technologies and its free itemized billing service.

BT responded in November 1986 with a sharp price reduction of 12 percent or more on long-distance calls over 35 miles. BT also reclassified some long-distance routes to the lower-cost "b1" tariff. Mercury responded swiftly by cutting its charges for calls on routes over 35 miles by a further 12 percent, thereby restoring the differential that existed before BT's move. Mercury regards the differential as being essential in view of the entrenched position of BT. After all, a customer would require a substantial cost saving to compensate for the cost of changing supplier. Moreover, BT has other advantages including customer inertia, the fact that Mercury is a relatively unknown entity, the reliance on BT for the provision of other telecommunications services, and the marginal extra difficulty of dialling on Mercury's network.

In August 1986 Mercury began its local service in the London area, which complements its provision of long-distance and international services and is of particular value to Mercury's important customers in the City. Mercury undercut BT's charges for local calls at peak and standard times (i.e. office working hours), but not for economy rate calls lasting four minutes or more. (A precise comparison of the two tariff structures is not straightforward because of the stepped nature of BT's charges versus the linear nature of Mercury's tariffs.) Again, Mercury's emphasis on business customers is apparent. The increases in BT's charges for local calls from November 1986 enhanced Mercury's competitiveness in this area.

How will competition between BT and Mercury evolve? The initial rounds of price competition between BT and Mercury give evidence of some rivalry between the two firms, but in our opinion the prospects for competition in the longer run are not so rosy. First, despite the interconnection ruling, conditions in the regulated duopoly are very favorable to peaceful coexistence. No more entrants will be licensed at least until the 1990s, and there would be some lag after that before any licensed new entrant could become fully operational. In the meantime, although Mercury may be able to gain a good return on its investments, it will take only a small share of BT's business. BT is unlikely to cut prices across the board in order to limit Mercury's penetration in one part of the market, and the regulatory mechanisms guard against selective price-cutting. Moreover, the view of Oftel that rebalancing has gone far enough may dissuade BT from further price cuts for long-distance calls. A price "umbrella" that facilitates implicit collusion may result, with Mercury offering some discount to compensate customers for the cost of changing suppliers. The conditions in the lucrative international market are also favorable to implicit collusion. In short, the two companies will be in a long-running relationship (a "repeated game" in economics jargon) that is protected from entry at least for some years. The initial skirmishes between them do not necessarily point to keen rivalry in the future. They have much to gain from peaceful coexistence, and the preconditions—notably the ban on entry—are favorable to it. If and when entry is allowed, new firms will face an entrenched duopoly. In section 8.5.2 we will consider why the Government chose to limit the competition faced by BT and Mercury.

8.4.5   Competition in Apparatus Supply

Liberalization of apparatus markets (telephones, PABXs, etc.) in 1981 has been followed by price reductions and improvements in the range, quality, and functional capability of products. Consumers have gained correspondingly. The advance of electronic and other technologies would have produced some of these benefits in any event, but the evidence is that the advent of actual and potential competition enhanced and accelerated the process. However, BT remains the dominant supplier of apparatus, and concern continues to exist about the prospects for effective competition in the future, especially after the acquisition of Mitel (see Gist and Meadowcroft, 1986). For example, BT's share of PABX supply *increased* from 65 percent in 1981 to 74 percent three years after liberalization and to 85 percent in 1985, partly because of BT's major move into the market for large PABXs. BT's share of the market for telephones, which it now supplies through a number of retail chains, was 83 percent in 1984–1985. However, recent surveys suggest that BT's share of the markets for PABX and telephone apparatus has since fallen as competition has grown.

As we discussed in relation to Mitel, a central issue is whether BT's dominance as a network operator distorts competition in the supply of apparatus. Oftel has attached a high priority to this question and has commissioned surveys of competition in apparatus supply. The sources of concern listed by Oftel included cross-subsidization of BT's apparatus supply business, preferential treatment of users of BT apparatus in providing network services, passing confidential information from BT's network business to its equipment business, using BT's advantages relating to approvals, compliance checking, and wiring, and denigrating rivals' products. Although these matters are covered by license conditions, enforcement is not straightforward. First, Oftel needs detailed and prompt information from BT if it is to investigate complaints effectively. However, progress toward the provision by BT of separate accounting information for equipment supply has been slow. Secondly, BT management has the difficult task of ensuring that BT employees comply with undertakings to Oftel regarding unfair practices. Thirdly, there may still remain uncertainties and doubts in the minds of customers about rivals' apparatus. BT's brands thereby enjoy the advantages of incumbency.

The DGT details the steps being taken by Oftel to promote effective competition in apparatus supply (Oftel, 1986a, paras 1.37–1.50). They include the following:

(i) a code of practice dealing with the passing of confidential network information;

(ii) BT's marketing guidelines on fair trading practices;

(iii) investigations of alleged predatory pricing and cross-subsidy;

(iv) development of more detailed accounting information;

(v) steps to modify BT's practices relating to wiring;

(vi) review of BT's acquisition and use of intellectual property rights;

(vii) review of competition to supply extensions to existing PABXs;

(viii) progress toward simplification of standards for apparatus.

The number of issues that Oftel is actively pursuing indicates once again its pro-competitive energy, but it also shows the numerous respects in which competitors may be disadvantaged by BT's dominant position as a network operator and equipment supplier. Liberalization has brought important benefits but, no matter how vigilant Oftel manages to be, we believe that truly effective competition cannot be guaranteed in the apparatus supply market, all the more so after BT's acquisition of Mitel.

8.4.6   Competition in Services

Network Services   Two important decisions regarding the competitive framework for network services have been the Government's decision in 1984 not to allow a joint venture between BT and IBM to provide data network services, and the development of a general license for value-added network services.

BT and IBM applied for a license to provide managed data network services through a joint subsidiary. The proposal would have linked computers of IBM customers on a network of BT lines, and services would have included electronic mail, ordering, and transactions. The venture would have used IBM's Systems Network Architecture (SNA) telecommunications standards, rather than the internationally agreed independent Open Systems Interconnection (OSI) standard. Oftel recommended that the Secretary of State should not grant the license, on the grounds that "a supplier of the size and power of a joint venture between BT and IBM would inhibit the entry to the market of other suppliers and therefore restrict competition in a way that would ultimately be against the interests of telecommunications users" (Oftel, 1985a, para. 1.15). The Government duly followed Oftel's advice but expressed its readiness to grant licenses to either company separately, or to other companies with adequate capability. Both BT and IBM have since launched VANS, and in 1986 Mercury formed a joint venture with the computer company ICL to compete in the market for business data communications services.

Clarification of policy toward the licensing of value-added and data services (VADS) occurred in May 1987 when the Department of Trade and

Industry issued a new 12-year licence for VADS. Recall that Professor Beesley, in his report published more than five years previously (Beesley, 1981), had recommended unrestricted resale of BT circuits, but that the Government decided to allow competition only in value-added services, at least until 1989. The question here is how to define "value-added." In some cases it is clear enough that a service does more than simply convey messages, and licenses can be granted in such cases, but in the interests of competition and efficient administration it is desirable that there should be a simple general license. The VADS license issued in 1987 extended liberalization as well as offering some welcome simplification. It provided for complete liberalization of all value-added services except telex, it allowed companies to sell capacity on their own networks, and it promoted the OSI standard. At the same time the DGT modified BT's and Mercury's licenses to try to prevent them from using their positions as network operators to restrict or distort competition from rival suppliers of value-added services.

Mobile Services   Since the introduction of the Cellnet (owned by BT and Securicor) and Vodaphone (owned by Racal) cellular radio networks in January 1985, there has been keen competition in the mobile services market. Demand has grown rapidly, and by mid-1987 the number of cellular radio subscribers was about 150,000 (Oftel, 1987, p. 56, table 6.1), well in excess of forecasts of demand. Congestion of the network occurred in London, and charges for peak-time calls to or from London were increased as Cellnet and Vodaphone sought to relieve the problems that arose. Cellular radio networks were extended to all major cities in 1986, and mobile telephone services were heavily advertised by the two rival suppliers. In his annual report for 1986 the DGT commented that "Experience with the cellular radio telephone systems illustrates the particular benefits that can be obtained when two or more competitors start from an almost equal base point" (Oftel, 1987, p. 2). Competition from independent equipment suppliers eager to win a market share has also been strong. BT made large price reductions for mobile telephones in February 1986, and Racal rapidly followed suit. A dispute arose between BT and Oftel later that year when BT introduced a range of mobile phones that had special features that worked only on its Cellnet network. Oftel said that the spirit of the license had been broken, and that in future it would recommend phones for approval only if all their features operated on both networks.

In 1986 licenses were granted to consortia applying to operate private mobile radio systems on Band III (part of the radio spectrum becoming available) and to run national wide-area radiopaging services. The number of wide-area radiopagers in use in the U.K. in mid-1987 was approaching 500,000 (Oftel, 1987, p. 57, table 6.2). In advising the Department of Trade and Industry which applicants to license, Oftel sought to promote effective competition and product variety. Enhancing the use of the radio spectrum in the provision of telecommunications services will be an important and exciting area for the industry in the future.

8.4.7   Labour's Policy of Renationalization

The Labour Party's policy is to bring BT back under social ownership if it is returned to power. This possibility may influence BT's share price, and hence its cost of capital, depending on the market's assessment of the probability of a future Labour election victory. If a Labour Government changed BT's policies towards what it saw as the social interest, the company's profit flow would decrease and the title to a share of that flow would fall correspondingly. This effect on BT's cost of capital could lead to underinvestment by BT (see section 4.2.3). The compensation to shareholders in the shipbuilding and aerospace companies renationalized by the Labour Government in 1977 was regarded by many as being unjust.

Labour's initial intention to renationalize on the basis of "no speculative gain" was modified and described in a little more detail in September 1986 when the party announced plans to issue nonvoting securities in exchange for the company's shares. These new securities would give control of BT back to Government without the need to spend large sums of public money. Indeed, it would be virtually unthinkable for a Labour Government to buy back BT's shares with cash (even at the 130 pence issue price), because the priority given to other ways of spending the billions of pounds would be much higher. Labour would antagonize hundreds of thousands of households if it paid substantially less than the market price of the shares before its election victory (although that price will be partly a function of what the market thinks a Labour Government would do if it won). In view of this the terms of the special securities would probably be related to the market price of the shares, but a cash alternative of 130 pence (the original offer price) might also be offered.

News of Labour's plans had a significant effect on BT's share price and contributed to its tumble from above 260 pence to below 200 pence in the summer of 1986. Indeed, BT became something of a political stock, with its share price significantly influenced by changing perceptions of the rival parties' electoral prospects. The share price rose sharply in the run-up to the 1987 General Election, and reached about 330 pence after the Conservative victory.

Closer to the main concerns of this book is the question of what Labour would do to the framework of competition and regulation in the telecommunications industry if it was re-elected in the future. The broad intention seems to be to integrate Mercury with BT's network, thus eliminating competition between network operators. It will be clear from what has gone before that we would regard this step as highly undesirable. The party has moved away from the postwar Morrisonian vision of state ownership, and envisages social ownership in the future as somehow providing more enterprise and responsiveness to economic circumstances. However, it is not clear how the objectives of managers of socially owned enterprise would be determined, or how they would be monitored, regulated, and rewarded for performance. In section 8.5.4 we shall assess future options for competition and regulation under social ownership.

8.5   Assessment of the Framework of Competition and Regulation

Our conclusions about the framework of competition and regulation developed in the 1980s for the British telecommunications industry can be summarized as follows. Throughout the period there has been a tension in policy making between two main objectives—the desire to promote the wellbeing of BT (and also Mercury), and the desire to promote effective competition and regulation. For the most part, the first of these objectives has been given more emphasis. Liberalization has occurred to a limited extent, but BT was transferred from public to private ownership with its dominant positions throughout the industry essentially intact and with a relatively light regulatory rein.

There was no restructuring of BT to promote competition, as happened to AT&T in the United States. On the contrary, BT's vertical integration has been extended by the acquisition of Mitel, which the Government allowed on terms favorable to BT. Mercury is to be the sole public network competitor at least until the end of the decade. There were delays before Oftel could determine the terms of interconnection between the BT and Mercury networks. The Government blocked an avenue of competition by refusing to permit simple resale before 1989, contrary to the recommendation of its adviser. The RPI – 3 constraint is generous to BT, as its burgeoning profits show, and BT enjoys, and has used, wide scope to alter relative prices within the basket of regulated services.

The objective of promoting the wellbeing of BT was favored by those in

Government wishing to maximize the proceeds from the sale of BT shares, their merchant bank advisers, and of course the management of BT. Especially in view of the Government's evident desire to privatize BT speedily, good relations with BT management were imperative, and they came to have considerable influence. Employees of BT, although their unions fought vigorously against privatization, also had a natural interest in having a competitive and regulatory environment that enhanced the profits and prospects of BT.

However, the interests of consumers and of some potential competitors in the industry lay more closely with the second objective—the promotion of effective competition and regulation. But these groups have a relatively muted voice compared with the interests less keen on competition. Nevertheless, they have found a champion in Oftel under Professor Carsberg. Oftel's powers are limited by virtue of earlier Government decisions (e.g. regarding Mercury and resale), and their force and scope are by no means clear, but Oftel has chosen to pursue the pro-competitive objective with considerable vigor. That is evident from the ruling on interconnection, the determination to produce better information for regulation, advice given to the Secretary of State on such matters as the BT/IBM proposal, and numerous statements that the DGT will not hesitate to go to the MMC to seek modification of license conditions if he has reason (and evidence) to do so.

Since BT and Oftel would prefer not to go to the MMC (other things being equal), there exists a kind of bargaining game between them in which negotiating strengths depend partly upon the assessment of what would happen in the event of an MMC reference. The attitude of the Secretary of State can also play a part. Relative information conditions are of particular importance, because Oftel's power rapidly diminishes the less it knows. We could almost describe the system as "regulation by negotiation," where the parameters of the negotiation are loosely defined by the 1984 Act, the licenses, and the conjectures regarding the attitudes of the MMC and the Secretary of State. Pro-competitive interests are especially fortunate that Oftel has chosen—as it need not have done—to adopt a vigorous stance. Oftel has by no means been captured by the interests that it regulates, at any rate so far.

There is more evidence of capture in the behavior of the Government when it set up the framework of competition and regulation. Here there is some irony. In theoretical discussion it is often the regulatory authority that frustrates government intentions by serving the interests of the regulated firm. Indeed, one of the advantages claimed for the RPI $- X$ was that it reduced the danger of capture by limiting the discretion of the regulatory body. In fact Oftel has been quite active in relation to the prices of services both within and outside the basket subject to control, and it has evidently not been captured. The Government, however, made a number of decisions that favored BT (and, to a lesser extent, Mercury), including their decisions on the horizontal and vertical integration of BT, limiting competition, and the price control formula. Before long these questions will be back on the policy agenda.

8.5.1 The Horizontal and Vertical Integration of BT

Whereas AT&T was split into component parts in 1984, BT was privatized as an integrated national unit with dominant positions in network operation (at local, long-distance, and international levels), the provision of telecommunications services of all kinds, and the supply (though not the manufacture) of customer premises equipment. BT was also the predominant U.K. buyer of switching and transmission equipment, although international competition is more effective in these markets. There are several ways in which BT could have been split up in order to promote effective competition and regulation before privatization (or indeed in the future). The operation of local and long-distance networks could be separated, perhaps with several local or regional network operators as in the United States. The division responsible for supplying customer premises equipment could be an independent entity, and the same is true of BT's interests in mobile radio and VANS. The Mitel manufacturing operation could also be under separate ownership, as it would have been if the proposed merger had been blocked.

Restructuring of this kind can enhance the effectiveness of competition and regulation by altering incentives and information conditions in such a way that private motives are directed more to social ends. First, if a dominant firm is divided into component parts, there may be scope for competition between those parts. In BT's case, however, the scope for competition between the parts is limited. For example, local network A would not compete with local network B head-on in the product market because each would enjoy a natural monopoly in its locality at the present state of technology. Nevertheless there may be scope for competition of other kinds. Companies A and B would compete in input markets, in capital markets, and for capacity to connect with long-distance networks. Furthermore, the ability to compare the performances of A and B would enhance the incentives of their managers and promote internal efficiency.

Secondly, the effectiveness of regulation would be enhanced because the monopoly of information is broken by restructuring the dominant firm. In the example of local networks A and B, some kind of yardstick competition could be used advantageously provided that the networks faced uncertainties that were correlated to some extent.

Thirdly, the separation of network and equipment supply operations would diminish the danger of anticompetitive behavior. Much of recent telecommunications policy has been concerned with the danger that BT will restrict or distort competition in apparatus supply by virtue of its dominant position as a network operator. Separating the two businesses would have diminished these worries by removing the *incentive* for anticompetitive behavior (unless the two parts acted collusively). Instead the task is now to regulate *conduct* by seeking to prohibit cross-subsidization, the passing of information, and so on. In a sense this involves attempting to simulate separation, but information and enforcement problems inevitably cause difficulties. The separation of ownership and management is perhaps a more effective and straightforward approach.

In the absence of restructuring, a greater burden falls upon the regulatory authorities. If the regime of competition and regulation proves unable to contain BT's market power effectively, then the option of restructuring might deserve consideration in the future. However, now that privatization has taken place, restructuring will be much harder to achieve because of vested shareholder interests, and it is without precedent in the U.K. The opportunity to restructure was available before privatization, but it was not taken up. BT's management and the Government's desire to privatize as profitably and speedily as possible stood in the way.

8.5.2   Limits to Competition

The Government deserves credit for the liberalizing measures that it has introduced in apparatus and VANS, but in important respects it has deliberately limited the extent of competition in the telecommunications industry. The two most important limitations of competition are the decisions not to license any public network operators other than BT and Mercury, and not to allow simple resale, at least until the end of the decade in both cases. It can also be argued that maintaining BT as an integrated unit was also inimical to competition, but that has already been discussed above.

A possible rationale for restriction of entry into the industry is the *natural monopoly* (or duopoly) argument—the desire to avoid "destructive competition," the wasteful duplication of facilities (see section 3.2). That justification would appear to entail blocking further entry for a long time—at least until demand and technology removed natural monopoly (or duopoly) conditions. It might even be at odds with the licensing of Mercury. The natural monopoly argument has at least three weaknesses. The first is that it is far from clear that cost conditions are naturally monopolistic with today's technologies. Secondly, if natural monopoly conditions do in fact exist, the removal of barriers to entry would probably not be followed by actual entry, but it would have desirable incentive effects on the incumbent firm or firms. This provides an argument for liberalization when there is uncertainty about whether natural monopoly conditions exist. Thirdly, freedom of entry generally has beneficial effects on the behavior of incumbent firms. As well as allowing the possibility of competition in the product market, it sharpens incentives for internal efficiency, and it tends to undermine the chances of collusion between incumbent firms.

The main justification offered by Government for limiting competition appears to be a version of the "infant industry" argument. The idea is that Mercury needs to be protected while it establishes a foothold in the marketplace. We find this a very weak argument. Mercury should be protected against anticompetitive behavior by BT, and it is unfortunate that resolution of the question of interconnection was held up for as long as it was, but it is not clear that Mercury should receive assistance beyond a guarantee that competition will be on fair terms. If, however, it is thought desirable to help Mercury, then help should be targeted directly to Mercury. A ban on further entry gives vastly more benefit to BT than to Mercury given the relative sizes of the two firms. Furthermore, it weakens the degree of competition between them. Few things undermine implicit collusion and peaceful coexistence better than the threat of entry, but that threat has been removed by the Government's decision to prohibit further entry for the time being. When that prohibition is ended, the question will arise of whether the next entrant will require protection of a similar kind. If the answer is positive, effective competition appears to be a very long way off, and if the answer is negative—and we believe it should be—then the case for shielding BT and Mercury from potential competition is shown to be somewhat spurious.

8.5.3   Price Control

We have argued that the RPI – 3 price control formula was very favorable to BT (and to those seeking to enhance the proceeds from the sale of its shares), and that it differed from Littlechild's proposed method of price control in important respects. Both the level and the form of the constraint can be criticized. As regards the level, setting X equal to 3 was generous to BT in view of the rapid pace of technological advance in supplying industries, the growth of demand, which can be met at low marginal cost, and the very large profits now being earned. The form of RPI − 3 is very simple because it is a single constraint that applies to a broad range of services. The price index gives a large weight to charges to business users, and, contrary to widespread initial belief, it does not represent the typical usage of domestic customers. BT has great scope to alter relative prices within the regulated basket, which it has exercised by cutting prices for long-distance calls and raising those for domestic calls and rentals. Such "rebalancing" can be justified on cost grounds, but it could make a nonsense of the regulatory regime if it were allowed to go unchecked. BT also enjoys market power in relation to some services that are outside the regulated basket.

Oftel has emerged as a vital supplement to the price control formula, despite the supposedly nondiscretionary nature of RPI − 3. The DGT has repeatedly stated that he will go to the MMC to seek a modification of the price control formula before its five-year term expires if he considers that BT's profits are excessive. Oftel has reviewed the pricing of individual services both inside and outside the regulated basket, and the question of rebalancing, by assessing rates of return using breakdowns of BT's costs.

The price control formula will come up for review in 1989 in any event. In his report, Littlechild (1983, p. 1) wrote that "Profit regulation is merely a 'stop-gap' until sufficient competition develops." While we agree with Littlechild that competition is by far the most effective means of protection against monopoly, we do not believe that its arrival is imminent in many sectors of the industry. Profit regulation is therefore not a stopgap. When the pricing formula is reviewed it will be adjusted on the basis either of information relating to BT, notably its rate of return, or of other information. Although data from Mercury and overseas network operators might offer some assistance in this regard, we believe that BT information will be paramount. Remarks by the DGT also suggest that BT's rate of return will be the principal consideration. It follows that the British RPI − X system is very similar to American-style rate-of-return regulation. Littlechild (1986, para. 10.21) himself confirms this point when he writes:

"It should now be evident that rate of return considerations are necessarily implicit in setting and resetting X. . . . The concept of a combination of the rate of return system and the RPI − X system, which is somehow different from RPI − X alone, thus reflects a misapprehension."

The true differences are ones of timing and of simplicity. As practiced in Britain, RPI − X involves a deliberate regulatory lag that is long (i.e. five years unless the DGT successfully intervenes sooner) and exogenous in the sense that the times of formal reviews are set in advance. This last fact has interesting implications for the behavior of the firm, because the incentive to cut costs would seem to diminish rapidly as regulatory review draws nearer.

Thus RPI − X by itself does not avoid the incentive problems of regulation, which arise essentially because of the monopoly of information of the regulated firm. That problem must be tackled directly by improving the quality of information from the firm, which Oftel has sought actively to do, and by exploiting alternative sources of information. Unfortunately they are unlikely to emerge until competition is allowed to develop more fully.

8.5.4   Public Ownership

If a future government took BT back into public ownership, the question of the framework of competition and regulation would still remain, albeit posed in a different context. As we explained in chapter 5 above, public enterprise in Britain has often been characterized by monopoly, unclear objectives, political intervention, and poor incentives and monitoring of managerial behavior. In the telecommunications industry we believe that it would be possible and desirable to alter all these features if BT were returned to public ownership. Competition should be extended rather than brought to an end. BT's objectives should be specified clearly in advance, and microeconomic efficiency should be the prime objective— macroeconomic, political, and social objectives are better met by other means. An independent regulatory body should monitor adherence to those objectives, and BT's managers and employees should face a system of incentives and rewards that promotes their achievement. In short, the issues of competition, regulation, and incentives should not be swept under the carpet if BT is returned to public ownership. In the telecommunications industry, as in others, they are crucial to economic efficiency irrespective of who owns the company.

The Energy Industries

9.1 Introduction

For most of the postwar period, major parts of the energy sector of the U.K. economy have been dominated by publicly owned enterprises. The bulk of economic activity in the electricity, gas, and coal industries has been placed in the hands of public corporations which have, to varying degrees, been protected from competition by statutory monopoly rights. Only in oil, where public ownership has been more limited, has the private sector been allocated the major role, and, even here, public policy has had a pervasive effect on the evolution of the industry.

Even before the advent of the privatization program, however, the structure of the energy industries was far from static. In the late 1940s and early 1950s primary fuel supplies were largely drawn from the coal industry. As well as being the principal source of energy for domestic space heating and for many of the country's major industries, coal was the basic input for both the generation of electricity and the production of gas. During the 1950s and 1960s this picture changed somewhat as relatively cheap imported oil became more readily available (see table 9.1). Petroleum products gradually increased their share of inland consumption of primary

Table 9.1 Inland consumption of primary fuels: total consumption (millions of tonnes of coal equivalent) and market shares, 1950–1985

Year	Total inland consumption	Market shares (percent)				
		Coal	Petroleum	Natural gas	Nuclear electricity	Hydro-electricity
1950	228.1	89.6	10.0	–	–	0.4
1955	253.9	85.4	14.2	–	–	0.4
1960	269.4	73.7	25.3	–	0.4	0.6
1965	303.3	61.8	35.0	0.5	2.0	0.7
1970	336.7	46.6	44.6	5.3	2.8	0.7
1975	324.8	36.9	42.0	17.1	3.4	0.6
1980	328.7	36.7	37.0	21.6	4.1	0.6
1985	326.9	32.2	35.2	25.2	6.8	0.6

Source: *Digest of U.K. Energy Statistics* (1986).

fuels until the early 1970s, by which time they had overtaken coal as the U.K.'s principal source of energy. The oil price shock of 1973 reversed this trend, however, and since that date the market share of oil has fallen significantly.

Apart from the substitution of oil for coal, another major change in energy markets resulted from the discovery and exploitation of substantial offshore reserves of gas and oil in the U.K. Continental Shelf (UKCS). This explains the steady expansion in the use of natural gas as a primary fuel input from the mid-1960s onwards and gave rise to a substantial restructuring of the gas industry which we will describe later. Not shown in the table is the later shift from imported to domestically produced oil which took place during the 1970s and early 1980s, and which in turn led to the emergence of new set energy policy issues.

These changing patterns in sources of energy have had major effects on the respective roles played by public and private producers over the last 40 years. Thus, prior to the development of UKCS reserves, public corporations were responsible for both the production and distribution of gas. However, since the bulk of offshore production of gas (and oil) has been undertaken by private producers, the public sector in the industry has, in the more recent periods, focused its attention chiefly on gas distribution and sales. Similarly, prior to privatization, the growth in the importance of petroleum products implied some overall diminution in the scope of the public sector's role in the *production* of primary fuels (although in electricity and coal public corporations have retained their production monopolies throughout the postwar period).

It is against this background that we will evaluate the U.K. Government's privatization program for the energy industries. We start, in section 9.2, with the gas industry, which was transferred to the private sector in 1986. The approach adopted by the Government in this case bears many resemblances to that followed in the telecommunications industry, and several of the points that we make echo arguments developed in chapter 8. Section 9.3 then considers the prospects for the privatization of the electricity supply industry. The ordering here is governed by the similarity of the economic issues surrounding electricity privatization to those surrounding the gas and telecommunications asset sales: in each case we are confronted by a network industry with significant elements of natural monopoly in parts of its operations. Thus, although the sale of state oil assets preceded Government plans for the privatization of electricity, and although the offshore oil and gas industries are closely linked, evaluation of the oil privatizations is deferred until section 9.4. This discussion is followed, in section 9.5, by an examination of some of the questions facing policy makers with respect to the future of the British coal industry, including questions about the likely consequences of partial or complete privatization. Finally, in section 9.6, we summarize our principal conclusions concerning competition, regulation, and privatization in the energy industries.

9.2   The British Gas Industry

In December 1986, British Gas became the second public utility company to be transferred to the private sector. Unlike in the British Telecom (BT) case, the Government did not retain a sizeable shareholding in the new company, but for the most part the two utility privatizations are marked by their similarities rather than their differences. Thus, for example, the sale of British Gas was accompanied by the creation of a new regulatory body, the Office of Gas Supply (Ofgas), and price controls have been established in markets where competition from other fuels is weak.

The organization of the material in this section is therefore similar to that in chapter 8. We begin with a short history of the gas industry in Britain (section 9.2.1) and an analysis of the industry's structure (section 9.2.2). These are followed, in section 9.2.3, by a discussion of the framework of competition and regulation that has evolved over the recent past, with particular emphasis being given to the Oil and Gas (Enterprise) Act 1982 and the Gas Act 1986—which were concerned with liberalization and privatization respectively—and to the Authorisation granted to the newly privatized British Gas by the Secretary of State for Energy. The final part of the analysis (section 9.2.4) comprises an assessment of the policies implemented by the Government in the course of the privatization exercise together with a few brief remarks on three of the main events in the nine months following the flotation of British Gas: the company's first conflict with Ofgas, its first major acquisition, and an attempt by large industrial customers of the company to elect Sir Ian MacGregor to the Board of Directors.

9.2.1   The History of the Industry
The first public supply of gas in Britain was made under a Royal Charter granted in 1812 to the Gas Light and Coke Company for street lighting in London. By 1850 the number of gas suppliers had grown to nearly 700, with the main application continuing to be street lighting. Thereafter the use of

gas in the home and in industry increased steadily until, by the mid-1930s, there were approximately 11 million gas customers.

The industry was nationalized in 1948. Prior to that gas supply was divided between municipal undertakings and commercial companies. The municipalities accounted for approximately 37 percent of the industry, and virtually all the remaining supply was in the hands of 509 commercial utility companies. The latter were subject to stringent statutory provisions designed to restrict profits and hold down prices, and a variety of schemes were in force to link prices to profits in ways intended to strike a balance between the interests of consumers and stockholders. In all there was a total of 1,046 gas companies and undertakings in existence at the time of nationalization.

The Gas Act 1948 led to the amalgamation of these companies and undertakings into twelve Area Boards, each of which was largely autonomous as regards the manufacture and supply of gas. In addition the Act created a central body, the Gas Council, which was allocated a supporting role in the industry. The statutory duties of the Council included the provision of advice to the Minister, organizing research programs, education and training, the manufacture and supply of gas fittings, and raising finance for individual Area Boards on the credit of the whole industry.

According to the Report of the Committee on the Gas Industry in 1945 (the Heyworth Report), the perceived advantages of nationalization mostly related to the attainment of various types of scale economies. Nevertheless, the Heyworth Committee concluded that there were no major *national* problems facing the industry, and that organization on a national scale to manufacture and distribute gas was therefore unnecessary for the achievement of the available economies. In particular, the Committee argued that a national grid was not practicable, that it was not economic to supply gas to every part of the country, and that selling prices could not usefully be fixed on a national basis. Given these arguments, the Labour Government opted for a regionally decentralized form of public ownership.

The reasoning of the Heyworth Committee, however, was subject to almost immediate challenge. As early as 1953 the Gas Council reported that the benefits of planning and control of production and distribution over far larger areas than was previously thought necessary were leading to more centralized forms of organization. Subsequently, changes in technology, including the introduction of natural gas, gave a further impetus to the trend towards centralization.

Until the 1950s gas was derived mainly from coal, but sharp increases in costs in the post-nationalization period led to a search for alternative methods of production. The first major technological advance, achieved in the late 1950s and early 1960s, was the production of high pressure gas through the gasification of oil. Next, in 1964, came the introduction on a commercial scale of imported natural gas, which was distributed through a high pressure pipeline from the Thames estuary to eight of the twelve Area Boards. Finally, substantial quantities of natural gas were discovered in the North Sea Basin in the mid-1960s, and these reserves provided the basis for the development of domestic production of natural gas.

When natural gas was first imported into Britain it was processed to make it suitable for use in existing appliances. However, the discovery of abundant reserves in the North Sea made it economic to embark upon a national program of converting all appliances to use natural gas. The program started in 1967, following the first landing of natural gas from the North Sea, and was completed a little over ten years later, by which time approximately 35 million appliances, operated by about 13 million customers, had been modified. In addition, the new circumstances led to the construction of a national high pressure gas transmission system to take North Sea gas from beachheads to the off-take points of the regional distribution systems.

As a result of these technological developments the industry was centralized in 1972. Under the Gas Act 1972 the Gas Council was renamed the British Gas Corporation (BGC) and it took over the operations of the 12 separate Area Boards. In addition, the Act gave the BGC increased power to search for and obtain supplies of gas and oil, although subsequently, in 1983 and 1984, it was required to dispose of the majority of its oil interests as part of the privatization program (see section 9.4). Until 1982 the BGC was also granted monopsony powers in respect of the purchase of North Sea Gas. However, that year saw the introduction of the Oil and Gas (Enterprise) Act, aimed at liberalizing the market by establishing common carriage provisions which, in principle, allowed other suppliers to transmit their gas through the BGC's pipeline network (see section 9.2.3).

In May 1985 the Government announced its intention to privatize the gas industry, and the necessary legislation (the Gas Act 1986) received the Royal Assent in July 1986. This provided for the complete business of the BGC to be transferred to a new company, named British Gas plc, and for the establishment of a framework of regulation for the industry. All the ordinary shares of British Gas were sold in December 1986 at a market capitalization of £5,602.5 million. Partly to reduce the magnitude of the share issue, however, the company was required to issue an unsecured

£2,500 million debenture to the Government, which was repayable in tranches in each of six successive years starting in 1987. In effect, therefore, the Exchequer will continue to receive proceeds from the sale until 1991.

9.2.2   The Structure of the Gas Industry

The major activities of the British gas industry are as follows:

(i) the production of natural gas, mostly from offshore fields;

(ii) transmission of gas to beachhead landing points;

(iii) transmission of gas from the beachhead to regional off-take points;

(iv) local distribution of gas to customers' premises;

(v) the sale of gas;

(vi) the sale, installation, and servicing of gas appliances.

Before considering these activities in more detail, it is worth noting that the nationalized BGC enjoyed monopoly positions in respect of activities (iii)–(v), and a monopsony position in respect of purchases of gas supplies. We will argue later that privatization has not materially altered this situation, and that British Gas will therefore continue to operate as a monopolist-cum-monopsonist for the foreseeable future.

Gas Supplies   Exploration for and extraction of natural gas, together with transmission to the beachhead, is mostly carried out by oil companies operating on the UKCS. However, British Gas has itself been involved in these activities since the mid-1950s, and by the early 1980s it had built up quite sizeable interests. As a result of the privatization program, these interests were reduced by the enforced sale of the BGC's 50 percent stake in the license for the small (onshore) Wytch Farm oil field in 1984, and of its stakes in five offshore oil fields and a further 20 offshore exploration blocks (which formed the initial assets of Enterprise Oil in 1983). Nevertheless, British Gas continues to have the largest single share of proven and provable gas reserves in the UKCS, amounting to about 15 percent of the total. Approximately 80 percent of the company's reserves lie in one offshore field, the South Morecambe gas field.

In the year ended 31 March 1986, British Gas obtained about 5 percent of its gas supplies from its own fields. However, with the exception of small volumes used in the manufacture of chemical feedstocks, *all* current UKCS production is either purchased or owned by British Gas. These sources account for about 75 percent of the company's supplies, the remainder being derived from the Norwegian sector of the North Sea.

One important feature of the market for gas supplies is the wide variation in the prices paid for gas from different fields. Most British Gas purchase contracts provide for an initial term of approximately 25 years, and the price payable for the gas is generally determined for the entire length of the contract via the specification of an initial base price and an explicit price variation formula. The latter provides for year-to-year changes in the price that are linked to variations in observable price indices for other commodities. Before 1980 most contracts linked these adjustments to changes in the U.K. Producer Price Index, but more recently the variation provisions have tended to make reference to the prices of competing fuels including heavy fuel oil, gas oil, and electricity.

The pricing provisions (and particularly the level of the base price) of gas purchase contracts reflect market conditions at the time they are concluded and, since fields come on stream at different dates, this partly accounts for the wide dispersion in the prices currently payable. For example, as exploration has proceeded additional supplies have increasingly been drawn from less accessible discoveries that have been more expensive to exploit. In principle, it would have been possible to link contract prices to changes in marginal production costs, but, in practice, such provisions would have had unfavorable incentive properties: offshore producers would then have benefited from the inefficient exploitation of later discoveries. A second important reason for the observed price dispersion is that gas purchased under contracts entered into before 1 July 1975 is exempt from U.K. petroleum revenue tax (see section 9.4).

Thus the first UKCS fields (the Early Southern Basin Fields) were relatively cheap to develop, and the contract terms were settled before both the first oil price shock in 1973 and the introduction of petroleum revenue tax. As a consequence, under the provisions of the long-term contracts, British Gas has been able to obtain supplies from these fields at prices well below levels that those supplies could have subsequently commanded if offered for sale on a spot market, and substantially below the levels applicable to contracts concluded during later periods.

Hence, although the average price paid by British Gas for supplies in the year to end-March 1986 was 17.2 pence per therm, prices for Early Southern Basin gas were much lower than this while prices for gas from fields developed in later periods were much higher. The anomaly arising from the differential application of petroleum revenue tax was partially corrected by the Gas Levy Act 1981, which introduced a tax (currently standing at 4 pence per therm) on gas purchased under contracts signed before July 1975. In 1985–1986 the levy was applicable to about 65 percent of gas purchases, and had the effect of raising the average cost of British Gas's supplies from 17.2 pence per therm to 19.9 pence per therm. Nevertheless, even allowing for the levy, the average cost of supplies continues to be well below the purchase prices settled in recent contracts. Gas from the Norwegian Frigg field, for example, is estimated to have commanded landed prices in excess of 30 pence per therm in the mid-1980s.

The proportion of gas taken from the Early Southern Basin Fields has declined over recent years and will continue to fall in the future. In the financial year 1981–1982 these fields accounted for 61 percent of supplies, but by 1985–1986 the figure was down to 44 percent and it is expected to decline to around 30 percent by 1991–1992. Upward pressure on average purchase prices from these shifts can therefore confidently be anticipated.

Transmission and Distribution   Natural gas enters the national transmission system at five coastal terminals. After treatment and measurement the gas is then carried at high pressure to over 100 regional off-take points, where it passes into the regional transmission system which conveys it to the main centers of demand. Finally it enters the local distribution systems, where pressure is gradually reduced until the gas reaches the meters of the 16 to 17 million customers.

The pipeline mileages in 1986–1987 were as follows: national transmission, 3,300 miles; regional transmission, 7,650 miles; local distribution, 135,000 miles. All this supply network is owned and operated by British Gas, and inspection, maintenance, and renewal of the network constitute a significant part of the total activities of the company.

Given the need to maintain pressures in the integrated pipeline network, preserving the balance between supply and demand at each point in the system is a vitally important function. The task is performed by two central control rooms (one concerned with overall supply strategy, including the management of off-takes from the various fields, and the other with day-to-day balancing of supply and demand throughout the transmission system) and 12 regional centers, each connected to the day-to-day control room and responsible for meeting demand within its own region.

Seasonal variations in demand for gas are quite marked—up to five times higher on a very cold winter's day than on the warmest summer day—and these are handled in one of five ways:

(i) varying the amount of gas taken from the supplying fields;

(ii) provision of seasonal supplies from fields specially developed for this purpose (e.g. South Morecambe);

(iii) making use of the Rough storage facility, a small field lying about 20 miles offshore, into which gas can be compressed during periods of low demand and from which gas can be withdrawn during seasonal peaks;

(iv) taking gas from liquefied natural gas storage installations and from underground storage cavities;

(v) interrupting supplies to certain large industrial and commercial customers who are willing to allow British Gas this option in exchange for lower unit prices.

Gas demand is also subject to wide variations during the course of the day—maximum demand may be up to four times the minimum level—and these are mostly catered for by approximately 1000 local storage units.

Gas Sales   British Gas supplies over 99 percent of the natural gas used in the U.K. Between 1975 and 1985 the total number of therms supplied by the company to the U.K. energy market (excluding transport) increased by about 50 percent, despite an overall fall in domestic energy consumption over this period of approximately 6 percent. Accordingly, the market share of gas rose from 28 to 42 percent. The market can be broken down into three broad sectors: domestic, industrial, and commercial. Their relative sizes in 1985–1986 are shown in table 9.2.

The principal domestic uses of gas are for home heating, water heating, and cooking, with central heating accounting for over 50 percent of domestic sales. The main competing fuels are solid fuel, oil, and electricity for heating purposes, and electricity for cooking. In the short term, and particularly with respect to central heating, competition amongst the various fuels is limited by (sunk) consumer investments in associated equipment.

Nevertheless, competition does take place over longer time periods, and between 1975 and 1985 gas increased its share of the domestic market from 40 to 58 percent, with the number of therms sold rising by more than 60 percent against a total market growth of around 13 percent. The most

Table 9.2   Breakdown of British Gas's sales, 1985–1986

Market	Therms sold (percent)	Sales value (percent)	Customers (percent)
Domestic	53.7	61.2	96.5
Industrial	31.6	24.6	0.5
Commercial	14.7	14.2	3.0

Source: *British Gas Prospectus* (1986).

important single factor in this change was the increasing use of gas for central heating: between 1980–1981 and 1985–1986 76 percent of the central heating systems installed in the U.K. were gas fired.

The industrial market for gas is conventionally split into two main categories: premium and nonpremium. The first comprises customers requiring a fuel that is clean and readily controllable, and does not have to be stored. In the premium market gas competes against gas oil and, to a lesser extent, against liquefied petroleum gas and electricity. The nonpremium market consists of customers whose principal requirement is crude bulk heat. Here gas competes against heavy fuel oil and coal, and, unlike in the premium market, purchase contracts usually allow British Gas to interrupt supplies at times of high system demand. In addition to these two main categories, gas is also supplied to the industrial market for use as a chemical feedstock in the manufacture of fertilizers, largely on an interruptible basis.

Demand growth in the industrial market has been much slower than in the domestic market. Between 1975 and 1985 the total number of therms sold rose by around 17 percent, although there was a slight decline between 1979 and 1985. However, the market share of gas increased steadily throughout the ten-year period, rising from 23 percent in 1975 to 36 percent in 1985.

One characteristic of the industrial market is the large volume of gas supplied per customer. In the accounting year 1985–1986, the three largest customers together accounted for 10 percent of the total number of therms sold by British Gas in *all* markets, and the largest customer (Imperial Chemical Industries) alone accounted for 7 percent of total sales. About 55 percent of the industrial market, representing about 12 percent of the total revenue of British Gas, is supplied on an interruptible basis. Since customers with interruptible contracts can be assumed to have the capacity to switch readily and quickly to alternative fuels, conditions conducive to effective competition amongst fuels exist in this area. It is also worth noting that, in the main, gas is supplied to customers under contracts that are individually negotiated.

The commercial market for gas largely comprises customers in the service industries and the public sector, including education (the largest single component, accounting for about 20 percent of commercial sales), shops, offices, public buildings, hotels, and restaurants. Over two-thirds of the gas consumed in the commercial sector is used for space heating, with water heating and catering being the next most important uses. For heating purposes gas competes chiefly with oil and electricity, while in catering electricity is the principal competing fuel.

About 50 percent of gas supplies to the commercial market are provided under individually negotiated contracts. The remainder, mostly to smaller-volume customers, is supplied according to published tariffs which consist of a standing charge and a rate per therm. Over the past ten years demand for energy in the commercial sector has been more buoyant than in the industrial market. The number of therms sold nearly doubled between 1975 and 1985, and, as in the domestic and industrial markets, the market share of gas rose steadily, from 19 percent in 1975 to 34 percent in 1985.

Appliance Sales, Installation, and Servicing   British Gas sells appliances from approximately 800 showrooms distributed throughout the country, which also serve as points where domestic gas bills can be paid. In 1985–1986 sales volumes were approximately as follows: central heating systems, 100,000; space heaters, 700,000; cookers, 500,000; other appliances, 100,000. Appliance sales have also been supported by installation and servicing activities. During 1985–1986 approximately 3.5 million appliances were covered by British Gas service contracts, and between 1981–1982 and 1985–1986 inclusive the company installed about 100,000 central heating systems and 1.6 million other appliances.

In its appliance sales and installation and servicing activities British Gas competes with privately owned retailers and a large number of independent service engineers. It does, however, derive a major competitive advantage from the existence of the large staff of engineers required for the provision of "essential" services that are part of its gas supply business, including dealing with gas escapes and other emergencies, installation and repair of meters, and safety checks on appliances. Since this latter type of work is highly seasonal, British Gas is able to offer "off-peak" labor at favorable rates for the installation and servicing of appliances in periods other than the winter months.

Financial Results   Table 9.3 sets out the current cost accounting (CCA) and historic cost accounting (HCA) profit and loss accounts for British Gas for the years ended 31 March 1986 and 31 March 1987, and table 9.4 provides a breakdown of the company's fixed tangible assets at the end of each of those years. In terms of revenues received, it can be seen that gas supply (transmission, distribution, and sales) is the predominant part of the business, and that, likewise, pipelines and related equipment dominate the company's asset structure. In terms of profits, the relative contribution of gas supply is even higher. The CCA operating profit of £688 million in 1985–1986, for example, can be broken down as follows: gas supply, £703 million; installation and contracting, £11 million; appliance trading, £12 million; exploration subsidiaries, –£43 million; other activities, £5 million. The principal component of the cost of sales was expenditure on gas purchases (including the gas levy) which totalled £3,896 million in 1985–1986, while operating costs include salaries, wages, and related costs (£1,202 million in 1985–1986) and depreciation (£431 million on a CCA basis in 1985–1986).

The increase in operating profit between the two years is largely attributable to a fall in gas purchase costs of approximately 9.5 percent, which in turn was a consequence of the impact of falling oil prices on the escalation provisions of gas purchase contracts. As a result, the company's rate of return—defined here as the percentage ratio of operating profit to average capital employed—rose from 4.1 to 5.8 percent on a CCA basis, and from 15.3 to 18.5 percent on an HCA basis.

9.2.3   The Framework of Competition and Regulation

Although the gas industry was highly fragmented prior to nationalization

Table 9.3   British Gas: profit and loss accounts, 1985–1986 and 1986–1987

	CCA (£ million)		HCA (£ million)	
	1986	1987	1986	1987
Turnover				
Gas supply	7,109	6,967	7,109	6,967
Installation and contracting	275	310	275	310
Appliance trading	278	300	278	300
Exploration subsidiaries	94	189	94	189
Other activities	21	28	21	28
Intragroup sales	–90	–184	–90	–184
Total turnover	7,687	7,610	7,687	7,610
Cost of sales	4,598	4,135	4,539	4,150
Gross profit	3,089	3,475	3,148	3,460
Operating costs	2,401	2,470	2,142	2,216
Operating profit	688	1,005	1,006	1,244
Net interest receivable	94	49	94	49
Gearing adjustment	0	8	0	0
Profit before taxation	782	1,062	1,100	1,293
Taxation	380	487	380	487
Profit for the year	402	575	720	806

Source: *British Gas Annual Report and Accounts* (1987).

Table 9.4   The tangible fixed assets of British Gas

	CCA (£ million)		HCA (£ million)	
	1986	1987	1986	1987
Land and buildings	1,190	1,279	363	390
Pipelines etc.	13,778	13,958	4,111	4,198
Gas and oil fields	1,609	1,518	1,420	1,431
Other	188	220	156	183
	16,765	16,975	6,050	6,202

Source: *British Gas Prospectus* (1986), *British Gas Annual Report and Accounts* (1987).

and contained large numbers of both municipal and private enterprises, competition in markets for gas sales was relatively limited: firms tended to operate in separate areas and to supply distinct groups of customers. Private companies were therefore subject to a variety of types of price and profit regulation.

Nationalization substantially reduced the number of firms in the industry, initially to the twelve Area Boards and later to a single public corporation. In the ensuing period product market competition remained notable by its absence, while regulatory policy evolved along the lines set out in chapter 5. By the 1970s the policy framework for the industry had been brought into line with that pertaining in telecommunications and electricity generation: there was a single national firm, protected from competition by statutory entry barriers and regulated by a department of central government. The underlying rationale for this approach was the familiar argument that the core activities of gas transmission and distribution constituted a natural monopoly, and that the operation of more than one firm in the market would therefore lead to cost inefficiencies. To protect consumers from the effects of the resulting market power, it was considered desirable that the industry should be publicly owned and controlled.

It is true, of course, that the BGC faced competition from other fuels in the wider market for energy, particularly in the longer term. Even here, however, competition was attenuated by the fact that two of the principal competing fuels, electricity and coal, were supplied by publicly owned industries whose pricing policies and competitive activities were themselves controlled by the Government. Moreover, Governments were also able to exercise control over the market prices of the various oil products by means of commodity taxes, and did in practice use these tax instruments to reduce the competitive pressures on the other energy industries, particularly coal (see section 9.5).

A slightly more surprising feature of the policy regime during the period of nationalization was the statutory monopsony position with respect to the purchase of gas that was granted to the BGC. Before reorganization of the industry in 1972 it would have been possible to have arranged for the Area Gas Boards to compete amongst themselves for gas supplies from the offshore producers. However, even during these early stages of the development of UKCS natural gas, it was the Gas Council that, on behalf of the Area Boards, entered into contracts with the firms involved in gas exploration and extraction. The 1972 reorganization therefore had little direct impact on competition in the market for gas purchases, although it did impede the possible later development of such competition as a deliberate policy measure.

One justification for the statutory monopsony in the purchase of gas was a desire to prevent appropriation of the rents associated with gas production by the offshore operators. This motive also helps to explain the attitude of British Governments to international trade in gas: both imports and exports have been strictly controlled and, while substantial imports have been allowed (most notably from the Norwegian Frigg field), exports by UKCS producers were effectively prohibited prior to privatization. As a result the market power of British Gas vis-à-vis UKCS producers was greatly strengthened, helping to maintain downward pressure on the prices producers could obtain for their supplies. However, the income-distribution problems connected with the accrual of rents on an exhaustible natural resource could easily have been solved by establishing appropriate taxes on producers, the solution that was later adopted for UKCS oil production when petroleum revenue tax was introduced. The award of a statutory monopsony position to the BGC appears to have been an extremely clumsy piece of economic policy.

The consequences of the gas monopsony might not have been overly detrimental if, in setting prices in the domestic, industrial, and commercial markets, British Gas had adopted a long-run marginal cost pricing policy, in accordance with the provisions of the 1967 White Paper on nationalized industries. In that event final selling prices would have reflected the marginal opportunity cost (the "efficient" price) of gas supplies, and customers would have been faced with accurate signals as to the value of gas they were consuming. In practice, however, the BGC based selling prices on the *average contract* price of its supplies. Because of the existence of the Early Southern Basin contracts, the effects of the oil price shocks on gas markets, and the escalating costs of extraction from less accessible fields, this average contract price has typically been well below best estimates of marginal opportunity costs between 1973 and 1987 (although falling world energy prices towards the end of the period may have narrowed the gap). Thus, in the early 1980s for example, a report by the consultants Deloitte, Haskins, and Sells (1983) concluded that the BGC was selling at less than the marginal cost of supply in all markets except the interruptible industrial market, Price (1984) estimated that prices to domestic and "firm" (i.e. noninterruptible) industrial customers were 12–17 percent below long-run marginal costs, and Newbery (1985) estimated that, although industrial prices appeared to be about right, domestic customers were paying up to around 20 percent too little at the margin.

It is likely, therefore, that much of the gain in the market share of gas between 1975 and 1985 was attributable to suboptimal pricing policies (a view that will receive support when we come to discuss electricity and coal pricing in later sections). That is, the changing market shares of the various fuels in this period may owe less to changes in their respective opportunity costs than to the failure of regulatory policy to establish and enforce appropriate pricing policies in energy markets.

Liberalization: the Oil and Gas (Enterprise) Act 1982   The statutory monopsony with respect to the purchase of gas from UKCS producers was nominally ended in 1982 by the Oil and Gas (Enterprise) Act which, along with the British Telecommunications Act 1981 and the Energy Act 1983, reflected a shift in public policy toward an increased emphasis on the use of competitive forces as a method of influencing the performance of nationalized utilities.

The Act provided for the use of the BGC's pipeline network by competing suppliers or by any other persons wishing to transport gas. It stipulated that the consent of the Secretary of State for Energy was required for gas to be supplied through pipes to *any* premises or for the use of the British Gas pipelines. However, it stated that consent would automatically be denied for supply to persons within 25 yards of a gas main unless that supply amounted to not less than 25,000 therms per annum. A person providing gas for himself was excepted from these requirements, as were supplies greater than or equal to 2 million therms per annum.

The Act did not attempt to specify the terms on which the BGC was required to provide pipeline services to other persons (the vital issue of "interconnection" discussed in chapters 3 and 8); these were left to be determined by negotiations between the BGC and the user. However, the user was afforded the right to make an application to the Secretary of State on this matter, and the Secretary of State was empowered to give directions to the BGC in respect of appropriate terms and conditions.

Thus, in theory, since 1982 UKCS producers have been free to negotiate direct sales of gas to larger consumers. In the event, however, no use has been made of the provisions of the Act to date, and the legislation has had no discernible effect on the degree of competition in the U.K. gas industry. The reasons for this apparent failure of policy are several and, taken together, they underline the point that, given the structure of the gas supply industry, much stronger liberalizing measures are required if significant competition is to be introduced into the market.

The obstacles facing a new entrant include the following.

(i) The 1982 Act effectively excludes new suppliers from the domestic market, which constitutes both the largest and most profitable market segment.

(ii) The lower-margin commercial and industrial markets are highly fragmented, tending to raise the penetration costs for a new supplier.

(iii) The largest customers are supplied on a contract basis: terms and conditions of supply are individually negotiated and are not published. Hence, there are significant incentives for British Gas to engage in predatory pricing in the event that new suppliers attempt to enter the market (price cuts can be localized, thereby reducing the impact of aggressive policies on total revenue).

(iv) With a large integrated supply system British Gas is able to offer superior security of supply than a potential rival. In obtaining gas from other sources the customer would typically need to make provision for back-up or top-up supplies from British Gas, and the latter has every incentive to impede entry by seeking to impose unduly onerous terms for this service.

(v) The new entrant must negotiate terms with British Gas for the use of the pipeline network. This provides scope for the dominant firm to impede entry by charging an excessively high price for the transport facilities. Although the rival supplier could appeal to the Secretary of State—and, since privatization, can now appeal to the Director General of Gas Supply—the uncertainties and delays that are involved serve to raise entry costs. Moreover, the need to negotiate for pipeline use provides British Gas with an early signal of the entrant's intentions, giving the dominant firm time to offer better terms to the targeted customer.

(vi) Finally, as already explained, British Gas's average gas purchase costs have generally been below marginal opportunity costs. Since all earlier supplies of gas from the UKCS were sold to the BGC under long-term contracts, the most likely type of new entrant would be an operator of an undeveloped or newly developed field who had uncommitted gas to offer. The unit gas costs of such an operator would, however, typically be much greater than British Gas's average purchase cost and, given the pricing policies of the dominant firm, it would be difficult for an entrant, even if more efficient than British Gas, to offer more favorable terms to the customer.

It is also worth noting that the Oil and Gas (Enterprise) Act did little to erode British Gas's monopsony position with respect to the purchase of UKCS gas supplies. The Act did not amend the "landing requirement" whereby all gas produced on the UKCS is required to be brought onshore in the U.K. Given the economics of gas production and transportation, the landing requirement continued to prevent the emergence of an effective export option for the offshore producers, and therefore blocked development of the more competitive gas market that would have been feasible had UKCS fields been able to build direct pipeline links to the continent.

The Gas Act 1986   The framework of the privatized gas industry was established by the Gas Act 1986. The Act has many features in common with the preceding telecommunications legislation although, for reasons to be discussed below, the resulting policy regime is likely to be even less conducive to the development of effective competition than in the case of telecommunications. As a result of the latter feature, the legislation was subject to a good deal of hostile criticism in Parliament and by the press, academics, consumer bodies, and potential competitors, although the impact of these various groups on its final form was extremely limited.

The main statutory provisions of the Act are as follows.

Section 1 empowers the Secretary of State to appoint the Director General of Gas Supply (DGGS), who in turn may appoint the staff of an Office of Gas Supply (Ofgas).

Section 2 establishes the Gas Consumers' Council, a consumers' "watchdog" body.

Section 3 abolishes British Gas's monopoly privilege with respect to the supply of gas through pipes, opening the way to the possible authorization of alternative suppliers.

Section 4 sets out the guidelines to which the Secretary of State and the

DGGS must have regard in carrying out their functions. In the original Bill that was presented to Parliament these included meeting all reasonable demands for gas, the protection of consumer interests with respect to prices, continuity and quality of supply, the promotion of efficiency in gas supply, and the protection of the public from dangers arising from the distribution and use of gas. However, Parliament later amended the bill so as to include a duty on the Secretary of State and the DGGS to act in the way best calculated "to enable persons to compete effectively in the supply of gas through pipes at rates which, in relation to any premises, exceed 25,000 therms a year." As with guideline (b), section 3, of the Telecommunications Act 1984 this gives additional scope for pro-competitive decisions by a regulator so inclined to act, although, unlike in telecommunications, the duty is only imposed with respect to one section of the market.

Section 5 makes supplying gas without an authorization a criminal offence (although clause 6 then exempts supplies of over 2 million therms per annum from this prohibition).

Section 7 empowers the Secretary of State to authorize a "public gas supplier" to supply gas through pipes to any premises within a designated area. The clause also provides for the inclusion in authorizations of certain conditions (for example, the payment of fees, and provision of information to the DGGS or the Gas Consumers' Council). Most significantly, except in special circumstances, it prevents authorizations for areas situated within 25 yards of the mains of another public gas supplier. Thus, given the initial authorization of British Gas, section 7 blocks the emergence of a competing public gas supplier in most of the relevant market.

Section 8 empowers the Secretary of State or the DGGS to authorize any person or persons to supply gas to specified premises when either the premises are not within 25 yards of a public gas supplier's distribution main or the supply involved is expected to exceed 25,000 therms per annum. Hence, section 8 has the effect of allowing the development of competition in supplies to large commercial and industrial customers.

Section 9 imposes general duties on a public gas supplier, including a duty to "avoid any undue preference in the supply of gas to persons entitled to a supply ... ." It remains to be seen how exactly this clause will be interpreted but, in general, it appears designed to prevent excessive price discrimination.

Section 10 imposes a duty on a public gas supplier, when the customer so requests, to give and continue to give a supply of gas of up to 25,000 therms per annum to any premises that are either within 25 yards of a distribution main or are already connected to such a main. However, since customers requesting in excess of 25,000 therms per annum are not "entitled to a supply," this has the effect of limiting the applicability of section 9; there is therefore no statutory duty on a public gas supplier to avoid undue preference in its dealings with large industrial and commercial customers.

Section 14 requires a public gas supplier to charge in accordance with fixed tariffs any consumer using no more than 25,000 therms per annum (labelled a "tariff customer"), and stipulates that a public gas supplier "shall not show undue preference" in fixing tariffs.

Section 19 empowers the DGGS, on application of another person, to give a public gas supplier directions securing to the applicant the right to use a pipeline owned by the public gas supplier, subject to such payments as may be specified. It therefore transfers some of the powers granted to the Secretary of State by the Oil and Gas (Enterprise) Act 1982 to the DGGS.

Section 23 empowers the DGGS to modify the authorization conditions imposed on a public gas supplier in cases where the latter raises no objections to the changes. If the public gas supplier does object, section 24 empowers the DGGS to refer the matter to the Monopolies and Mergers Commission (MMC).

Section 25 requires the MMC to report on the matters referred to them, and section 26 obliges the Director to modify authorization conditions to remedy any adverse effects identified by the Commission.

Section 27 enables orders (by the Secretary of State) under certain provisions of the Fair Trading Act 1973 or the Competition Act 1980 to modify authorization conditions.

Section 49 provides that, on a transfer date to be appointed by the Secretary of State, *all* the property, rights, and liabilities of the BGC are to become those of a successor company (i.e. British Gas).

It can be seen then that, as in the case of telecommunications, regulatory powers are divided between the Secretary of State, the DGGS, and the MMC. However, although the procedures for granting and amending authorizations/licenses and for enforcing compliance are broadly similar in the two cases, the powers to secure effective competition are generally weaker in the gas industry. New entry into the domestic market is blocked, and the DGGS has a duty to "enable" competition only with respect to supplies to the larger customers in the commercial and industrial markets. There is therefore little prospect that an alternative national public gas supplier will emerge to compete with British Gas in the way that Mercury has managed to do in the telecommunications industry.

The Gas Act also contains no provisions that will help to increase competition in the market for gas purchases, although in March 1986 the Secretary of State announced that: "The Government is prepared to consider applications for waivers of the landing requirement on a case by case basis. In doing this, it will take into account considerations relating to the security of the U.K.'s gas supplies, without any presumption that exports should not take place in present circumstances." In view of the facts that (a) existing UKCS production is committed to British Gas under long-term contracts, (b) foreseeable new field developments are relatively few in number and most frequently small in magnitude, (c) gas utilities in Northern Europe have already secured the supplies they require for the next decade, and (d) direct exports would involve the construction of costly pipeline links, it is unlikely that U.K. producers will be able to take advantage of the new opportunities on any significant scale. That is, liberalization has come too late to have any substantial short- to medium-term effects, and the monopsony power of British Gas will not be materially affected for many years to come. Moreover, while the longer-term implications of liberalization are to be welcomed, it is not clear that the export opportunities will be maintained indefinitely: the ministerial statement is qualified by the "in present circumstances" condition.

British Gas's Authorisation   Given the market power allowed to British Gas by the 1986 Act it might have been expected that the accompanying Authorisation, granted under clause 7 of the Act, would have been a lengthy and detailed document that attempted to establish a strict regulatory regime for the private company. In the event, however, the Authorisation is extremely brief, reflecting the Government's preference for regulation "with a light hand." Its main features are summarized below under the headings of accounting procedures, price control, common carriage, and other provisions.

Accounting procedures   The first substantive condition of the Authorisation requires British Gas to prepare separate accounts for its gas supply business. This is defined to include procurement, treatment, storage, transmission, and distribution of gas for sale and safe delivery through pipes to customers in Great Britain, and the conveyance of gas for third-party suppliers. The gas supply business therefore accounts for the great bulk of the activities of the company, and excludes only such operations as appliance trading, installation and contracting activities, exploration and production, and the provision of consultancy services.

As a consequence of this provision, the DGGS will have extremely poor accounting information upon which to base his decisions. For example, it will be difficult to assess whether or not British Gas is willing to make its transmission grid available to third-party suppliers on reasonable terms, since there is no requirement to treat the transmission system as a separate cost center. Similarly, without adequate accounting information it will be hard to judge the extent of any cross-subsidization or price discrimination that might be taking place. Hence, enforcement of the duty to "avoid undue preference," which is imposed on a public gas supplier by clause 9 of the Gas Act, will be impaired. Finally, the absence of a requirement to prepare separate accounts for regional distribution and sales systems will limit the ability of the DGGS to use company information as a basis for checking the internal efficiency performance of British Gas; the Government failed to take the opportunity to increase the number of yardstick indicators available to the DGGS.

Price control   The most detailed condition of the Authorisation sets out the formula that is to determine the level of prices charged to tariff customers. In each relevant year the average price per therm is constrained to lie at or below a "maximum average price" per therm which is defined as follows:

$$M_t = [1 + (RPI_t - X)/100]P_{t-1} + Y_t - K_t,$$

where M_t is the maximum average price per therm in year t, RPI_t is the percentage change in the retail price index between October of year $t-1$ and October of year t, $X = 2$ percent,

$$P_{t-1} = [1 + (RPI_{t-1} - X)] P_{t-2},$$

except that P_1, the value for 1986–1987, will be equal to the average price in 1986–1987 less the average cost of gas in that year, Y_t is the gas cost per therm in year t, and K_t is a correction factor per therm to be made in year t.

In effect, the formula divides the maximum price per therm into two principal components. The *gas component* Y is the average cost to the company of obtaining gas, mostly made up of payments to suppliers and including the gas levy. For gas produced from the company's own fields the price is deemed to be the market price as determined by the Inland Revenue for taxation purposes. The *nongas component* P is an amount per therm, changes in which are limited to the percentage change in the retail price index less two percentage points (X). Thus, in order to increase its profit margin, British Gas must reduce its nongas unit costs (labor, capital, etc.) by more than 2 percent per annum, a figure that presumably reflects the

Goverment's initial perception of the magnitude of the combined effects of scale economies and improvements in internal efficiency that might reasonably be expected over the next few years.

Since the formula links maximum prices in a given financial year to the retail price index and gas costs in that same year, in setting prices British Gas must necessarily rely on forecasts of the latter two variables. The correction factor K therefore allows for any undercharging or overcharging in one year to be corrected subsequently via a formula that incorporates an interest charge on the amount of the correction and an adjustment to take account of any change in the number of therms supplied from one year to the next. The purpose of the correction factor is simply to prevent British Gas from benefiting from forecasting errors and to provide incentives against intentional manipulation of forecasts aimed at improving financial performance (without such a factor the company would gain from consistently overestimating changes in its gas costs and in the retail price index).

Since gas tariffs are generally composed of two parts—a fixed element (the standing charge) and a price per therm—the pricing formula allows for some rebalancing of the structure of charges by British Gas. However, the Authorisation also constrains any cumulative percentage increase in the standing-charge component to be no greater than the cumulative percentage change in the retail price index from its base level in December 1985. This restriction is one of several amendments to the original draft authorization, which required only that British Gas use its best endeavors to secure the aforementioned outcome. It is designed to ensure that small consumers, for whom the standing-charge element comprises a substantial fraction of their overall purchases, are protected against substantial increases in prices resulting from changes in tariff structures.

It should be noted, however, that connection charges for new tariff customers are *not* regulated: British Gas is required by the Authorisation only to publish the principles upon which such connection charges will be established. In addition, as already explained, the pricing formula applies only to tariff customers of the company. With respect to contract customers, Condition 5 of the Authorisation states that:

"The Supplier shall, at the time when this Authorisation comes into force, publish:
(a) a schedule of the maximum prices payable for gas supplied at that time to contract customers and shall publish a revised schedule at the time of any changes to those maximum prices; and
(b) a general statement of the Supplier's policy as regards its willingness to enter into negotiations for prices for gas supplied to contract customers."

Thus, apart from this minimal provision of information, contract prices are completely unregulated, even though competition from other fuels is relatively weak in several parts of the noninterruptible industrial and commercial markets.

With respect to modifications of the formula, British Gas has been granted the right to request disapplication of the price control condition with effect from a date not earlier than 1 April 1992. If it does so, the price control condition will cease to apply unless the DGGS chooses to make a reference to the MMC and the MMC concludes that abandonment of the condition can be expected to operate against the public interest. The DGGS himself has the right to modify the Authorisation at any time, including the right to vary the pricing formula, provided that British Gas agrees to the changes and the Secretary of State does not object. In the absence of such agreement, the DGGS may refer the matter to the MMC and, if the MMC subsequently proposes modifications to the condition, the DGGS is obliged to act on those proposals. In effect, then, if both the DGGS and MMC are agreed that a change would be desirable, it is possible for the pricing formula to be altered at any future date.

Taken as a whole, the pricing constraints imposed on British Gas can hardly be described as stringent. The implicit target of a 2 percent per annum reduction in nongas costs should not prove to be onerous. Some demand growth over the five-year period was predicted in the prospectus for the share issue and, given the existence of scale economies, this should lead to reductions in real unit costs even in the event that internal efficiency is not improved (see section 8.3.5). Moreover, the nationalized BGC was set a target of reducing its real net trading costs per therm by 12 percent between financial years 1982–1983 and 1986–1987 and managed to meet this target within the first three years of the four-year period.

Unlike in telecommunications, the pricing formula for British Gas also contains a "cost-plus" component: changes in the average purchase cost of gas can automatically be passed on to tariff customers, thus providing insurance for the company against movements in beachhead prices (caused, for example, by fluctuations in international oil prices). The underlying rationale for full insurance (as opposed to partial indexation of the maximum price to gas costs) is presumably that, in the short run, these gas costs are noncontrollable—long-term contracts imply that purchasing decisions in the immediate future will have very little impact on the overall average—so that customers can be given accurate signals about movements in gas input prices without seriously weakening the regulated firm's incentives to reduce costs. However, the signals provided to customers are based upon the *average* purchase price of gas, rather than marginal opportunity costs, and only by accident will the two approximately coincide.

Common carriage   The two conditions (numbers 9 and 10) of the British Gas Authorisation that set out regulations concerning the use of the company's pipeline network by third parties are both extremely short, and together they add up to only about 300 words. British Gas is required, after consulting the DGGS, to prepare a statement setting out general information for the guidance of those persons who might wish to negotiate with it for the conveyance of gas, giving examples of the prices which it would expect to be paid for such conveyance in typical circumstances, and a general description of the principal matters which it would expect to be the subject of those negotiations. Thus the DGGS has no powers to set the appropriate rates independently, although section 19 of the Gas Act 1986 gives persons interested in having their gas conveyed in this way the right to make representations to the DGGS, in which event the Act enables him, among other things, to "specify the sums or the method of determining the sums" he considers should be paid in consideration for the transport services. In principle, therefore, a pro-competitive DGGS will have some scope for encouraging new entry into nontariff markets, although, for reasons already explained, British Gas will continue to enjoy considerable powers to impede the emergence of third-party suppliers.

The Authorisation also requires that British Gas prepare a statement concerning its policies with respect to the supply of gas ("back-up gas") to a third-party supplier in the event that the third-party supplier's gas is temporarily unavailable. The intention here is to remove the barrier to new entry arising from the capacity of the incumbent dominant firm to offer customers greater security of supply than a small more specialized newcomer. Again, while the Authorisation requires only that British Gas publish guidance information about its policies, including a description of the method by which it proposes to calculate the charge for supplying back-up gas, the Gas Act empowers the DGGS, upon receiving representations from a third-party supplier, to give directions with respect to the terms and conditions of the relevant transaction.

Only time will tell whether or not these powers of the DGGS will be sufficient to encourage use of British Gas's pipeline network by competing suppliers on any significant scale. However, there are few grounds for optimism on this score. Quite apart from the incumbent firm's ability to manipulate information flows upon which terms-of-access determinations will necessarily depend, a number of other formidable entry barriers will remain, including the inability of newcomers to enter the tariff market, the lack of regulatory constraints on British Gas's pricing policies in the contract market, and British Gas's access to gas supplies at prices below marginal opportunity costs.

Other provisions   The remaining conditions of the Authorisation relate, for the most part, to a variety of disparate matters, including provision of information to the Director General and to the Gas Consumers' Council, provision of emergency service, codes of practice for tariff gas supplies and payment of bills, provision of services for the elderly and disabled, provision of information to customers on the efficient use of gas, supply of gas to public lamps (!), and the payment of fees (which, among other things, are used to finance Ofgas, the Gas Consumers' Council, and relevant references to the MMC).

The Authorisation also sets out the circumstances in which it (the Authorisation) can be revoked by the Secretary of State, the most important of which is failure of British Gas to comply with orders made under the Gas, Fair Trading or Competition Acts and/or bankruptcy of the Company. Revocation of the Authorisation is the ultimate sanction that can be applied by the Secretary of State and, since use of this power would effectively signal an almost total collapse of the regulatory regime, the consequent damages would be sufficiently great that the deterrent effects of its threatened use are likely to be significant only in rather extreme circumstances.

9.2.4   Assessment of the Framework of Competition and Regulation
The privatization of British Gas illustrates the tension in policy making between accommodating the short-term interests of major pressure groups (including the management of the enterprise concerned, new shareholders, and the firm's customers) and the longer-term benefits associated with promoting competition and establishing an effective regulatory regime. Given the political background to the U.K. privatization program, it is perhaps unsurprising to find that, in practice, the shorter-term interest group pressures have been accorded the greater weight. What is more surprising is just how little weight was, in the event, attached to competitive and regulatory objectives. To an even greater extent than in the telecommunications case, British Gas has been transferred to the private sector with its monopoly and monopsony powers intact: the philosophy of "regulation with a light hand" has been implemented in an extreme form,

and major opportunities to improve incentives in the industry have been missed.

Policy failures are evident in at least four major areas. First, there was no attempt to restructure the British Gas Corporation prior to privatization. Second, the pricing formula for tariff customers preserved the existing pricing philosophy of the BGC, which was closer to an average cost than a marginal cost tariff structure. Third, little effort was made to promote effective liberalization by encouraging actual and potential competition to the dominant supplier. Fourth, Ofgas has been granted only very limited regulatory powers, and there are considerable uncertainties surrounding longer-term developments in regulatory policy.

In each case, with the possible exception of the lack of clarity with respect to the long-term regulatory approach, the major beneficiary has been the senior management of the BGC, now the senior management of British Gas. It was management that had most to lose from restructuring, from reassessment of pricing policy, and from the diminution in market power associated with more effective competition and stronger regulation. Although it can be argued that consumers of gas also benefited in the short run from the decision to retain average cost pricing, the overall consequences of this outcome are less clear: in the longer term consumers are likely to suffer from the allocative inefficiencies associated with suboptimal pricing and market power, as well as from the absence of incentives for greater internal efficiency that would have been produced by more competition. Taking account of the impact of privatization on taxpayers and groups such as UKCS producers of gas, our general conclusion is therefore that an excessively high side payment has been made to the incumbent management to ensure managerial cooperation in the process of transferring ownership.

Restructuring The options for restructuring the BGC prior to privatization have been evaluated by Hammond *et al.* (1985). The two principal alternatives considered were the following:

(a) regionalization, involving the creation of 12 separate regional gas companies and an enterprise (possibly a public corporation) that would own and operate the national transmission system;

(b) separation of *all* pipeline operations, including local distribution networks, from the gas supply business, involving the creation of one or more pipeline companies that would transport gas for firms (e.g. offshore producers) competing for final customers.

Hammond *et al.* concluded that the second option was largely impractical so far as supplies to domestic consumers are concerned and that, particularly since it could be combined with vertical separation of pipeline operations and gas supply in parts of the industrial and commercial markets, regionalization offered the most attractive alternative to the sale of the BGC in its pre-privatization form (i.e. the course actually followed by the Government).

In effect, regionalization would have returned the industry to something approximating its structure prior to the 1972 Gas Act (augmented by the national transmission system) and was therefore an eminently feasible option. Relative to the creation of a private sector monopoly-cum-monopsony covering both transmission/distribution and gas supply, it would have had a number of advantages, including the following.

(i) Reduction of monopsony power: regional distribution companies would have had to compete in the purchase of supplies from UKCS and foreign producers.

(ii) Increased likelihood of efficient cost-related regional price variations: distribution companies would have not been able to engage in the geographic cross-subsidization currently practiced by British Gas.

(iii) Enhanced effectiveness of regulation: each distribution company would have had monopoly power in its own region, but Ofgas would have been able to draw on information from several independent sources, opening up the possibility of yardstick competition.

(iv) Greater capital market competition: regional companies would have faced a more plausible threat of takeover than does British Gas and shareholders would have had more information upon which to base their assessments of managerial performance, both factors that might serve to improve incentives towards internal efficiency (but see section 2.2.3 for some qualifications concerning the takeover threat).

(v) Lower barriers to entry: vertical separation of the national transmission and area distribution networks would have put UKCS producers wishing to supply large industrial and commercial customers on a par with the regional companies when negotiating for rights to use the national high pressure pipelines, and, unlike British Gas, the common carrier would not have had direct financial incentives to exclude new entrants from the gas supply business.

One of the problems that would have faced policy makers in the event that the regionalization option had been adopted would have been the need to revise existing gas supply contracts. This could have been accomplished in one of a number of different ways, including the creation of a state-owned wholesale agency to hold existing contracts, auctioning off the contracts to the regional companies, and cancellation of the contracts followed by renegotiation between distribution companies and offshore producers.

Whichever course was followed, the likely consequence would have been a sharp increase in the prices paid by the regional companies via Early Southern Basin contracts. As a result, average gas purchase prices, and hence final selling prices, would quickly have been moved toward marginal opportunity costs, with beneficial effects for allocative efficiency. Moreover, the hike in prices would have facilitated new entry since established gas distribution companies would not then have access to inputs at prices that are substantially below the costs of developing new gas fields, a situation that currently has the effect of impeding potential competition.

The additional rents accruing from the revision of the Early Southern Basin contracts would also have provided a useful supplement to Exchequer revenues. The rents would have accrued directly to the state in the event that either the wholesale agency option or the auction option had been adopted. Cancellation, followed by renegotiation, of contracts would initially have left the additional returns in the hands of offshore producers, but they could readily have been clawed back via modifications to the oil and gas taxation regime.

Given the feasibility of the regionalization option and its several attractive characteristics, why then did the Government prefer to create a privately owned national monopolist-cum-monopsonist? Three major considerations appear to have been involved. First, legislation to restructure the industry, including provisions for the revision of existing contracts, would inevitably have slowed down the privatization process. Thus, although revenues from the exercise would almost certainly have been greater, they would have accrued at a later date and, given the attachment of the Government to public sector borrowing targets, the delay might have made it more difficult to attain short-term fiscal objectives. Moreover, delay might have raised doubts about the feasibility of accomplishing privatization within the lifetime of the incumbent Government (which, in the event of a Labour Party victory in the subsequent election, could have led to an indefinite postponement).

Second, the senior management of the British Gas Corporation was hostile to any restructuring of the industry. This attitude can partly be explained in terms of managerial preferences for a quieter life and for greater company size, and partly by genuine beliefs that full integratration yielded potential gains in internal efficiency. Irrespective of the underlying motivations, however, the fact of managerial hostility to restructuring would have complicated the task of privatization and contributed to delays in policy implementation.

Finally, as argued above, the revision of gas purchase contracts necessitated by restructuring would almost certainly have led to an increase in final selling prices. Thus gas consumers might have faced a significant price hike in the immediate post-privatization period. Although the community as a whole would have been likely to benefit, and gas consumers themselves would have reaped longer-term gains from greater competition and more effective regulation, this is an example of a situation where the detriments (higher prices in the short run to consumers) would have been much more visible than the benefits (including marginally lower tax rates and lower prices in the longer term). Hence the electoral consequences of restructuring might have appeared unattractive to the Government.

The decision not to reorganize the gas industry prior to privatization therefore represents a victory for political expediency over considerations of longer-term economic efficiency. In chapter 2 we examined the weaknesses of political decision making in the context of the control of public enterprise, and in chapter 4 we considered the impact of interest group pressures on regulatory processes. Both discussions are relevant to the process of privatization, which involves major political choices and can be viewed as encompassing the initial decisions about the structure of the new regulatory regime. Thus the decision not to restructure the British Gas industry can be interpreted as a response to interest group pressures from management and consumers that was motivated chiefly by electoral considerations. Economic efficiency objectives were accorded a lesser priority, with detrimental consequences that will become increasingly apparent in the longer term.

The Pricing Formula   With respect to the tariff market, both the level and form of the pricing constraint are open to criticism. The gas component part of the tariff (Y) links allowable prices to the *average* cost of gas purchases and, the gas levy notwithstanding, the existence of the Early Southern Basin contracts indicates that domestic tariffs are likely initially to be below levels required for the attainment of allocative efficiency. On the other hand, the annual cost-reduction target implicit in the nongas component of the formula ($X = 2$ percent) does not appear to be very demanding in the light of the BGC's performance in the period immediately prior to privatization.

These decisions concerning the two major components of the formula can partly be justified as an attempt to achieve a gradual movement of final selling prices towards allocatively efficient levels. As the Early Southern Basin contracts expire average purchase costs of gas will rise and, other things being equal, these average costs will move towards the cost of supplies from new fields. Further, by setting X at a relatively low level, allowable prices will rise (fall) more (less) quickly than if a more stringent target had been imposed. Thus, over the course of the next few years it might be hoped that selling prices will reach a more efficient level.

It is likely that the interests of consumer groups were a major factor in the decision not to couple privatization of the gas industry with an immediate upward adjustment of the price level. It should also be noted, however, that the decision was also very much in line with managerial preferences. Lower initial prices will contribute to further short-term increases in market share (a goal that was actively pursued by the BGC management), and the relatively generous cost-reduction target should allow the managers of British Gas to achieve a steady improvement in profit performance, thus enabling them to present themselves in a favorable light to shareholders.

While the distortions resulting from an inappropriate choice of the average price level may only be temporary, the pricing formula embodies more permanent deficiencies with respect to the incentives provided for the construction the tariff *structure*. To see this, suppose that British Gas serves a number of different submarkets with differing marginal costs of supply. For example, the submarkets may be defined in terms of geographic (areas of the country) or temporal (time of day or year) characteristics. For simplicity we will assume that marginal costs are independent of output, demand is a function of the average price charged in each submarket (thus ignoring both interdependent demands and the complexities associated with multipart tariffs), and demand elasticities are constant and identical in all submarkets.

The pricing formula then confronts British Gas with a constraint of the form

$$\bar{p} \sum_i q_i \geqslant \sum_i p_i(q_i)q_i,$$

where $\bar{p}$ is the maximum allowable average price for all supplies. A profit-seeking firm will therefore aim to maximize

$$\sum_i (p_i - c_i)q_i + \lambda(\bar{p} \sum_i q_i - \sum_i p_i q_i),$$

yielding the first-order conditions

$$[p_i(1-e)-c_i](1-\lambda) + \lambda(\bar{p}-c_i) = 0,$$

where e is the inverse demand elasticity. Comparing two submarkets j and k such that $c_j > c_k$, we therefore find that

$$\frac{1-m_j(1-e)}{1-m_k(1-e)} = \frac{\bar{m}_j-1}{\bar{m}_k-1} < 1,$$

where $m_i = p_i/c_i$ and $\bar{m}_i = \bar{p}/c_i$. It follows immediately that

$$m_k < m_j.$$

That is, the proportionate mark-up of price over marginal cost is lower in the lower-cost market.

Another, more intuitive, way of looking at this result can be obtained by rewriting the price constraint in the form

$$\bar{p} \geq \sum_i s_i(q)p_i(q_i),$$

where s_i is the share of total output accounted for by the ith market. Thus the (regulated) price index is calculated using weights equal to the output shares of the various markets and, by increasing outputs in low-price markets and reducing outputs in high-price markets, the firm can increase the weights attached to the former and reduce the weights attached to the latter. Since this change in weights tends to reduce the value of the index, by acting in the way described the firm can, in effect, loosen the pricing constraint.

The result can usefully be compared with the structure of mark-ups required to maximize welfare subject to a constraint on the firm's profit level: the Ramsey price structure. On the assumptions made, the latter implies that the proportionate mark-ups should be the same in all markets: $m_k = m_j$. Thus, compared with the Ramsey rule, the pricing formula gives British Gas incentives to apply higher mark-ups to higher-cost supplies and lower mark-ups to lower-cost supplies. Not only will this distort competition with other fuels such as electricity but also, over time, it will affect the investment program of the company. For example, overcharging for gas at the winter peak would eventually lead to a level of capacity provision that was suboptimally low.

In several jurisdictions in the United States regulators have been active in promoting more efficient price structures for monopolistic utilities, and the issue is considered to be an integral feature of the regulatory process. In Britain, however, little attention appears to have been paid to the problem:

as we have shown, the incentives provided by the pricing formula are perverse, and the DGGS has been afforded relatively few means of addressing the issue. One possibility is that the DGGS could take a strong line with respect to the enforcement of the "avoidance of undue preference" provision of section 9 of the 1986 Gas Act, but this might be politically unpopular and it could prove difficult to persuade the courts as to the merits of the appropriate interpretation of the legislation. While it is also possible that the issue will eventually be referred to the MMC, our interim judgment is that the initial framework of U.K. regulation is seriously deficient on this important point.

Competition   Since the British Gas Authorisation effectively blocks entry into the domestic market, in the foreseeable future the only prospect for the development of increased competition in gas supplies lies in markets for larger industrial and commercial users. The Oil and Gas (Enterprise) Act 1982 formally removed certain statutory barriers to entry into this market but, because of the continued existence of other substantial obstacles to the emergence of potential competition, has had little practical effect on competitive behavior. Nor has the situation been materially affected by later Government measures that have accompanied the privatization of the industry.

The first difficulty arises from the access of British Gas to low price inputs from the Early Southern Basin fields. These supplies depress the average purchase costs of British Gas, and mean that the incumbent firm can undercut a rival that draws on supplies from a newly developed field and yet still make an accounting profit from the relevant transaction. Thus, although such price discounting might be judged to be predatory if gas inputs were priced at marginal opportunity costs, it is highly unlikely that the behavior would, in practice, satisfy any of the conventional tests for predation (e.g. price less than the average variable cost of supply).

The potential competitor's position is also weakened by two further factors. First, because British Gas is not required to account separately for the various parts of its business, it will in any case be extremely difficult to apply even conventional cost-based tests for predation. Second, U.K. competition law is lenient in its treatment of predatory behavior. If a reference is made to the MMC the best that a complainant can hope for is that, after a lengthy inquiry, the Secretary of State will, on a positive recommendation of the Commission, act so as to prevent such behavior from occurring in the future. That is, U.K. legislation is remedial rather than penal, and does little to *deter* predatory actions by a dominant incumbent firm.

Finally, control of the use of the pipeline network affords British Gas a considerable strategic advantage over potential rivals. An entrant must negotiate with British Gas for conveyance of its supplies, thus providing the incumbent with advance notice of its rival's intentions and giving the former time to offer more favorable terms to the targeted customer. Moreover, in the unregulated parts of the gas market, the DGGS has no formal powers to restrict the use of this type of localized reactive pricing strategy by the incumbent firm. For example, the legislation only requires British Gas to avoid undue preference among customers with demands of less than 25,000 therms per annum, and the company is therefore free to charge radically different prices to its various large customers.

Looked at from the viewpoint of a potential entrant then, the prospects are not encouraging. The entrant faces a dominant incumbent firm which has an "artificial" cost advantage (deriving from existing long-term supply contracts), control of the distribution network, and virtually unlimited freedom in its pricing policy. Moreover, in the absence of an effective export option, any attempt at new entry risks offending the newcomer's only alternative customer: British Gas continues to enjoy monopsony power over UKCS supplies.

As a consequence of these various problems, our conclusion is that, even in the industrial and commercial markets, the prospects for increased competition in the supply of gas are bleak. The outcome is particularly unsatisfactory because there were a number of ways in which the legislation accompanying privatization could feasibly have been used to promote greater competition. For example, it could have provided for the following:

(i) a revision of gas purchase contracts to channel economic rents to the Government rather than to pass them on to customers in the form of lower (British Gas) prices;

(ii) the provision of separate accounts for the various parts of British Gas's gas supply business and for the company's transmission/distribution activities;

(iii) the allocation of stronger powers to the DGGS with respect to the prevention of predatory pricing and price discrimination in the contract market.

In the event, these opportunities were not exploited and, in opting for light regulation of British Gas, the Government has created a market structure that is inimical to the development of greater competition.

Regulation   Although the regulatory framework established for the gas industry has numerous weaknesses, the resulting structures are, fortunately, not permanently fixed. Regulatory policy can be expected to evolve over time and, as the Director General of Telecommunications (DGT) has shown, an active regulator can use the discretion afforded by the initial regime to remedy some of the legislative deficiencies. Nevertheless, any proclivities of the DGGS to foster competition and strengthen regulatory controls *will* be checked by the initial conditions: there is no equivalent to Mercury in the industry, entry based on the introduction of new technologies and products is much less likely than in telecommunications, and the formal powers of the DGGS are not great.

In the course of time, many of the features of the regulatory framework, including the pricing formula, will no doubt be reviewed by the MMC. In arriving at its judgments, the MMC is required to apply very widely drawn "public interest" criteria, and there is therefore substantial uncertainty attached to the recommendations that it might make. With respect to pricing, it is extremely likely that cost data, supplied by British Gas itself, will be one of the factors influencing future decisions, and the record of monopolies and mergers cases examined by the MMC suggests that the rate of return on capital will play a significant role. However, the precise weight that will be attached to the rate of return (as compared with other performance indicators) remains unclear.

To the extent that British Gas's average costs do have a positive influence on allowable prices in subsequent indexation periods, there will be some attenuation of incentives for cost reduction. As a review of the pricing formula becomes imminent the company might tend to hold back on cost-saving projects for fear that the consequence of cost reductions will be less favorable prices in the subsequent period. At this point, relatively long gaps between reviews can have negative consequences (see section 4.2.2): the gains from manipulating cost levels upwards in the period immediately preceding the review are greater the longer the duration for which the subsequent prices are expected to hold.

Expectations that the rate of return will be taken into account when fixing regulated prices also lead to incentives for cross-subsidization by British Gas. The company might be tempted to depress its overall rate of return by charging lower prices in the unregulated industrial and commercial markets in the hope of thereby being allowed higher prices in the regulated tariff market. By failing to require separate accounts for the regulated and unregulated parts of British Gas's business, the Authorisation serves to encourage this type of strategic behavior (because the behavior is more difficult to detect). Further, the strategy is made more attractive by both its deterrent effect on potential competitors and its contribution to the managerial goal of increasing the company's share of the total energy market.

Despite the fact that the rate of return on capital is likely to be an influential factor in the regulatory review, it would be wrong to conclude that overinvestment will inevitably be a major problem in the industry. The MMC's public interest guidelines are an open invitation to consider adjustments of prices towards shorter-run marginal costs. Hence, the management of British Gas will necessarily have to consider the possibility that, in the event of the emergence of excess capacity, it will not be able to recover the full economic costs of investment expenditures. In addition, as we have shown in section 4.2.3, if short-run marginal costs are an influential factor in regulatory decisions, British Gas may have incentives to limit its capital expenditures since, by so doing, it can exert an upward pressure on allowable prices. Finally, to the extent that the pricing formula gives the company incentives to overprice at demand peaks, this too will be a force pushing in the direction of underinvestment in the longer term (although it can be argued that, since under public ownership British Gas tended to overinvest and to underprice peak supplies, the shorter-term implications of these directional shifts may be by no means detrimental).

Whether or not underinvestment will eventually be a major problem depends to a large extent upon expectations about the role that will be accorded to the rate of return in the MMC's deliberations. The introduction of an explicit rate-of-return criterion into these deliberations would help mitigate some of the difficulties but would not, in itself, be a panacea; much depends upon the level at which the allowable rate of return is set. Suppose, for example, that a "fair" rate of return is defined that is only *slightly* above the cost of capital, that the firm will never be allowed prices that would lead to performance significantly exceeding this level, and that prices will be adjusted below the level implied by the "fair" rate in the event of excess capacity. The outcome is then likely to be underinvestment. In favorable states of the world (demand high in relation to capacity) the firm cannot earn more than the (relatively low) allowed rate of return, whereas in unfavorable states (demand low in relation to capacity) it can expect to earn significantly less. Hence there is an obvious bias in favor of limiting capacity in order to reduce the probability of unfavorable states. On the other hand, if a more generous rate of return was allowed, the incentives for "rate-base padding" (see section 4.2.1) would have a stronger positive effect on capital expenditures, which would more substantially offset the bias arising from demand uncertainty.

What these various arguments suggest is that, in its present form, the U.K. regulatory regime might well lead to significant suboptimalities in investment programs. Our own judgment is that, in the longer term, the problem is more likely to be underinvestment than overinvestment. In addition to the factors already mentioned, this view is based on three further considerations.

(i) The presence of substantial uncertainty as to the evolution of the future conduct of regulatory policy is itself a factor tending to raise the private cost of capital to a regulated firm above the corresponding social cost.

(ii) Although it is now probably fairly low, the nonzero probability of renationalization of the industry on terms unfavorable to shareholders (e.g. in the event of a return to political power by the Labour Party) serves to depress the anticipated return on new investment. Similarly, and perhaps of much greater importance, a future non-Conservative government might attach a lower weight to profitability criteria in regulatory decisions.

(iii) The monopoly position enjoyed by British Gas, coupled with high barriers to entry into the industry, imply that any tendency to underinvestment is unlikely to be checked by competitive threats from actual and potential competitors.

We conclude that the most fundamental weaknesses of U.K. regulatory policy are associated with an excessively short-term view of the underlying economic issues. The Government has been content to focus upon the initial post-privatization period, leaving many fundamental issues unresolved. The resulting absence of any clear durable bargain between Government and the regulated firm is to be regretted, as also is the failure to promote greater competition (the benefits of which would also have been of a longer-term nature). What has happened is that one of the major deficiencies of the U.K. control system for nationalized industries—preoccupation with short-term political issues (see chapter 5)—has been duplicated in the policy framework set for the regulated privately owned gas industry.

Recent developments   Given the short time that has elapsed since the privatization of British Gas, there is as yet little evidence concerning the actual impact of the new regime established in 1986. The first report of the DGGS was issued in February 1987 (Ofgas, 1987), but, as was only to be expected, it was largely devoted to a general review of issues and priorities. In the summer of 1987, however, a number of events occurred that, in different ways, touch upon problems that we have discussed in this section.

The first was a dispute between Mr James MacKinnon, the first DGGS, and British Gas concerning the DGGS's rights to acquire information relevant to the pricing formula. In June 1987 British Gas announced that it intended to cut average prices to domestic customers by 4.5 percent in the tariff period commencing 1 July. A major factor in this decision was the fall in gas purchase costs that had occurred as a result of the fall in world oil prices (see the figures in table 9.3), and, since this was relevant to the calculation of the maximum allowable price (via the gas cost component Y of the pricing formula), the DGGS asked British Gas to provide him with details of the terms of the various supply contracts. British Gas refused, reportedly on the grounds that the information was commercially sensitive, and stated that the DGGS was entitled only to a single figure: the company's own estimate of the average purchase price in the relevant tariff year. This position was maintained, despite an offer by Mr MacKinnon to examine the data on British Gas's own premises. The DGGS then threatened legal action and, subsequently, at its first annual shareholders' meeting, British Gas announced that it would, after all, be willing to provide Ofgas with the information requested.

What is remarkable about the dispute is that it should have arisen at all. If British Gas believed that it had a right to withhold relatively objective data pertaining to a major component of the pricing formula, the conflict signals how much more difficult it will be for the DGGS to obtain information that is more susceptible to manipulation and is not directly relevant to the determination of the maximum allowable average price. For example, the DGGS will need cost breakdowns to assess whether or not British Gas is unduly discriminating among tariff customers and to give rulings on terms and conditions for the conveyance of third-party gas through British Gas's pipelines, yet neither the 1986 Act nor the initial Authorisation explicitly requires the company to provide such information. In short, the dispute highlights the relatively weak position of the DGGS, and continuing difficulties with respect to the acquisition of information can be anticipated.

The second event of note was the proposed acquisition by British Gas of an approximately 33 percent stake in Bow Valley Industries, a Canadian oil and gas company, together with an option to increase its holding to up to 51 percent by the end of March 1990. The proposal, announced in early August 1987, did not involve any fundamental competition or regulatory policy issues, but Bow Valley does have a 14 percent stake in the UKCS Brae Field, which has total initial proven and probable reserves of 118 million barrels of oil and 275 billion cubic feet of gas. The chief executive of

British Gas declared at the time that the acquisition was the first of what might be many such transactions and indicated that oil and natural gas exploration and development would be an area of major importance for the company in the future.

The issue raised here is the extent to which British Gas will be allowed to expand by acquisition into upstream activities in the UKCS, reversing the process that occurred when the company's oil interests were transferred to Enterprise Oil prior to the flotation of the latter in 1983. Vertical expansion would strengthen British Gas's already formidable hand in its dealings with other UKCS producers, and any significant move in this direction would warrant investigation by the MMC. In addition to its effects on competition, there are also concerns about the implications of vertical integration for the incentives provided by the price control formula. Because gas purchase costs can be passed through into retail prices, British Gas might have weaker incentives than an independent producer to be cost efficient in its exploration and development activities. Moreover, since transactions between the production and distribution/sales parts of the company would not be at arm's length, there would be scope for manipulating transfer prices in negotiations with the Inland Revenue.

Finally, the summer of 1987 saw a major dispute between the Board of Directors of British Gas and some of the company's larger industrial customers. The latter were disgruntled both by what they saw as excessively high industrial gas prices—particularly in relation to the input prices obtained by their overseas competitors—and by the wide disparities in prices charged to different firms. Following complaints to the Office of Fair Trading and the European Commission in Brussels about British Gas's pricing policies in the contract market, a group of industrial customers nominated Sir Ian MacGregor, former chairman of both British Steel and British Coal, for a seat on the Board of Directors. The move was strongly opposed by Sir Denis Rooke, the Chairman of British Gas, who argued that it would be wrong for a director to be appointed to look after one section of customers. In the event, British Gas's shareholders supported the Chairman and Sir Ian was not elected to the Board.

Whatever the merits of the industrial customers' case with respect to the average level of gas prices, the incident serves to highlight the existence of significant pockets of market power in the contract market. The customers concerned felt that they could not easily switch either to other fuels such as electricity, coal, and oil, or to other suppliers of gas. Indeed, if these alternatives had been perceived to be available it would be difficult to explain why the complainants would have risked offending a major supplier by behaving as they did. Although there are good reasons, explained above, for doubting that industrial gas prices are in fact high in relation to the marginal opportunity cost of supply, the industrial customers do, nevertheless, have a point. The existing regulatory regime leaves British Gas with a free hand in the contract market and provides little assurance that third-party gas suppliers will be able to obtain access to the pipeline network on reasonable terms. In such circumstances, industrial users will rightly feel that they are subject to the discretionary behavior of British Gas and, whether or not the incumbent firm chooses to exercise its market power to raise prices significantly above costs, the outcome will be perceived to be unfair. Thus, irrespective of its likely effects on economic efficiency, stronger regulation, aimed at establishing and enforcing "fair rules of competition," would be a desirable development.

It is also noteworthy that, in pursuing their case, the industrial customers pressed their complaint with the Office of Fair Trading and the European Commission, and not with Ofgas. This was because the contract sector of the market is subject to general competition law. The DGGS has virtually no jurisdiction in the area and does not have the power to refer matters relating to gas supply to contract customers to the MMC. Given the interdependences between the contract and tariff sectors, the existence of significant market power in parts of the former, and the expertise that will gradually be acquired by Ofgas, we believe that this division of responsibilities is misguided and potentially damaging. Regulation would be more effective if the DGGS were granted wider powers to make references to the MMC and to modify those conditions of the Authorisation that are concerned with behavior in the contract market. Alternatively the existing division of responsibilities could be ended by placing all regulatory policy in the hands of the Office of Fair Trading.

9.3   The Electricity Supply Industry

The 1987 Conservative Election Manifesto contained a commitment to privatize the electricity supply industry (ESI) but did not provide any detailed information as to how and when this was to be done. Given the size of the industry and the complexity of the issues involved, it is likely that the preparatory stage of the policy process will be of longer duration than in most of the earlier privatizations and that the transfer of ownership will not occur until around the end of the decade. Because of the anticipated timetable, therefore, our analysis in this case will largely focus upon the broad structural issues raised by the prospective privatization of the industry, rather than upon the fine detail of the policies that might be implemented.

Our discussion comprises five sections. The history and structure of the industry in Britain—we omit discussion of Northern Ireland, where the picture is somewhat different—is briefly described in section 9.3.1. Existing regulatory structures and policies are examined in section 9.3.2, while section 9.3.3 is devoted to an analysis of problems surrounding policies to promote competition in the industry. We then turn, in section 9.3.4, to the central topic of the discussion: an analysis of the various structural options that are available to the Government. Finally, section 9.3.5 contains a summary assessment of the prospects for privatization.

9.3.1   History and Structure of the Industry in Britain

Like the gas industry, prior to nationalization electricity supply in Britain was divided amongst a large number of municipal undertakings and commercial companies, each of which was centered on a particular area of the country and, if privately owned, was extensively regulated. Private ownership was, however, much more common on the distribution side of the industry, public utilities having been dominant in electricity generation from a relatively early date, and regulatory activities were more centralized than in gas. Thus, for example, the Electricity (Supply) Act 1919 established the Electricity Commission to promote, regulate, and supervise the supply of electricity on a national scale, while the Electricity (Supply) Act 1926 set up the Central Electricity Board to construct and operate a national system of interconnected generating stations.

Although interwar legislation introduced a substantial measure of public ownership and control over the generation and supply of electricity in bulk, it had little impact on the distribution of electricity to final customers: in the mid-1940s there still existed about 560 separate suppliers, of which approximately one third were privately owned. Full nationalization only occurred in the wake of the Electricity Act 1947, which established the Central Electricity Authority (CEA) as a public corporation responsible for the generation and supply of bulk electricity and created fourteen Area Boards, each constituted as a separate public corporation responsible for the distribution of electricity in its own region.

Following the 1947 Act the organization of the industry became highly centralized: the CEA, for example, was entrusted with general control over the Area Boards with respect to policy and finance. It was not long, however, before moves were afoot to amend this structure. The Electricity Reorganisation (Scotland) Act 1954 reduced the number of Area Boards to twelve by setting up two independent Scottish Boards, each vertically integrated in the generation and distribution of electricity. A little later the Herbert Committee (1956), established to inquire into the working of the industry, criticized the organization of the industry on the grounds that (a) it was overcentralized and (b) it would be better to separate the executive and supervisory functions of the CEA. Partly as a result of the Herbert Committee's recommendations, the Government introduced legislation (the Electricity Act 1957) to restructure the industry, and it is this Act that has determined the principal organizational features of the industry for the subsequent 30 years.

In brief, the 1957 legislation implemented the Herbert Committee's recommendation that the functions of generating and supplying bulk electricity should be separated from the functions of coordinating and controlling the supply system as a whole. As a consequence the Central Electricity Generating Board (CEGB) was established to handle the former tasks. The Area Boards were also accorded greater autonomy, particularly with respect to financial matters. However, although the Herbert Committee had envisaged the continuation of the CEA as a regulatory watchdog body, none of whose members would be drawn from the Electricity Boards, the Government balked at this recommendation. The principal reason for this reluctance to adopt the Committee's position appears to have been an unwillingness to relinquish direct ministerial control over the industry: the CEA would have had substantial powers of supervision and decision, and ministerial influence would have been relatively indirect, operating via powers of appointment and the capacity to make parliamentary orders.

Hence, in place of the CEA, the Government opted for the establishment of the Electricity Council, which is a forum where the general policy of the ESI is discussed and which consists of a chairman, two deputy chairmen, the chairman and two other members of the CEGB, the chairmen of the twelve Area Boards, and up to three other members directly appointed by the Secretary of State. The Electricity Council is therefore a federal body, entrusted with consultative and deliberative functions rather than with powers of direction, control, or supervision.

The Electricity Act 1957 was concerned with reorganization of the industry in England and Wales only; Northern Ireland and Scotland continue to have their own independent boards. As already noted, in the Scottish case the two organizations—the South of Scotland Electricity Board and the North of Scotland Hydro-Electric Board—each have responsibility for both generation and distribution activities, although they jointly operate a power-pooling scheme for the use of generating capacity.

Consumers' interests in England and Wales are represented by 13 distinct organizations. The Electricity Consumers' Council, set up in 1977, operates at the national level while 12 Area Electricity Consultative Councils, one for each Area Board and established by the 1957 Act, are concerned with regional issues.

It can be seen therefore that, in England and Wales, the organization of the industry provides for vertical separation between the generation and transmission of bulk electricity (undertaken by the CEGB) and distribution and retailing activities (undertaken by the Area Boards, which are also responsible for contracting and appliance marketing operations). The CEGB is required by statute to meet directly the electricity requirements of British Rail and, with the authority of the Secretary of State for Energy, it provides direct supplies to a further small and restricted group of industrial customers. It also purchases bulk supplies of electricity from the South of Scotland Board and Electricité de France. These various transactions, however, account for only a small fraction of the CEGB's revenues and costs (although the possibility of increasing the capacity of cross-channel transmission links, to take advantage of excess generating capacity in France, offers prospects for significant future growth) and, for the most part, its activities can be viewed as the generation and supply of electricity to meet the requirements of the Area Boards. In turn, the Area Boards, while purchasing some electricity from private producers and being allowed in certain circumstances to generate their own power, obtain almost all of their supplies from the CEGB. In principle, therefore, the relationship between the CEGB and the Area Boards, considered as a group, is one of bilateral monopoly. In practice, however, the role and composition of the Electricity Council facilitates coordination between the two sides of the industry, with the CEGB in the dominant position, and in many respects the resulting behavior is little different from that to be expected from a single fully integrated public corporation.

The terms on which electricity is sold by the CEGB to the Area Boards are set out annually in the former's Bulk Supply Tariff (BST). Direct sales to customers by the CEGB have also generally been on terms linked to the BST charges. Although, viewed from the perspective of the ESI as a whole, the BST tariff rates are internal transfer prices, they are nevertheless the key pricing instruments of the industry. By and large the Area Boards structure their own retail tariffs around the BST rates, albeit with a good deal of simplification and averaging, since these rates are the principal determinants of the Area Boards' own cost structures.

To date, there has been little use of the publicly owned national and regional transmission/distribution grids by private producers of electricity. Much of the privately generated electricity emerges as a by-product of other production processes—for example, a firm might make use of steam from its manufacturing plant to drive a generator—and is consumed on site. Until recently entry into the market was restricted by statute: the Electric Lighting Act 1909 prohibited persons other than Electricity Boards from commencing to supply or distribute electricity as a main business, while the Electricity (Supply) Act 1919 restricted the establishment and extension of generating stations.

As part of its legislative program to promote liberalization in energy markets, however, the 1979–1983 Conservative Government sought, in the Energy Act 1983, to reduce the barriers to entry facing private producers of electricity. Among other things, the Energy Act repealed the aforementioned provisions of the 1909 and 1919 Acts and required the Area Boards to purchase electricity from persons other than the CEGB at rates to be set out in published tariffs, known as Private Purchase Tariffs (PPTs). In other words, the Act created a "put option" for private producers at the designated rates. In addition, the legislation required the CEGB and the Area Boards to make their transmission and distribution networks available to others on terms which were to be set out in published tariffs, and which were to be calculated so as to yield only a normal rate of return on the capital involved.

We will analyze the Energy Act in more detail in section 9.3.2 below, but it can be noted immediately that, as yet, the legislation appears to have had very little effect on the structure of the ESI. Private producers have not come forward in any numbers either to make use of the electricity grids to transport supplies directly to customers or to sell electricity to the Area Boards under the terms set out in the PPTs. Nor is there any sign that entry threats have substantially intensified. As a consequence, the generation and distribution of electricity in Britain has continued to be dominated by a group of public corporations that faces very little competition from either established or potential rivals.

9.3.2   Regulation of the Electricity Supply Industry

The ESI currently operates within the policy framework laid down by the 1978 White Paper on nationalized industries (see section 5.4). Thus, for example, the Government has set out the following targets for the industry as a whole:

(i) a financial target, defined in terms of operating profit as a percentage return on average capital employed, calculated according to current cost accounting conventions, and equal to 2.75 percent for the three years from 1985–1986;

(ii) an annual external financing limit, which in 1986–1987 called for a repayment of loans totalling £1.416 billion;

(iii) a required pretax real rate of return of 5 percent on new investment as a whole;

(iv) performance objectives, of which the most important has taken the form of a target reduction in real controllable unit costs of 6.1 percent over the period from 1983–1984 to 1987–1988.

Subject to these various constraints, and in line with the provisions of the 1967 and 1978 White Papers, the ESI's public corporations have attempted to construct tariff structures that broadly reflect long-run marginal costs. Thus, the 1987–1988 BST contained two fixed charges, two capacity charges (reflecting marginal capital costs), and no less than 36 unit rates (reflecting marginal operating costs) that differentiate between time of day, day of the week, and season of the year. While there have been a number of criticisms of the detailed implementation of marginal cost pricing policies (see Slater and Yarrow, 1983), it is fair to say that the ESI has made a more serious attempt than most of the other nationalized industries to meet this aspect of public policy objectives. However, one major policy failure is worth explicit mention: successive Governments have used their influence over the terms of the CEGB's purchase contracts with British Coal to shield the domestic coal industry from international competition. The contracts between the two public corporations have forced the CEGB to purchase its principal input, accounting for around 40 percent of its total costs, at rates that are typically well in excess of international market levels and have limited the extent to which it can make use of imported coal. The extent of the subsidy can be gauged from table 9.5, which shows estimates of the premiums over the Rotterdam spot market price that were paid by the CEGB between 1979 and 1983. The consequences of this policy are that accounting costs in the ESI have been inflated above opportunity cost levels and, since it is the former that influence the level and structure of electricity prices, incorrect cost signals have therefore been passed forward to electricity consumers.

Perhaps the most interesting aspect of the financial regime imposed on the ESI in recent years is the similarity of many of its features to those embodied in the regulatory framework adopted for the privatized gas industry. As argued in section 5.4, the 1978 White Paper shifted the

Table 9.5 Estimates of the percentage premium paid for coal by the CEGB

Year	1979	1980	1981	1982	1983
Premium (percent)	14.3	36.4	8.1	16.3	35.4

Source: Molyneux and Thompson (1987).

emphasis of policy objectives from pricing and investment guidelines derived from first-best welfare principles to increased profitability and cash flow. Thus, between financial years 1980–1981 and 1986–1987 the financial target was increased from 1.7 to 2.75 percent and the external financing limit was reduced from $+£187$ million to $-£1,416$ million. The resulting impact on the industry has been akin to the type of change that could have been expected in the event of privatization: management has been confronted with greater pressures to improve financial performance.

Similarly, the performance target covering reductions in real controllable unit costs is analogous to the X factor in the gas pricing formula. For the ESI, the major cost component that is classed as noncontrollable is its expenditure on coal inputs. Hence, if the ESI were set a pricing formula of the $RPI - X + Y$ form, where Y was linked to the average purchase price of coal, the outcome would not be dissimilar to that implied by an appropriate combination of the financial and cost-reduction targets. Unless accompanied by regulation of the rate structure, however, such a pricing formula approach would represent a step backward with respect to the incentives for temporal price differentiation (for the reasons outlined in section 9.2.4).

Against the view that the current regulatory structure for the publicly owned ESI is similar to that adopted for the privately owned gas industry, it might be argued that, under public ownership, the financial pressures on management are less severe than those that would be demanded by the capital market. For example, both the financial target (2.75 percent) and the required rate of return on investment (5 percent) appear low in comparison with comparable private sector rates of return. The situation is, however, less clear cut than it might appear at first sight. In the first place, as a result of excess capacity in the industry as a whole and of an inefficient plant mix (partly the consequence of unanticipated movements in fossil fuel prices in the 1970s), the book value of assets at replacement costs is almost certainly much greater than the underlying economic worth of the assets. Second, despite the rate-of-return criterion, investment programs are in practice largely constrained by the need to agree external financing limits with the Government, and, given the pursuit of tight fiscal policies, it is likely that the "implicit" required rate of return for the public sector has been in excess of 5 percent over the last few years. In any event, because of the existence of excess capacity the number of new investment projects initiated by the industry has been relatively limited during this period, and capital expenditures have been little affected by the choice of target value. With growing demand, however, investment decisions are again becoming more important, and we will discuss the implications of privatization for the industry's cost of capital in section 9.3.4.

In reality, with the exception of the period covering the 1984–1985 coal miners' strike, the cash flows generated by the ESI over the past five years have been substantial. For purposes of comparison it can be noted that in 1979–1980 it was estimated that a CCA rate of return of around 1.25 percent was equivalent to an HCA return on average net assets of 9.8 percent (Monopolies and Mergers Commission, 1981a, para. 3.8), and that in 1985–1986 operating profits plus depreciation amounted to £2.749 billion, equal to about 25 percent of turnover, while the Government benefited to the tune of over £1.9 billion in the form of interest payments on debt, corporation tax, and the external financing limit. To produce these cash flows the Government, via its control of the financial constraints, has forced prices above short-run marginal costs.

If, therefore, the industry is to be privatized, there does not appear to be a strong case for an initial hike in prices on allocative efficiency grounds, despite the apparently low level of the current financial target. Nevertheless, in November 1987 the Government announced that it would again be increasing the financial target for the ESI in England and Wales to 3.75 percent in 1988–1989 and 4.75 percent in 1989–1990, the net effect of which is likely to be an increase in real electricity prices of around 8 percent over the two years. The reason given for the increase was that prices would have to be raised to attract adequate finance for the major power station construction program that is anticipated in the 1990s. However, if this argument is taken at face value, it implies a remarkably pessimistic view of the cost reductions that are likely to be be attained by a privatized industry, particularly since it is known that coal input costs are of the order of £750 million above the level that could be achieved if the domestic coal market was liberalized (see section 9.5). Moreover, it is by no means clear why consumers should be asked to pay in 1988 for an investment program that will not be in place for several more years—unless, that is, the policy decision also reflects an appreciation of the potential underinvestment problems that are associated with privatization (see section 4.2.3). The most cynical view of the policy announcement is, of course, that it simply reflects an attempt to increase the sales proceeds that will be realized when the public corporations come to be transferred to the private sector.

However, whatever the motives for the decision, it is safe to conclude that it does not show privatization in a particularly favorable light.

Had the recommendations of the Herbert Committee concerning the role of the CEA been adopted in the 1950s, the similarity between the regulatory regimes of the publicly owned ESI and the privately owned gas industry would have been even greater: the CEA would have functioned as an independent supervisory agency acting at arm's length from Government departments and from the regulated firms, in very much the way that Ofgas and Oftel operate currently. Ironically, therefore, the regulatory model adopted for gas and telecommunications in the mid-1980s is similar to one that was rejected for the ESI by a Conservative Government in the mid-1950s.

As the trend in cash flows to the Exchequer shows, the tightening of financial constraints on the ESI since 1979 has certainly had the desired effect of improving financial performance. On the other hand, the implications for allocative and cost efficiency are less clear. Excess capacity in the industry, overpriced coal inputs, and gas pricing policy all point to the conclusion that the level of electricity prices has been suboptimally high when judged against allocative efficiency criteria. With respect to internal efficiency, although (real) unit controllable costs have recently been reduced by 4.6 percent between 1983–1984 and 1986–1987, the record of productivity performance has not been impressive. Between 1978 and 1985 total factor productivity increased by an average of 1.4 percent per annum, little different from the rate achieved between 1960 and 1978 which itself was slightly below the manufacturing average over this earlier period. Given the strong productivity gains in U.K. manufacturing during the 1980s, recent improvements in the ESI therefore appear to have lagged behind those in other major industrial sectors of the economy. Thus the substantial improvement in financial performance does not appear to have been matched by corresponding gains in internal efficiency, an outcome consistent with the argument developed in sections 5.5 and 5.7 that public corporations with market power have been allowed to meet tighter financial targets by raising prices rather than by reducing costs.

It is with respect to this last point that significant differences between the regulatory frameworks for the publicly owned ESI and the privately owned gas industry *do* emerge. Unlike the electricity corporations, British Gas is unable to raise its prices to tariff customers above the levels specified in the price control formula (i.e. the price level, rather than the rate of return or the EFL, is the policy instrument), and, coupled with pressures emanating from the capital market to increase profits, this may produce greater short-run incentives to reduce unit costs. It should be noted, however, that, despite weaknesses in the framework of control for the nationalized industries, it is by no means clear that the operational efficiency of the ESI—the dimension of performance most likely to be improved by regulation of the RPI − X type—can be classed as poor. In its 1981 investigation of the CEGB, for example, the MMC (Monopolies and Mergers Commission, 1981a) concluded that "we are satisfied that the Board has an effective operational planning system and that the out-turns are adequately monitored," while Pryke (1987) points out that "the thermal efficiency of its [the CEGB's] fossil-fuel stations compares favourably with that of other countries, and the availability of its big generating units, which used to be so poor, is now relatively high by international standards." (See Henney (1987) for a dissenting note, however.)

The dimension of internal efficiency in which the performance of the ESI has more clearly been deficient is investment costs. Thus both time and cost overruns in the construction of new power stations in general, and of nuclear plants in particular, have frequently been substantial, and the MMC report noted that "the weaknesses and failings on power station construction sites discussed in earlier reports still exist." Because of the long periods associated with the planning and construction of new capacity, it is too early to assess whether or not the changes brought about by tighter financial constraints have yet had, or are likely to have, a material effect on investment costs. What can be said, however, is that, with respect to new investment, moving to a system of price regulation of the type now used in the telecommunications and gas industries might easily create at least as many problems as it would solve (see sections 4.2 and 9.3.4).

9.3.3 Competition

Between 1947 and the early 1980s successive Governments showed little or no interest in policies designed to increase competition in the ESI. In part, this can be explained by the natural monopoly characteristics of electricity transmission and distribution and by the difficulties of promoting competition among independent generating companies that are connected to a single supply network. Since public policy has more recently shifted to a (nominally) pro-competitive stance in its approach to electricity generation, it will be useful to say a few words about the latter difficulties before going on to evaluate the impact of liberalization on the industry.

There is little doubt that the establishment of a regional or national power network can potentially be of great benefit to consumers of electricity. To be included among the gains are the following effects (see Joskow and Schmalensee, 1983):

(i) the realization of plant-level scale economies through the consolidation of geographically dispersed loads;

(ii) increased reliability of supply via the consolidation of uncertain loads and uncertain plant performance characteristics;

(iii) efficient production, achieved by coordinating the operations of plants with differing marginal costs of supply;

(iv) lower total capacity requirements resulting from the aggregation of demands with differing load characteristics;

(v) economies from the coordination of maintenance schedules;

(vi) economies in responding to emergencies such as plant and transmission failures.

However, the existence of an integrated power system poses certain problems for the development of competition in electricity generation. To prevent system failures, electrical equilibrium must be maintained at all points in the network: the power "demanded" at each point must be equal to the power "supplied." It follows from this that, unlike most markets, a company generating electricity at a particular point in the network *cannot* direct its output to a designated point of demand. Hence, the performances of the various generating sets attached to the system are, in a very direct and obvious way, interdependent.

In practice, it has proved difficult to handle these network interdependences in an efficient manner through the use of a fully decentralized set of contractual relationships. Large networks, whether they be comprised of publicly owned or privately owned firms, therefore typically make use of some centralized "planning" authority that makes allocative decisions (e.g. which power stations are to generate electricity at a particular moment) on a command or fiat basis. However, the establishment of central coordination (to overcome the externalities associated with full decentralization) is in conflict with the goal of promoting greater competition through the encouragement of more individualistic decision making. In other words, the technology of electricity supply creates a policy dilemma—the benefits of coordination among firms have to be balanced against the benefits of competition—and the question of how this trade-off should be resolved is one of the most important issues in electricity economics.

To date the role of competition in the British ESI has been extremely limited. Until 1983 the CEGB was protected from competition by statutory barriers to entry, but the most significant of these were removed by the Energy Act which sought to introduce competitive pressures into the industry whilst preserving the CEGB's centralized control of the network through its ownership of the national transmission grid. With respect to purchases of power from private producers by the industry's Area boards the relevant clause of the Energy Act states that

"The principles on which tariffs are fixed and prices proposed by an Electricity Board ... shall include the principle that a purchase by the Board ... should be on terms which
a) will not increase the prices payable by customers of the Board for electricity supplied to them by the Board, and
b) will reflect the costs that would have been incurred by the Board but for the purchase."

With respect to the use of publicly owned transmission and distribution facilities by private suppliers, the relevant clause states that

"The principles on which tariffs are fixed and prices proposed by an Electricity Board ... shall include the principle that charges should be no more than sufficient to provide a return on the relevant assets comparable to any return that the Board expects to receive on comparable assets."

The first of these two clauses relates only to purchases of electricity by Area Boards. Thus, in effect, the Act stipulates that the PPTs (setting out the terms on which Area Boards are willing to purchase electricity from private producers) should reflect the avoidable costs of the *Area Boards*, and not the avoidable costs of the CEGB. Since the purchase costs of the Area Boards are largely governed by the rates of the BST, we should therefore expect to see prices offered to private producers that are closely in line with BST rates.

The CEGB's response to the Energy Act was to restructure the BST in a way that compelled the Area Boards to offer less favorable terms to private producers than to the CEGB. In 1984–1985, the first tariff year after the introduction of the Act, a new system service charge was introduced into the BST which incorporated cost elements that had previously been treated as capacity related and hence had been considered to be components of long-run marginal cost. The charge was allocated among Area Boards on the basis of each Board's maximum demand in the tariff year 1982–1983. Since this procedure was retained in subsequent tariff years, it implied that any changes in maximum demands in the years subsequent to 1982–1983 had no effect on the allocation of the system service charge. Hence, as far as an individual Area Board was concerned, the system service charge became an unavoidable cost from 1984–1985 onward and, as such, was to be excluded when constructing its PPT. The result is that, unless an Area Board completely disconnects itself from the CEGB, the per unit charge paid to the CEGB is significantly in excess of that paid to a private producer for supplies with similar load characteristics.

Under the most favorable of the PPTs that are available to a private producer, an approximate estimate of the disparity between average PPT prices and average BST prices is given by the percentage of the CEGB's revenues from Area Boards which is accounted for by the system service charge. The resulting estimates are shown in table 9.6. The figure for 1983–1984 shows the corresponding figure for the old service charge component of the BST in the last tariff year *not* covered by the Energy Act, and the table reveals the sharp upward movement in the relative importance of fixed (i.e. unavoidable) charges in 1984–1985, followed by further upward shifts in the subsequent years. Thus, by 1986–1987 private producers were being offered terms that, at best, were nearly 10 percent less favorable than those demanded by the CEGB.

In 1987–1988 the CEGB took an additional substantial step in the same direction by introducing a "nonmarginal" energy charge, nominally aimed at recovering that fraction of its coal costs that could be attributed to the protection of the domestic coal industry. This substantially raised the fixed cost component of Area Board payments to the CEGB and, although the Government prevented Area Boards from reducing their PPT rates by a corresponding amount, the prices available to the CEGB's potential rivals fell by approximately 5 percent and the gap between average BST and average PPT rates increased further.

In defense of its tariff manipulations, the CEGB can claim that the Energy Act was incorrectly formulated, in that economic efficiency requires that private producers be offered terms based on its *own* short-run marginal costs since, for example, to offer more when the industry already has excess capacity would simply stimulate the construction of additional

Table 9.6 The CEGB's system service charge revenues as a percentage of all revenues from Area Boards

Year	1983–1984	1984–1985	1985–1986	1986–1987
Percentage	1.0	7.8	8.7	9.5

Source: *CEGB Annual Report and Accounts* (1984, 1985, 1986, 1987).

surplus plant. This reasoning has some merit, although the supply/demand balance in the South of England indicates that incremental generating capacity or transmission capacity (to transport electricity from the surplus areas of the North and Midlands) will be required in the near future. Nevertheless, the ease with which the CEGB has been able to achieve its purpose (i.e. deterrence of new entrants) vividly illustrates the market power of a lightly regulated dominant firm.

Substantial difficulties also confront a potential entrant who wishes to make use of the publicly owned electricity grids to supply consumers directly. As in the gas industry, the charges for the "transportation" of electricity and for connection to the grid are set by the corporations themselves (rather than by regulators), the incumbent firms have sufficient flexibility in pricing policy to respond to entry threats by selective price discounting, and entrants are at a comparative disadvantage with respect to the security of supply they can offer to any given customer.

Thus, faced with a situation in which the incumbent firm can effectively determine the terms available from the major distributors of electricity and/or can offer selective discounts without triggering regulatory interventions, our conclusion is that, notwithstanding the intentions of the Energy Act, private producers of electricity continue to face substantial barriers to entry into the industry. Significant levels of new entry, based upon either the generation of electricity as a main business or the development of combined heat and power schemes, have not yet been observed in Britain. Nor can they be expected in the future in the absence of additional pro-competitive policy measures to ensure that new entrants can gain access to the the markets for their outputs on fair terms. Thus far, policies to liberalize the market have been limited in scope and have had little practical effect.

9.3.4   Prospects for Privatization
In its post-election evaluations of policy options for the ESI, the most important initial questions to be settled by the Government concern the organizational structures to be adopted for the privately owned companies. British Telecom (BT) and British Gas were sold as single units, but there is little prospect that the same model will be followed for electricity supply, if only because there is already some vertical separation between generation and distribution in England and Wales (but not in Scotland). Hence, in electricity, the pressures towards "structural conservatism" point in the same direction as the economic arguments concerning competition and regulation: away from a solution based

upon the creation of a single fully vertically integrated electric utility company.

Given this point, we will proceed by assuming initially that, in the course of privatization, the current division between the distribution and generation of electricity in England and Wales is retained. This leads to separate discussions of policies towards the Area Boards and the CEGB. In both cases, however, options involving some *horizontal* restructuring of the existing public corporations will be examined. Next, we will consider the potential merits of vertical integration at either the national or regional level and, since it plays such an important role in the economics of the industry, we will pay particular attention to the future of the national transmission system. Finally, we will examine the rather different position of the industry in Scotland, before setting out a brief assessment of the main policy options.

Privatization of the Area Boards   Since cost conditions in electricity distribution effectively rule out the possibility that incumbent firms can stringently be constrained by the development of actual or potential competition, privatization will entail the replacement of existing public monopolies with regulated private monopolies. In these circumstances the principal potential benefits of privatization are twofold:

(i) it might help to promote increased competition in electricity *generation* by introducing profit incentives for the distribution companies to shop around for low cost supplies;

(ii) it might introduce greater incentives for the reduction of distribution costs.

With respect to (i), as we pointed out earlier, institutional arrangements in the publicly owned ESI have created close relationships between Area Boards and the CEGB in which the former have played a relatively subservient role. For example, Area Boards have not challenged the manipulations of the BST that have been designed to deter new entry into generation. In contrast, there would have been fewer incentives for privately owned profit-seeking distribution companies to have been quite so cooperative with the CEGB on this matter, since the effect of entry deterrence is likely to be higher wholesale electricity prices in the longer run. Thus privatization of the Area Boards can be expected to lead to reduced barriers to entry into electricity generation.

It should be noted, however, that the underlying problem—an excessive degree of vertical integration, leading to reduced competition in generation—has little to do with ownership *per se*. Abolition of the Electricity Council and its replacement with a regulatory body independent of the public corporations (along the lines of the Herbert Committee recommendations) would have been one alternative way forward. Moreover, a dominant electricity generating company would, if unregulated or only lightly regulated, continue to possess substantial market power in its dealings with both distribution companies and actual or potential competitors. Hence, although it may be a step in the right direction, privatization of the Area Boards is neither a necessary nor a sufficient condition for *significantly* enhanced competition in electricity generation.

Similar remarks apply with regard to the introduction of incentives for reductions in distribution costs. In section 2.4 it was shown that an unregulated private monopoly will not necessarily be more cost efficient than a public corporation, and in chapter 4 we noted how regulation itself may introduce distortions in a private firm's choice of inputs, leading to costs that are higher than minimum feasible levels. The lesson to be drawn from the earlier analysis is therefore that the conduct of regulatory policy will have a crucial bearing upon the cost performance of the industry, a message that is reinforced by evidence from the U.S. experience. How then will privatized distribution companies be regulated?

The evolution of U.K. policy to date indicates the establishment of a regulatory authority to monitor an initial pricing formula (for domestic sales at least) of the $RPI - X + Y$ form. Here X would be a number based upon an estimate of the opportunities available to the companies for reductions in real controllable costs and Y would be linked to some index of the unit cost of bought-in supplies of wholesale electricity. The Y factor introduces an immediate conflict between the desire to allow changes in wholesale electricity prices to be passed on to final customers and the desire to establish strong incentives for distribution companies to seek out and promote cheaper supplies of wholesale electricity. *Partial* indexation of retail to wholesale prices is one possible way of coping with the problem, or, if privatization is accompanied by price controls on wholesale prices, Y might be set equal to changes in the maximum allowable average price (rather than the *actual* prices paid by Area Boards, which could be lower). However, the introduction of yardstick regulation (see below) is potentially the most effective way of improving this and other, more important, trade-offs.

As we showed in section 4.4, the use of a single pricing constraint can be reconciled with satisfactory incentives toward the adoption by firms of efficient tariff structures provided that the weights used in the construction of the regulated price index are set appropriately. Although extensive and detailed demand and cost information would be required to compute the optimal weighting pattern for the index, it should be possible to arrive at some approximation to this pattern on the basis of existing Area Board data.

With respect to price regulation, in our view the most important single issue to be settled concerns the nature of the process that will be used to review and amend the pricing formulas set for the privatized electricity distribution companies. If, as we anticipate, the telecommunications and gas precedents are followed, it will be the MMC that periodically conducts the regulatory reviews. However, the MMC's rather general public interest guidelines, together with the absence of credible long-term guarantees to investors, are potential sources of uncertainty and may lead to a bias towards underinvestment in privately owned utilities. Hence, we favor a more explicit approach to the framing of longer-term policy that, in relation to adjustments of the price control formula, would attach significant weight to the criterion of a "fair" rate of return on capital. In electricity distribution the existence of a number of similar utilities implies that rate-of-return regulation can be combined with the provision of reasonably strong incentives for cost reduction, and that it need not lead to a substantial bias towards overcapitalization. This is possible because of the absence of an "information monopoly" that would block the application of regulatory yardsticks.

To illustrate, consider an explicit regulatory bargain in which the totality of investors in privatized distribution companies is guaranteed a fair rate of return on capital, but in which the prospective allocation of returns among the different firms is made dependent upon their relative performance. In the initial indexation period each company is set a pricing constraint that, on best available information, will allow it to earn the fair rate of return. Because of differences in internal efficiency and of unanticipated demand and cost movements, however, it is to be expected that at the end of the period some companies will have performed better than others. If, by the time of the first regulatory review, a given company had achieved a higher rate of return than the average for the industry as a whole (by, for example, obtaining lower wholesale prices or reducing distribution costs), it would be allowed to set prices in the subsequent period at a level calculated to permit it to retain some, but not all, of its relative financial advantage. At the same time the set of allowable prices for the 12 companies as a whole would be fixed so as to yield no more than a fair rate of return on the total capital employed in electricity generation. Put simply, the *relative* prices of the distribution companies would be determined by past relative performance, while the *average* level of retail electricity prices across the country would be determined by the criterion of a fair rate of return (see section 11.3.5 for a fuller account of this procedure).

This system of regulation for retail electricity prices has the following advantages.

(i) The incentives for strategic overinvestment are relatively slight since each company is able to capture only a fraction of the profit gains that such behavior would produce for the industry as a whole.

(ii) Since the benefits of better than average performance with respect to cost reduction would persist over several review periods it is possible, depending upon the (policy-determined) speed at which rates of return are equalized, to induce quite strong incentives for improvements in internal efficiency.

(iii) By opting for relatively short indexation periods, it is possible to ensure that average prices across the country closely track average costs whilst preserving the aforementioned cost-reduction incentives.

(iv) *Either* retail electricity prices can be indexed to movements in *average* wholesale prices across the country, rather than to the input prices of a single distribution company, thus preserving shorter-term incentives to acquire cheaper supplies, *or*, if the period between price reviews is reasonably short, such indexation can be abandoned entirely without significant loss.

The incentives provided by yardstick regulation can, of course, be eroded by collusion amongst distribution companies with respect to cost-reduction and investment programs. Similarly, the benefits would be lost if, prior to privatization, the Area Boards were amalgamated into a single national distribution company. Here we face a classic trade-off between the number of firms in the industry and the realization of potential scale economies (see section 3.2.1). Larger numbers tend to impede collusion and, in this case, facilitate the development of competition in cost-reduction activities by enabling regulators to devise more effective incentive structures (because the supply of information is less monopolized). Although, in the course of the privatization debate, it has been suggested that there might be scale economy benefits from the creation either of a single distribution company or of a smaller number of Area Boards than currently exists, little or no evidence has been put forward in support of this position. In view of the clear detriments of horizontal integration, therefore, and assuming that privatization of electricity distribution is to proceed, we would favor the preservation of current organizational structures.

Moreover, again assuming that a substantial transfer of ownership is to take place, we believe that there is a case to be made for the retention (at least initially) of some of the Area Boards in the public sector. The major benefits of the yardstick approach derive from innovations in regulatory policy and are not an automatic consequence of the transfer of ownership. Coupled with the introduction of performance-related pay for managers, the approach could equally well be applied to publicly owned corporations. Indeed, a mixture of publicly and privately owned distribution companies would create a greater diversity of interests and incentive structures in the industry that might serve to hinder the development of collusive arrangements (cf. arguments surrounding the role of the British National Oil Corporation developed in section 9.4.4 below).

In addition to the scale economies point, a second argument that has been put forward in favor of greater horizontal concentration in electricity distribution is that larger companies are required to offset the market power of the CEGB (the countervailing-power argument). Again we have little sympathy with this view. Given the opportunities afforded by privatization to reform the regulatory and competitive structures of the ESI, the better way of proceeding is to tackle the problem of monopoly power in generation through measures to increase competition in the upstream part of the industry and/or enhance the effectiveness of regulatory policy, and it is to these issues that we now turn.

Privatization of Electricity Generation   At the moment, the CEGB is responsible for both the generation *and* transmission of bulk electricity in England and Wales. Thus, in addition to its generating assets, the CEGB owns and operates the national high voltage transmission system known as the national grid, and it is this latter aspect of its business that can safely be classified as a natural monopoly activity. However, it is extremely unlikely that, considered as a *separate* operation, electricity generation also constitutes a natural monopoly; in many countries the production of electricity is undertaken by a relatively large number of different companies, and international evidence does not indicate the existence of any clear cost-efficiency benefits associated with single-firm production. Hence restructuring of this side of the U.K. industry prior to, or in the course of, privatization is an option that merits serious consideration, and we will examine ownership transfer based on three alternative forms of organization: A, continuation of the CEGB in its present form (i.e. sale of the CEGB's power stations in a single block); B, the creation of regional generating companies; C, the creation of two or more nonregional generating companies from the CEGB's existing assets.

For each alternative, there is also the question of what to do with the national grid. Since the respective merits of the options are contingent upon decisions about the future of the transmission system, we will offer some preliminary remarks on this issue in the evaluation of each alternative.

Option A   A single sale of the CEGB's full portfolio of assets (generating sets plus transmission links) would not require restructuring of the upstream parts of the industry, and is the option that would permit the most rapid transfer of assets to the private sector. Unsurprisingly, the management of the public corporation has expressed a strong preference for this approach, suggesting that the arguments against restructuring that were successfully deployed in the case of gas privatization are also directly relevant to electricity. The economic case is largely based upon claims that internal efficiency would be damaged if smaller-scale generating companies were established. Thus, for example, it might be argued that there are economies of scale in day-to-day operations arising from the the centralized despatch of power stations according to their respective marginal operating costs and in longer-term investment planning arising from the coordination of plant construction programs.

However, while arguments for the existence of significant economies of coordination are generally sound, the attainment of such benefits does not *necessarily* require the creation or retention of a single company responsible for *all* electricity generation and transmission activities. As experience in the U.S. and elsewhere shows, coordination can be achieved by cooperation amongst a number of separate companies (e.g. centralized despatch of generating stations via power-pooling arrangements). Although, as argued earlier, such cooperation might tend to impede the development of effective competition, the trade-off with competition could be improved by entrusting coordination functions to a separate transmission company, since it is in the organization of energy flows through the grid network that many of the benefits of scale reside.

In defense of the proposition that single-firm production is, nevertheless, the superior option, France is often quoted as an example of a country where substantial scale economies have been reaped as a consequence of this form of industrial organization. Electricité de France has focused heavily upon nuclear plant, basing capacity expansion around pressurized water reactors (PWRs). By relying upon a single type of reactor, the publicly owned industry has been able to obtain low unit costs from "learning" effects in plant design, construction, and operation (economies of replication), and from the construction and operation of several large reactors on a single site (economies of colocation). Moreover, it can be argued that such benefits would have been substantially reduced if the structure of the French industry had been less concentrated because, for example, many of the "learning" advantages are internal to the firm concerned and cannot easily be transferred to other organizations.

For a number of reasons, however, these scale economy arguments in favor of single-firm production are not entirely convincing. First, it is one thing to demonstrate the existence of *potential* benefits of large size but quite another to show that a highly concentrated industrial structure will necessarily provide sufficient incentives for their *realization*. Thus, for example, the CEGB's own performance record counts against the point that lower construction costs follow fairly automatically from larger scale (see section 9.3.2).

Second, even accepting the existence of economies of replication and colocation, there is little evidence to suggest that the minimum efficient scale for an electricity generation company is of the order of 50 GW or more (the net capability of the CEGB was 52.4 GW in early 1987). The smaller Belgian industry has pursued a strategy similar to that of the French, with not dissimilar results, and American studies have tended to place minimum efficient scale (whether at the firm or system level) at a much lower level of capacity than 50 GW (see Joskow and Schmalensee, 1983). The continued existence of successful smaller companies in countries with more fragmented wholesale electricity markets also provides corroborative evidence for this view.

Finally, economies from learning or experience are much more significant for nuclear technologies than for other methods of generating electricity: older well-established fossil fuel technologies do not exhibit these effects to anything like the same extent. It is therefore impossible to divorce evaluation of the likely effects of privatization from views about the prospects for nuclear generation in Britain. Currently, the CEGB hopes to obtain permission to build a series of PWRs, but its investment appraisals are based upon the 5 percent required rate-of-return criterion laid down in the 1978 White Paper. One effect of privatization would be to increase significantly the discount rate applied to investment projects, perhaps to something of the order of 10 percent real or more. At these higher rates of discount the economic case for nuclear power is far from clear (see Yarrow, 1988), and should future plant construction be based upon fossil fuel technologies the learning-effects argument would lose most of its force.

Much depends, therefore, upon whether a large-scale nuclear program in Britain is considered desirable. The Government is firmly committed to an expansion of nuclear capacity and, if this position is taken as given, it strengthens the case against a comprehensive break-up of the CEGB. Nevertheless, a pro-nuclear policy stance does not in itself establish a decisive case for the retention of a single generating company. Rather, it points only towards the development of organizations that would be larger than those appropriate to fossil fuel technologies, and there is always the option of creating a company or public corporation responsible exclusively for nuclear generation in England and Wales (which accounted for around 20 percent of total supply in the mid-1980s), leaving smaller competitors to operate with the alternative technologies. Moreover, since a single privately owned generating company would have considerable market power, it would be necessary to regulate the monopolist's wholesale electricity prices, leading to potential suboptimalities in investment expenditures of the type analyzed in section 4.2.3. The investment problem is likely to be serious for electricity generation in general, and for nuclear generation in particular, because of the high capital intensity of the industry, the long gestation lags in the construction of plant, and the durability of physical assets. Thus, for example, to the extent that a regulated private monopolist would face uncertainty about the future course of regulatory policy, would be concerned that *ex post* welfare-maximizing regulators might not allow full recovery of sunk capital costs, and would be tempted to hold back investment programs so as to be in a better position to bargain with regulators (e.g. so as to argue that the necessary investment could not be financed without higher prices), there could be a tendency towards underinvestment coupled with a bias against more capital-intensive nuclear plant.

This concern about possible suboptimalities in investment programs—which is a concern associated with *all* systems of price regulation—is reinforced in this case by analysis of the incentives for a private monopolist to engage in strategic behavior aimed at influencing regulatory decisions. With only one firm in the market, when making its decisions the regulatory body must necessarily rely upon cost information from the monopolist, which information can be manipulated by the latter to its own advantage. The result is that the agency relationship between regulators and the monopolist involves a relatively unfavorable trade-off between cost efficiency and allocative efficiency, and this is one of the major deficiencies of the single-firm solution to the structural problem.

An associated weakness of the option under consideration is that it also enhances the ability of the incumbent firm to engage in anticompetitive behavior aimed at influencing the decisions of rivals. In particular, it tends to facilitate strategic moves to block or impede the entry of competing electricity generation companies. In our own view, it is upon this question of entry conditions that the relative merits of option A ultimately rest. In principle, regulatory policies could be introduced to limit this aspect of the market power of a dominant incumbent firm and, if successful, they would strengthen competitive pressures with respect to the construction of new capacity, which is precisely the area in which greater competition would be most beneficial. Moreover, entry threats would weaken incentives towards underinvestment in the industry and, over time, new entrants would provide valuable information to regulators. Thus, if potential competition can be increased, many of the disadvantages of the option under discussion will be reduced in significance.

We have already argued that the 1983 Energy Act had little impact on entry conditions because of the CEGB's ability to manipulate tariffs to the disadvantage of its potential rivals. In the United States, however, the Public Utilities Regulatory Policies Act (PURPA) has led in many States to substantial new entry into the industry. Indeed, if anything, the rate of new entry has tended to be excessive. The differences in results between the two countries are chiefly attributable to the fact that the terms and conditions of supply contracts are much more closely regulated in America. We conclude, therefore, that, if the CEGB's power stations are sold in a single block, it will still be possible to increase competitive pressures in electricity generation provided that strong regulatory measures are enforced to ensure that rival producers have access to markets on reasonable terms. However, as we will argue below, this difficult regulatory task would itself be facilitated if there was some initial restructuring of the CEGB.

Option B The creation of a group of regional generating companies from the existing assets of the CEGB would be a less straightforward administrative exercise than the creation of a single generating company. However, in comparison with option A, the advantages of this type of restructuring include the following:

(i) the immediate introduction of interutility competition in the market for bulk electricity;

(ii) an increased likelihood that bulk electricity prices would reflect regional variations in costs of supply;

(iii) a reduction in the market power of incumbent generating companies relative to potential competitors;

(iv) a reduction in the power of companies vis-à-vis the regulatory agency;

(v) an increase in the information available to regulators, facilitating the development of more effective regulatory incentive structures based on comparative yardsticks;

(vi) greater capital market pressures for internal efficiency arising from the increased information available to shareholders and the greater vulnerability of smaller companies to takeover threats in the event that their performance is poor.

These advantages would pertain whether or not existing transmission links were transferred to the new companies. Since it would lead to a decision-making structure rather similar to that adopted by the CEGB in the past, the integration of generation and transmission would facilitate the continued realization of coordination benefits, many of which occur at the regional level. Thus, the 1981 MMC report (Monopolies and Mergers Commission, 1981a) noted that the CEGB operated seven area grid control centers, and that

"… in the short term, costs are first optimised separately by each Area, including running spare, based on Area demand estimates. Costs are placed in a national context by means of inter-Area transfers."

On the other hand, compared with structures based upon the separation of generation and transmission, control over the high voltage grid would give privatized companies an enhanced ability to deter new entry. Although this ability could be limited by strict regulation of terms of access to the networks, the regulatory task would be rendered more difficult by the existence of vertical integration.

Whatever the decision concerning ownership of the high voltage network, as a consequence of transmission costs each generating company would possess market power in its own area of the country and, in the short to medium term at least, complete deregulation of bulk electricity prices would be undesirable if only because of existing bottlenecks in the transmission network. Nevertheless, given the short distances between the major centers of population in England and Wales, in the longer term this local market power would be attenuated by the threat of cross-entry, based either on the construction of new transmission lines or of new power stations in the locality to be served (on the assumption that any regional company would be allowed to construct incremental generating capacity in a market area served largely by one of its rivals).

In practice, however, competition among regionally concentrated generating companies might be restricted less by the magnitude of transmission costs than by the development of tacit collusion among the firms. Indeed, regionalization is almost an open invitation to the newly privatized companies to practice geographic market sharing, and regulators would need to be particularly vigilant in attempting to prevent this particular abuse of market power. In this task they would be supported by the competitive threats afforded by new entrants to the market and by profit-seeking distribution companies with incentives to promote the development of competing sources of supply, although it would likely take several years before these constraints on incumbent generating firms were fully effective.

One objection that has been made to regional restructuring of electricity generation is that there is currently a considerable mismatch of generation capacity and consumption among different regions of England and Wales (Henney, 1987). For example, the maximum demands of the London and South Western Area Boards in 1985–1986 were 3906 MW and 2324 MW respectively, while the capacities of plants within their areas were 976 MW and 431 MW respectively. Even if regional integration of generation, transmission, and distribution (the "power-board" approach) were being contemplated, however, the force of the objection is unclear: economic efficiency does not require that each region be self-sufficient. Thus, for example, it may be cheaper to meet growing demand in southern England by increasing the capacity of transmission links to areas of surplus generating capacity such as the Midlands or Northern France than to build more power stations in the South.

In fact, the existence of major interregional flows of bulk electricity is the basis of one of the arguments *for* regionalization, at least when the latter is compared with existing arrangements. At the moment the demand-related charges of the BST are uniform across the country and, given transmission costs, there is reason to believe that significant regional price discrimination is taking place (e.g. price–cost differentials may be lower in the south of the country than in the Midlands and North). The creation of independent generating companies would, however, provide incentives for the rapid elimination of these arbitrary disparities.

Option C   While regionalization of electricity generation would initially leave the new companies with substantial local market power, it can be argued that a swifter transition to a more competitive market for bulk electricity would be possible if the CEGB were to be broken up into a series of companies which each possessed a geographically dispersed portfolio of power stations. Either the whole or a part of the generating assets of the CEGB could be disposed of in this way. For example, the CEGB owns eight relatively old nuclear reactors based on the Magnox design which are soon due for decommissioning, and which therefore might be considered inappropriate candidates for transfer to the private sector. Alternatively, *all* nuclear power stations could be retained in the public sector and a mixed-ownership system could be developed.

If option C were to be pursued, there would clearly be no case for transferring the national transmission grid to one of the newly privatized generating companies. Nor, unlike in the regionalization option, would there be any sensible way of dividing the grid among several firms. Either a separate transmission company/corporation would need to be created or, in the event of partial privatization, transmission functions could be entrusted to a publicly owned generating corporation (as in Sweden).

In deciding the initial number and sizes of the independent companies, policy makers are again confronted by the familiar trade-off between competition and scale and internal coordination benefits. Cost conditions in electricity generation are such that the creation of a large number of very small companies would almost certainly be undesirable, since it would lead to significant losses in operational efficiency and longer-term difficulties with respect to investment planning. However, precise determination of the optimal number and size of the generating companies is a matter on which it is hard to be confident. Henney (1987) suggests that 4–5 GW is about the right capacity level for each company—which is in line with earlier research in the United States (Christensen and Greene, 1976; Huettner and Landon, 1978)—but it should be noted that this view is based upon the assumed exclusion of nuclear plants from the privatization program.

Despite this uncertainty, in the longer run the costs of making wrong decisions about the initial post-privatization industrial structure may not be too severe. *If* effective competition is established, market structure can be expected to change over time: mergers can be allowed if it becomes clear that firms are inefficiently small, and entry can take place if an insufficient number of companies is created at the time of privatization. Industrial structures are not set in stone, and it is precisely because it provides more information about relative performance and greater flexibility of response to that new information that competition should be encouraged.

One of the major benefits claimed for option C is that, by facilitating the rapid introduction of strong competitive pressures into the industry, it would open up prospects for the deregulation of wholesale electricity prices. Regulatory policy could then concentrate its attention on distribution and transmission activities, where the natural monopoly problem is significant. There is a certain amount of question begging in this line of argument, however, and it is appropriate to draw attention to some of the limitations of the proposal.

First, of the three privatization options under discussion, it would involve the most severe administrative problems, and it could prove difficult to arrange the transfer of the bulk of the CEGB's assets on a single date. On the other hand, if privatization proceeded in stages the first private companies to be established would find themselves competing with a dominant and potentially hostile public corporation which might still have control of the transmission grid. Close and strict regulation of the wholesale electricity market during the transitional phase would therefore be desireable.

Second, and of rather greater significance, is the problem of ensuring that the coordination among generators of electricity—which is necessary for the attainment of secure supplies of electricity at least cost—is accomplished by methods that do not facilitate anticompetitive collusive behavior. As noted earlier, one of the features of electric power systems is that demand and supply must instantaneously be balanced throughout the network if system security failures are to be avoided. Thus if, at a given time and a given location, demand runs ahead of supply, the consequence will be cessation of supply over some given section of the network. Put more technically, failure of markets to clear imposes substantial external costs: hence the preoccupation of engineers with system security.

In principle, coordination problems can be solved by means of contracts between independent generation, transmission, and distribution companies. However, given the existence of external effects and technologies dependent upon large inputs of durable and specific capital equipment, there are few grounds for confidence that decentralized contractual processes will lead to particularly efficient outcomes (see Williamson, 1975). Moreover, the problem is exacerbated by the fact that parts of the industry (distribution and transmission) will necessarily be regulated, so that downstream regulatory distortions could easily induce upstream inefficiencies in electricity generation. Finally, to the extent that contractual problems are overcome, the result may be associated with relatively weak competition amongst the supplying firms. It is worth noting, for example, that the existence of several firms engaging in similar economic activities is neither a necessary nor sufficient condition for effective competition, and that an unregulated cartel would not be a particularly attractive outcome.

We conclude, therefore, that while there is a strong case for reducing horizontal concentration in electricity generation it would be wise to proceed with some caution in this direction. Exclusive reliance on structural remedies would carry many risks and, in particular, immediate deregulation of bulk electricity prices would be unlikely to induce a swift transition to a competitive and efficient industry.

Vertical integration of generation, transmission, and distribution   Thus far, whilst addressing some of the issues connected with the integration of generation and transmission activities, we have only examined policy options that are based upon maintenance of the current separation between generation/transmission and distribution. It remains to be considered whether or not there are merits in proposals that envisage further vertical integration in the industry.

The case for the integration of the upstream and downstream parts of the ESI rests upon the existence of interdependences between the activities of the distribution and generation companies. For the most part, these pertain to longer-run investment decisions. Decisions concerning the construction and location of new power stations are necessarily affected by the likely evolution of the transmission and distribution systems, and vice versa. Thus, in meeting incremental demand, explicit cooperation between upstream and downstream companies may yield long-run cost savings. Such coordination may, of course, be perfectly feasible via the market transactions of independent companies and, on the whole, the major interdependences that occur are between investments in generation and transmission capacity, rather than investments in generation and distribution (i.e. lower voltage) capacity. Nevertheless, the existence of vertically integrated electric utilities in the U.S. and elsewhere (including Scotland) suggests that the possible benefits of such arrangements cannot entirely be discounted.

With respect to vertical integration, there are two options for restructuring the ESI that deserve brief consideration: D, the creation of a single fully integrated electric utility company; E, the creation of regional fully integrated utility companies.

Of these, the former would be much the easier to implement. Informal vertical integration already exists in the ESI, in that coordination of activities takes place through the Electricity Council. Amalgamation of the CEGB and the Area Boards would be a relatively straightforward operation, and, since the Electricity Council produces consolidated accounts for the industry, the resulting company could be presented to the capital market as an organization that already has a performance track record.

In all other respects, however, we believe that option D is dominated by each of the other alternatives we have put forward, including E. For example, in comparison with option A, it would preclude the development of competition in the purchasing of wholesale electricity, raise entry barriers, and prevent the use of regulatory yardsticks in electricity distribution. In compensation for these clear and obvious detriments, full horizontal and vertical integration of the industry would offer some potential, if speculative, benefits by way of possible economies of coordination, but most of the latter could be realized if a privatized CEGB were allowed to own and operate the transmission system.

Similarly, the bulk of the gains from internalized coordination could be achieved through the establishment of regional vertically integrated companies. With respect to option E, the six advantages of regionalization (relative to A) which were listed earlier would also continue to hold. Each of the benefits, however, is attenuated by the vertical integration of generation, transmission, and distribution. Thus, for example, relative to the regional solution based on vertical separation, the absence of independent distribution companies would lead to less competition in the wholesale electricity market, increase the market power of the private companies, and reduce information flows to the regulatory body.

Whether or not the coordination benefits of vertical integration at the regional level are sufficiently large to offset these losses is a question that is difficult to resolve on the basis of available evidence. The past performance of the (fully integrated) South of Scotland Electricity Board compares reasonably favorably with that of the CEGB, but the relevance of this observation is limited by the fact that it pertains to a different framework of regulation and competition than the one envisaged for the industry in the post-privatization period. Because of implications for competition and regulation, however, we would suggest that any initial presumption should be in favor of the organizational separation of electricity distribution.

Transmission   If the Area Boards are privatized separately, a decision to sell CEGB's full complement of generating capacity as a single block would weaken the case for separating its transmission assets. Vertical separation of transmission activities might tend to increase short-run operational costs and hinder the development of an efficient pattern of investment in new plants and transmission lines. Set against these losses could be benefits from increased competitive pressures (it would be easier to arrange fair terms of access to transmission links for rival electricity generating companies) but these latter advantages would be restricted by the continued existence of a dominant incumbent CEGB with considerable market power and, in any case, smaller new entrants could bypass the national transmission system by supplying directly to distribution companies. In this case, therefore, there is respectable argument for leaving both generation and transmission with the CEGB and simply introducing stricter regulation of the terms on which the transmission facilities of the dominant company are made available to others.

A similar point can be argued with respect to the regionalization option: the simplest approach would be to divide up existing transmission facilities among the new companies on an area basis. Each company would then be responsible for the despatch of power stations in its own locality and for negotiating interutility transfers of power. However, in this case the arguments for the vertical integration of generation and transmission carry less force. Thus, particularly in the light of the existing disparities between capacity and demand in different regions of the country it might be more efficient to establish a national system of coordinating supplies based upon the creation of a private company or public corporation that would own and control the national grid.

Establishment of a separate national transmission and control company becomes a more interesting option in the event that the Government decides to split the CEGB into several independent generating companies that are not regionally concentrated. The transmission company (or public corporation) would own the national grid, organize central despatch of generating units, coordinate maintenance schedules for power stations, arrange for financial payments to utilities based upon cost savings arising from central despatch, and provide for the maintenance and development of the transmission system. It is clear that the resulting entity would have considerable market power, and that its ownership structure and methods of operation would be of crucial importance for the overall performance of the industry.

In the United States the activities outlined are most frequently organized by means of power pools (i.e. formal and informal arrangements among independent utilities to coordinate some or all of their investment and operating activities). Adopting a similar model in the U.K. would involve some or all of the private generating and distribution companies taking ownership stakes in the transmission company. The participation of generating companies and, perhaps also, distribution companies in this exercise does, however, raise fundamental questions about the feasibility of increasing effective competition in wholesale markets. Again we stress the conflict between the desire to coordinate the activities of individual utilities (so as to obtain the cost advantages associated with efficient use of an integrated network) and the desire to promote more individualistic decision making (so as to promote interutility competition). As a result of this problem, there is a danger that close control of the coordination activities of the transmission company by the generating and distribution utilities would facilitate collusive anticompetitive behavior by incumbent firms. To illustrate, established generating companies could seek to exclude new entrants to the industry by setting unfavorable terms for the services offered by the transmission company to newcomers.

Although distribution companies would not have similar incentives to reduce competition in the supply of bulk electricity, ownership and control of transmission activities by these firms would also present certain difficulties. In particular, it would promote collusion on the buying side of the wholesale market and tend to increase monopsony power. Given the substantial sunk costs in electricity generation, such buying power can have substantial damaging effects on economic efficiency. For example, the ability of distribution companies to drive down prices towards short-run marginal costs can cause underinvestment problems in electricity generation that are closely akin to those described in section 4.2.3. Although long-term contracts provide one means of alleviating this difficulty, the costs of contract specification and enforcement are such that it is difficult to imagine all supplies being provided on this basis; spot markets would be retained to allow flexibility of response to unforeseen contingencies. Hence inefficiencies associated with monopsony power could well remain. (In this context it can be noted that the performance of the British gas industry—where producers supply a single buyer and long-term contracts are the norm—is not entirely encouraging.)

In the light of these various points, we believe that, if a separate transmission firm is to be established, there is a strong case for independent ownership (possibly public) and control of the resulting entity. The independence of the firm from the generating and distribution companies would assist in the development of a more competitive market in bulk electricity, and public ownership might be the best way of dealing with the considerable market power that the firm would possess.

However, irrespective of whether an independent transmission company is a regulated private monopoly or a public monopoly, there remains considerable doubt as to whether suitably strong incentives for efficient operation can be established and, given the importance of the role that such an entity would be expected to play, this is a point of some significance for the future development of the industry. In principle, vertical separation has much to recommend it, but in practice the technology of the ESI points to the conclusion that there are no easy ways of improving the fundamental economic trade-offs. Again we would warn against excessive reliance on structural remedies alone. Whatever structural option is chosen, it is likely to be the conduct of regulatory policy that will have the most significant effect on industrial performance.

Privatization in Scotland   The ESI in Scotland is about a tenth the size of the industry in England and Wales and is characterized by full vertical integration of generation, transmission, and distribution, with the two Scottish Electricity Boards operating a power-pooling arrangement. The South of Scotland Electricity Board (SSEB) is much the larger of the two Scottish public corporations, and has a plant mix more heavily weighted towards nuclear stations than that of the CEGB: in 1986–1987 the SSEB obtained nearly 50 percent of its requirements from nuclear stations, and a further 1.4 GW of nuclear capacity, equivalent to about 30 percent of the current maximum demand, is under construction. As its name suggests, the North of Scotland Hydro-Electric Board (NSHB) concentrates on generating power from hydroelectric capacity in the Highlands.

With a maximum demand in 1986–1987 amounting to less than 5 GW, the Scottish market is too small to permit the creation of several competing generating companies without simultaneously incurring significant cost penalties. One option for privatization would be to split distribution and generation and attempt to encourage competition in the wholesale market between the privately owned Scottish generating company (or companies in the event that the NSHB is sold separately) and the newly created generating company or companies in England. The SSEB is already connected to the grid in England and Wales and there is some trading of supplies with the public corporations further south. The capacity of the transmission link is extremely limited, however, and in the foreseeable future there appears to be little prospect of strong competition being developed in this way. Similarly, given that there is soon likely to be very substantial excess capacity in Scotland and that the plant mix is heavily weighted towards nuclear sets with relatively low marginal operating costs, the prospects for significant new entry of smaller producers (via combined heat and power schemes, for example) are also poor.

With respect to the Scottish market, therefore, it should be recognized that the opportunities for increasing competition in in the short to medium term will be limited, and hence that the case for any immediate restructuring of the industry is weaker than in England and Wales. If privatization proceeds on the basis of existing organizational structures, however, this lack of competition points to the need for stringent regulation of the industry. Thus, for example, the private firm(s) should be required to provide separate accounts for its generation, transmission, and distribution activity, so that the regulatory authority can more easily compare its performance in each operation with that of (nonintegrated) companies in England and Wales, and, in addition to control of average prices, regulators should be active in attempting to monitor price *structures*.

Provided that the "regulation with a light hand" precedent, which was established during the course of privatization of the gas industry, is not followed and that electricity generation and distribution continue to be the responsibilities of different firms in England and Wales, retention of a vertically integrated structure in Scotland also has some positive aspects. The effects of changes in the structure of ownership, regulation, and competition that are currently envisaged for the industry in England and Wales are difficult to predict, partly as a result of the fact that much of the experience and knowledge gained from observation of past performance will be of only limited value in the new environment. In these circumstances there is a sound case for allowing some structural diversity: performance under different conditions can be assessed empirically, and lessons for the subsequent development of public policy can be learned. In particular, if separate distribution companies are to be retained in England and Wales, the performance of the Scottish company might cast some light on the question of the relative merits of vertical integration.

This last point is one aspect of a more general set of arguments that is as relevant to the future of the industry in England and Wales as it is in Scotland. The changes likely to be brought about by privatization are substantial and will lead to a period of rapid learning. The encouragement of diversity in the industry will not only increase the rate of acquisition of policy-relevant information, but will also tend to facilitate structural changes that may later be deemed desirable in the light of the new knowledge. That is, in periods of rapid learning flexibility of response is at a premium, indicating that it would be unwise for the Government to commit itself wholeheartedly to an industrial structure that is likely to be resistant to change.

9.3.5   Assessment

Throughout our discussion of the ESI we have emphasized the fundamental policy trade-off between the benefits of coordination among electric utility companies and the benefits of greater competition in the industry. Each of the five options we have considered seeks to resolve this trade-off in a different way, based upon a particular mix of horizontal and vertical integration in the industry.

On balance, we believe that horizontal integration has been carried too far in Britain and that there is a strong case for promoting the development of more competition in the market for wholesale electricity. The size of the CEGB's operations appears to be well in excess of empirical estimates of the minimum efficient scale for a generating company and, although international comparisons of performance must always be handled with care, the past record of the U.K. public corporation, relative to less concentrated industries overseas, affords little support for the claimed benefits of horizontal integration. These points also apply *a fortiori* to the possibility of creating a private monopoly responsible for generation, transmission, *and* distribution, the solution least conducive to the development of competition in the industry and the one that would lead to the most severe regulatory problems.

Unfortunately, the links between industrial concentration and the degree of competition in the marketplace are by no means straightforward, and the technology of the ESI creates pressures towards collusive behavior. For this reason, we are skeptical of proposals to increase competition and improve efficiency that place nearly all the emphasis on structural reforms. Rather we see the conduct of regulatory policy as being the most important single influence on the future performance of the industry. In particular we would stress the contributions that regulatory policy can make (a) to increasing rivalry among electricity distribution companies via the use of yardstick competition and (b) to creating a "level playing field" on which new entrants can compete fairly against incumbent generating companies. In the absence of measures to achieve these two goals, structural remedies are likely to have disappointing effects, whereas if the two goals can be attained competition in bulk electricity markets will be substantially increased regardless of the initial structural conditions. On balance, we favor some divestiture of CEGB assets prior to privatization simply because, by improving information flows to regulators, it would facilitate the development of more effective regulatory policies, *not* because it is likely *per se* to have substantial effects on competition in wholesale electricity markets.

We would also suggest that the trade-off between coordination and competition also points to the potentially beneficial effects of retaining parts of the ESI in public ownership, particularly if the Government decides to separate electricity generation and transmission. In that event, there would be merit in keeping coordination activities (associated with the operation of the transmission system) in the public domain so as not to facilitate collusion amongst incumbent privately owned utilities, including collaboration to impede new entry. In many countries electricity supply is characterized by a mix of public and private ownership, and to treat privatization as an all-or-nothing issue is to create an arbitrary and unnecessary constraint on policy decisions. Indeed, one of the weaknesses of the U.K. privatization program to date has been that, in its enthusiasm for private ownership, the Government has opted for policies that allow the rapid transfer of complete industries to the private sector, frequently with scant regard for the more fundamental issues of competition and regulatory policy.

Our own perspective is somewhat different. For the most part, we see the introduction of privately owned companies into industries such as electricity supply as one instrument (among several) for improving industrial performance indirectly through the promotion of greater competition and better regulation. In the particular case of the ESI, we believe that this points to partial step-by-step privatization, involving limited asset disposals (to increase actual competition and regulatory information immediately) and strong regulation by an independent body (to prevent monopolistic abuses and increase the effectiveness of potential competition). Both sets of measures would be consistent with the continuation of a significant level of public ownership in each part of the ESI (i.e. in generation, particularly nuclear, and distribution, as well as in transmission). By creating greater diversity, a mixed-ownership system would also facilitate the acquisition of policy-relevant information and make it easier to adjust industrial structure as knowledge and circumstances change. Moreover, that such an approach is feasible is shown by the structure of the industry in Sweden.

Finally, it is relevant to note that questions arising from the proposed privatization of the ESI should not be considered in isolation from other major issues of energy policy. Thus, we have drawn attention to problems connected with the future of nuclear power in Britain. Roughly speaking, privately owned generating companies are likely to be less favorably disposed towards nuclear power than the CEGB has been in recent years (discount rates used in investment appraisals will tend to rise), and the magnitude of this change in incentives is likely to be greater the smaller is the private company. In turn, decisions concerning the choice of generating technologies will have major implications for the future of the British coal industry (to be discussed in section 9.5). If coal import policy is liberalized, privately owned electricity generation companies would exert strong pressure on British Coal to reduce its prices toward international price levels. In similar circumstances, however, a publicly owned generating board is likely to pursue exactly the same policy (the CEGB has already demonstrated its desire to move in this direction). Other things being equal, therefore, the net effect of privatization on the demand for domestically produced coal could well turn out to be positive. Perhaps, then, it is the National Union of Mineworkers and antinuclear environmentalists—rather than a strongly pronuclear government—who should be the strongest advocates of a change of ownership of the ESI!

9.4   The Oil Industry

In terms of both the number of share flotations and the net proceeds realized from the sales, between 1979 and 1987 disposals of oil assets accounted for a larger fraction of the privatization program than any other single industry. The sale of British Petroleum shares in 1979 was the first of the major flotations of this period, and the 1987 disposal of the residual 31.5 percent Government stake in that company (together with the associated rights issue) was at the time the largest ever equity offering on any of the world's stock markets. Substantial proceeds were also obtained from the privatizations of Britoil and Enterprise Oil (see section 7.1).

In this section we will first set out some background information on the development of the U.K. offshore oil industry (in section 9.4.1), before going on to examine public policy toward the industry in general (in section 9.4.2), including the growth of public ownership during the 1970s, and the later privatization policies in particular (in section 9.4.3). Finally, section 9.4.4 comprises our assessment of the contribution of oil privatization to the attainment of the Government's objectives and an account of the key role played by oil asset sales in the evolution of the privatization program.

9.4.1   Historical Background
Public ownership of parts of the oil industry dates from before the outbreak of the First World War, when the U.K. Government took a controlling interest in British Petroleum (BP) with the purpose of promoting greater security of supply of oil, principally for the Navy. Domestic production of oil has, however, only occurred on a significant scale since the mid-1970s,

the first reserves of oil in U.K. waters having been discovered in 1969. We will therefore restrict our attention to this relatively recent period.

The early development of the U.K. offshore industry was stimulated by two factors: the Gröningen gas discovery in the northern Netherlands at the end of the 1950s, which increased the perceived likelihood of the existence of substantial reserves of oil and gas below the North Sea, and the 1958 Continental Shelf Convention. Once ratified by a sufficient number of nations, the latter enabled governments to settle international boundaries, extend national petroleum legislation to offshore areas, and issue petroleum exploration and production licenses.

In Britain, the first round of licensing took place in 1964. The U.K. sector of the North Sea was divided into quadrants of one degree latitude and longitude, each of which was subdivided into thirty blocks of approximately 10 km × 20 km. The Department of Energy invited companies, either individually or as consortia, to apply for the right to explore the designated blocks, and 348 such blocks were initially allocated. Since 1964, there has been a succession of licensing rounds and, for the most part, rights have been awarded on a discretionary basis whereby applicants are judged on factors such as technical competence, financial standing, operational record, and proposed exploration programs. On a few occasions, however, a small proportion of the available blocks has been allocated by means of an auction.

The earliest UKCS discoveries, starting in 1965, were of gas fields but, between 1969 and 1974, 18 oil fields were found in the U.K. sector, and the recoverable reserves from these deposits eventually allowed Britain to become self-sufficient in oil. The first oil to come ashore was from the Argyll field, in June 1975, to be quickly followed by oil from the large Forties field in December of that year. By the end of 1980, a total of 15 fields was on stream, producing about 1.6 million barrels of oil per day.

By the end of 1985 over 1,000 exploration wells had been drilled in the U.K. sector, leading to over 200 significant discoveries of oil and/or gas. Thirty offshore oil fields were in operation, and the production level had reached 2.65 million barrels of oil a day. However, by the mid-1980s, it was believed, possibly prematurely, that most of the major oil fields in the "mature" areas of the North Sea (the Central and Northern North Sea Basins and the East Shetlands Basin) had already been discovered. In their exploration activities, therefore, oil companies have been turning increasingly to the "frontier" areas of the UKCS, where water depths are frequently greater, and to the development of improved technologies for extracting oil from smaller marginal fields.

9.4.2 Public Policy and Public Ownership

Public policy towards the offshore oil industry in the 1970s appears to have had two principal objectives: first to secure financial returns for the Exchequer, and second to exert some control over the production companies with respect to matters such as the rate at which new fields were brought on stream, the subsequent output (and, hence, depletion) rates, and the destination of the final output (security of supply having become an important policy consideration in the wake of disruptions in the international market in 1973). In pursuit of the first objective, the Government relied largely on fiscal policy in the form of a system of taxation uniquely applicable to the offshore industry and designed, among other things, to recover rents accruing from the rights granted to companies to exploit the oil and gas fields.

In brief, the offshore tax regime has comprised three main elements:

(i) a royalty levied at a rate of 12.5 percent of the value of deliveries of oil;

(ii) petroleum revenue tax (PRT), initially set at 45 percent in 1975 and increased in stages to 75 percent in 1983, which is charged on the revenues less expenses (including royalties) arising from offshore production;

(iii) corporation tax, charged in the standard way but with royalties and PRT counting as allowable deductions.

The oil taxation regime also contains a large number of special provisions that need not detain us here. The main point to note is simply that the Government has generally sought to obtain rents from the industry only after the oil and gas have been landed. That is, unlike in the United States, auctioning of natural resource rights has not been a preferred method of raising revenue. This approach has been popular with the offshore producers because it both delays rental payments and transfers some of the exploration risk to Government.

With respect to Government control over exploration, production, and sales, the years since the first licensing round in 1964 can usefully be divided into three periods. From 1964 to 1974 rapid expansion of exploration activity was encouraged, and a total of 863 blocks were allocated in four rounds of licensing. Between 1974 and 1979, a period of Labour Government, the exploration process was restrained, and only 86 blocks were allocated in two rounds (1977 and 1978). The mid-1970s also saw the introduction of two major pieces of legislation: the Oil Taxation Act 1975, which established PRT, and the Submarine Pipelines Act 1975, which, among other things, introduced depletion controls to enable the Government to cut back production from developed fields if it so wished and conferred powers to set up the British National Oil Corporation (see below). The third period, which commenced in 1979, has been characterized by a withdrawal of the Government from direct involvement in exploration and production activities and, particularly since 1983, the introduction of tax concessions for new fields, designed to increase the level of exploration.

Public ownership in the offshore oil industry has occurred in three ways:

(i) through the Government's equity stake in BP, one of the leading North Sea exploration/production companies;

(ii) through the stakes in oilfields held by the BGC and the National Coal Board;

(iii) through the holdings of the British National Oil Corporation (BNOC).

In each case, ownership has (a) supplemented the Government's tax returns from the offshore industry and (b) provided a means by which, in theory, it could influence the development of the industry. Only in the case of BNOC, however, was public ownership specifically established for these purposes.

In creating BNOC, it was the then Labour Government's intention that it (BNOC) should take a 51 percent stake in all North Sea oil developments. BNOC had an initial capital of £600 million and was required to pay all its revenues into a new account, called the National Oil Account, into which the royalties due from private sector offshore activities were also to be paid. BNOC was allowed to draw on this account to finance its activities, and was given a number of other advantages relative to private sector companies, including exemption from PRT.

In the event, because of anxieties that nationalization of 51 percent of the oil industry would seriously weaken the incentives for private sector exploration and development activities and anxieties about the financial burden on the Exchequer implied by a commitment to meet 51 percent of the development costs of all new fields, BNOC's original objective was watered down. Existing North Sea operators were required to conclude agreements with BNOC that gave the latter rights to participate in the developments (but not necessarily an ownership stake) and to purchase 51 percent of the resulting output at market prices. The right of purchase was justified in terms of the national interest in obtaining secure supplies of oil.

Nevertheless, despite this backtracking by the Government, BNOC did acquire substantial North Sea interests during the second half of the 1970s, and both retained and augmented many of its original privileges. In 1975 BNOC obtained the oil interests of the National Coal Board under the provisions of the Petroleum and Submarine Pipelines Act, and purchased

16 percent and 20 percent stakes respectively in the Thistle and Ninian fields from the financially distressed Burmah Oil Company. By June 1976 it had acquired stakes in the Hutton, Dunlin, Murchison, and Brae fields, and was later given a 51 percent stake in the 86 blocks allocated in the fifth and sixth licensing rounds. Finally, in 1978, BNOC's privileges were further extended when it was given first right of refusal to buy stakes in blocks awarded to private companies in earlier licensing rounds whenever such stakes came on to the market.

By 1979, then, the activities of BNOC comprised two quite distinct types of operation. BNOC had quickly become a substantial exploration/development/production enterprise in its own right. In addition, however, it was also a major oil-trading enterprise, buying oil from other producers under the terms set out in the various participation agreements that had been concluded, and selling the product on into competitive markets.

9.4.3   Privatization in the Oil Industry

In opposition, the Conservative Party had declared its intention to dispose of assets acquired by BNOC during the 1970s. The return of a Conservative Government in 1979, however, coincided with a period of both rapidly rising oil prices and increasing anxieties about security of supply, stimulated largely by unfolding political developments in Iran. It was decided, therefore, that in the short term at least BNOC should remain in business as both a production and trading operation. The immediate changes in public policy were consequently rather modest. The Government placed a fraction of its equity stake in BP on the market in October 1979, following the precedent set by the Labour Government in 1977, to raise finance for its expenditure programs (net receipts totalled £276 million). In addition, an emergency program was introduced that included taking royalties from the private sector in oil rather than in cash, suspending restrictions on gas flaring (which served to limit production in some fields), organizing a new more extensive licensing round to encourage further exploration, and ordering companies to cut their exports from the U.K.

Although BNOC was retained, the Secretary of State for Energy announced in 1979 that it was to be stripped of a number of its powers. Henceforth, for example, it would have no right to sit on an operating committee in the industry if it had no ownership interest in the relevant field, it would lose its privileged position in the licensing rounds, and it would lose its special access to the National Oil Account (see Redwood, 1984). Partially to compensate for the loss in Government revenues associated with deferral of asset sales, about £610 million of BNOC oil was sold forward in 1979–1980 for the short-term benefit of the public account (an exercise that was repeated in 1980–1981). Proposals to issue an oil revenue bond, with interest payments linked to BNOC's performance, were also considered.

Throughout this period, however, there was no abandonment of the earlier plans to dispose of BNOC's North Sea assets. By 1981, conditions in international oil markets were more settled, and the higher prices that were then prevailing had the advantage of making BNOC a very profitable enterprise that would be attractive to private investors. Moreover, the gradual expansion in the scope of the Government's privatization program led to the development of more ambitious plans for asset sales in the offshore industry. Thus, when the pre-privatization policy measures eventually arrived, they encompassed the oil interests of the BGC as well as those of BNOC.

In August 1982, the production assets of BNOC were transferred to a new company, Britoil (leaving the trading interests of the BNOC still in place), and in November 1982 51 percent of the shares in Britoil were sold to the public, yielding net proceeds of £536 million to the Exchequer. At that time, the share issue was, by a substantial margin, the largest undertaken as part of the privatization program. Further sales of offshore interests then followed in quick succession. The year 1983 saw the disposal of additional Government shares in BP (generating net proceeds of £556 million), and the establishment of Enterprise Oil, the company formed from the oil interests of the BGC under the terms of the 1982 Oil and Gas (Enterprise) Act. In June 1984 Enterprise Oil was sold, yielding net proceeds of £381 million, and, later in the same year, disposal of BGC's interests in the (onshore) Wytch Farm oil field produced a further £82 million. In August 1985, £450 million (gross) was obtained from the sale of the remaining 49 percent Government holding in Britoil, and, finally, the sale of the residual Government stake in BP in 1987 yielded £5,725 million (gross).

As noted above, the creation of Britoil did not involve the simultaneous winding up of the trading activities of BNOC, and, up until 1985, BNOC continued to buy and sell oil and to exercise its influence over North Sea developments through those of its powers, afforded by the various participation agreements, that remained. In 1985 this residual form of direct Government intervention in the marketplace was ended by the abolition of BNOC and its replacement by the Oil and Pipelines Agency (OPA). The function of the OPA is to administer the Government's pipeline and storage system and the disposal of royalty in kind, and to maintain emergency lifting arrangements which become effective in the event of a threat to the U.K.'s oil supplies. Thus, although the disposal of royalty in kind necessitates the continuation of some Government trading activities, the intention was, and still is, that these will be conducted at a relatively low level compared with the scale of operations of BNOC.

9.4.4 Assessment

Initial plans to dispose of North Sea assets, formulated during the period between 1974 and 1979 when the Conservative Party was in opposition, appear to have been strongly motivated by the view that the public ownership of stakes in offshore exploration, development, and production activities was inimical to the efficient development of the industry. Thus it was argued that public corporations would be inefficient in their own operations and would impede the activities of private producers in a competitive market. In support of the case against public ownership, it can also be argued that such ownership was not and is not a necessary condition for the exercise of general control over the initial build-up and later decline in offshore operations. Thus, rates of exploration, development, production, and depletion can be influenced by Government control over licensing round allocations, the tax regime, and the regulatory framework surrounding the industry. In particular, for example, in emergency any government can take powers to force private companies to obtain and move oil in ways that serve to protect national supplies.

Given that UKCS producers have little influence on international oil prices, there are few grounds for concern that privatization of oil assets has led, or will lead, to abuse of market power in the final product market. Nor in examples such as those of BP and Enterprise Oil are there reasons to oppose privatization on regulatory policy grounds: in neither case was public ownership of the relevant assets a major factor in the development of public policy towards the industry. In these cases, then, the decisive factor should indeed be the likely effects of ownership on internal efficiency, and the case for privatization is consequently a strong one (although we are doubtful that the resulting gains will be particularly large: BP, for example, was already a quoted company operating at arm's length from the Government).

The situation with respect to BNOC, however, was rather different in that BNOC was specifically designed to be an instrument of regulatory policy. In assessing the privatization of BNOC, it should first be noted that, as in other examples of economic regulation, the relationships between the

Government and UKCS producers can be viewed as giving rise to a particular set of agency problems. In its dealings with the oil industry, the Government's objectives have included the appropriation of rents associated with the valuable natural resources in the UKCS and the achievement of production plans that are consistent with balance of payments goals and with the maintenance of secure supplies. As in all agency problems, however, the attainment of these objectives depends heavily upon the quality of information that is available to the Government. Thus, one argument in favor of some public ownership of the industry is that the nationalized enterprise(s) can be used both to gather policy-relevant information and to impede strategic manipulation of information flows by colluding private producers.

On this view, perhaps the most useful function of BNOC was to improve the efficacy of the regulatory process by acting as the "eyes and ears" of the Government in the offshore industry. Hence, even if the public corporation was not efficiently managed and did, through its operations, make life more difficult for private producers, these points do not, by themselves, constitute a decisive case against state ownership: any detriments have to be set against the potential information gains. Moreover, given the large magnitudes of the rents associated with UKCS oil reserves, the fact that many North Sea operators are foreign owned, and the importance of oil as a primary fuel input, the economic value of additional information to the U.K. Government is likely to be substantial. We conclude, therefore, that the detriments of public ownership would need to be demonstrably high before it could safely be concluded that public ownership of some parts of the offshore industry was unmerited.

Perhaps the best epitaph for BNOC has been supplied by Redwood (1984), who has been one of its strongest critics. In his assessment, Redwood concludes that BNOC "made no net positive contribution at all to the development of the North Sea," but he also states that

"... BNOC carried out the task to which it was appointed by the Labour Government with distinction and verve. It did get its hands on assets; it did, in the end, attract staff from various quarters who were able to make their contribution to North Sea development. Its asset position was strong. It did in the end enable the Conservative administration to sell off shares at a very good price."

In the light of this performance record and because of the high value of oil industry information to Government, we would be more reluctant than Redwood to conclude that BNOC made no net positive contribution to public policy. More to the point, we conclude that it is unlikely that privatization of BNOC has made, or will make, significant positive contributions to the better conduct of regulatory policy towards the industry.

This, however, is not the whole story. Although the impetus for plans to wind up BNOC may have had their origins in particular views about regulatory and industrial policies, following the election of the Conservative Government in 1979 the emphasis rapidly shifted towards the contribution that asset sales could make towards the financial objectives of the Government. Thus, the disposal of shares in BP, the forward sales of BNOC oil, the creation and sale of Enterprise Oil, and the sale of the BGC stake in Wytch Farm can all be interpreted as decisions motivated chiefly by the desire of the Government to reduce the public sector borrowing requirement (PSBR), a motivation that is most clearly revealed in the case of the forward sales of BNOC oil.

Nevertheless, from a wider perspective, it is possible that the oil privatizations have had important *indirect* effects on the conduct of microeconomic policy, and that their historical significance is far greater than our narrowly focused evaluation would imply. Thus the oil asset sales served as a link between the earlier policies of the 1974–1979 Labour Government and the major privatizations of the utility industries that commenced in 1984 with the sale of BT. The initial disposal of BP shares in 1979 followed the precedent set by the Labour Government in 1977, and, as with the development of many other aspects of economic policy (including the use of monetary targets and the introduction of cash limits for nationalized industries), represented a continuation and extension of pre-existing approaches rather than a radical break with what had gone before. Likewise, the forward sale of BNOC oil was a relatively small incremental change, but it led fairly easily towards the notion of privatization which, in the case of Britoil, might be seen as the ultimate forward sale.

Prior to privatization, and again motivated by the objective of reducing the PSBR, the Government toyed with the idea of introducing a BNOC oil revenue bond, the returns on which would be linked to the Corporation's performance. A similar option was considered for the then publicly owned BT, the activities of which were also causing concern because of the level of borrowing entailed by its substantial investment program. The facts that, in the end, privatization of BNOC appeared preferable and that, even in difficult market conditions arising from falling oil prices, a large share issue was managed with reasonable success almost certainly gave some encouragement to the Government to pursue a similar course in the telecommunications industry. Thus, while privatization of BT was indeed a radical departure from the earlier policy tradition, the path towards it was smoothed, and no doubt made to appear less daunting, by the history of oil asset sales.

9.5   The Coal Industry

The coal industry is the only part of the energy sector which, by the end of 1987, had been left untouched by actual or proposed privatization policies. However, there is every reason to believe that the Government is attracted by the prospect of at least partial privatization of the industry at some future date. To complete our discussion of the energy sector, therefore, in this section we consider some of the options that are available to the Government with respect to the conduct of policy towards the industry. We start (in section 9.5.1) with an outline of the rationale for the creation of the National Coal Board (NCB) in 1946 and an analysis of some of the general characteristics of the NCB's subsequent behavior. (In 1987 the NCB was renamed the British Coal Corporation but, for convenience and to avoid possible confusion, we will use the older title throughout the discussions.) This is followed (in section 9.5.2) by an outline of major policy developments in the period since 1946. Finally, we consider the prospects for implementing policies of liberalization and privatization in the industry (section 9.5.3).

9.5.1   Coal Nationalization
The British coal industry was taken into public ownership in 1946. Before nationalization the structure of the industry was atomistic: production was undertaken by a large number of relatively small private companies. However, since cost conditions are far removed from those that characterize a natural monopoly, for the most part the case put forward for nationalization was not based upon perceived economies of scale resulting from increased concentration. Rather, the principal motive for the introduction of public ownership was to provide an institutional structure conducive to the implementation of the Government's policies for an industry that had suffered a substantial decline in its fortunes.

The production of coal in Britain peaked in 1913 at a figure of 292 million tonnes per annum. During the interwar years the industry was in steady decline so that, by the mid-1940s , output had fallen to around 190 million tonnes per annum. The drop was almost entirely attributable to losses in export markets, as domestic consumption of coal had remained roughly constant over the period. Partly as a consequence of depressed market conditions, there was little investment in the industry and the capital stock became gradually more dilapidated. According to Robson (1960): "Poor leadership, conservative management, backward technology and inadequate investment characterized the British coal industry during the twenty-five or thirty years prior to nationalization."

The output fall which resulted from the loss of international markets placed strong downward pressures on the the wages of mineworkers during the interwar period, leading to embittered labor relations that culminated in the major national strike of 1926, an event of great political and economic significance in British twentieth century history. One of the policy responses to these problems was the Coal Mines Act of 1930, introduced by the Labour Government of the time to create a "distress cartel" in the industry. Among other things, the Act fixed a maximum permitted output for the country as a whole, and established procedures for allocating quotas to individual collieries and for penalizing deviants. Firms were allowed to trade in production rights but, since quotas were fixed on a quarterly basis, there were strong incentives for less efficient mines to be kept open so as to maintain their commercially valuable allocations.

One aim of the 1930 legislation was to hold up the price of coal and thereby alleviate the pressure on mineworkers' wage rates. However, cartelization exacerbated the longer-term problems of the industry by delaying the exit of uneconomic capacity and reducing the incentives for new investment in the more efficient coal mines. By the mid-1940s, therefore, the Government faced a choice among three major policy options: (a) continued state intervention to support prices in a privately owned industry, (b) deregulation to allow market forces to impose the required structural adjustments, and (c) nationalization. The first option would have delayed the "modernization" of the industry, while the second would have opened up major conflicts in the labor market. The Attlee Government therefore had no hesitation in choosing nationalization, by which means it hoped to be able to combine a program of new investment with continued support of mineworkers' wages. At that time, given the difficulties faced by the industry, the move was not particularly controversial: the Conservative opposition did not resist nationalization with any vigor.

Transfer of the coal industry to the public sector was accomplished by the Coal Industry Nationalisation Act of 1946. This established the NCB as a monopoly supplier in Britain, and the relevant statute contains one of the most famous phrases in the legislative history of the nationalized industries: the NCB was given the duty of ". . . working and getting the coal in Great Britain, to the exclusion (save as in this Act provided) of any other person." A further provision of the Act required the NCB to supply coal "at such prices as may seem to it best calculated to further the public interest in all respects." However, as in the statutes of the other major public corporations, the legislation placed restrictions on pricing policy in the form of a break-even constraint: the NCB was required to operate "so that its revenues shall not be less than sufficient to meet its outgoings properly chargeable to revenue account (including interest) on an average of good and bad years."

Given the political background to coal nationalization, in the years following 1946 the NCB appears to have interpreted the public interest guideline with respect to pricing policy as meaning that, as one of its aims, it should seek to promote as favorable a trade-off as possible between miners' wage rates and employment in the industry. Thus it would not be wholly inaccurate to characterize the Board's pricing/output objective as the maximization of output subject to the break-even constraint, and the consequences of this policy are illustrated in figure 9.1.

In the diagram, MC is the industry's marginal cost curve at a given wage rate. The marginal cost curve is drawn with an upward slope because of the existence of disparities in the costs of production among mines (which in turn are the result of, for example, site-to-site variations in geological conditions). The curve DD' shows the demand curve for the NCB's output. Equilibrium price p and output q are determined by the condition that the shaded area between the price line and the marginal cost curve to the left of

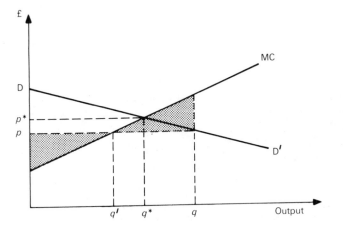

Figure 9.1   Output determination in the coal industry

point q' is equal to the equivalent shaded area to the right of point q' (the break-even constraint). Thus, relative to the allocatively efficient equilibrium, shown by (p^*, q^*) and characterized by the equality of price and marginal cost, price is lower and output is higher.

Changes in wage rates will shift the marginal cost curve and hence influence the equilibrium levels of price, output, and employment. However, at any given wage rate, employment is higher than in the case of marginal cost pricing, so that the National Union of Mineworkers (NUM) is presented with a more favorable trade-off between wages and employment in its bargaining with the NCB. In other words, the derived demand curve for labor is shifted outwards, as illustrated in figure 9.2, which shows wage/employment equilibria for union preferences that are represented by indifference curves linking the two variables.

In economic terms, what has happened in the industry is that the rents available from production at low cost sites have been used to subsidize high cost capacity. It is not necessarily the case, however, that the rents have been fully dissipated by the maintenance of this high cost capacity. As figure 9.2 shows, it is likely that part of the rents have been captured by workers in the form of higher wages. An underlying cause of this outcome has been the failure of Governments to impose any charges or compensatory taxes on the NCB in return for its rights to extract coal: the 1946 Act simply allocated ownership rights in all deposits to the Board.

Returning to the diagrams, it should immediately be apparent that the

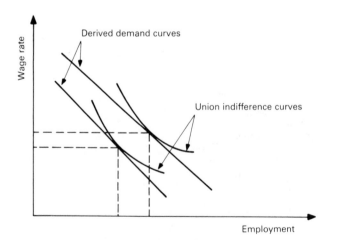

Figure 9.2   Wage and employment determination

NUM stands to benefit from any outward shift in the demand curve or loosening of the break-even constraint. To the extent that NCB managers prefer higher to lower output and obtain benefits from the quieter life associated with the satisfaction of workers' interests, they too will stand to gain from such changes. What the diagrams do not capture is the ability of the NCB and NUM to influence public policy in ways that ease the pressure of the demand and financial constraints confronting the industry, but we will return to this point in the discussion below.

9.5.2 Policy Developments since 1946

Following nationalization, coal output in Britain increased to a postwar peak in the mid-1950s. Thereafter output declined rapidly until the early 1970s and more slowly in the period up to the year-long miners' strike in 1984–1985 (see table 9.7). The first part of the fall is largely attributable to the drop in home consumption of coal caused by the availability first of relatively low priced oil and later of natural gas (which not only competed with coal in markets for final consumers but also eliminated the derived demand for coal arising from the production of town gas). The oil price shock of 1973 helped restore coal's competitive position but, although the NCB was subsequently able significantly to slow the rate of decrease in its share of the domestic energy market, falling energy demand meant that output continued to decline, albeit at a slower pace than before.

The response of successive Governments to these trends in energy markets was to continue and extend the protection afforded to the domestic coal industry. As already explained, the NCB was protected against

Table 9.7 Output from NCB mines

Year	Output (million tonnes)
1947	187.5
1950	205.6
1955	211.3
1960	186.8
1965–1966	177.0
1970–1971	135.5
1975–1976	114.5
1980–1981	110.3
1981–1982	108.9
1982–1983	104.9
1983–1984	90.1
1984–1985	27.6
1985–1986	88.4
1986–1987	99.0

Source: *British Coal Corporation, Annual Report and Accounts* (1987).

competition from other domestic coal producers by the monopoly position established for it by the 1946 Act. A small private sector did survive, but has, in effect, been regulated by the public corporation. At the time of nationalization there were about 1,400 collieries in Britain, and the NCB granted licenses to nearly 500 of the smallest (i.e. those having no more than 30 workers underground) to continue in private production. Similarly, while the production of opencast (strip-mined) coal has remained in the private sector, the NCB's property rights in coal reserves give the public corporation overall control of the operations. On larger sites the private producers act as contractors for the NCB; on smaller sites they are licensed by the NCB to produce *and* sell the coal. As in the case of deep-mined coal, however, the private licensees must pay royalties to the NCB, the levels of which are wholly at the discretion of the latter. In 1986–1987, opencast mines had an output of 13.3 million tonnes and licensed mines contributed a further 2.0 million tonnes.

Since it rapidly became clear that this monopoly position would fail to protect the NCB against further substantial declines in output and employment, the period since 1946 has witnessed a series of supplementary policy measures designed to afford additional support to the domestic industry. Steps to increase the demand for domestically produced coal have included the following.

(i) Government pressure on the publicly owned electricity industry—which is by far the largest customer of the NCB—to purchase more coal from the NCB. (NCB sales to the CEGB and SSEB totalled 79.5 million tonnes in 1986–1987.) This has been done in two ways. First, at various times ministers have used their powers to influence the CEGB's investment program towards greater reliance upon, and earlier construction of, coal-fired generating stations. Second, the CEGB has been discouraged from purchasing a greater fraction of its coal inputs from lower-cost overseas suppliers. Thus, for example, in response to a threatened coalminers' strike in 1981, the Government "persuaded" the CEGB to limit its imports of coal to around 3 to 4 million tonnes per annum, against a backgound of an import level of about 7.5 million tonnes in 1980 and of CEGB plans to build one or more terminals to increase its import capacity to something of the order of 15 million tonnes per annum (Robinson and Marshall, 1988). Thereafter, under the terms of the revised joint understanding (between the CEGB and the NCB) which was to run for a period from 1983 to 1987, the CEGB undertook to purchase at least 95 percent of its estimated coal requirements from the NCB (Boyfield, 1985).

(ii) Specific taxation of fuel oil, a substitute product that had become increasingly price competitive during the 1950s and 1960s.

(iii) Government grants to firms that convert to coal from oil and gas.

Support for the domestic coal industry has also been forthcoming in the form of a variety of supply-side policies. These have included the ready provision of finance for major investment programs, even when the latter have been based on highly optimistic demand projections, and the provision of various types of subsidy, including the implicit subsidies contained in relatively undemanding financial targets. The best example of the supply-side approach is the *Plan for Coal*, drawn up in 1974 following the oil price hike of 1973, the coalminers' strike of 1973–1974, and the arrival of a new Labour Government.

The *Plan for Coal* set various targets for investment, capacity, and output over the ten-year period from 1975 to 1985. It was estimated that total home energy demand would reach 400 million tonnes per annum of coal equivalent in 1983, and that, of this total, the NCB's deep mines would account for 120 million tonnes. Accordingly, to offset closures of older collieries, estimated to run at an average of 4 million tonnes of capacity a year, a major investment program to develop new capacity was set in place. At the same time, it was projected that labor productivity would grow at a rate of 4 percent per annum.

The outcome was that, by 1983, the last full year before the statistics became distorted by the 1984–1985 strike, domestic energy demand was only 330 million tonnes of coal equivalent per annum (17.5 percent below the forecast), of which, despite the effect of CEGB purchasing policy, NCB deep mines contributed about 100 million tonnes (16.7 percent below forecast). Although real investment expenditures were well in excess of those called for in the *Plan*—£6.5 billion in 1983 prices, against a projection of approximately £4.4 billion—the targets for capacity expansion were not met. Closure of older capacity averaged only about 1.7 million tonnes per annum, and, partly as a consequence of this, labor productivity growth averaged around 2 percent per annum (see Boyfield, 1985).

In recent years, mostly as a consequence of the combination of overinvestment in new capacity and the relatively slow rate of closure of inefficient collieries, the NCB's continued viability has depended upon large injections of Government finance. In 1983–1984, for example, operating losses were covered by subsidies, known as deficit grants, amounting to £875 million. There were also separate social grants, totalling £459 million, intended to help in meeting costs incurred in closing

Table 9.8 NCB financial results, 1985–1986 and 1986–1987 (£ million)

	1985–1986	1986–1987
Turnover	5,340	4,515
Other income	4	1
Operating costs (net)	(4,719)	(4,147)
Operating profit	625	369
Interest charges	(437)	(386)
Social costs	(691)	(798)
Terminal depreciation	(66)	(62)
Tax	(1)	(0)
Extraordinary items	(0)	(12)
Minority interests	(1)	(0)
Profit (loss) after tax, interest, and restructuring costs	(571)	(889)
Grants		
Social grants	513	594
Readaptation grants	8	7
Deficit grants	50	288
	571	889

Source: *British Coal Corporation, Annual Report and Accounts* (1987).
A £342 million strike recovery provision has been deducted from operating costs in 1985–1986. All figures are on a historical cost basis.

uneconomic capacity, encouraging the movement of miners from one colliery or coalfield to another, and improving the pension benefits of miners willing to accept voluntary redundancies. The total level of explicit subsidy was therefore £1.334 billion. More recent figures are shown in table 9.8. Thus, in 1985–1986 and 1986–1987 social grants plus deficit grants amounted to £563 million and £882 million respectively, although the former figure is slightly distorted by the carry-forward from the previous financial year of £342 million provision for strike recovery costs.

The 1984–1985 miners' strike was principally a conflict about the rate of closure of older less efficient collieries, with the NUM resisting the plans of the NCB's new chairman, Ian MacGregor, to improve the financial position by reducing the "tail" of highly unprofitable mines. After a year-long and very bitter struggle, the NUM lost the battle, and closures have since proceeded at a more rapid rate. In the short run the strike imposed severe financial costs on the Exchequer. The NCB's deficit rose to £2.225 billion in 1984–1985, and there was also a sharp deterioration in the financial positions of the nationalized electricity and steel industries. This deficit forced the enactment of the Coal Industry Act 1985 which allowed the Government to fund NCB losses up to a total of £2 billion and provided additional finance to compensate redundant miners and to defray the costs of colliery closures.

In the longer term, the accelerated rate of closure of higher-cost capacity can be expected to lead to some improvement in the finances of the NCB as unit costs are reduced. However, the NCB still has ambitious programs for the development of new larger collieries on greenfield sites with substantial relatively accessible reserves. If the NCB is to remain in public ownership, therefore, there will continue to be substantial calls on the Exchequer for funds to finance these developments.

9.5.3 Prospects for Liberalization and Privatization

Since coal is an internationally traded commodity and since the industry is not, in any case, a natural monopoly, there is considerable scope for increasing competition in the U.K. market. This could be achieved in the context either of public ownership or of full or partial private ownership. We will therefore first assess the measures that might be taken to promote greater competition, together with the likely consequences of those measures, before going on to consider the ownership question.

The simplest, and probably the most powerful, pro-competitive policy change that could be implemented would be to lift the implicit limitations on imports, thereby substantially reducing barriers to entry into the U.K. market. In practical terms, the most important effect of such a move would be that the CEGB would be free to obtain its coal from the cheapest source, which in turn would remove one of the sources of distorted electricity prices (see section 9.3.2). More generally, U.K. coal prices would be driven down towards levels prevailing on international markets. Although the average production cost of NCB deep-mined coal is substantially above that of major exporting countries such as the United States, Australia, and South Africa, a free-trading policy would not lead to the swift demise of the domestic industry, for two reasons. First, transport costs, particularly to inland sites, give the NCB an offsetting cost advantage in delivering coal to domestic power stations, many of which were built in or around the coalfields precisely so as to minimize these costs. Second, there are wide intercolliery variations in unit production costs, so that many mines could continue to operate profitably at the lower prices. Moreover, the great majority of the larger coal-fired power stations are located close to the lower-cost coalfields, particularly in the Midlands and parts of Yorkshire, so that the two factors tend to reinforce one another. For these reasons, Robinson and Marshall (1988) estimate that the level of imports would be unlikely to exceed 20 million tonnes per annum for at least a decade (imports amounted to 12.1 million tonnes and 9.9 million tonnes in 1985–1986 and 1986–1987 respectively).

In the absence of increased subsidies, however, the fall in selling prices induced by liberalization would increase the speed at which higher-cost uncompetitive mines were closed, leading to a more rapid contraction in output and employment. Given lower labor productivity in these mines, the consequences would be substantially greater for employment than for output. At this stage the Government would, as now, be faced with choices concerning the level of subsidies and grants. Unfortunately, the social costs of a rapid contraction in employment are likely to be high (which is a major reason why successive Governments have chosen to support the industry). Employment in the industry is concentrated in villages and small towns away from the main urban centers and in regions of the country where unemployment has tended to be higher than the national average. In many cases, therefore, redundant mineworkers face poor prospects of finding alternative jobs. Put another way, the resource cost of labor (i.e. other outputs foregone) is lower than the wage rate.

On balance, we favor liberalization because it would make the trade-off between the social costs and benefits of support more explicit than is currently the case (and thereby facilitate more informed decision making) and would avoid unnecessary allocative inefficiencies in the fuel choices of the industry's customers. This position is, however, conditional upon liberalization being accompanied by policies designed to correct distortions between private and social costs. Resource costs of labor that are below existing wage rates provide a justification for employment subsidies in the short to medium term, while the distributional effects of contraction call for the continuation of redundancy payment schemes in those cases where efficiency considerations do, nevertheless, point to colliery closures. Above all, public policy in this area should be based upon calculations of the avoidable social costs of production, rather than on the often arbitrary financial costs appearing in the NCB's internal accounts.

Turning to domestic competition in the industry, there appears to be little case for the preservation of a system in which the NCB can effectively control the activities of its potential rivals. In particular the limitations on the sizes of private licensed producers of both deep-mined and opencast coal should be abolished. The MMC (1983b) recommended that the limit on the size of reserves that can be worked by private opencast operators be raised to 100,000 tonnes (from the 50,000 tonne figure established in 1981, which in turn represented an increase on the previous 35,000 tonne limit), but, since environmental effects can be taken into account on a case-by-case basis, it is difficult to see the case for any *general* limit.

Unfortunately, such measures are unlikely to have much effect on competition if the NCB retains its monopoly control over the issuing of licenses and the setting of royalty levels since it can use these instruments to restrict competition. This point goes to the heart of the liberalization issue. At present the NCB is accorded a regulatory role that is inconsistent with the development of fair competition between it and rival producers. Thus, whether or not the NCB is eventually to be privatized, we would advocate that it be stripped of these powers by removing its property rights over unworked coal reserves.

One solution to the problem would be to vest the property rights in the Crown, as is done in the case of oil and gas reserves. The regulatory function would then be restored to the state, which would allocate rights to work the coal and, in the process, set taxes, royalties, working obligations, and environmental constraints. In this framework, the NCB would compete on equal terms with any other firm wishing to exploit coal reserves, whether by deep-mining or strip-mining methods. Royalties and taxes would accrue directly to the state, which would derive additional revenues if, as would be preferable, the rights were allocated by auction rather than by discretionary methods.

By freeing existing producers from direct control by the NCB, these changes in the licensing system would immediately increase domestic competition. Opencast mining currently accounts for about 13–14 million tonnes of output and, adding in the small amount of privately produced deep-mined coal, the competing private sector would account for around 13 percent of domestic consumption of the commodity. In the longer term, private producers could compete with the NCB for the development of the substantial unworked reserves that are known to exist in the U.K. and, as the NCB closes its higher cost capacity, could be expected to achieve a growing market share. Such competition also leaves open the possibility of joint ventures between the NCB and private companies, particularly in the exploitation of major reserves, where a combination of the NCB's technical expertise and private sector managerial expertise and finance might sometimes be an attractive proposition.

The remaining question to consider is whether privatization of the NCB, either in its existing form or on a part-by-part basis, would generate significant benefits over and above those likely to emerge from liberalization. Given the existing financial state of the industry and the undoubted hostility of the NUM, there is little prospect that capital markets would view a single flotation of the NCB as an interesting proposition. The figures in table 9.8 illustrate some of the difficulties, but they do not reveal the full extent of the problems. Thus, in 1986–1987, before allowing for social costs of £798 million, the NCB's mining activities had an operating profit of £311 million, of which no less than £244 million was contributed by opencast operations (equivalent to a rate of return on average capital employed in opencast operations of 118.9 percent). Moreover, on a CCA basis operating profit in that year was only £62 million, largely because of the much larger depreciation provisions implied by the CCA method. Finally, none of these figures take account of the implicit subsidy associated with CEGB purchases of coal at prices well in excess of international market levels, which has recently been estimated by the CEGB to amount to about £750 million per annum. The NCB's deep-mining activities are therefore still highly unprofitable at competitive price levels.

While it might technically be feasible to find investors who would place a positive price on NCB shares on the basis of Government promises to continue industrial support for a designated period, there would be consequential moral hazard problems and the danger that the creation of a heavily subsidized private industry would create an unappealing precedent. For these reasons, full privatization is an option that the Government appears to have ruled out within the near future.

In the longer term, if a slimmed-down coal industry can be restored to profitability, a flotation of the public corporation might become a more attractive option. It can be argued that in these circumstances there would be something to be gained—in terms of internal efficiency, improved investment appraisal, and the like—from the introduction of the profit motive. Given that we have earlier argued that, as a general principle, a presumption in favor of private ownership is justified where effective competition exists and where other forms of market failure are insubstantial, and given that a restructured coal industry may eventually satisfy these conditions, we have some sympathy with this view (but see the caveat in the final two paragraphs of this section). It is, however, ironic that it would be necessary for the major problems to be resolved and for the major internal efficiency gains to be attained in the context of public ownership *before* the benefits of private ownership could be realized.

Although the financial position of the NCB as a whole inhibits early flotation as a single entity, the existence of collieries, and even whole coalfields, that are profitable at existing prices, and at least potentially profitable at the prices that would prevail in a more competitive market, implies that partial privatization is feasible in the shorter term. However, whilst recognizing that the survival of very small privately owned deep mines shows that large scale *may not* be a necessary condition for low cost production, we believe that the creation of an atomistic ownership structure, which would return the industry to its pre-nationalization form, would not be the best option. Although coal production is not a natural monopoly, some economies of scale do appear to exist in areas such as management and research and development. Thus, as the pre-nationalization record shows, a highly fragmented market structure might deliver rather poor performance.

If early privatization were to be favored, therefore, a better alternative would be to transfer collieries to private ownership in blocks, where the size of a single block might be as large as a whole coalfield. High cost mines and coalfields would continue to be publicly owned, but their significance would diminish over time as they were closed at a rate that reflected the Government's evolving perceptions of the balance between social costs and benefits of closure. Coupled with policies of liberalization, this type of approach would lead to the rapid emergence of strong competition in the domestic market, without necessitating the abandonment of significant scale economies.

In practical terms, however, associated with *all* of the ownership transfer options we have considered is an underlying danger that makes it appropriate for us to conclude by sounding a warning note. As pointed out earlier, the proceeds from privatization are higher the greater the degree of monopoly afforded to the newly created company or companies. In the case of coal, preoccupation with this financial point could be particularly significant, not because Government is likely to want to maximize the proceeds from the transaction(s). but rather because the *feasibility* of privatization is dependent upon the creation of profitable companies.

Given that, even in the absence of effective competition, many collieries are unprofitable, if a high priority is given to privatization public policy will be biased towards measures that serve to enhance the industry's financial performance. To the extent that such measures involve policies to reduce unit private costs there are grounds for concern that divergences between private and social costs will be discounted. Moreover, policies that protect the domestic industry from competition also serve to enhance financial performance and therefore increase the prospects that flotation(s) would find favor with the capital market. Thus, as the experience with BT and British Gas demonstrates, preoccupation with ownership transfer might work against the adoption of the most effective policies for regulatory reform and the promotion of competition. We therefore conclude that it is appropriate to give priority to the latter policies. In particular, implicit restrictions on imports should be lifted and the regulatory functions of the NCB with respect to the issuing of licenses and the setting of royalties should be transferred to the state. Only after these issues (together with associated questions concerning appropriate levels of subsidies and grants) have been settled should the issue of privatization be considered.

9.6 Concluding Comments

Evaluation of past and prospective privatizations in the U.K. energy industries raises a wide and disparate set of economic issues. For example, in gas and electricity policy makers are faced with classic natural monopoly problems, in coal the issues center on the problems surrounding an industry in decline, and in oil Governments have been concerned to maximize their revenues from the offshore industry while promoting the rapid development of domestic production to improve the balance of payments position and guarantee secure supplies. Each case, however, illustrates the importance of one or more of the general economic arguments that run throughout our analyses. Thus, as elsewhere, the energy industries demonstrate the crucial roles played by public policies with respect to the encouragement (or discouragement) of competition and the development of appropriate regulatory frameworks, underlying both of which are fundamental questions concerning the links between information, incentives, and economic performance.

Our first general conclusion is that too little has been done to promote increased competition in the gas, electricity, and coal industries. Since 1979 there have been some moves towards liberalization, but these have generally been ineffective. In gas and electricity the intentions of the Oil and Gas (Enterprise) Act and the Energy Act have been thwarted, largely because the legislative provisions left dominant incumbent firms with considerable discretion over terms of access to the distribution networks and did virtually nothing to restrict predatory behavior in the event that, access problems notwithstanding, entry does actually take place. The outcome must therefore be classed as a policy failure. Privatization of British Gas did nothing to remedy this defect and, if anything, has made the position worse by strengthening the incentives of the incumbent firm to deter new entry. Further, opportunities to increase competition in gas by restructuring the industry at the time of privatization were not taken.

In the coal industry case, there is a long record of protectionist measures designed to insulate the domestic industry from competitive pressures. Over time, these have imposed considerable resource costs on the U.K. economy by delaying the reduction in production capacity. On social cost grounds, the case for policy interventions to smooth the transition to a lower production base is a good one, but the adjustment process, extending over most of the twentieth century, has been unduly protracted. Moreover, the instruments adopted (e.g. the allocation of monopoly rights to the NCB and the restriction of imports) have been inappropriate; it would have been better to allow more competition and to deal with the consequences by direct financial subventions. In section 9.5.3 we set out various means by which competition in domestic markets can be increased. If implemented, these would lead to an increase in private production in the industry, but they do not require that the NCB be privatized. Indeed, to the extent that preoccupation with early privatization would lead to the assignment of a higher priority to measures aimed at increasing the (private) profitability of the industry, it might actually stand in the way of desirable developments in public policy.

Turning to regulatory issues, our judgment is that the framework of control established for British Gas represents, to date, the nadir of the U.K. privatization program. Not only did the Government fail to learn the lessons from the BT case but also regulatory policy appears to have taken a step backward. In pursuing the objective of "regulation with a light hand," the Government has created a private monopolist with even more market power than BT and a regulatory body, Ofgas, with rather less power than Oftel. Thus, for example, the ability of Ofgas to promote competition will be extremely limited and its accounting information will be poor.

A similarly cavalier attitude towards the problem of acquiring better policy-relevant information is also evident in the Government's approach to the oil industry. Although several of the asset sales (e.g. BP, Enterprise Oil, and Wytch Farm) give no substantive grounds for concern about the future conduct of regulatory policy, this conclusion does not hold in the important case of BNOC/Britoil where little weight seems to have been given to the information-gathering role that can be played by a publicly owned offshore operating and trading company.

For the future, the prospects may be a little brighter. There has been no great rush to privatize the electricity and coal industries and, in the former case, the signs are that a thorough appraisal of the policy alternatives, including possible restructuring of the industry, will be conducted before final decisions are made. Such appraisals are particularly to be welcomed since, as we have explained, striking an appropriate balance between competition and regulation is perhaps more difficult in electricity supply than in any of the other industries we have considered.

Unfortunately, however, there remains a variety of pressures against adoption of radical measures to increase competition in, and to strengthen the regulation of, industries such as electricity supply. These include political preferences for speedy privatization to meet Parliamentary timetables and both increase and bring forward the realization of sales proceeds, managerial preferences for the preservation of large organizations with monopoly power, and investor preferences for the flotation of companies with predictable profit streams and observable (past) track records. In the past, when they have come into conflict with policy proposals aimed at establishing greater competition and/or tighter regulation—as they did in the telecommunications and gas cases—these pressures have generally prevailed, and the November 1987 Government announcement of increases in real electricity prices over the next two years is indicative that they are still at work. There is therefore a chance that the prospect of a brighter future may turn out to be a mirage. Indeed, by creating a new interest group (shareholders) that is well disposed to monopoly power and regulation with a light hand, and by strengthening the preferences of Government for these same outcomes (because they facilitate the administrative process accompanying privatization and permit the early realization of *capitalized* monopoly rents), there is a danger that privatization could lead to a less competitive and more poorly regulated industry than the one that might be expected to develop if the current policy approach—based on the rapid and complete transfer of state assets to the private sector—were to be abandoned. Although they have proved elusive in the past, increased competition and improved regulation might, in fact, more readily be achieved in the context of continuing public ownership of a part, but not the whole, of the ESI (and, indeed, of the other energy industries).

10.1   Introduction

Some of the most radical reforms in the privatization program have occurred in the transport industries, particularly air and road. British Airways, the British Airports Authority (now BAA), National Freight, Sealink ferries, Associated British Ports, and subsidiaries of the National Bus Company have been transferred to the private sector, along with the aerospace companies British Aerospace and Rolls-Royce. The scope of competitive forces in transport has been widened by the deregulation of coach and bus services, and by some steps toward the liberalization of domestic and international air services. New methods of regulation have been introduced, for example in the operation of airports. These developments, and the debates about ownership, competition, and regulation that have attended them, are the concern of the present chapter.

The next section describes the privatization of British Airways, and the steps that are being taken to introduce some competition on domestic and international routes. However, the company was sold with its dominant position—in terms of market share, routes, access to airports (especially Heathrow), and fleet—substantially intact, and its market power is bolstered further by the acquisition of British Caledonian, hitherto its principal U.K. competitor. An important question is whether the new threats of entry, and policy against possible anticompetitive practices, will be effective in constraining the market power that British Airways derives from its established (and now strengthened) market position.

Section 10.3 is concerned with the privatization of BAA and the regulation of airport pricing. No attempt was made to promote competition between airports: monopoly was simply transferred to the private sector. The valuable part of the sale was not so much the air traffic activities, but the prime site property and shops at airports together with their duty-free tax concessions. We consider possible inefficiencies of resource allocation arising from the pricing and investment policies for airports, and we examine the merits of the proposal that BAA should have been split into competing units prior to sale.

Section 10.4 describes the radical deregulation of express coaching and local bus services introduced by the Transport Acts of 1980 and 1985. In these industries the reform of the competitive and regulatory environment took place before privatization, which occurred in the form of the piecemeal transfer of subsidiaries of the National Bus Company, often in the form of management buyouts. The deregulation of express coaching was followed by a bout of keen competition, but the incumbent firm, National Express, soon reasserted its dominant position, although competition between coach and rail has been a longer-lasting consequence. The deregulation of local bus services has so far had little impact in many areas, but there have been dramatic results in some areas, where intense (and possibly unstable) competition is happening. We assess the prospects for competition, though it is too early to judge what results deregulation is likely to have in the longer term.

Finally we consider some options for privatizing British Rail, including the possibility of separating the ownership of its track and trains. The railway network is not at present on the agenda for privatization, because it is not profitable (it relies on subsidies for many of its operations) and because prospects for competition are extremely bleak. However, public subsidy and monopoly are not incompatible with private ownership of production facilities, and a future Conservative Government may decide to privatize and reform rail transport just as it has for road and air transport in recent years.

10.2   Airlines

Although British Airways (BA) was always a prime candidate for privatization, it was not transferred to private ownership until early in 1987, following long delays due to competition lawsuits brought by Laker and renegotiation of the Bermuda 2 Agreement with the United States regarding North Atlantic routes. BA was finally offered for sale on 30 January 1987 at a price of 125 pence per share, which valued the company at £900 million. The Government was careful to point out the risks of the airline business, and saw the issue as a way of deepening rather than widening share ownership. In other words, the BA share offer was presented more as one for existing owners of shares than for first-time buyers. Nevertheless the offer price was seen as being very attractive, and demand from individuals, U.K. institutions, and foreign buyers was strong. The issue was massively oversubscribed, and, when dealings began on 11 February, the share price opened at 118 pence before closing at 109 pence—a premium of 44 pence (68 percent) above the partly paid price of 65 pence.

BA was an attractive candidate for privatization because it was profitable, and a change in its ownership raised far fewer problems for policy regarding competition and regulation than the privatization of utility companies such as British Telecom (BT) and British Gas. BA had been managed according to broadly commercial criteria in the public sector, and an elaborate system of domestic and international regulations already existed. The sale of BA nevertheless raised important questions about competition and regulation. First, there were fears that BA, as the dominant U.K. airline, would exploit its dominant position more energetically in the private sector, for example by predatory pricing to exclude rivals from certain routes. This danger could be met by the structural remedy of reducing BA's relative size (e.g. by route transfers) and/or by sufficiently tough measures to prevent anticompetitive conduct. Secondly, the sale of BA influenced Government policy making on competition and regulation in the airline industry generally. The Government cannot easily change its airline policy in a manner unfavorable to BA once privatization has taken place, because it would be accused of breaking the commitments made at the time of sale. Moreover, BA in the private sector might be able to resist change more easily than when it was in the public sector, although it must be said that the management of BA under Lord King appears to have exerted a considerable influence on Government policy in the run up to privatization. The U.K. Government advocates competition and deregulation in the domestic and international airline industries, but in the event it privatized BA without reducing its market power substantially.

We begin this section by outlining some of the main features of competition and regulation in the airline industry. We then describe the position of BA, including its extensive international route network, its main center of operations at Heathrow, and the recent strong improvement in the company's performance. Next we describe Government policy as set out in the 1984 White Paper *Airline Competition Policy* (Department of Transport, 1984b), which followed the major review of the subject by the U.K. Civil Aviation Authority (CAA) (Civil Aviation Authority, 1984). Finally we consider the BA–British Caledonian merger proposal announced in July 1987, and we offer our assessment of airline competition policy and its relation to the privatization of BA.

10.2.1 Competition and Regulation in the Airline Industry

Throughout the world the airline industry is heavily regulated. As well as the necessary regulation of safety, security, and environmental (e.g. noise) standards, there is a high degree of *economic* regulation. Governments are closely involved with the allocation of routes, the licensing of airlines, the setting of fares, and airports policy. Following the deregulation of the domestic airline industry in the United States in 1978, moves towards liberalization are being made in many countries, but progress is slow and patchy. The deregulation of international routes is inhibited by the need for multilateral renegotiation of air services agreements between governments, and domestic deregulation depends on the attitudes of particular governments. The limited extent of liberalization so far bears witness to the strength of many existing airlines in resisting the arrival of effective competition.

The fortunes of airline companies are nevertheless quite volatile. Profits are very sensitive to demand because of the high fixed (though not necessarily sunk) cost of operating a fleet of aircraft. The marginal cost of carrying additional passengers on a route is low, and "load factors" (i.e. the extent to which aircraft are full) are of critical importance. Demand uncertainties are therefore magnified in terms of their impact on profits. There is also much uncertainty on the cost side, because financing charges and fuel costs account for a large proportion of total expenditure, and both tend to be volatile. Finally, there is exchange rate uncertainty. Competition (where it exists) further affects these uncertainties, because price is free to oscillate more than in a highly regulated regime. But competition sometimes diminishes profit uncertainty insofar as price movements tend to be correlated with cost changes so that the volatility of profit margins is dampened.

The nature of competition and regulation varies from route to route. It is instructive to begin with the most liberal domestic regime—the United States—where deregulation occured in 1978. (Safety regulation of course remained.) Bailey (1986) reports on the experience of deregulation in airlines and other industries (see further Graham *et al.* (1983) and Bailey *et al.* (1985)). On average air fares fell significantly, and cross-subsidies were eroded as prices came more into line with costs. Productivity improved, and the wages of airline employees were sharply reduced. Consumer choice widened and more price/quality options became available. However, these mostly desirable consequences of deregulation have recently been followed by more disconcerting events. Competitive failure and merger activity (in which the authorities have been reluctant to intervene) have caused an increase in concentration, with the six largest airlines increasing their market share from 73 percent in 1978 to 84 percent in 1986. Fears have been expressed that the initial bout of competition will be followed by cosy oligopoly unless antitrust policy is sufficiently vigilant. A particular danger is that airlines derive local market power from their "hub and spoke" networks centered on major airports. American experience in the past decade has important lessons for other countries (and groups of countries) that are moving towards liberalization. The rapid restructuring of prices demonstrates the inefficiency and inertia that regulation can sustain, but the recent trends towards a more concentrated market structure show that there are forces in the industry that might threaten the benefits of liberalization unless they are somehow held in check.

Domestic routes in the U.K. have also been substantially deregulated in the 1980s. Regulatory barriers to entry have been diminished, and competitors providing services on both new and existing routes have entered the market. However, policy on access to airports (especially Heathrow) can pose difficulties for competitors. Restrictions on fare setting have been relaxed, and approval of fares by the CAA is no longer required; notification is sufficient. Pricing is subject to regulation only insofar as it is found to be anticompetitive, for example predatory pricing.

It is not yet possible to make a definitive assessment of the effects of airline deregulation in the U.K., but the initial evidence suggests that its impact has been positive, if not dramatically so. Traffic volume has grown, and independent operators such as British Midland have increased their market shares at the expense of British Airways. Competition has grown on some routes, and services have consequently improved. Fares on U.K. routes have tended to come down since liberalization, at least on the main trunk routes, and they are generally lower than on comparable routes in Continental Europe. Special discount fares have become more prevalent, and are perhaps the most obvious manifestation of increased competition.

The economic regulation of international scheduled sevices is for the most part based on bilateral "air services agreements" between governments, which give each government the power to designate one or more of its national airlines to operate the service in question. Air services agreements often specify capacity limits for incumbents, require fares to be approved, and regulate entry. Many fares are coordinated by the airline cartel IATA. Thus the identity and behavior of route operators is determined to a large extent by government decision rather than competitive forces. Airlines may compete to be awarded the routes by government, but that competition is essentially rent-seeking activity.

To win government designation for an international route, a British airline must obtain a licence for that route from the CAA and permission from the foreign government. In Europe (see McGowan and Trengrove, 1986) the U.K. has negotiated relatively liberal air services agreements with the Netherlands, Belgium, and Luxembourg, which deregulate fares, capacity, and entry. The agreements with West Germany and Switzerland are pro-competitive to a limited extent, but other European countries—notably Denmark, Greece, Italy, Portugal, and Spain (who have state airlines)—are more hostile to deregulation of European air services. The Civil Aviation Act 1982 lays down the criteria to which the CAA must have regard in granting licenses, which include efficiency, profitability, consumer benefit, and so on. Competition for licenses to operate new routes is more effective than competition for licenses on existing routes, because revocation of licenses is relatively rare. Thus there is a considerable incumbent advantage. However, bilateral liberalization policies are offering some opportunities for entrants to seek to gain access to routes already flown. For example, in mid-1987 the CAA granted route licenses for scheduled services between Gatwick and nine European cities to Air Europe, a charter airline owned by the International Leisure Group. The CAA also granted some routes to British Caledonian. These licenses are subject to approval by the European countries concerned, but this is likely to be given in most of the cases in question and it is clear that competition to British Airways is growing in this area.

Some attempts to liberalize European civil aviation in the EEC as a whole have also been made, but they have so far met with little success. The national airlines have in the past enjoyed effective immunity from the provisions of EEC competition law (Articles 85 and 86 of the Treaty of Rome), but in 1986 the European Court ruled, in a case brought by the Nouvelles Frontières travel group, that the air transport sector was in principle subject to Community competition rules. Following this judgment, the European Commission began litigation against national airlines alleging a variety of anticompetitive practices. It remains to be seen whether this action against cartelization will succeed in the Court. At the same time the governments of the Member States deliberated a compromise package that would have brought a very modest degree of competition to European routes. However, talks broke down at the end of June 1987 (because of a dispute about the status of Gibraltar airport). Thus the initiative for reform now seems to lie with the Commission. If their action succeeds, liberalization may go much further than that proposed in the compromise package that failed to win acceptance.

Services between the U.K. and the United States are governed by the "Bermuda 2" air services agreement, which is more liberal than most international agreements, although fares, capacity, and entry are regulated to some extent. Competition on North Atlantic routes has been quite keen, and the major airlines have had to respond to low cost operators such as Laker, Virgin, and People's Express, which have met with varying degrees of success. There has also been some competition with other European airlines such as Air France on North Atlantic routes.

Airports policy is another important element of the framework of competition and regulation, because the demand for the services of an airline is influenced by the location of the airports it uses and the ease of transferring to connecting flights. This last factor gives rise to a kind of "network externality" inasmuch as flights to or from busy airports are especially desirable. This gives a competitive advantage to an airline with rights at a major airport hub.

10.2.2 British Airways

BA's main business is the operation of international and domestic scheduled passenger air services. It also runs charter services (through its British Airtours subsidiary) and cargo services. Its international route network, which covers 145 destinations in 68 countries, is arguably the best in the world, and measured by passengers carried BA has a larger share of the market for international scheduled services than any other airline. Its center of operations is at Heathrow, the world's busiest international airport. At the end of 1986 BA had a fleet of 163 aircraft. Of these the 51 long-haul aircraft for intercontinental routes included 31 Boeing 747s and seven Concordes, and 70 of the 112 short-haul aircraft were also Boeings.

Until 1984 BA was a public corporation run by a Board appointed by the Secretary of State for Transport. It became a public limited company on 1 April 1984 in readiness for privatization, but almost three years elapsed before its shares were sold to private hands. In the public sector BA's financial performance had been poor for some years, but a strong improvement in its performance occurred after Lord King became Chairman in 1981 and assembled a new management team. Table 10.1 gives information on BA's turnover and profits for the past six years. The improvement from 1982 to 1984 is especially notable. Demand growth and currency movements were helpful factors, but internal efficiency measures were the driving force. The number of BA employees fell by almost a third—from 54,000 to 36,000—in the early 1980s, and labor productivity consequently rose substantially. Modernization of the fleet of aircraft made for fuel efficiency improvements, and computerization provided

Table 10.1 BA's financial performance, 1982–1987

Year to 31 March	Turnover (£ million)	Operating surplus (£ million)	Pretax profit (loss) (£ million)
1982	2,241	12	(108)
1983	2,497	185	74
1984	2,514	268	185
1985	2,943	292	191
1986	3,149	198	195
1987	3,263	173	162

Source: *British Airways Prospectus* (1987) and *Annual Report and Accounts* (1987).

further efficiency gains. At the same time BA's marketing approach changed, and services became more customer oriented. The fall in profits in 1986–1987 was due largely to the reduction in transatlantic traffic in the summer of 1986 following the Chernobyl and Libyan incidents. It does not reflect a deterioration in BA's operating efficiency.

It is worth emphasizing that the main improvements in financial and productivity performance occurred two years or so *before* privatization, while BA was still in the public sector (on productivity trends see table 5.6 in chapter 5 above). BA was clearly a leading candidate for privatization at the time, but the monitoring and incentive systems of private ownership (see chapter 2 above) were not in place. BA's experience therefore shows that public ownership is no bar to major efficiency gains. It may well be that the impending prospect of privatization fostered keener commercial objectives in BA's management, but it is not clear that it was essential for that to happen. We attach importance to the fact that BA was operating in an industry where competition existed and was growing at least in major business segments, and where performance comparisons with other airlines were readily available. In short, the changing framework of competition and regulation, together with the energy of Lord King's new management team, were key factors.

Finally we should briefly describe the litigation which delayed BA's flotation. Late in 1982 the liquidator of Laker Airways brought a treble damages suit for $1 billion in the U.S. courts against BA and other airlines alleging that they had conspired to put Laker out of business. Similar actions were initiated in 1984 and 1986 by creditors of Laker. The cases have all been either settled or dismissed. An important question that arises from the Laker cases is the extent to which BA is subject to American antitrust laws in relation to its transatlantic services. Given that American antitrust law is tougher than U.K. or EEC competition law relating to airlines, this issue has a significant influence on the framework of competition and regulation faced by BA on some of its major routes. The U.S. courts have held that international airline services are within their jurisdiction, but the U.K. Government has maintained that American antitrust law is not applicable to air services authorized under the Bermuda 2 agreement. The matter has not yet been fully resolved. It is an interesting example of how international frameworks of competition and regulation can affect a privatized U.K. firm.

10.2.3 Government Policy for Airlines

Following a review carried out by the CAA (Civil Aviation Authority, 1984), the U.K. Government set out its airline policy in the White Paper on *Airline Competition Policy* (Department of Transport, 1984b). This document established the framework in which the privatized BA was to operate for the foreseeable future.

In the White Paper the Government stated four main objectives in addition to the maintenance of high standards of safety:

(i) to encourage a sound and competitive multi-airline industry;

(ii) to promote competition in all markets both internationally and domestically;

(iii) to ensure adequate safeguards against anticompetitive or predatory behavior by airlines;

(iv) to privatize BA.

However, the Government's response to the CAA's report on airline policy was by no means radically pro-competitive.

The CAA made several recommendations designed to promote competition by reducing the extent of BA's dominant position in the U.K. airline industry and enhancing the scope for independent airlines to compete effectively. Among other things, the CAA recommended the following:

(i) there should be at least one airline fit to replace BA on any major intercontinental route if necessary, and additional competition by British airlines on those routes should be licensed where possible;

(ii) BA's routes to Saudi Arabia and Harare should be transferred to British Caledonian;

(iii) BA's scheduled service routes from Gatwick should be taken over by other British airlines;

(iv) BA's routes from provincial airports should be taken over by other British airlines.

The Government rejected the proposed route transfers, taking the view that the independent airlines had grown and would continue to be able to do so provided that fair competition prevailed. Instead, the Government favored a voluntary agreement between BA and British Caledonian to exchange routes and boost British Caledonian's financial strength. In the event, the two airlines agreed to exchange BA's routes to Saudi Arabia for British Caledonian's faltering routes to South America.

This exchange was much less favorable to British Caledonian than the CAA proposal. Moreover, the fall in oil prices in 1986 badly affected the profitability of the Saudi Arabian routes, while ironically the South American routes picked up. In the event the exchanges did not achieve the objective of securing British Caledonian's independence, and the company became vulnerable to takeover. The BA takeover is discussed in section 10.2.4 below. The CAA proposals would have given British Caledonian a greater chance of survival as an independent force in the industry.

The Government also turned down the proposals that other airlines should take over BA's scheduled service routes from Gatwick and provincial airports. It was argued that BA's presence enhanced the stature of those airports. The other British airlines would have benefited from the changes recommended by the CAA, and so they were among the losers in relative terms. However, BA offered to provide independent airlines other than British Caledonian with up to £450,000 per route to help to develop up to 15 new European routes from regional airports. There is a good case for saying that the interests of consumers (i.e. air travellers) were also damaged by the Government's decision not to restructure BA to promote competition. We shall pursue this question when we consider the BA–British Caledonian merger proposal and offer an assessment of policy in the next section.

The Government's response to other recommendations by the CAA was more favorable. It welcomed the proposal that domestic fares should cease to require specific approval by the CAA, and the proposed introduction for a two-year experimental period of an area licensing facility allowing airlines to fly between any two points in the U.K. The Government also endorsed the CAA's intention to use its licensing powers to increase the range and market penetration of European scheduled services from Gatwick Airport. However, the Government did not agree that CAA powers needed strengthening in order to promote effective competition and to guard against the danger of anticompetitive behavior.

10.2.4 Concluding Remarks

By international standards the U.K. Government has been relatively liberal in its attitude towards deregulation, and its stated objectives are pro-competitive. However, its negative response to the CAA's proposals to reduce BA's dominance was not in keeping with its pro-competitive intentions. It is hard to avoid the conclusion that the Government was greatly influenced by the impending privatization of BA and by the company's management in particular. Lord King forcefully opposed reductions in BA's relative size, and stressed that the company was already undergoing a tough efficiency drive that involved a sharp decrease in staff numbers. With privatization so close at hand, BA's management was in a strong position in its dealings with the Government, and the CAA's proposed route transfers were successfully avoided.

What options could the Government have chosen to promote its stated competitive objectives more fully? (See Ashworth and Forsyth (1984) and Forsyth (1984) for a fuller discussion of this question and related issues.) Broadly speaking, routes (including landing rights) can be allocated to airlines in two ways—by government franchise or by market forces. There is scope for competition even in the case of highly regulated routes, provided that airlines compete effectively for the government franchises. Competition can occur when a new route becomes available and if existing routes come up for regular renewal. It is essential for effective competition that there should be several airlines capable of competing in this way. Otherwise competitive disciplines will be undermined by incumbent advantages or the danger of collusion between the few. In fact, however, BA faces little competition on many major routes, and it enjoys the great advantage of privileged access to Heathrow. BA's size in relation to the independent British airlines means that there is no prospect of the independents displacing BA on a large number of its existing routes. Moreover, it is Government policy that it will not lightly revoke licences currently in use in any case.

The route transfers proposed by the CAA can be criticized on the grounds that they would have done little to promote competition directly, but they would have had the indirect benefit of strengthening the position of the independents in a way that enhanced the prospects of realistic competition between British airlines—competition both *in* the market and *for* the market. This last point calls attention to the criteria upon which routes (including landing rights) are awarded. These are usually loosely defined, and the CAA has relatively little information (about efficiency etc.) to go on. The monopoly rents can be considerable, and airlines therefore have an incentive to engage in socially wasteful rent-seeking activity. Ashworth and Forsyth (1984) discuss the possibility of auctioning franchises to routes or groups of routes. Such a system offers several advantages. Routes would be granted according to a clear-cut criterion. Efficiency would be encouraged insofar as routes would tend to be allocated to the airlines best able to operate them, and efficient operation of those routes would be further stimulated. Wasteful rent-seeking activity would also be discouraged.

A further step in the same direction would be to allow airlines to sell or trade the route franchises that they owned. This again would enhance the efficiency of both the allocation and the operation of routes, because a mechanism would exist for the mutually advantageous transfer of routes from less efficient to more efficient operators. Moreover, the transfer mechanism would advantageously exploit the information of the airlines, which is naturally greater than that available to regulatory authorities. As before, the operation of a system of this kind would require a multi-airline industry capable of providing adequate actual and potential competition. It would also require changes to airports policy, which we shall consider in the next section.

Market forces have more play in routes, such as domestic routes, where deregulation is happening. Competition can occur in the market, rather than for the market via the regulatory process of route allocation. Sunk costs need not be high, because aircraft can be leased and in the case of existing operators can be switched from route to route. However, entry barriers can result if some airlines enjoy privileged access to important airports, as BA does in the case of Heathrow. Access is privileged in the sense that BA pays less for its landing rights than others would pay for them: it is enjoying a scarce input at below market prices. Furthermore, strategic entry barriers can result if incumbent operators can credibly threaten predatory behavior against new entrants. The ability of an airline such as BA to withstand an episode of predatory pricing is so much greater than that of most independents that this is a serious concern. Of course the Laker litigation was about exactly this question. The need for vigorous policy against anticompetitive behavior is self-evident. It is disturbing that the CAA believes that its powers need strengthening in this regard, but that the Government is satisfied that they do not. However, the Government has ended the immunity of domestic and charter services from the provisions of the Competition Act 1980.

British airline competition policy was thrown into turmoil in July 1987, only a few months after privatization, when BA and British Caledonian announced their intention to merge. BA's agreed bid for its principal U.K. competitor was valued at £237 million, a considerable premium over British Caledonian's net asset value of £97 million at 31 October 1986. In favor of the merger it was contended that British Caledonian was in a precarious financial plight and vulnerable to takeover (probably foreign) in any event. In the year to October 1986 it made a pretax loss of £19.3 million owing to the adverse effects of falling oil prices on its Saudi and Nigerian routes, and the fall in traffic caused by the Chernobyl and Libyan incidents. Nevertheless the airline was set to return to profitability in 1987, and it would have enjoyed a sounder financial position if the Government had accepted the CAA proposals described above. Secondly, it was argued that the merger would cut overhead costs, reduce duplication of some services, and encourage more business from passengers transferring between flights. Thirdly, it was contended that the competitive threat from giant American airline combines required the union of the two main British airlines.

However, the merger posed very serious threats to competition. Under the terms of the original bid BA would come to dominate Gatwick as well as Heathrow, its share of international scheduled services would rise from around 82 to 93 percent, and its share of U.K. domestic services by U.K. airlines would rise to about 60 percent. Moreover, the merger threatened to make a mockery of the Government's airline competition policy set out in the 1984 White Paper and reaffirmed so recently in the BA share prospectus. The first objective of that policy was "to encourage a sound and competitive multi-airline industry." The case for referring the merger to the Monopolies and Mergers Commission (MMC) was overwhelming, and despite intensive and controversial lobbying by BA, the Secretary of State duly accepted the recommendation of the Director General of Fair Trading to make a reference. In order to avoid prolonged and damaging uncertainty, the MMC was given three months, rather than the usual six, to produce its report.

The MMC reported in November 1987 that under revised terms proposed by BA the takeover was not against the public interest. Thus the way was cleared for BA to make a new bid for British Caledonian. BA proposed that the merged company would surrender British Caledonian's five domestic route licenses and some European route licenses. However, the merged firm intends to reapply for those route licenses in competition with independent airlines. BA also proposed to withdraw British Caledonian's objections to Air Europe's applications for some European routes, and not to oppose bids by other airlines for long-haul route licenses where multiple designation is possible. However, BA intends to keep all

British Caledonian's intercontinental routes. The preponderance of the merged firm in the British airline industry—in terms of fleet, crew, and existing route network—is such that competition for the surrendered routes is unlikely to be fully effective. Following a battle with Scandinavian Airline Systems (SAS), BA finally won control of British Caledonian in December 1987.

We have to conclude that the record of the U.K. Government in promoting competition in airlines is mixed. Its declared attitude towards the deregulation of domestic and international (especially European) services contrasts favorably with the illiberal attitudes of some other countries. But in the case of BA its actions were less than actively pro-competitive. BA's dominance of the U.K. airline industry has been maintained, and indeed extended by the takeover of British Caledonian, its principal competitor. That event undermined a central element in previously stated airline competition policy, but might have been averted if the Government had strengthened British Caledonian's chances of survival as an independent competitive force by accepting the CAA's recommendations on route transfers in 1984. In BA's case as in others, we believe that the desire to enhance the proceeds from privatization, and the strong bargaining position of management, played no small part in shaping the framework of competition and regulation for the industry.

10.3   Airports

The privatization of BAA (formerly the British Airports Authority) in July 1987 is perhaps the clearest example of the Conservative Government's preference for regulated private monopoly over public monopoly. Given the Government's decision not to divide BAA into potentially competing parts, its privatization had virtually nothing to do with competition. Moreover, since the great majority of those working on BAA premises were already employees of private firms (shops, banks, restaurants, etc.) or will continue to be public employees (air traffic controllers, customs officers, etc.), the privatization did not do a great deal to increase the scope of private operations at airports. Mainly it was about the transfer to private hands of valuable *assets*—runways, terminals, car parks, prime shopping sites, and tax concessions.

This section has four parts. The first describes Government airports policy as set out in the 1985 White Paper, which gives useful background, for example concerning plans for the future development of airport capacity in the U.K. We then outline BAA's main activities, its financial performance, and its pricing policies. Thirdly, we describe the new regime of price regulation, and finally we offer an assessment of BAA's privatization. The unusual method of selling BAA's shares, which combined an offer for sale and a tender offer, has already been discussed in chapter 7 above.

10.3.1   Airports Policy

The privatization of BAA is just one element in Government airports policy, and it should be viewed in the wider context. The central problem for airports policy over the years has been to accommodate the rapidly growing demand for air travel without undue damage to the environment. Proposals to establish a third major airport near London, successively at Maplin or Stansted, and plans to extend capacity at Heathrow and Gatwick have been the subject of intense controversy. The role of the regional airports in national policy has also been much debated. A series of public inquiries has taken place, and discussion documents and White Papers have been issued. The most recent is the 1985 White Paper on *Airports Policy* (Department of Transport, 1985), which is the focus of this section. The White Paper has two main parts: the first considers the development of airports in the U.K., and the second outlines reform of their ownership and regulation, notably the privatization of BAA.

Airport capacity is determined by two principal constraints: the capacity of airport terminals to handle passenger movements, and the capacity of runways safely to handle aircraft movements. Expansions in terminal capacity at London's main airports (i.e. the fourth terminal at Heathrow and the second at Gatwick which opens in 1988) have made runway capacity the binding constraint. The White Paper estimated that the effective capacity of London airports in 1995 would be 64.5 to 70.5 million passengers per annum (mppa), with Heathrow and Gatwick respectively accounting for about 60 percent and 32 percent of that capacity, and Stansted and Luton making up the residual.

The Government's principal measure to meet the anticipated growth in demand was to approve planning permission for the development of terminal facilities at Stansted up to a capacity of 15 mppa. This development is to occur in two phases of 7–8 mppa each, with the second phase requiring Parliamentary approval. The capacity limit is determined by terminal space: Stansted's runway could handle 25 mppa (depending on aircraft size and mix), and further development of the airport to utilize runway capacity might occur in the more distant future. The Government reaffirmed the policy that Gatwick should remain a single-runway airport, and stated that the possibility of a fifth terminal at Heathrow would be kept under review. A modest development of Luton Airport was also proposed.

The measures above are concerned with meeting demand in the southeast, but the White Paper also envisaged a greater role for the regional airports where capacity is less intensively used. Outside London the two "gateway international" airports for long-haul services are Manchester and Prestwick. Together with Aberdeen and Birmingham they handle about 70 percent of regional traffic. The smaller regional airports include Newcastle, East Midlands, Leeds, Liverpool, Cardiff, Bristol, Teesside, Glasgow, and Edinburgh. The regional airports jointly handle about a third of passenger traffic at U.K. airports. Domestic traffic accounts for approximately 45 percent of their business, and international scheduled and charter traffic account for about 10 percent and 45 percent respectively.

The Government stated its belief that airports should be free to compete as far as possible, and its concern to encourage the growth and development of regional airports. It declared its readiness to approve financially justified capital expenditures for expansion of regional airports, and its intention to develop Manchester as a regional hub airport. The regional airports also have a part to play in relation to the partial liberalization of airline services (see section 10.2.3). Finally on airport development, the White Paper discusses airports for business aviation, including the new "Stolport" (i.e. short takeoff and landing airport) in the East London dockland, and helicopter ports.

The White Paper made proposals for reform of the structure of ownership and regulation of airports, which were carried into law by the Airports Act 1986. The BAA has a near monopoly of airports in the southeast by virtue of owning the main three of the four London airports (Heathrow, Gatwick, and Stansted), and it owns Scotland's four principal airports (Aberdeen, Edinburgh, Glasgow, and Prestwick). The Government chose to sell BAA as a single entity, rather than dividing it into potentially competing parts. Selling the seven airports separately would have diminished BAA's dominance, but the Government took the view that the resulting advantages were not substantial and were outweighed by serious disadvantages. We shall assess this and other questions in section 10.3.4 below, but next we shall describe BAA's main activities.

10.3.2 BAA's Activities

The BAA owns and operates the principal airports in Britain. It was set up under the 1965 Airports Authority Act, and initially comprised the four Gateway International Airports—Heathrow, Gatwick, Stansted, and Prestwick. The BAA took over the regional airports at Edinburgh, Aberdeen, and Glasgow in the 1970s; most other regional airports are owned and operated by local authorities. The BAA's seven airports together handled 55.3 million passengers in the year to 31 March 1987, which was 73 percent of U.K. air passenger traffic, and £25 billion worth of cargo traffic, which was 85 percent of the cargo tonnage passing through U.K. airports. Heathrow handles the majority (over 57 percent) of BAA's passenger traffic. It is the busiest international airport in the world, and is used by more than 70 airlines flying to over 200 destinations. In terms of numbers of international passengers Gatwick has just become the second-busiest airport in the world. Passenger traffic growth is a crucial determinant of BAA's future profits. For more than 20 years it has been quite steady at an average rate of 6.4 percent, and growth is set to continue. The Department of Transport predicts annual growth rates of between 3.4 and 6.1 percent for London's airports, and between 2.1 and 5.7 percent for other U.K. airports, until the end of the century. BAA has 7,500 employees, but they are only a tenth of the number that work on BAA's premises.

Profits have also grown strongly over the years. Unlike other nationalized industries, BAA has always been in the black, and in the year to 31 March 1987 it made a pretax profit of £90 million on a current cost basis, and £124 million on a historic cost basis, on total income of £439 million. About 48 percent of that income came from charges for airport traffic services provided by BAA to airlines. Airport charges include elements for each departing passenger, aircraft landing, and aircraft parking. Airport charges have been subject to price regulation since 1 April 1987 (see section 10.3.3). BAA's air traffic activities require large sums of capital expenditure to expand and improve airport capacity—runways, terminals, roads, and car parks. BAA plans to spend over £850 million over the next five years on projects such as the refurbishment of Terminal 3 at Heathrow, the new terminal at Gatwick, and the expansion of Stansted airport (see above). Other expenditure on air traffic services includes the cost of security, operational safety, and emergency services, which together account for a third of BAA's workforce.

The remaining 52 percent of BAA's income in 1986–1987 came from commercial activities. Most of this income (£158 million, i.e. about 36 percent of BAA's total income) came from concessionaires who sell goods and services to the public, including duty-free drink and tobacco, tax-free goods, books and newspapers, insurance and banking facilities, car rental services, car parking, and catering services. Most concession income (£88 million in 1986–1987) comes from duty-free and tax-free shops. Concessions are usually put out to competitive tender, and BAA typically receives a percentage of the concessionaires' turnover. Other commercial income comes from rents and services provided to tenants such as airlines and hotels.

Although traffic and commercial activities account for an approximately equal share of BAA's income, most costs are incurred in relation to traffic activities. In the year to 31 March 1987 BAA made a current cost trading profit of £131 million on commercial activities, and a trading loss of £36 million on traffic activities. (On the historic cost basis the commercial profit was £140 million and the traffic loss was £9 million.) The allocation of joint costs (e.g. on terminals) between traffic and commercial activities is not a precise science, and BAA may have an incentive to increase the reported loss on traffic activities (especially in view of past litigation over traffic charges by a number of airlines), but by any reckoning there is a substantial cross-subsidy from commercial activities to traffic activities. BAA makes a loss on its primary business, which it more than recoups by its income from its highly desirable shopping areas, which is enhanced by the tax privileges currently enjoyed by duty-free and tax-free shops, and by the relative lack of competition between them.

Under public ownership the BAA's stated policy for traffic charges was to apply long-run marginal cost (LRMC) pricing. Although LRMC prices are helpful in making investment appraisals, their use in practice can cause large losses in allocative efficiency in industries where capacity constraints are long term. The usual argument for using LRMC prices rather than short-run marginal cost (SRMC) prices is that SRMC prices can be very volatile when capacity is periodically adjusted to match demand, with undesirable consequences for uncertainty and investment planning. However, the capacity limits at airports (e.g. for Heathrow landing slots at peak times) are long term in nature, and there is a strong case for using SRMC pricing to ration demand at peak times more efficiently and increase revenues to cover overheads.

Furthermore, it is questionable whether the BAA under public ownership did actually pursue its stated policy of LRMC pricing. Starkie and Thompson (1985) concluded from their investigation that LRMC pricing was not consistently applied. They used cost data relating to the expansion of terminal facilities at Heathrow and Gatwick to assess LRMC.

This information was prepared by BAA in connection with the lawsuit initiated by a number of airlines in 1980 who alleged that BAA's traffic charges were discriminatory and too high. The British and American Governments were also in dispute at that time about airport charges at Heathrow. The litigation was settled out of court and a Memorandum of Understanding between the two Governments was signed in 1983. The memorandum stated that the British Government would look "for no more than a reasonable rate of return on investment" in formulating financial targets for BAA, and that no distinction would be drawn between sources of revenue (whether traffic or commercial) in computing rates of return. This is known as the "single-till" principle. Starkie and Thompson found that, even after changes in pricing structure in 1983, BAA's traffic charges at Heathrow and Gatwick were in general below LRMC (let alone SRMC), that Stansted was unjustifiably cross-subsidized, and that LRMC pricing would allow traffic income to cover traffic expenditure. These criticisms also apply to the traffic charges of the privatized BAA, because the regulatory regime has the effect of perpetuating the pricing structure that prevailed under public ownership. The regulatory regime is described in more detail in the next section.

BAA's policies regarding commercial activities were the subject of an inquiry by the MMC (Monopolies and Mergers Commission, 1985). Most commercial activities are not operated directly by BAA but are subcontracted or franchised to private sector firms—banks, caterers, newsagents, and so on. In many cases the BAA effectively auctions monopoly rights by tender: there is competition for the market rather than competition in the market (see section 4.6.1 above on franchising). In other cases the BAA grants concessions to competing suppliers, for example car hire firms or oil companies refuelling aircraft at Heathrow. Franchising is well suited to achieving productive efficiency, but the BAA faces a dilemma regarding allocative efficiency. Competition between concessionaires supplying similar product ranges (e.g. rival bookshops) would enhance allocative efficiency insofar as it eliminates monopolistic exploitation, but it would reduce the BAA's revenues by diminishing the value of the franchises. This is basically the same as the trade-off between competition and revenue maximization that the Government faces when privatizing a firm. Of course competition would not always promote allocative efficiency. Space in terminal buildings is scarce, and competition in one service might entail the undesirable disappearance of another: there is a trade-off between competition and diversity. However, the MMC concluded that the danger of monopolistic abuse in commercial services was real, and they expressed reservations about the BAA's attitude to competition. However, a majority of the MMC panel found that the BAA was not pursuing a course of conduct which operated against the public interest. Professor K.D. George dissented from this view. He concluded that BAA effectively restricted or prevented competition to its concessionaires, even where such competition would be possible, in a manner contrary to the public interest. The MMC made a series of recommendations concerning, among other things, the promotion of competition in tendering, the establishment of performance indicators, and the presentation of detailed accounting information to show separately the results of traffic and commercial activities at each airport. The MMC finally remarked that privatization might increase the difficulty of containing BAA's ability to exploit the captive nature of the concessionaires' market, and they concluded that their recommendations should be applicable to the privatized BAA.

A separate distortion of allocative efficiency arises from the tax privileges accorded to duty-free goods. Duty-free shops are a major source of revenue. They account for about 20 percent of BAA's total income. A large fraction of the proceeds from the privatization of BAA therefore reflect the capitalized value of a tax distortion. There is no economic justification for the tax anomaly: it is arbitrary and inefficient, and there is no distributional reason for giving perks to international travelers who are prepared to add bags of drink and cigarettes to their luggage in already crowded aircraft cabins. (It might be more sensible, though still anomalous, to give duty-free perks to arriving passengers rather than to those departing.) Given the BAA's policy on traffic charges (see above), the tax distortion also has the effect of cross-subsidizing traffic activities, thereby adding to allocative inefficiency. The future of duty-free sales is uncertain. Duty-free tax privileges in Europe may be abolished after 1992 as part of fiscal harmonization within the EEC. This prospect is serious for BAA because about half of its substantial income from duty-free goods comes from intra-European sales. However, 1992 is also the date at which the regulation of BAA's airport charges will be reviewed. Loss of income from duty-free goods could then be made good by allowing an increase in traffic charges, quite consistently with the single-till principle. The regulation of BAA is our next topic.

10.3.3 Regulation of BAA

Many aspects of BAA's behavior are subject to Government regulation. Airports are licensed and periodically inspected by the CAA to ensure that their operators are competent and that safety standards are upheld. Airports are subject to environmental regulation, especially regarding noise, and they are required to carry out airport security measures. The Government also has powers of traffic regulation, and may influence the use of U.K. airports by making rules on traffic distribution between airports, limiting aircraft movements, and allocating landing and takeoff slots between airlines at airports where capacity is constrained. Runway and terminal developments are subject to planning regulation. However, the main concern of this section is the economic regulation of airport pricing.

The Airports Act 1986 subjects all U.K. airports above a certain size to economic regulation, and their operators are required to obtain permission from the CAA to levy airport charges. Economic regulation takes the form of conditions attached to these permissions. All BAA's seven airports are subject to economic regulation, and the three London airports are "designated," which means that they also have to meet some mandatory conditions regarding airport charges and the information to be published in their accounts. Section 39 of the 1986 Act states that in carrying out its duties as economic regulator, the CAA must act

". . . in the manner which it considers best calculated

(a) to further the reasonable interests of users of airports within the UK

(b) to promote the efficient, economic and profitable operation of such airports

(c) to encourage investment in new facilities at airports in time to satisfy anticipated demands by the users of such airports

(d) to impose the minimum restrictions that are consistent with the performance by the CAA of its functions. . . ."

The CAA must also have regard to the U.K.'s international obligations, including the Chicago Convention on nondiscrimination between airlines of different nations, the Bermuda 2 agreement, and the 1983 Memorandum of Understanding with the American Government concerning airport charges (see above). If the CAA and an airport operator cannot agree on certain conditions, the matter is referred to the MMC, which must also have regard to the above objectives in its decision making.

The centerpiece of the economic regulation of BAA is the price formula which limits the airport charges at the three London airports collectively, and at Heathrow and Gatwick individually. The formula is a version of $RPI - X$ price regulation, which has been described in earlier chapters in relation to telecommunications and gas (see sections 8.3 and 9.2.3 respectively). Regulation applies to average revenue per passenger from specified charges (principally on landing and departing aircraft, on passengers, and for baggage handling), and X was set equal to unity. To be more precise the formula is

$$M_t = \left(1 + \frac{\mathrm{RPI}_t - 1}{100}\right) Y_{t-1} - K_t$$

where M_t is the maximum average revenue per passenger allowable in year t, RPI_t is the percentage change in the Retail Price Index between September in year t and the preceding September, Y_{t-1} is the specified average revenue per passenger in the previous financial year $t - 1$ and is defined as

$$\left(1 + \frac{\mathrm{RPI}_{t-1} - 1}{100}\right) Y_{t-2} + S_{t-2},$$

where S_{t-2} is the allowable security costs per passenger in year $t - 2$, and K_t is a positive or negative correction factor to adjust for any discrepancy between the actual and the maximum allowed average revenue per passenger two years previously.

The correction factor is needed because it is impossible for BAA to predict all elements of the formula a year ahead, and without it BAA would have an incentive to forecast incorrectly so as to manipulate the formula in its favor. The security factor in the formula allows BAA to recoup 75 percent of any additional costs necessarily incurred as a result of changes in Government policy toward airport security. In sum, the formula applies RPI – 1 to average (airport charge) revenue per passenger, with an allowance for 75 percent of any extra security costs and a factor to correct for past forecasting errors.

The formula came into effect on 1 April 1987 and was based on average revenue per passenger in the previous year. It will be reviewed by the MMC every five years, with the first review in 1992. The CAA can alter pricing conditions within five-year periods only with BAA's consent. The Secretary of State for Transport can override the formula in order to meet the U.K.'s international obligations.

Regulation of airport charges is not the only element of economic regulation. At its five-yearly reviews of designated airports the MMC must also report on whether their "operational activities" (i.e. activities that are carried out for the benefit of, or paid for by, airport users) are being conducted in a manner contrary to the public interest. The broad definition of operational activities embraces the bulk of BAA's operations, including commercial activities. The CAA has the duty of imposing conditions to remedy conduct found by the MMC to be against the public interest. The

CAA also has powers to impose conditions in relation to "aviation-related activities" (aircraft landing, takeoff, and parking, and the handling of passengers and their baggage) in order to remedy or prevent anticompetitive conduct such as discriminatory or predatory pricing. If the airport operator objects to such conditions, the matter is referred to the MMC. Finally, there are conditions which increase the information available to the CAA by requiring BAA to publish detailed accounts annually for each of its seven airports.

10.3.4   Assessment

The main effect of privatizing BAA was financial: the Government sold assets yielding future flows of property income to private hands in exchange for a lump sum. The sale was not so underpriced as some other major privatizations, but it was a poor financial deal for the general public insofar as the assets were sold for less than the stock market's judgment of their value. The privatization of BAA offers little prospect of efficiency improvement. The large majority of employees at airports work for private companies (retailers, banks, caterers, etc.) anyway, BAA's commercial activities were already conducted so as to maximize profits, and its traffic activities continue to be subject to heavy regulation. Allocative inefficiencies in pricing policy are to persist, the Government will continue to control major investment plans through planning legislation, and no competitive stimulus has been injected. Below we shall consider how privatization affects the regulation of BAA's activities, but first we ask whether more could have been done to promote competition in airport services.

Competition   BAA's airports face a limited degree of competition from overseas airports such as Amsterdam, Frankfurt, and Paris, but the most natural way to enhance competitive forces would be to promote competition between airports within the U.K. This could have been achieved by dividing the ownership of BAA's airports so that, for example, Heathrow and Gatwick could have competed for custom. BAA management argued vigorously against separate ownership, and the Government also took the view that any advantages that it offered were outweighed by serious disadvantages. In the Airports White Paper they argued that effective competition between airports was limited in any case, partly because the desire of airlines operating scheduled services to facilitate interconnections between flights tended to make one airport dominant in a regional group (as Heathrow is in the London area).

Secondly, the Government argued that the London airports were an integrated system (notwithstanding the fact that Luton Airport is separately owned), and that the prospects for each airport would be unduly sensitive to Government policy (on licensing, planning consents, and so on) in the event of separation. The separate sale of the London and Scottish airport groups was also rejected, on the grounds that it would do nothing to promote competition but would jeopardize efficiency and delay privatization. These considerations, together with management influence and the likely dampening effect of separation (via increased competition) on sales proceeds, held sway and BAA was privatized as a single entity.

Nonetheless, the case for separating ownership in order to promote competition is considerable (see Starkie and Thompson, 1985, especially chapters 5 and 8). Although capacity constraints imply that competition would have less effect at peak times (there is no incentive to undercut a rival if you have no spare capacity to meet extra demand), the same is not true off-peak. For example, competition for charter and long-haul discount-fare traffic at off-peak times could benefit many actual and potential passengers greatly and ensure fuller utilization of capacity. Secondly, separation of ownership would have sharpened the capital market pressures on airport managements by giving shareholders a keener interest in the comparative financial performance of different airports. Takeover threats would also have been strengthened, but in any case they have been ruled out by Government measures including its "special share" (which gives a veto on takeover), limitations on shareholdings, and restrictions on the disposal of airports. Thirdly, separate ownership would have increased the information available to the regulatory authority (the CAA) and would have permitted the possibility of some "competition via regulation" (as described in section 4.6.2).

Regulation   The first problem with the regulation of BAA pricing is that it perpetuates the inefficiencies in resource allocation that have prevailed in the past (see section 10.3.2 above). Traffic charges are generally too low (for example, there is heavy rationing at peak times at Heathrow and Gatwick), and traffic operations are cross-subsidized by commercial activities. Commercial income is boosted by the market power of concessionaires, and a large proportion of it derives from arbitrary tax concessions to duty-free and tax-free goods. As a result, international travelers enjoy lower-cost airport charges (not to mention cheaper cigarettes and drink) at the expense of the Exchequer, and large amounts of retail space, which could be used by competing retailers, are absorbed by goods for which demand is inflated by tax concessions. The British Government is not entirely to blame for this bizarre state of affairs, which was enshrined by the "single-till principle" of the 1983 Memorandum of Understanding following pressure from the U.S. authorities. It remains to be seen whether the tax concessions will be removed in the European Community after 1992 and whether airport charges will rise if the cross-subsidy is thereby reduced.

Although the inherited pricing policy and the single-till principle imply that traffic charges are inefficiently low (especially at peak times), the RPI − 1 constraint appears quite consistent with substantial profit growth by BAA, even if productivity does not improve by 1 percent per annum. It is projected that passenger traffic at the London airports will rise by about 4 to 5 percent annually, and traffic and commercial income are therefore set to grow strongly. Moreover, many of BAA's activities are not subject to RPI − 1 regulation, including traffic activities at the Scottish airports and commercial activities generally.

BAA also retains discretion concerning *relative* prices within the price formula, which applies only to *average* (traffic) revenue per passenger at the three London airports. The constraint is similar to the "average price per therm" control faced by British Gas (see section 9.2). In each case the company has a strategic incentive to expand business segments with low marginal costs. For example, cutting traffic charges to off-peak charter operators would tend to reduce average revenue per passenger and relax the constraint on charges to high revenue passengers at peak times. In an otherwise perfect world, this encouragement to changing relative prices would be undesirable (see section 4.4 on departures from Ramsey pricing), but in practice it may be desirable insofar as it partly offsets the existing subsidy to peak-time travelers and the incentive for BAA to exercise market power in relation to off-peak travelers.

It is difficult to assess the likely effect of privatization upon the investment behavior of BAA. In an unregulated market, a dominant firm would find it profitable to restrict capacity below the socially desirable level in order to raise price and extract monopoly profits. A tendency to underinvestment can also arise insofar as private and social discount rates differ (e.g. because of political and regulatory uncertainties). But price regulation can have contrary effects. Many peak charges are held below market levels. The 1983 Memorandum of Understanding on airport charges speaks of a reasonable rate of return on assets, and we have noted elsewhere that RPI − X control has some similarities to rate-of-return regulation. BAA may therefore have some incentive to expand capacity for strategic reasons (see section 4.2.1 above on the Averch–Johnson effect), though we believe that the tendency to underinvestment is likely to be more powerful. However, we must not ignore the close Government involvement with airport investment policy, which is dictated by concern for the environment and the promotion of British aviation. Notwithstanding the change of BAA's ownership, it will ultimately be the Government that decides major aspects of future expansion plans.

This point is underlined by the fact that the major investment decisions for Britain's airports announced in the 1985 White Paper were implemented immediately *before* BAA's privatization (see section 10.3.1 above and Starkie and Thompson (1986) on the commercial viability of the expansion at Stansted). If the privatization of BAA had been motivated by a belief in the superiority of market forces and private decision making, it would hardly have been appropriate for the Government to initiate such an important investment program so soon before the sale.

We conclude that, above all else, the privatization of BAA was simply the transfer to private hands of a monopoly with valuable property assets. The sale did something to extend share ownership, but in the process there was a transfer of wealth from the Government (representing the general public) to successful applicants for shares because most of the shares were offered for less than their worth as subsequently judged by the market. The case for promoting competition and enhancing the effectiveness of regulation by separating the ownership of BAA's airports was rejected, and, as management had urged, the group was sold intact. The Government will continue to influence and regulate key aspects of BAA's behavior, notably investment programs, and allocative inefficiencies in the pricing structure will persist. It is hard to see how the privatization of BAA will improve the economic efficiency of airport operations: it was primarily a financial operation designed to serve other objectives.

10.4   Express Coaching and Local Bus Services

The framework of competition and regulation for coach and bus services in Britain has been radically reformed by recent legislation. The Transport Acts of 1980 and 1985 dismantled the regulatory structure that had lasted for 50 years, and opened up new possibilities for competition. In some areas liberalization has had immediate effects on pricing, passenger choice and demand, the range of services offered, the nature of cross-subsidies, and the number of competitors in the marketplace. But in most areas deregulation has had little apparent effect in its first year. In the longer term the blessings of deregulation may be mixed, and important questions for policy remain.

Does liberalization guarantee effective competition, or will incumbent operators prevail over their rivals and come to exercise local market power on their route networks? Is there a danger of "destructive competition," leading to inefficiency and possibly even to chaos? What will be the nature of competition between long-distance coach services and rail?

There is also the question of the ownership of the public sector coach and bus operators—notably those within the National Bus Company—that have dominated the industry. There was a wide range of options for privatization concerning both the structure of the firms sold to private hands and the methods of sale. The Government has chosen the option of structural reform and has favored management buyouts as a way of privatizing parts of National Bus.

Great uncertainty surrounds the future of both competition and ownership in the coach and bus sectors, and too little time has elapsed since deregulation to make a confident prediction of how events will unfold. However, the industry is a particularly interesting part of the privatization program because the policy of radical liberalization and structural reform is very different from that followed in the major utility industries and in airports and airlines.

We begin this section by describing the main operators in the industry and the regulatory structure in which they operated before 1980. We then outline the main provisions of the 1980 Transport Act, which deregulated express coaching, and we review the development of competition in that sector. Next we look at the 1985 Transport Act, which extended deregulation to local bus services where competition began in October 1986. Finally we consider the options for privatizing National Bus. Limitations of space prevent us from providing much more than a sketch of what is happening in the industry. For fuller accounts the reader is referred to Davis (1984), Kilvington (1985), Kilvington and Cross (1986), and Jaffer and Thompson (1986) on express coaching, the MMC report (Monopolies and Mergers Commission, 1982a) on bus services, the 1984 Government White Paper on *Buses* (Department of Transport, 1984a), Meadowcroft and Pickup (1987) on the initial effects of bus deregulation, and Mulley and Wright (1986) on the privatization of National Bus. We draw from these sources in what follows.

10.4.1 The Industry before 1980
The 1930 Road Traffic Act instituted a system of heavy regulation that lasted essentially unchanged for 50 years. The Act was motivated by concern about passenger safety and the danger of destructive and

inefficient competition (see sections 3.2.1 and 3.3.1), and accordingly it provided a regime of control over both quality and quantity. Quality regulation embraces vehicle safety, maintenance arrangements, mechanical inspection, professional competence, the fitness and working hours of drivers, and so on. The system of quality regulation, which is supervised by the independent Traffic Commissioners, has not been weakened by the recent legislation.

Before 1980 the Traffic Commissioners also had extensive powers regarding the number, identity, and behavior of firms supplying public passenger road transport services. A firm seeking to provide a service had to obtain a route license from the Commissioners, who also had powers over fares and timetabling. The Commissioners were empowered to grant licenses only if they were satisfied that they were positively in the public interest. Thus the burden of proof lay with the potential entrant, who was likely to be opposed in his application by incumbent operators of bus and rail services. The whole procedure was costly, lengthy, and prone to inertia. In effect, existing operators were shielded by regulatory barriers to entry.

Incumbent operators of bus services were left free to exercise their local market power in a variety of ways. There was no pressing need to cut costs, reduce inefficiency, or respond to consumers' changing preferences with innovative solutions. There was ample scope for cross-subsidization between routes and between times of day. Industry performance appeared tolerably good in the early years, but its drawbacks began to emerge in the 1950s as car ownership became more widespread. The vicious circle of higher fares, fewer passengers, and growing losses became apparent, and an increasing number of bus services came to rely heavily on funds from central and local government. Public funding was inevitably required to subsidize loss-making services judged to be socially desirable (such as many rural bus services), but the pattern of subsidy was hidden from view and was in all probability an inefficient way of meeting the social ends that it sought to achieve.

Public sector operators have in the past dominated coach and bus services, and of course rail services. Competition from the private sector came from a number of independent bus operators and from taxi services, which were also subject to extensive regulation. The main public sector operators have been the National Bus Company, local government Passenger Transport Executives (PTEs), municipal operators, the Scottish Bus Group, and London Regional Transport.

National Bus was created effectively as a nationalized industry under the

Transport Act 1968. It took over many bus and coach services then in public ownership. Its local bus operations were divided into four regional units which owned numerous local operating companies (see Mulley and Wright (1986, tables 3 and 4) for statistics on their recent performance). Two subsidiaries of National Bus—the Bristol Omnibus Company and the Trent Motor Traction Company—were part of the recent investigation by the MMC into the efficiency of local bus services (see Monopolies and Mergers Commission, 1982a). The National Express and National Holidays divisions of the company operate scheduled express services and holiday tours, and the National Travelworld travel agency business has about a hundred retail outlets. In the year to 31 December 1985, on the eve of its privatization, the National Bus Company made an operating profit (after interest and tax charges) of £17.6 million on a turnover of £807 million, of which 79 percent was received from passengers. (In that year there was also an extraordinary charge in preparation for privatization—relating to deferred taxation, pension fund deficiencies, and closures—of more than £100 million.) At the year end the company employed nearly 49,000 staff and operated a fleet of more than 14,500 buses and coaches. In 1985 the company operated 616 million vehicle miles in service, of which local bus services accounted for 75 percent and National Express 12 percent; there were 1,440 million passenger journeys.

Under the 1968 Transport Act the county council PTEs were required to meet passenger transport needs in the English metropolitan counties and in Strathclyde in Scotland. Councils in nonmetropolitan counties had similar functions under the 1978 Transport Act. They operated some bus services directly and some by agreements with other operators (public or private). The 1985 Transport Act modified the duties of county councils (and the successors to the metropolitan county councils, which were abolished in recent local government reform) by requiring them to secure the efficient provision of necessary transport services not provided by a free market. A number of district councils operate bus services as well. An example is the City of Cardiff Council, which was also part of the MMC investigation referred to above. The City Council has statutory powers to operate bus services under local Acts of Parliament. The Council has a Transport Committee composed of local councillors, and day-to-day operations are run by a Transport Department. Arrangements in London are different again. In 1984 the London Regional Transport Act was passed, which transferred responsibility for London transport from the Greater London Council to the new London Regional Transport. The Act provided for greater competition (e.g. via tendering) and for more private sector involvement. In view of these recent changes the further deregulation of bus services in London has been deferred.

Bus companies are financed by revenues from fares and by subsidies from local authorities (some of which are ultimately paid by central government). The main kinds of subsidy are revenue support grants and concessionary fare subsidies for groups such as the elderly. The level of subsidy has tended to rise steadily over time, and became particularly acute in the London area. The White Paper on *Buses* (Department of Transport, 1984a, table 15) found that in 1982–1983 (when total industry turnover was some £2.4 billion) the proportions of bus operators' income from fares, concessionary fares payments, and revenue support were 62 percent, 10 percent, and 28 percent respectively. In London the figures were 46 percent, 11 percent, and 44 percent. However, National Bus and the Scottish Bus Group obtained 76 percent of their income from fares.

Until recently, a typical arrangement would involve the authority specifying what services it wanted and meeting the operator's reported costs. In the absence of potential competition, the poor incentives for cost efficiency of such cost-based contracts are well known. In addition such schemes have allocative efficiency problems because there is no clear way of relating the cost of individual services to the private and social demand for them. These twin efficiency problems were a central part of the motivation behind the reforms instituted by the 1980 and 1985 Transport Acts. We will consider the deregulation of local bus services in sections 10.4.4 and 10.4.5, but first we will describe the deregulation of express coaching.

10.4.2   Deregulation I: The 1980 Transport Act

The 1980 Transport Act was the first step in the deregulation of the markets for coach and bus services. The Act had four parts, dealing respectively with public service vehicles, the privatization of the National Freight Corporation (NFC), pension schemes in British Rail (BR) and the NFC, and various miscellaneous items. Our main concern is with Part I of the Act, the purposes of which were as follows:

(a) redefining and reclassifying public service vehicles;

(b) abolishing road service licenses for express carriages as redefined;

(c) making it easier for applicants to obtain road service licenses, and restricting the power to attach thereto conditions as to fares;

(d) providing for the designation of areas as trial areas in which road service licenses are not required for stage carriage services;

(e) making new provision for securing the fitness of public service vehicles;

(f) substituting a system of public service vehicle operators' licenses for the system of public service vehicle licenses; and

(g) providing an appeal against a refusal by the London Transport Executive to enter into an agreement with a person other than the Executive for the provision of a London bus service.

The Act defined "public service vehicles" as vehicles adapted for more than eight passengers at separate fares in the course of business. Public service vehicles were classified into three types:

(i) stage carriages (vehicles used for local bus services);

(ii) express carriages;

(iii) contract carriages.

An express service is defined as one where passengers travel at least 30 miles measured in a straight line. The Act abolished road service licenses for express services, and thereby removed regulatory barriers to entry into the express services market.

Regulatory barriers to competition in local bus services were diminished by three measures. First, the onus of proof regarding the granting of licenses by traffic commissioners was reversed. Thus Section 5(2) of the Act stipulates that the commissioners "shall grant the licence unless they are satisfied that to do so would be against the interests of the public." Secondly, regulatory controls on pricing were relaxed. Section 7(3) requires the traffic commissioners not to exercise their powers over pricing conditions to licenses "unless satisfied that the proposed exercise of those powers ... is essential in the interests of the public." Thirdly, the Act provided for experiments in more radical deregulation by giving the Minister power to designate "trial areas" in which the licensing requirement for local bus services was dropped. The initiative here lay with the local authorities, because the Minister could use his powers of designation only upon their request. Operators of bus services in trial areas were required to inform the relevant local authorities and the local public about new, changed, or discontinued services.

The Act relaxed quantity regulation by removing (in the case of express services) and easing (in the case of local bus services) restrictions on the conduct of participants in the market. Entry was made freer and price controls became less strict. But quality regulation was retained and strengthened by tighter standards on vehicle fitness and by switching the focus of regulation onto the operators themselves, rather than their behavior. Section 21 of the Act states that the traffic commissioners should grant a public service vehicle operator's license only if they are satisfied as to the good repute, financial standing, and professional competence of the potential operator.

In section 10.4.4 we will describe how the 1985 Transport Act made the second major step to a liberalized framework for competition. But first we shall examine the rise and fall of competition in express coaching after the 1980 Act.

10.4.3   Competition in Express Coach Services

At the time of deregulation in October 1980 the market for scheduled express coach services in England and Wales was dominated by National Express, the publicly owned subsidiary of the National Bus Company, and the Scottish Bus Group enjoyed a similar position in Scotland. No independent operators ran major networks. However, deregulation was followed rapidly by new entry. A major new entrant was British Coachways, a consortium of ten independent companies who planned to attack the heart of National Express business by operating a wide network of intercity express services. Other independent operators introduced services from their local regions to London, and many new firms entered market niches operating commuter coaches, holiday coaches, excursions, and tours.

The immediate result was a phase of intense competition. British Coachways' fares were set at roughly *half* those previously charged by National Express. The response was swift—National Express promptly matched the low prices charged by the entrant. The nature of express services altered rapidly, with the emphasis shifting to frequent, rapid, and direct services with fewer stopping points on the main trunk routes. This change is shown graphically by the coach timetables reproduced as illustrations 1–4 in Kilvington and Cross (1986). For example, typical journey times between London and Manchester were cut from $5\frac{1}{2}$ to 4 hours as a result of the elimination of intermediate stops and better use of the motorway. Smaller towns became less well served, and many services were discontinued. Nevertheless demand expanded strongly, and the number of passengers traveling on National Express rose by more than 50 percent despite the advent of competition and the suspension of less popular services. Demand growth was most spectacular on the principal trunk routes, and it has been estimated that demand trebled in some cases. Much of this business was due to switching from rail travel, and we shall consider the response of BR below.

The bout of intense competition between express coach operators was over in a matter of months, and National Express regained its dominant position. Members of the British Coachways consortium were beginning to withdraw from the market as soon as April 1981, only six months after deregulation, and their challenge had effectively disappeared by 1983. The demise of the consortium has been attributed to a number of causes, including the nature of their competitive strategy, the incumbent advantages enjoyed by National Express, and its aggressive response to entry.

The essence of British Coachways' strategy was to compete on price, but National Express enjoyed numerous nonprice advantages by virtue of its incumbent position, and once it matched British Coachways (and other independents) on price, the entrants' prospects became very bleak. The three main advantages enjoyed by National Express were its established nationwide network, its goodwill and customer awareness, and its privileged access to major terminals such as Victoria Coach Station in London. Technical cost factors were probably not such an important consideration. There is little evidence that National Express possessed absolute cost advantages, or that economies of scale or scope characterize production technology in coaching. Nor are the sunk costs of running a coach service on a given route particularly great, because the coach can be switched to other duties with relative ease.

Marketing advantages are quite another matter. Whereas National Express was well known throughout the country, the entrants were little known except perhaps in their home regions. Therefore National Express could achieve higher load factors and frequency of service—and hence lower unit costs—by serving customers from both "ends" of a route, rather than relying mainly on the home base. The entrants could have attempted to promote customer awareness of their services by massive marketing campaigns, but that would have entailed enormous sunk costs and would have reduced timetabling flexibility. Such marketing advantages were compounded by the policy of National Bus (the parent of National Express) of not allowing competitors to have access to its coach terminals, notably Victoria Coach Station. There is an analogy here with the issues of vertical integration and interconnection in telecommunications: National Express denied interconnection rights to its competitors and hence they were put at a disadvantage. The entrants had to find alternative terminal facilities, such as a derelict goods yard near King's Cross railway station. As well as being less pleasant and less well known than Victoria Coach Station, these facilities were less suitable for passengers wishing to change coaches. (Davis (1984) states that 24 percent of passengers arriving at Victoria change coaches there.) This kind of problem is recognized in the

1985 Transport Act, which forbids discriminatory practices in relation to bus stations for local bus services.

Given the nature of its incumbent advantages, it is not surprising that National Express responded aggressively to competition right from the start, before its rivals could build up goodwill and customer awareness. The entrant's pockets could not withstand the effects of the incumbent's sharp price-cutting strategy for long, and National Express had good reason to believe that short-run revenue losses would soon be recouped by the return of its market dominance. The policy adopted by National Express bears some signs of a campaign of predatory pricing, but, whether or not this is so, the competition authorities stood by and did nothing.

Some independent operators on trunk routes have survived, but they have generally done so by pursuing policies of product differentiation and specialized niche entry. They have tended to serve just one or two routes and have differentiated their product by using luxury coaches. Many have entered into agreements with National Express. Policies of this kind are exactly the opposite of those attempted by the British Coachways consortium. They have been more successful because they considerably diminish the incumbent firm's incentive to respond to entry in an aggressive manner. The independent sector has also fared better in Scotland, where the Scottish Bus Group was less responsive to competition than National Express was south of the border.

Although the period of intense competition on trunk routes was short lived, deregulation also brought about some longer-term changes. Fares did rise after the price wars, but not to the levels at which they had been before deregulation. Profitable routes have become better served, and services have been reduced and withdrawn on less profitable ones. Journey times between major population centers have been reduced, but at the expense of those living in between them. Most significantly there has been keener competition between coach and rail, which was given a boost by the rail strike in 1982 which encouraged many new customers to travel by coach. Kilvington and Cross (1986, table 5) list a number of initiatives by BR in response to coach competition after deregulation. They include schemes to reduce rail fares for off-peak travelers (e.g. Railcards for families, under 24s, and senior citizens) and intercity saver fares. These moves were aimed at the groups and the times of the day and week where coach competition is most threatening and where marginal cost is low as a result of spare capacity. BR's policies of targeted discounts have been successful in expanding demand, but the overall effect of coach deregulation on BR (and hence on Government) cash flows has been significantly negative. Consumers of rail services have benefited, and allocative efficiency has improved insofar as fares for various services have moved more closely into line with the relevant costs.

The independent sector has been more successful in commuter coaching, seasonal (mainly summer) business, and excursions and tours, than it was in challenging the intercity network business of National Express. The rail strike in 1982 gave commuter coach services an important boost, and the market has expanded steadily since then. Because commuter traffic is at peak times, BR cannot respond so aggressively. Deregulation has added to competitive pressures in seasonal and excursion business, but there was some freedom of entry into those sectors before the 1980 Act. Independent operators have tended to compete (on quality as well as price) more strongly with each other, and they have also faced some new competition from the public sector in the shape of an extension of the activities of municipal bus undertakings.

In broad terms the deregulation of express coaching has so far achieved a mixed record of success. Fares have fallen on average, and services have become more responsive to consumer demands. However, some consumer groups have lost out as their areas have become less well served. Competition between the public sector operators in coach and rail has become keener to the general benefit of the traveling public. There have been some surprising and ironic consequences of deregulation. Far from enabling private sector entrepreneurs to exploit profitable opportunities at the expense of the public sector incumbents, National Express swiftly emerged victorious in the battle for intercity services, where barriers to entry gave it important advantages over competitors.

The experience of competition in express coaching has several important lessons. First, it was the threat of potential competition, and not any change in ownership, that transformed the behavior of National Express. Secondly, competition within the public sector is perfectly feasible, as the responses by BR show. Thirdly, the removal of regulatory barriers to entry is no guarantee that effective competition will prevail. Accompanying measures to safeguard the competitive process are also required.

10.4.4   Deregulation II : The 1985 Transport Act

In July 1984 the Government set out its plans for the second major step to deregulation in the White Paper on *Buses* (Department of Transport, 1984a). Its proposals were enacted in the Transport Act 1985, which received Royal Assent in October 1985, and competition in local bus services began a year later. The main provisions of the Act concerning competition, regulation, and ownership were as follows. First, the deregulation in 1980 of express coaching, and of local bus services in trial areas, was extended to bus services throughout the country (except London). Secondly, the Act brought about important structural changes in the industry by providing for the reorganization and privatization of the National Bus Company. Thirdly, the bus operations of PTEs and local councils were reformed by providing for their transfer to separate companies. Fourthly, the Act altered financing arrangements, notably in relation to tendering for subsidized services, travel concession schemes, and grants for rural services.

Part I of the Act abolished road service licensing, and in its place introduced the requirement that local bus services (outside London) should simply be registered with the Traffic Commissioners for the relevant area. Under section 7 of the Act the Commissioners may apply traffic regulation conditions to local services, but only so as to prevent danger to road users or to reduce severe traffic congestion. Such conditions may relate to the routes, stopping places, and stopping times of services, and they must be applied equally to all actual and potential operators of local services in an area. Part I of the Act also deregulated taxi and hire car services to some extent, and it modified certain public service vehicle licensing requirements. Regulation of road passenger transport continued in London, where a system of "London local service licenses" was instituted in Part II of the Act. London was treated differently because of the recent events concerning the transfer of control from the Greater London Council and the establishment of London Regional Transport.

Part III of the Act dealt with the structural reform and privatization of the National Bus Company. The Company was required to submit to the Government its proposals for transferring its operations to the private sector, and the Secretary of State for Transport was given powers to modify those proposals. A three-year time limit was set down for the disposal program to be carried out. Section 48 of the Act gave the main objective of the Company in this regard as being "to promote sustained and fair competition, both between companies which are Bus group or former Bus group companies and between any such companies and other persons engaged in providing bus services ... ." However, the Company was also told to have regard to the effect of any program on "the net value that may be expected to be secured" from the asset disposals—a rather different consideration. In addition, the Company was required to give employees of any undertaking being sold a reasonable opportunity of acquiring (perhaps jointly with others) a controlling interest in its equity share capital.

Part IV of the Act was concerned with the powers and duties of Passenger Transport Authorities, PTEs, and local councils in relation to local transport services. In formulating and carrying out the transport plans for their areas, these authorities were given the duty of not inhibiting actual or potential competition between operators of local services. The Act required PTEs to transfer their bus undertakings to companies owned by their Passenger Transport Authorities and provide for their division into smaller self-standing companies. There was similar provision for the formation of companies to run council bus undertakings.

Part V of the Act covered financial provisions. Section 89 requires authorities responsible for expenditure on public transport to invite tenders for subsidized services on a competitive basis. As well as promoting efficiency by competitive contracting (see section 4.6 above), this measure makes more visible the pattern of subsidies in local bus services. The Act allows local authorities to establish travel concession schemes for children, elderly people, and the disabled, and gives all eligible service operators the right to participate in such schemes. Powers were also given for grants to be made for services in rural areas.

Two related principles motivated many of the central reforms instituted by the 1985 Act—the promotion of effective competition for the custom of passengers and public transport authorities, and the separation of the "expenditure" and "supply" functions of the latter bodies. These principles are supported by many of the incentive arguments set out in this book. It is too soon to judge how full deregulation will work in practice, but we now go on to describe some of the turbulent events that have occurred so far.

10.4.5   Competition in Local Bus Services

Only three councils applied to be designated as trial areas for the deregulation of local bus services under the 1980 Act—those in Devon, Norfolk, and Hereford. The full deregulation brought about by the 1985 Act, which came into effect on 26 October 1986, was therefore based on very few experiments. Moreover, the evidence from the trial areas must be treated with care because they were not representative of the country as a whole, competition could be on a limited scale only, and the conduct of participants in the experiments may have been affected by the public attention that they received at the time.

The most interesting trial area was the town of Hereford, which was the only major urban center to be deregulated at the time (Devon and Norfolk excluded their urban areas from the experiment). Competition between the three operators there took a variety of forms. As well as competition on price and service there were allegedly attempts to disrupt rivals' services by the tactics that are said to have been common before regulation was instituted by the 1930 Act. Such tactics included racing to stops, refusing to set down passengers at intermediate stops for fear of being overtaken, blocking rivals' vehicles, duplicating rivals' timetables, early arrival to pick up passengers waiting for rivals' buses, painting over rivals' timetable displays, intimidating passengers intending to use rivals' buses, and deviating from routes. Since full deregulation in 1986 there have been allegations of tactics of this kind in those areas where competition has occurred. (They have been a prominent theme in our local newspapers in Oxford, which happens to be a notable example of competition.)

However, competition in commercial bus services has not been widespread since deregulation. In their study of the initial effects of deregulation in metropolitan areas, Meadowcroft and Pickup (1987) found that there has not been substantial competition on the road between existing major operators, or from existing independents, or from new entrants. Established operators have tended to remain in their existing territories, and new entrants, although perhaps 200 in number nationwide, are typically small and not directly in competition with incumbent operators. However, among the metropolitan areas, competition has been extensive in the Strathclyde region and substantial new entry has occurred in Manchester. (It is also possible that there is more competition, including competition on fares, outside the metropolitan areas.)

Meadowcroft and Pickup suggest four possible reasons why competition in commercial services has not been more widespread in the immediate aftermath of deregulation. The first is that barriers to the entry and growth of rival operators might be arising from incumbent advantages in relation to access to bus stations (recall the discussion of National Express and Victoria Coach Station above) and special ticketing arrangements (e.g. travelcards) which increase customer loyalty to incumbent firms with large networks.

Secondly, the superior efficiency of incumbent firms might partly explain why competition has not been more extensive. Entry threats can be an effective discipline on incumbent firms even though entry is not actually occurring. Since part of the case for deregulation was that incumbents were supposedly inefficient, this explanation does not seem very likely on the face of it, but as yet there is not enough evidence on the cost savings being achieved by incumbent operators to make a detailed assessment of the question.

Anticompetitive behavior by incumbent operators—or the threat of it—might be another factor deterring entry and growth by rival firms. Aggressive pricing has been the incumbent's response to entry in very few areas but in general fares have not changed appreciably since deregulation. Nonprice strategies have also been used. A common tactic has been to proliferate services, often by using minibuses, on the routes where competition has emerged (or is thought likely to emerge). Bus users on these routes gain from more frequent services so long as the competition lasts, but the proliferation is not necessarily efficient and it can cause bad congestion in town centers. Moreover, if the proliferation of services is essentially part of a predatory response to entry, the benefits might quickly disappear if and when the rival operators are seen off.

Fourthly, competition might grow in the years to come. At the time of writing less than a year has elapsed since deregulation, and many potential entrants might have adopted a strategy of "wait and see" until some uncertainties have diminished. To say the least, the early experience of deregulation has varied greatly from place to place, and it is too soon to make firm judgments about the future pattern of market structure and conduct.

Nevertheless the extent of competition so far has been disappointing. The problems of disruptive and unstable competition on the commercially viable routes where competition is occurring are immense, and it is unclear how they can be resolved without the return of local market dominance. Bus competition is peculiarly prone to such problems for several reasons. First, it is easy for bus operators to disrupt the operations of their rivals with relative impunity. They rely on the common resource of finite road space, and tactics such as physical obstruction are easily implemented and hard to prevent. Secondly, potential customers are highly visible because they stand in queues in public places. Similarly, the positions of rival buses are clear for all to see. Such visibility and identifiability of both customers and suppliers gives rise to incentives to race to stops, to refuse to set down passengers at stops where few people are waiting, and so on. Thirdly, competition in bus timings tends to be unstable for the reasons set out in the theoretical literature on product differentiation that dates back to Hotelling. The number of passengers waiting at a stop depends on how much time has elapsed since the last bus stopped there. It is therefore desirable to arrive at a stop just before a rival does (this is a kind of "minimum product differentiation"). It is impossible for all competitors to do this profitably, and an unstable situation results. In short, equilibrium may fail to exist. The instability problem would not be so severe if bus timings (i.e. "product locations") were fixed once chosen, but they are not entirely so. Timetables can readily be changed subject to registration procedures, and enforcement of adherence to timetables is no easy matter, especially given the random nature of traffic flows in town centers, although the 1985 Act does give Traffic Commissioners powers to prevent operators from running services that they have failed to operate in accordance with their registration.

The picture has been somewhat different, but also mixed, on routes that are not commercially viable. (It should be noted, however, that there is no clear-cut distinction between commercial and uncommercial routes: the two can interact in several ways, but space does not permit a discussion of this here.) Even where there is no competition *on* a route there can be competition *for* the route as a result of the requirement in the 1985 Act that subsidized services should be put out to competitive tender. This form of "competition via regulation" seems to be working well in some places. For example, the Hereford and Worcester County Council began competitive tendering in 1981. As a result the number of routes requiring subsidy and the average level of subsidy both fell significantly. However, competition for contracts has so far been less successful in many areas. There has been only one bidder (i.e. no competition) for a large proportion of contracts, and incumbent operators have been awarded the overwhelming bulk of contracts (see Meadowcroft and Pickup, 1987). Nevertheless there is evidence that competition for tendered services has led to significant cost savings, and its scope might be realized more fully in the future. Tendering can provide excellent incentives for productive efficiency by using competitive forces to overcome the informational disadvantage of the buyer of the service (the local authority). It can also improve allocative efficiency by clarifying the true cost of the service, although the ultimate choices of which routes are served and timetables still rest with the local authority. The problems of asset handover, contract specification, etc. that often bedevil franchising (see section 4.6.1) are not so great in relation to rural bus services.

Rather ironically we are therefore left with the provisional conclusion that the 1985 Act appears to have succeeded more by instituting "competition by regulation" for uncommercial services than by releasing competitive forces by deregulating commercial services. However, we must repeat that it is too soon to assert any conclusion about the longer-term effects of deregulation with confidence.

10.4.6   The Privatization of National Bus

The structure and scope of the operations of the National Bus Company were briefly described above. Four broad options for its privatization are analyzed by Mulley and Wright (1986):

(a) the sale of National Bus as a single entity;
(b) splitting the company into its four local bus regions;
(c) dividing the regions into subsidiary companies;
(d) further dividing the subsidiaries into "sub-subsidiaries" that could compete in local areas.

If the overriding objective was to maximize sales proceeds, then option (a) would be best. The company would be large enough to be floated on the Stock Exchange, and its profit prospects would be enhanced by the likelihood that potential rivals would be inhibited from competing strongly with so powerful an incumbent (recall what happened in express coaching). But privatizing the company as a whole is the least attractive option on other counts. It would do nothing to increase the number of competitors, the scope for entry deterrence (and threats thereof) would be large, capital market incentives (in the form of takeover threats or bankruptcy) would be weak, managers and employees would not control their local businesses, and political interference might continue. Those disadvantages are avoided or reduced by breaking up the company into smaller parts, although that strategy makes Stock Exchange flotation unattractive because of the small size of the resulting companies. Nevertheless the Government has favored this approach by its policy of breaking up the company and encouraging employee/management buyouts.

The question remains of how far to split up the company. If larger units are sold, the proportionate equity stake of any individual or group of employees will be correspondingly smaller, and their return on investment will be less related to their own efforts. On the other hand, the risks and rewards associated with smaller units are likely to be less attractive to employees and their financial backers. The choice between options (c) and (d) is a crucial determinant of whether there is effective competition at the local level. Option (d) would break local market power—at least initially—and would therefore tend to reduce expected returns and raise risks to a marked degree. But it is doubtful whether employees would wish to commit substantial resources, as well as their human capital, to such risky ventures.

In the event a version of option (c) was adopted. The National Bus Company Group was restructured in preparation for its disposal program so that it became a financial holding company, no longer providing central services for subsidiaries. In place of its regional structure, National Bus's operating companies were grouped into seven portfolios. A few of the operating companies were further divided into smaller units. Following this restructuring, the company is being sold as 52 separate local bus companies, six coach operating companies, and eight engineering companies. National Express, National Holidays, National Travelworld, and the Coach Station subsidiary are also to be privatized.

The disposal program was about halfway through by mid-1987 and should be essentially complete in 1988. The great majority of local bus operations have been sold to their management teams. Management buyouts are favored by the provision of £50,000 for their legal expenses and by allowing their bids to fall 5 percent below outside offers. The prices paid for the companies are confidential, but the revenues from privatization are likely to exceed £300 million. Sales proceeds could have been even larger if the National Bus Company had been sold as a single entity, but on this occasion the maximization of revenues has not been the Government's main aim.

10.4.7 Assessment

In contrast with its policies for the major utility industries, the objectives motivating the Government's recent bus transport policies have been admirably pro-competitive. The wholesale removal of regulatory barriers to entry—first in express coaching and then in local bus services—have been radical measures to promote competition. They have been accompanied by important steps to put the bus operators at arm's length from the public transport authorities, most notably the introduction of compulsory tendering for subsidized services, which introduces "competition via regulation." In particular, privatization (of National Bus) has occurred *after* the establishment of a more competitive industry structure.

However, experience has shown that there are severe problems in sustaining efficient and effective competition in coach and bus services, despite the apparent absence of natural monopoly cost conditions. In express coaching, National Express rapidly disposed of competitive challenges on its prime intercity routes by virtue of its aggressive pricing and its incumbent advantages in marketing and access to terminals. This underlines the point that the legal possibility of entry is not enough to guarantee effective competition. In the face of a powerful incumbent firm, effective competition is fragile indeed, and requires a strong competition policy of a kind not yet present in Britain. In addition, it would have been desirable to allow competitors to National Express better access to key coach stations. Again we see how vertical integration can thwart competition.

Other difficulties have attended the deregulation of local bus services, at least in its early months. In many places, deregulation has had little visible impact because incumbent operators have not been faced with competitive challenges. In other areas competition has been intense, but sometimes chaotic, unstable, and inefficient. It was most unlikely that radical reform of the industry would be followed immediately by stable competitive equilibrium, but there are reasons to believe that instability may persist or that local market dominance will be reasserted. This belief receives some support from the historical experience of what happened before regulation was instituted by the 1930 Act, and from the features of bus competition discussed above—the ease of disrupting rivals' operations, the visibility of potential customers and competitors, and the instability of competition in bus timings. It is to be hoped that local authorities and the traffic commissioners will be able to contain malpractices between rival operators without impeding effective competition, but it is not yet clear that this will happen.

The introduction of competitive tendering for subsidized services appears to have been somewhat more successful in achieving its aims. As Kilvington (1985) observed on the Hereford trial area: competition for the market is seen to perform more adequately than competition within it. Market forces have been used to enhance the effectiveness of the regulation of operators on noncommercial routes, and have helped public decision makers by providing better information about the costs of various services.

We shall conclude this section with two points on the question of ownership. The first is that public ownership was evidently no impediment to aggressive competitive responses by National Express and local bus companies (and even by BR). It was the advent of actual and potential competition that transformed their behavior, and not any change in ownership.

The second point concerns the privatization of the National Bus Company. Market power in bus services is extremely localized, and even though National Bus subsidiaries are being sold separately, rather than as a single national company, the prospects for sustained effective competition may be poor. Established incumbent firms may soon be able to see off the competition in many areas, especially in view of the features of bus competition referred to above. The danger is that market power at local level will not be broken and that privatization will simply lead to its being exercised by private rather than public operators. If that happens, the call will be for reregulation, not deregulation, and we will have turned full circle.

10.5 Railways

Railways in Britain were in private ownership until 1948, when nationalization consolidated various regional companies into a single state-owned entity. There is private ownership of railways in some other countries, for example the United States, and the Japanese National Railway company is in the process of being privatized. However, the bleak prospects for competition and profitability on the railways in Britain today are such that BR is the most difficult transport industry to privatize. Some of the nonrail activities (e.g. hotels) at the periphery of its operations have been sold to private hands, but its basic rail network business remains firmly in the public sector and immune from competition (except from other modes of transport such as coach and air).

The scope for effective competition on the railways is limited by the presence of fixed and sunk costs (see Starkie, 1984). Fixed costs are large because of the infrastructure (track, stations, etc.) that must be provided before any trains can run on a route. Duplication of infrastructure would generally be inefficient, and natural monopoly cost conditions therefore characterize physical network provision. Infrastructure costs are largely sunk because the assets are of minimal value for other purposes, and we saw in chapter 3 above how the sunkenness of costs mitigates against freedom of entry, especially when there are natural monopoly cost conditions as well. However, the cost conditions relating to the operation of services on the physical network are less inimical to competition. To operate a service it is necessary to have trains, staff, and rights of way (including rights to set down and pick up passengers and/or goods at stations). Although there are inevitably some sunk costs in hiring staff and buying or leasing rolling stock, they are small in relation to the massive sunk costs of establishing network infrastructure.

For there to be any hope of competition in rail services, it would therefore be necessary to give actual and potential operators of services equal access to the railway infrastructure. Starkie (1984) proposes a framework in which the ownership of track and trains is separated. Divided ownership might lose economies of vertical integration (see Williamson, 1975), but there were examples of it in Britain prior to nationalization, and private wagons carry much of BR's freight traffic even today. A similar separation is essentially what happens in other transport industries such as coach and air. Starkie envisages a division of BR into two groups. One company—"British Rail" in the strict sense—would own the infrastructure and would be responsible for train control and overhead administration. Another company or companies—"British Trains"—would own the rolling stock and would compete in the running of train services. The Rail company would charge competing operators of trains for the use of its track and stations. For example, it could charge direct costs at times of spare capacity and could auction rights of way at peak times.

A less radical step than enforced vertical separation of track and trains would be to allow BR to remain vertically integrated but to require it to grant access on fair terms to competing operators. Such a framework would be closely analogous to the regimes that have been established for the gas, electricity, and telecommunications networks. The issue in all these cases is interconnection—what constitutes "fair terms" for access to the network of the vertically integrated firm, and can they be effectively enforced? Continued vertical integration imposes a heavy regulatory burden, as the experience of those industries since liberalization shows, and it is evidently a very difficult task to create and maintain conditions for effective competition. Vertical separation of the kind proposed by Starkie for rail is a more direct route to the objective of promoting competition. Unless that objective can be met, privatization appears an unattractive prospect because the absence of competitive forces would compound the huge burden of regulation.

Another obstacle to privatization is that BR is heavily reliant on public funds. In the year to 31 March 1987, almost a quarter of BR's turnover (£786 million out of £3,183 million) came from Government grants. BR made an operating surplus of £69.9 million, and a surplus of £2.4 million after interest charges. This financial result was substantially better than results in previous years. The Government grant of £786 million was £110 million lower than the grant in 1985–1986, and BR's aim is to reduce the subsidy by a further 25 percent to £555 million in 1989–1990 by cost-cutting measures.

There are several possible justifications for Government grants to rail services, including the social desirability of services in less populated areas, the reduction of traffic congestion on roads, and the need to finance the deficits resulting from allocatively efficient pricing (i.e. $P = MC$) in natural monopoly cost conditions. Grants are not inconsistent with privatization—as we saw in connection with subsidies to bus services in rural areas—but privatization would make their administration considerably more difficult. Moreover, the industry's need for grants would make the proceeds from privatization small and highly dependent on expectations about future subsidy policies.

The lack of competition and the presence of sunk costs (unless there is vertical separation of track and trains) imply that competitive tendering for uncommercial rail services is unlikely to work satisfactorily. In coach services there are low sunk costs, there are many actual and potential suppliers, and the service is not too difficult to specify. The fulfillment of these conditions in rail services is less likely, and franchising—or "competition for the market" (see section 4.6.1)—might encounter serious difficulties. Bidding for franchises would probably not be competitive, problems of asset handover might be considerable (depending who owns the assets), and the needs of integrated network operation would imply that sizeable areas would have to be franchised, with corresponding problems of contract specification and administration.

In conclusion, it is evident that the difficulties of establishing effective competition and regulation in the railway industry are an unappealing combination of many of the problems faced in other industries. There are natural monopoly cost conditions, massive sunk costs, and a vertically integrated incumbent firm with huge incumbent advantages. Even if competition could be promoted, it might be prone to the instabilities (e.g. in timetabling) apparent from the deregulation of local bus services. An alternative to a privatized BR operating in a partly competitive environment would be a private BR monopoly subject to heavy regulation. But the regulatory problems would be enormous, especially in the absence of competitive yardsticks. In addition, rail services are distinctly unprofitable in overall terms (although some services are commercially viable), and the proceeds from privatization would not be large. Taken together, these factors suggest that the privatization of BR—in whatever form—should and will be a remote prospect. A more fruitful path is to concentrate on improving incentives and regulation in the industry under public ownership, and (without too much hope) perhaps also to facilitate private competition as an experiment in some parts of the industry where it might stand a chance.

Chapter 11

The Water Industry

11.1 Introduction

In February 1985 the Minister for Housing and Construction announced in the House of Commons that the Government intended to examine the possibility of a "measure of privatization" in the water industry. An initial discussion paper was published in April of that year, and, after studying the responses to its contents and examining the issues, the Government presented a White Paper on water privatization to Parliament in February 1986. The White Paper set out a number of reasons for the decision to proceed with privatization in the industry and laid down the basis for the legislative proposals that the Government intended to put to Parliament "as soon as possible."

The original timetable called for the introduction of a paving Bill transforming the publicly owned water authorities into public limited companies in late 1986, completion of the legislative stage by mid-1987, and the flotation of the resulting companies, either individually or in groups, from late 1987 onwards. In the event, with a General Election impending in either 1987 or the first half of 1988 and the legislative proposals proving more difficult to implement than had originally been anticipated, the Environment Secretary announced in June 1986 that privatization of the water industry was to be deferred.

The Conservative Election Manifesto of 1987, however, reaffirmed the Government's intention to proceed with water privatization, and, following that party's victory in the June 1987 General Election, the proposals were quickly revived, albeit with a number of significant modifications that we will discuss below. The paving legislation will now be introduced to Parliament in 1988, and, if all goes to plan, it can be expected that flotations of the resulting companies will commence in 1989 or 1990.

Although the general thrust of Government policy toward the industry is now clear, many issues of detail remain to be resolved, particularly with respect to methods of regulation. The water industry shares many of the network and natural monopoly characteristics of telecommunications, gas supply, and electricity supply, and much of our earlier analysis is therefore immediately applicable to this particular case. Rather than simply repeat these earlier arguments, however, we will, in this chapter, focus rather more on the special features of water supply and on their implications for regulatory policy. Three examples will suffice to illustrate the sorts of points we have in mind. First, the opportunities for increasing competition in the services provided by the industry are generally less favorable than in most of the other cases of privatization we have considered, and, in the search for improved economic efficiency, greater weight must necessarily be placed upon the development of effective regulation. Second, since the publicly owned water authorities have themselves been entrusted with regulatory functions with respect to a number of environmental issues, privatization necessarily involves a substantive reappraisal of the conduct of important aspects of environmental policy. Finally, at the moment, charges for many of the services supplied by water authorities are *not* quantity related (e.g. most domestic water supply is unmetered).

Even where regulatory issues are broadly similar to those we have considered in previous chapters, the trade-offs confronted in the water supply industry serve to bring certain dimensions of the problems into sharper focus. Two problems in particular merit special attention. The first concerns the quality of service provided. Given the structure of the industry, it is extremely unlikely that profit-maximizing firms, subject to price controls alone, would face an incentive structure conducive to the efficient choice of quality standards. As a consequence of this market failure, effective regulation will require that the privatized industry be subject to strict quality controls as well as price controls, and, in setting price and quality constraints, regulators will be compelled to take into account the trade-off between the two variables: higher quality standards will, by raising costs, lead to higher prices. Any notion that regulation need only concern itself with price controls is therefore fundamentally misguided, and should be abandoned at the outset.

The second issue of particular interest in the water supply case is the potential use of regulatory yardsticks. Unlike in telecommunications, gas, and electricity generation, the pre-privatization industry is already regionalized and current policy proposals rely upon the continuation of this structure. Thus, regulators will have access to information from a group of independent private companies and, as in electricity distribution, this will afford opportunities for the implementation of more efficient incentive structures. It remains to be seen whether or not these opportunities will actually be realized, but the existing structure of the industry at least invites a thorough appraisal of the approach. In the analysis that follows, therefore, we will attempt to develop some of our earlier remarks on yardstick regulation.

In the light of these various points, the material in the remainder of this chapter is divided into three sections. Section 11.2 provides an account of the recent history and structure of the industry, up to and including the abortive attempt at privatization in 1985–1986. In section 11.3, after considering the scope for increasing competition in water supply (including the introduction of franchising) and the position of the existing statutory water companies, we concentrate upon three of the major issues that will arise in connection with the regulation of a privately owned industry: price controls, quality controls, and the use of regulatory yardsticks. Finally, section 11.4 contains an assessment of current Government proposals for the privatization of the industry.

11.2   The Water Industry in Britain

The proposals concerning water privatization that were set out in the 1986 White Paper related only to the industry in England and Wales (i.e. they did not include Scotland). This restriction, and the subsequent delay in the implementation of the policy, is partly explained by the evolution of the organizational framework of the industry in the postwar period. Before examining both the functions/activities of the existing public corporations and recent policy developments, we will therefore first consider this structural history. The key year in this period was 1973, when the industry in England and Wales was reorganized into ten regional water authorities.

11.2.1   The Organization of the Industry

Prior to 1973, the water industry in England and Wales was dominated by three categories of organization: water undertakings, sewerage and sewage disposal authorities, and river authorities. Responsibility for the supply and distribution of water was placed in the hands of the organizations in the first of these categories. Until the mid-1950s there existed over a thousand separate water undertakings, but thereafter numbers were substantially reduced by a process of consolidation aimed at achieving economies from increased scales of operation. Thus, by the early 1970s the number of water undertakings had fallen to 198, of which 64 were run by individual local government authorities and 101 by joint boards comprising more than one local government authority, and 33 were statutory privately owned water companies.

The sewerage and sewage disposal authorities were responsible for the treatment and disposal of water-borne wastes, and were run either by individual local government authorities or, in a relatively few cases, by joint boards of local authorities. Over 1,300 such organizations were in existence at the beginning of the 1970s.

The river authorities, of which there were 29 in 1971, came into being in 1965, and were responsible, among other things, for water conservation, land drainage, fisheries, control of river pollution, and, in some cases, navigation. Thus, for example, the river authorities controlled abstractions of surface and underground water (whether by water undertakings or by other parties) by means of a system of licensing, and regulated discharges of wastes into river systems through the allocation of discharge consents. The authorities were entitled to construct reservoirs, but not pipeline networks or treatment works, which were the responsibility of the water undertakings.

In addition to these principal types of institution, a number of other organizations were active in the industry prior to 1973. These included the Water Resources Board (a national agency entrusted with data collection, research, and planning for the industry as a whole), the British Waterways Board (responsible for canals and some river navigation), navigation authorities, and national drainage boards.

It can be seen, therefore, that the institutional structure of the water industry in England and Wales prior to 1973 was highly fragmented, with water supply, sewerage, and regulatory functions divided amongst a large number of relatively localized organizations. In many ways the structure resembles that of the prenationalization electricity and gas industries: public ownership was predominant but Government involvement in the industry occurred via local authorities. Likewise, the 1973 reorganization of the industry can usefully be compared with the nationalization (centralization) of the energy sectors that had taken place in the 1940s: the principal aim was to achieve economies of scale and scope associated with larger more integrated operations.

The guiding principle of the Water Act 1973, which established nine regional water authorities in England and the Welsh Water Authority, was that a single body should plan and control all uses of water in each river catchment, a principle generally known as "integrated river-basin management." Each water authority was entrusted with responsibility for water supply, sewerage, sewage disposal, water resource planning, pollution control, fisheries, flood protection, water recreation, and environmental conservation in its own area. Thus, not only were the major activities of water supply, sewerage, and sewage disposal consolidated but they were also bundled together with a wide range of environmental and regulatory functions.

While the integrated river-basin management principle suggests the establishment of a separate authority for each river basin, the actual areas allocated to the water authorities by the 1973 Act reflected a compromise between this underlying principle and potential economies of scale and scope. Thus, given the small sizes of river systems in England and Wales, in practice the area covered by each of the water authorities typically contains more than one river basin. The important point, however, is that the legislation created organizations based on river catchment areas, rather than on artificial administrative boundaries that required separate bodies to be responsible for different parts of the same river system.

In principle, it would have been possible for the new water authorities to carry out their allocated functions whilst preserving local authority ownership of the bulk of the assets of the industry. If that course had been followed the authorities would have been responsible for contracting out water supply, sewerage, and sewage disposal to local authorities. In the event, however, it was decided that local government assets should also be transferred to the water authorities, although the Water Act 1973 made provision for local authorities to act as agents with respect to the discharge of sewerage duties. Thus, the new water authorities came into possession of substantial physical assets in the form of water mains, sewers, treatment works, and the like. Since the asset transfer was internal to the public sector, no compensation for the loss of assets was paid to local authorities—an outcome that has now become controversial in view of the impending privatization of the industry and the anticipated sales proceeds that will be derived by central, rather than local, government.

Following reorganization some local authority involvement in the control of the water authorities was retained in the form of representation on the boards of the new organizations. Until 1983 the authorities were run by relatively large boards with a majority of local authority representatives. However, the position was changed by the Water Act 1983, which provided for smaller boards that were designed to facilitate the introduction of a more commercial approach to the conduct of the businesses and all of whose members are appointed by ministers. The Act therefore served further to shift control of the authorities from local to central government and, in effect, it was only in 1983 that water became a full-fledged nationalized industry.

The statutory (privately owned) water companies escaped reorganization in 1973, and were left to operate as before. They are unregistered companies, incorporated by individual Acts of Parliament (hence the title statutory), whose shares are quoted on the Stock Exchange. They are, however, subject to strict regulatory controls, which include restrictions on the amounts of share and loan capital that can be raised, the methods by which new share capital can be raised (which must be by auction or tender), rates of dividend on share capital, rates of interest on loan capital, amounts that may be put to reserve and contingency funds, and amounts of accumulated surpluses that may be carried forward from one year to the next. As with the prewar regulation of private gas and electricity companies, this regime was designed to prevent the exploitation of market power.

The continued operation of the statutory water companies was guaranteed by section 12 of the Water Act 1973. Where a statutory water company operates within the area of a water authority the legislation obliges the latter to discharge its water supply and distribution functions through the company. There now exist 28 such companies, which collectively supply water to about 25 percent of the households in England and Wales. They are not, however, involved in activities such as sewerage and sewage disposal.

Given the history of coexistence of publicly and privately owned firms in the British water industry, in evaluating the prospects for further privatization it would clearly be useful to know how the past performances of the two types of firms have compared. Unfortunately, most probably as a consequence of the difficulties in obtaining comparable data, there is little systematic evidence on this issue. Thus, studies of the type conducted in the U.S. water industry (see section 2.5) are notable for their absence in Britain, and we are therefore compelled to treat the question as unresolved.

The structure of the water industry in Scotland is somewhat different from that in England and Wales. Twelve Regional and Island Councils (local authorities) are responsible for water alongside other local services, and an organizational structure based upon administrative boundaries has therefore been preferred to one based upon the integrated river-basin management principle. We do not want to dwell upon the reasons for this particular decision, but simply note that factors such as differences in political institutions, physical geography, and settlement patterns contributed to the outcome. The important point to note, however, is that, as a consequence, the physical assets of the water industry in Scotland are not currently owned by public bodies that are responsible to the central government. Hence, any legislation to privatize the industry in Scotland would require the disposal of *local* government assets. Given that most local government in Scotland is not controlled by the Conservative Party, and irrespective of whether the final destination of the sales proceeds would be the Exchequer or the relevant local authorities, it is unlikely that such a move would be politically attractive. Thus far, therefore, the Government has shown no inclination to grasp this particular thistle.

11.2.2   Functions and Activities of the Water Authorities

Taken together, the water authorities in England and Wales currently employ around 50,000 people and have an annual turnover in excess of £2.6 billion. Their capital expenditure in 1986–1987 was over £900 million and the value of total net assets, calculated on a replacement cost basis, is estimated to exceed £27 billion. These assets include about 139,000 miles of water mains, 141,000 miles of sewers, 6,500 sewage treatment works, and 800 water treatment works. Thus, the industry is highly capital intensive, with assets per employee of over £0.5 million in 1987 prices.

As explained above, implementation of the principle of integrated river-basin management in 1973 has led to a situation in which the authorities are required to carry out a very wide range of functions. These can be grouped into three general categories: *operational activities* (the supply of water, and the treatment and disposal of liquid wastes), *environmental regulation* (the planning and regulation of water resources and uses, control of the quality of river and drinking water, control of waste disposal, fisheries, and navigation), and *community services* (whose beneficiaries are not identified for charging purposes, and which include land drainage and flood protection, highway drainage, wildlife conservation, amenity, and recreation).

Of these categories, operational activities account for the great bulk of both costs and revenues, and it is upon these functions that most of our analysis will be focused. Nevertheless, the question of how best to deal with the environmental regulation and community service functions in the context of private ownership of the industry has substantial implications for any evaluation of the overall benefits of privatization, and we will touch upon this issue at various points in the following discussion. It will therefore be useful to set out in more detail the principal features of each of the existing activities of the water authorities. Briefly, they are as follows.

Water conservation   Water authorities have the statutory duty of water conservation, with each authority having control of the function in its own area. This involves the planning of water resources, provision to meet demand for water, and the ownership and management of reservoirs, aquifers, and gathering grounds.

Water supply and distribution   This function consists of the pumping and treatment of raw water, and the ownership and management of treatment works, service reservoirs, and the mains network. It is partially discharged through the statutory water companies.

Control of drinking water quality   Drinking water standards are laid down by the European Community Drinking Water Directive, and these must, in law, be enforced by the Government. The water authorities are required to meet these prescribed standards but, where it is satisfied that there is no public health risk, the U.K. Department of the Environment is permitted to authorize delays or derogations.

Sewerage   Water authorities have a statutory duty to provide public sewers to drain their areas effectively. They are also required to endeavor to make arrangements to discharge this function through local authorities acting on an agency basis, and this type of relationship with local authorities is the norm in the industry. The activity consists chiefly in owning and maintaining the sewer network, and thereby providing a means of transporting domestic water-borne wastes, surface water run-off, and liquid trade-effluent discharges either to a treatment works or, less frequently, directly to a receiving watercourse.

Sewage treatment and disposal   This involves the ownership and management of treatment works, wherein water-borne wastes are rendered acceptable for discharge into watercourses, and the disposal of sludge residues from the process.

River management   Among the duties of the water authorities falling under this heading are planning the use of rivers, monitoring the quality of river water, and licensing any abstractions of water from rivers.

Regulation of discharges   The water authorities are entrusted with the allocation of rights ("consents") to discharge wastes into watercourses, although, in the case of discharges by the authorities themselves, consents are granted by the Secretary of State for the Environment.

Land drainage, flood protection, and sea defense   The authorities have a statutory duty to exercise general supervision over all aspects of land drainage and flood protection in their areas, and have some powers to carry out improvement and maintenance work on their own account.

Navigation   Obligations imposed upon the authorities with respect to navigation include duties to keep channels open for traffic, to license boats using the rivers, and to make and police bylaws governing the use of rivers for navigational purposes.

Fisheries   Water authorities have the duty to maintain, improve, and develop fisheries, and to regulate the use of these fisheries via the allocation of licenses and the passing of bylaws.

Nature conservation   Water authorities have duties to have regard to the preservation and conservation of flora and fauna, to further nature conservation, and to protect sites of special scientific interest.

Amenity and recreation   The authorities are required to secure the use of water and land associated with water for the purposes of recreation (principally angling and boating).

By way of drawing attention to the multifarious duties carried out by the water authorities under the integrated river-basin management system, the 1986 White Paper quoted the example of Thames Water, which is the largest and most profitable of the authorities in England and Wales. The River Thames catchment area covered by the authority supports 3,500 water abstractions: 1,200 for agriculture, 500 for water supplies (by the Thames Water Authority itself and by the eight statutory water companies that operate, either entirely or partially, within its area), and 1,800 for industrial and other uses. These abstractions are regulated and managed by Thames Water to ensure that they do not unduly lower the level of the river and thereby threaten natural life in the area or substantively interfere with recreational use of the river and its tributaries. The Authority now issues about 193,000 rod licenses per annum for fishing and there are about 19,000 boats which are registered to use the river. Finally, Thames Water must regulate discharges into the river and its tributaries so as to prevent pollution that would have detrimental effects on water supplies, wild life, and recreational activities.

As noted above, however, in financial terms it is the operational functions that dominate the activity of the water authorities. This can be

Table 11.1 Water Authorities' operating and capital expenditures in 1984–1985

Function	Operating expenditure		Capital expenditure	
	Amount (£ million)	Percentage	Amount (£ million)	Percentage
Water supply	579	46.0	261	33.0
Sewerage	161	13.0	239	30.0
Sewage treatment	366	29.0	148	18.5
Water resources	54	4.5	27	3.0
Land drainage	54	4.5	58	7.0
Environmental	40	3.0	3	0.5
Other	–	–	61	8.0
Total	1254	100.0	797	100.0

Source: Department of the Environment (1986).

seen from table 11.1, which provides a breakdown of operating and capital expenditures by the ten authorities in 1984–1985. Thus, in that year, the main activities of water supply, sewerage, and sewage treatment accounted for 88 percent and 81 percent of operational and capital expenditures respectively.

A similar picture emerges if the activities of the water authorities are broken down according to their contributions to turnover. Table 11.2 provides illustrative figures drawn from the accounts of the Severn Trent Authority for 1984–1985, which show that water supply and sewerage charges together accounted for about 83 percent of total turnover. In contrast, income from land drainage and environmental activities amounted to only about 5 percent of the Authority's income. The table also illustrates the point that much of the income of the water authorities is derived from the provision of unmetered services. Thus, charges for the great majority of domestic consumers are based not upon the quantities of services supplied, but rather on the rateable value of the relevant dwelling. That is, the amount payable by each household is some designated fraction—which varies from area to area and is changed each year by the water authorities—of the property's rateable value, which in turn is estimated on the basis of the rent that the property is anticipated to command if let on the open market. However, since the Government plans to abolish the domestic rating system, unless current legislative proposals are withdrawn this method of charging will necessarily be in need of reform in the near future, a point to which we will return in section 11.3.3.

11.2.3 Recent Policy Developments

The story of recent Government policy towards the water industry in

Table 11.2   Analysis of turnover for the Severn Trent Water Authority, 1984–1985

Charge	Amount (£ million)	Percentage
Unmeasured water supply	86	23.7
Measured water supply	48	13.2
Unmeasured sewerage	156	43.0
Measured sewerage	13	3.6
Trade effluent	15	4.1
Water abstraction	14	3.9
Other water resources, water supply, and sewerage	11	3.0
Land drainage	12	3.3
Environmental service charge	6.6	1.8
Other environmental	1.4	0.4
Total	363	100.0

Source: Littlechild (1986), based on Severn Trent Water Authority Accounts, 1984–1985.

England and Wales is a familiar one. The ten authorities are subject to the system of control set out in the 1978 White Paper on nationalized industries, and have therefore been controlled by means of a mixture of financial targets, external financing limits, performance targets (the most important of which have taken the form of target reductions in real operating costs), and investment criteria. In addition, a number of the authorities have been subject to efficiency audits by the Monopolies and Mergers Commission (MMC). In Scotland, central government's influence on the industry is less direct, operating through more general financial controls on local authorities that include cash limits on capital expenditure and, in certain cases, rate-capping (i.e. placing limits on levels of local taxation).

As with most of the other nationalized industries, policy since 1979 has rested on the view that, in the past, the internal efficiency performance of the authorities had left much to be desired, and the general approach has been to attempt to make the enterprises operate along more commercial lines (the reorganization of the boards of the authorities by the Water Act 1983 is one illustration of the general drift of public policy). In particular, and again in line with developments in other parts of the public sector, priority has been given to reducing the financial contribution of the water industry to the public sector borrowing requirement.

The changed emphasis of public policy since the late 1970s has had substantial effects on the performance of the water authorities. The upward trend in real operating costs in the 1970s has been reversed, and, as can be seen from table 11.3, despite continued demand growth for water there was a reduction in manpower of approximately 18 percent between 1979 and 1985, an outcome that again stands in contrast with the earlier trend.

Equally striking has been the turnaround in the proportion of capital expenditure financed from internal sources. In 1974 virtually the whole of the industry's capital program was financed by borrowing. By 1980–1981 this proportion had been reduced to around 60 percent, and by 1986–1987 to around 10 percent. This has been achieved both by improvements in operational efficiency, and by holding back planned investment programs: in 1986–1987, for example, the authorities sought permission for capital expenditures that were 13 percent above those eventually allowed. However, price increases forced by the imposition of tighter external financing limits and higher financial targets have also made a significant contribution to higher cash flows and hence to the greater availability of internal funds. Thus, over recent years, increases in water charges have tended to run well ahead of the general inflation rate.

Despite the gradual tightening of financial constraints on the water authorities, the latter appear to have been relatively generously treated in comparison with many other nationalized industries. In 1986–1987 the financial target, expressed as the ratio of operating profits to net assets on a current cost accounting (CCA) basis, was set at a level of only 1.6 percent, which represents an increase from the 1.4 percent return in 1985–1986, and from 1.0 percent in 1984–1985. Financial results for the authorities in 1985–1986, calculated on a historic cost accounting (HCA) basis, are shown in table 11.4. While operating profit was about 21 percent higher than in the previous year, it can be seen that, assuming the replacement cost of net assets is of the order of £27 billion, the resulting rate of return on capital (i.e. the ratio of historic cost profit to the replacement cost of assets) was, by most standards, extremely low, standing at about 3.7 percent. On a fully consistent CCA basis, and largely because of the much higher CCA depreciation charge, the rate of return was lower still (less than 2 percent). Thus, unless further very substantial improvements in internal efficiency can be made and/or there are significant further price increases, it is

Table 11.3 Water Authority manpower as at 31 March each year

Year	1976[a]	1979	1982	1985
Number of employees	60,649	63,221	60,586	51,785

Source: Department of the Environment (1986).
a. Figures prior to 1979 were calculated on a slightly different basis.

Table 11.4 Financial results for the Water Authorities, 1985–1986

Authority	Turnover (£ million)	Operating profits (£ million)	Net profits (£ million)	Capital expenditure (£ million)	Loans outstanding (£ million)
Anglian	297.0	138.7	39.4	122.0	838.0
Northumbrian	111.0	58.1	7.7	39.0	421.0
North West	362.0	146.7	36.5	167.0	905.0
Severn Trent	391.0	149.0	51.7	125.0	805.0
Southern	177.0	77.7	38.5	70.0	286.0
South West	88.0	39.4	23.2	41.0	136.0
Thames	501.0	184.3	149.9	194.0	269.0
Welsh	187.0	46.0	12.2	55.0	432.0
Wessex	106.0	64.1	18.8	54.0	232.0
Yorkshire	248.0	99.3	35.6	100.0	509.0
Total	2468.0	1003.3	413.5	967.0	4833.0

Source: Water Authority Annual Reports and Accounts.

unlikely that the returns on new investment in the industry will appear attractive to profit-seeking private investors.

The 1986 White Paper on the privatization of the industry did not provide any detailed information about how the Government intended to tackle these fundamental financial issues. Indeed, for the most part, the document was concerned only with setting out the Government's plans in the most general of terms, leaving detailed decisions to be made at a later stage. The outline program was as follows:

(i) restructure the ten water authorities in England and Wales as "water supply public limited companies" (WSPLCs);

(ii) establish a system of regulating the WSPLCs;

(iii) modernize water and sewerage law;

(iv) permit domestic water metering trials on a compulsory basis;

(v) improve the legislative framework for the control of drinking water and river water quality.

The ten water authorities were then to be transferred to the private sector in their existing forms. Thus it was planned that the various regulatory functions relating to environmental matters would be retained by the WSPLCs. However, the exercise of these functions by private bodies was to be underpinned by a clearer strategic framework of national policy for the water environment and by a system of finance whereby the costs of providing environmental services could be recovered by a mixture of direct charges (e.g. for consents to discharge wastes into rivers) and general charges (e.g. for public goods).

The White Paper was also unspecific about the future of the privately owned statutory water companies. While their continued existence was not immediately threatened, paragraph 43 stated that:

"The Government sees advantage in ending the constitutional link between the water companies and the authorities once they become WSPLCs, and in bringing the companies under the same form of financial regulation as will apply to the WSPLCs. At the same time the companies would be able to convert to PLC status, and take advantage of the greater scope for enterprise that this would offer. The Government will be discussing these proposals further with the companies."

With respect to regulation more generally, the 1986 proposals envisaged a framework of control that would broadly be in line with the regimes established for the telecommunications and gas industries. Thus, the main water services were to be regulated by a Director General of Water Services (DGWS) through long-term licenses granted to the WSPLCs. The White Paper expressed a preference for price controls over limitations on profits or dividends (the approach that had earlier been adopted for the statutory water companies), explicitly recognized the need for regulation of water quality standards, and reaffirmed the principle that cross-subsidization among services should be avoided. It also indicated an awareness of the opportunities for the adoption of yardstick regulation of the industry. Thus, in paragraph 56 it was stated that:

"The regulatory system will enable comparison of performance to be made between WSPLCs, and this will both act as an impetus to improvement and—by providing a yardstick for investors to make judgements—facilitate competition between WSPLCs on the capital market."

However, it was not precisely spelt out how these various principles were to be implemented.

The ambitious legislative program outlined in the 1986 White Paper quickly ran into timetable difficulties. Problems that emerged included the following.

(i) Existing water industry legislation is spread over many different acts and statutes, and the consolidation required by the privatization proposals was therefore a complex and lengthy technical task.

(ii) It proved difficult to clarify the respective roles of the water authorities and the Government with respect to the discharge of (environmental) regulatory functions, and there was considerable opposition from a variety of interest groups to the notion that privately owned companies should act as environmental regulators.

(iii) On the original timetable, the Government would have been faced with the prospect of attempting to guide complex and controversial legislation through Parliament at a time when the next General Election was likely to be imminent.

(iv) The legal right of the Government to sell assets which it had acquired, without compensation, from local authorities in 1973 was questioned, and the local government trade union NALGO brought a court case against Thames Water for spending money on furthering the case for privatization before Parliamentary authority had been given.

(v) Given the low levels of profitability of most of the water authorities, major questions concerning both the writing-off of debts to improve financial viability and the methods of flotation to be adopted needed to be resolved before the asset transfers could proceed.

The cumulative effect of these problems was that, less than six months after the publication of the White Paper, the decision was taken to defer the proposed privatization of the water industry. As noted earlier, the legislative program was revived after the June 1987 General Election, and the paving Bills will come before Parliament in 1987–1988. The Government has announced one major change in its approach to the issue, however. In contrast with the 1986 plans, it is now intended that the water authorities will be stripped of most of their functions relating to regulation of the environment, and it is proposed that these will instead be allocated to a new body, provisionally entitled the National Rivers Authority. Again, precise details of the Government's plans have not yet been finalized, but it is clear that the general effect of the policy would be to restrict the functions of the WSPLCs to the main operational activities of water supply and distribution, sewerage, and sewage disposal.

Not surprisingly, most of the managements of the water authorities have reacted with some hostility to this proposal, since it entails a significant diminution in their roles. Thus, whereas the chairman of Thames Water was initially a keen advocate of privatization, he has now become an opponent of the Government's policy. More important, the separation of regulatory functions from water supply and sewerage responsibilities implies the abandonment of the integrated river-basin management principle, and a reversion to an industry structure that more closely resembles the pre-1973 situation (although it is planned that there will be only one river authority, rather than the 29 that existed before reorganization). Thus, while the separation of regulatory and operational functions is eminently sensible in the context of an industry that is privately owned—which is presumably why the Government modified its original proposals—the decision serves to demonstrate a lack of compatibility between private ownership and integrated river-basin management. It follows that, to the extent that the latter has substantive merits—as has consistently been argued by Governments in documents up to and including the 1986 White Paper—privatization will necessarily have substantive detriments. The decision also reopens questions concerning the most appropriate structure for a privatized water industry: given that the functional scope of the existing public enterprises was determined by the integrated river-basin management principle, if the latter is to be abandoned it is natural to ask whether there is any justification for retaining these existing areas and organizations and, more generally, whether further restructuring would be beneficial.

11.3   Regulatory Issues in the Water Industry

To accompany the 1986 White Paper on privatization, in January 1986 the Government also published a report by Professor Littlechild that had been commissioned by the Department of the Environment. The Littlechild Report examined a variety of issues relating to the regulation of privatized water authorities on the assumption, specified in the terms of reference for the study, that the authorities would be privatized in substantially their present form, and that responsibility for economic regulation would be placed with an independent regulator whose position would be similar to that of the Director General of Oftel. Given both the availability of this document and the extensive discussions of similar regulatory issues in earlier chapters, in this section we will not attempt to cover as wide a range of questions as Littlechild, but will rather focus upon those areas where water privatization raises either particularly difficult or particulary interesting problems. In one sense, however, our discussion is broader than Littlechild's, since we need not restrict ourselves by the assumption that the water authorities will be privatized in their present form (indeed, the 1987 Government announcements indicate that, in at least one important respect, they will not be).

11.3.1   The Scope for Competition

It appears to be accepted by both the Government and industry analysts that the the scope for increasing competition in the supply of water and sewerage services to final customers is extremely limited, and we can see no reason to dissent from this general consensus. Natural monopoly conditions derive from the established local networks of pipes and sewers.

In effect, there are two separate monopolies—water supply and distribution, and sewerage—and it is an open question whether factors such as the interrelated demands for the two services make the combined activities a natural monopoly. Both functions are now carried out by the water authorities, but before 1973 there was clear separation between water undertakings and sewerage and sewage disposal authorities. Moreover, statutory water companies are not involved in the latter activities. What little evidence on relative performance that there is appears to be consistent with the view that, to the extent that there are economies from the integration of the two principal activities of the industry, the resulting benefits are not of decisive importance. Thus, vertical separation appears to be a viable structural option.

Irrespective of the degree of integration, however, the natural monopoly problem remains, and competition in the provision of the basic "transportation" services (of both water and water-borne wastes) only appears feasible in boundary areas along the borders between neighboring enterprises. Clearly, the greater the number of individual competing firms, the greater is the scope for this type of boundary competition. However, settlement patterns are such that it is difficult to imagine that such spatial competition could be turned into a potent force other than by creating an industry structure so fragmented that substantive scale economies would be lost. Thus, unlike in telecommunications (where Mercury competes with British Telecom) and energy (where the various fuels are partially substitutable for one another), the prospects for introducing even modest amounts of product market competition in the provision of the transportation services of the water industry are bleak.

In theory, as in other network industries, it is possible to envision the separation of pipeline operations from, for example, the water supply (sales) business. Different water supply companies would then be able to compete for customers using the common pipeline network. However, because of the increased costs of coordination, the option is likely to be unattractive as far as domestic consumers are concerned (cf. the discussion of restructuring in the gas industry in section 9.2.4). While competition for the custom of large industrial and commercial users would be more feasible to arrange, it also has to be recognized that any resulting benefits from increased competition in supply are likely to be considerably less than in other utility industries. Unlike gas and electricity, the costs of "producing" water suitable for domestic consumption are relatively low in relation to the value added at the transportation stage.

Of rather greater significance, however, are the opportunities for promoting competition in the downstream operation of sewage treatment. Currently, the water authorities collectively own around 6,500 sewage treatment works which, prior to re-organization in 1973, were operated by a large number of different local authorities. Scale economies are not sufficiently great to justify high levels of either national or regional concentration in this activity, and it would be possible to have a relatively large number of firms, whether publicly or privately owned, competing for contracts from publicly or privately owned water authorities/companies.

More generally, competition in the industry could be increased by the more widespread adoption of franchising. Water authorities already discharge some of their functions via both the statutory water authorities (water supply and distribution) and local authorities (sewerage). Apart from sewage treatment, it would also be possible to contract out economic activities such as the maintenance and construction of the pipeline networks themselves. Thus, although natural monopoly conditions hold in the basic transportation services of the industry, and although there are strong arguments for maintaining the organizational link between pipeline operations and the provision of service to final consumers (at least for smaller customers), this does not necessarily imply that forward and backward integration from these activities is desirable. On the contrary, as a matter of general principle public policy should seek to isolate the natural monopoly elements and to prevent the firms entrusted with these activities from extending their monopoly powers into other areas. By limiting the degree of vertical integration, extensive use of franchising and contracting out would therefore serve to expand the domain of economic activity in which effective competition can be introduced.

Finally, there is also scope for increasing competition in activities other than the basic services of the industry. These operations comprise a wide range of commercial services, stretching from the production and sale of bottled mineral water to overseas consulting. They are, however, only fringe activities of the authorities and, while opportunities for expansion do exist, they are likely to remain of relatively minor importance for the foreseeable future.

11.3.2 The Statutory Water Companies

Within both the existing framework of regulation and control of the water industry and the structures likely to be proposed by the Government for a privatized industry, the position of the statutory water companies appears to be somewhat anomalous. Full implementation of the integrated river-basin management principle in 1973 would have required the transfer of these companies to the public sector, followed by the amalgamation of each company with the water authority responsible for its area. No doubt political pressures on the then Conservative Government spoke against this option and contributed to the survival of the companies. Whatever the reasons for it, however, their continued existence has been a source of complication for later proposals to privatize the industry.

If anything, the anomalous position of the companies will be accentuated by privatization of the water authorities. Under the approach set out in the 1986 White Paper, one central problem would have been the determination of the charges that the companies would have had to pay to the authorities for water abstractions. With the water authorities in private hands, there would have been a danger of monopoly pricing for the companies' basic input which could have left the latter at a substantial disadvantage. Strict regulation of such charges would therefore have been necessary. The problem is likely to be eased considerably by the revised Government proposals for the industry that were put forward in 1987. Thus, if a National Rivers Authority is to be responsible for the licensing of water abstractions (a function undertaken by the river authorities before 1973), the successors to the statutory companies will be on a par with the privatized water authorities in the market for water abstractions.

However, a second, more important, difficulty remains. Given the Government's preference for price rather than dividend controls, the existence of the statutory water companies (and their future, assumed survival as PLCs) implies that any future DGWS will be faced with the prospect of regulating not ten but 38 different sets of tariff structures for final customers, with wide variations in cost conditions amongst the various companies. While we are generally favorable to the idea that increased numbers of firms can assist regulators by providing them with greater information, the control of such a large number of tariffs (and standards of service) by one office may cause serious administrative problems that could potentially detract from the quality of decisions, particularly if the new regulatory body is of a similar size to Oftel and Ofgas.

11.3.3 Price Controls and Investment Problems

Assuming that some variant of the RPI – X approach is to be adopted for the regulation of privatized water authorities, the Government is faced with a range of questions similar to those considered in previous chapters. For example, at what levels should both X and the initial prices be set, and, given that the authorities supply several different services, which of these should be covered by the price controls? There is also the issue of whether the regulatory constraint should be applied in aggregate to all the services so covered, or whether there should be a separate constraint for each service supplied. If the former approach is adopted, it gives rise to the further question of how the appropriate weightings applied to each service in the calculation of the aggregate price index should be determined.

In the case of water supply, these various issues are complicated by the fact that a large proportion of the revenue of the authorities derives from unmetered services. The current pricing system for unmetered supplies can be regarded as a special case of a two-part tariff comprising a fixed "connection" charge and a variable unit charge, in which the fixed component is set at a level linked to property (rental) values and the per unit component is set at zero. For most domestic consumers, therefore, the only dimension of choice that is affected by charges is whether or not to receive water and sewerage services: once connected to the system, additional services are charge free. Since water and sewerage services are basic necessities, this means that, to a first approximation, domestic demand is independent of the charges that are levied, and that the water authorities therefore effectively face a completely inelastic demand for much of their output.

It is possible to argue that the market power that would accrue to privatized water authorities under a system in which they can, in effect, levy taxes on domestic consumers is one of the reasons why the introduction of metering for domestic water supplies might be beneficial. Thus metering can be seen as a way of increasing the price sensitivity of demand, and hence of reducing market power. However, because of the lack of substitutes for the basic services of the industry, it is unlikely that the elasticity of demand for water would be very high at the unit price levels likely to pertain in the event that metering was introduced, and the water authorities would therefore still continue to enjoy very considerable market power.

The more fundamental potential advantage of domestic water metering is the contribution it might make to improvements in allocative efficiency. There is an obvious tendency towards overconsumption of goods and services that are provided free of charge at the margin, although the avoidance of metering costs has to be set against this detriment of the existing system when determining the overall balance of advantage between the two alternative methods of charging. Again, much depends upon the the price sensitivity of demand: the greater the reduction in consumption induced by a given increase in per unit charges the greater will be the cost savings to the supplying firms.

An additional factor that is currently stimulating increased interest in the possibility of domestic metering is the Government's plan to abolish the domestic rating system and replace it with a system of local taxation based upon a community charge levied at a fixed rate per head of the population (i.e. a poll tax). In principle, the community charge approach can be used for unmetered water supplies simply by levying a per capita fixed charge on consumers, so that a given household's water bill would be equal to the number of adult members of that household multiplied by the per capita community charge for the relevant locality. However, since one of the aims of the proposed change in local taxation is to link taxes more closely to the quantity of local services consumed by households, this underlying principle points in the direction, where feasible, of increased use of unit charges.

In the light of these points, it is not surprising to find that the paving legislation for water privatization provides for the introduction of compulsory water-metering trials—that is, households in the sample areas would be compelled to accept metering—aimed at assessing the costs and benefits of introducing unit charges to domestic consumers. Earlier, in 1984, the Department of the Environment had commissioned a steering group, chaired by Mr R. Watts, Chairman of Thames Water, to "report to the Government on the possible extension of water metering generally to households." The subsequent report (Watts Report, 1985) concluded that, on best available evidence, the net benefit of introducing metering for the average domestic consumer was likely to be close to zero but that, because of underlying uncertainties about the price sensitivity of demand and the cost savings that could be achieved from reduced volumes, further research based on metering trials was warranted.

The net benefit calculations in the Watts Report were based upon an assumption that, in the event that metering was introduced, unit charges would reflect the marginal cost of supplies. Since it is unlikely that this would turn out to be the case in practice, the conclusions about the benefits of metering are probably overoptimistic. There is a much more fundamental weakness in the Report, however, in that, while its purported aim was to examine "whether the social gain from charging domestic water consumers according to usage exceeds the social costs of replacing the existing rate-related charging system with a relatively expensive charging system based on individual metering," at no point in the document is the concept of consumers' surplus mentioned. Thus the social gains from metering are equated with the cost savings to the water authorities that would flow from the reductions in quantity demanded induced by a positive unit price, while the social costs are equated with the costs of metering. Properly calculated, however, social costs should include the consumers' surplus losses associated with the decline in consumption. The magnitude of these losses is difficult to estimate, depending as they do on both the slope and the curvature of the demand curve over the relevant price interval, but, unless demand is completely inelastic (in which case there is no allocative efficiency case for metering anyway), they will certainly be positive. Thus, if the other calculations in the steering group's report are taken at face value, once consumers' surplus losses are taken into account the correct conclusion is that the net social benefits of metering the average domestic consumer are *negative*.

The Watts Report serves to highlight an important difference between the decision criteria of publicly and privately owned enterprises that is germane to the water privatization debate. Profit-seeking privately owned WSPLCs *will* ignore consumers' surplus losses when evaluating investments in metering equipment, since such losses will be irrelevant to the incremental profit calculations. It is hard to be certain as to how the metering issue would be settled by a privately owned industry; much depends upon the anticipated effects of the decision on the regulated price level (which determine the revenue consequences of the decision). Nevertheless, and particularly if regulators allow post-metering prices that protect the firms' pre-metering revenues, there is a real prospect that a privatized water industry will shift to a metering system for domestic consumers in circumstances where the net social benefits of such a policy will be negative (the methodology of the Watts Report is indicative of the likely bias in this direction). If this happens, the consequential net loss in economic welfare should be treated as one of the costs of the privatization policy.

It remains to be seen whether or not extensive metering of domestic water supplies will in fact be introduced at some point in the future. Whatever the outcome, the relatively long timescale that is involved indicates that, if the Government's privatization of the industry proceeds as planned, in the short to medium term price controls for the industry will need to allow for the fact that much of the output of the WSPLCs will be unmetered. In general, this will tend to exacerbate the regulatory problems associated with ensuring that the tariff structures of privately owned multiproduct monopolies are allocatively efficient. Suppose, for example, that an authority provides two similar services, one metered and one unmetered, with charges per unit volume equal to p_1 and p_2 respectively. Suppose further that the total costs of supply are $C(q_1 + q_2)$, where q_1 and q_2 are the respective volumes, and that the WSPLC is regulated by an aggregate average revenue constraint of the type adopted for British Gas, implying that

$$p_1 q_1 + p_2 q_2 \leqslant \bar{p}(q_1 + q_2)$$

where $\bar{p}$ is the maximum allowable average charge per unit volume.

Since service 1 is unmetered and, by assumption, revenues are derived from a fixed charge, q_1 will be constant (i.e. independent of p_1). If the average revenue constraint is binding, it yields a simple expression for p_1 that can immediately be substituted into the firm's profit function. Hence, profit is simply equal to

$$\bar{p}(q_1 + q_2) - C(q_1 + q_2),$$

which can be maximized with respect to q_2. As a result, and assuming that the maximum allowable price is consistent with non-negative economic profits, the firm will have an incentive to keep expanding its metered supply if there are scale economies in production: marginal revenue is constant (equal to $\bar{p}$) and greater than marginal costs. Price in the metered market will, of course, fall with increasing volume sold, but any lost revenues will be more than covered by the rise in charges in the unmetered market that are permitted by the average revenue constraint. As a consequence, unmetered consumers will cross-subsidize metered supplies.

We conclude, therefore, that water industry regulators will need to play close attention to the *structure* of charges for the different services of privatized water authorities. Whether this is done via an aggregate price constraint based on a rather more sophisticated weighting system than the average revenue constraint just described, or by the introduction of a series of constraints for individual services, is a matter that is essentially of secondary importance. In both cases, regulators will require extensive information about the relevant demand and cost structures. As in the telecommunications and gas industries, the notion that regulators can make do with relatively simple cost and demand information and need not concern themselves with the fine detail of the tariff structures of the monopoly firms is, to say the least, misguided.

Apart from questions relating to the price structures of multiproduct monopolies, privatization of the water authorities will also raise difficult issues connected with the setting of appropriate *average* price levels. The Littlechild Report and the 1986 White Paper devote attention to the issue of whether or not price controls should be relatively uniform across the ten different authorities or should be tailored to the individual circumstances of each authority. We will consider this question in section 11.3.5 below, but here we focus on the rather different issues surrounding the low levels of profitability in the water industry. In particular, we ask whether privatization of the water authorities will provide appropriate incentives for new investment in the industry.

We have discussed theoretical issues connected with investment incentives for regulated monopolies in section 4.2, and the water industry serves as a good illustration of some of the difficulties that can arise. The basic services of the industry are highly capital intensive and its assets are extremely durable. Given the physical state of some of these assets, demand growth, and consumer demands for increased water quality and service standards, to operate efficiently the industry will require a continuing and substantial program of new investment which, after privatization, will only be forthcoming if investors expect to receive market rates of return on their capital expenditures.

The American "solution" to this investment problem has been to establish implicit bargains between society and regulated firms, whereby the latter are promised a reasonable rate of return on capital employed. In an attempt to avoid some of the undesirable incentives associated with this type of cost plus contract, U.K. policy has nominally taken a slightly different approach based around the RPI $-$ X formula. However, in capital-intensive industries where there is little competition, the U.K. approach to regulation itself has serious drawbacks and, in the context of water privatization, two problems are particularly serious.

The first is associated with the lack of any long-term guarantees as to the decisions that will be taken when the pricing formulas come to be reviewed. The durability of capital assets implies that rates of return on new investment will, for the most part, be a function of these review decisions rather than of the price levels and indexation provisions established at the time of flotation. In the absence of clear guidance as to the long-term conduct of regulatory policy, and in the absence of precedents from earlier periods, private investors will rightly be concerned that they will not be allowed to recover the costs, including an appropriate return on capital, of their investment expenditures. Hence, because of lack of credibility with respect to future public policies, there is a real danger of underinvestment in a privatized industry. Moreover, incentives for underinvestment are strengthened by the potential payoffs from strategic behavior by the regulated WSPLCs. Thus, in order to influence later regulatory decisions, firms may deliberately underinvest since, by confronting regulators with supply shortages and relatively poor service standards, they will be in a stronger position to argue that higher prices are required to finance the desired improvements. In contrast, if high expenditures to improve standards are incurred at the outset, regulators will later treat these items as *sunk* costs and firms would have to rely more heavily on arguments of fairness in supporting their case for higher prices, which arguments may not always be persuasive to public bodies facing consumer pressures for lower prices. To offset these biases, therefore, we can see no alternative to the explicit introduction of rate-of-return criteria in regulatory decisions but, until this is done, the uncertainties associated with regulatory policy are likely to have negative effects on investment in the industry.

The second difficulty that is particularly acute in the case of water privatization is the low level of profitability of the industry. Table 11.5 shows the profit position in 1984–1985, and it can be seen that, in CCA terms, the water authorities were, after subtracting interest charges, making significant losses. The extent of the problem can be gauged by considering the case of Thames Water, the most profitable of the authorities. In 1984–1985, Thames made a 1 percent current cost rate of return on net assets and, in the accounts, current cost depreciation for that year amounted to £126 million, or about 2.8 percent of the replacement cost of net assets (approximately equal to £4.5 billion). Thus, if the real cost of capital had been raised from the implicit value of 3.8 percent to, say, 10 percent, the authority would have had to increase operating profits by about £280 million, from £55 million to £335 million. Even assuming a zero price elasticity of demand, on a turnover of £455 million this would have implied an average increase in charges of over 60 percent. Alternatively, operating costs (equal to £268 million) would have to have been reduced to approximately zero!

Although water authority charges have, in real terms, been steadily increasing in the pre-privatization period, it is unlikely that the

Table 11.5 Profits of the Water Authorities in 1984–1985

	Historical cost (£ million)	Current cost (£ million)
Net available income for financing capital	1,023	1,023
Less depreciation	202	719
Operating profit before interest	821	304
Less interest	565	565
Overall profit	256	−261

Source: Vass (1986).

Government will be politically attracted by price hikes of the magnitudes suggested by the above calculations (despite the increased sales proceeds that they would generate). Much more likely, therefore, is the prospect that the authorities will be privatized with initial price levels that will imply rates of return on assets that are low by the standards of private industry. This outcome need not be unduly damaging: past investment expenditures are sunk costs and what matters to private investors is the allowed rate of return on new incremental investment. It does, however, pose some difficult problems for regulators when the price control formulas come to be reviewed. In effect, what is required is that, for purposes of calculating future rate bases (an exercise that we believe to be inevitable in the longer term), the values of existing assets are written down to levels commensurate with the initial prices, but that post-privatization investment expenditures and depreciation provisions should then be calculated according to standard accounting conventions. However, once again it is difficult to see how the extensive and detailed forms of regulation practiced by U.S. authorities can be avoided.

11.3.4 Quality of Service

As both the 1986 White Paper and the Littlechild Report explicitly acknowledge, any regulatory body for the privatized water industry will need to exercise control over the quality of water and of more general service standards of the new WSPLCs. The underlying problem is that a profit-seeking regulated monopolist will not typically be confronted with incentives that lead to quality choices that efficiently meet consumers' demands.

The point is illustrated in figure 11.1. Point E_1 shows an initial equilibrium where the regulated firm is producing a volume of output q_1 that is sold at a (controlled) price $\bar{p}$. The initial demand curve $D_1 D_1'$ is drawn on the assumption of a given quality-of-service level, denoted s_1. Consider now the effect of an increase in service quality to s_2, which is assumed to shift the demand curve outwards to $D_2 D_2'$, leading to a new equilibrium at E_2. The effect of the change is to increase (gross) consumers' welfare by the sum of the shaded areas A and B and, if a cost–benefit analysis were being conducted, this sum would be compared with the incremental costs, including the costs of producing the extra output, associated with increased quality. Thus, for example, if incremental costs are C, the increase in quality would be beneficial if $A + B > C$. The gain in revenue to the regulated firm, however, is equal to area B, and the quality improvement will only be made if $B > C$. It follows that, at any given price,

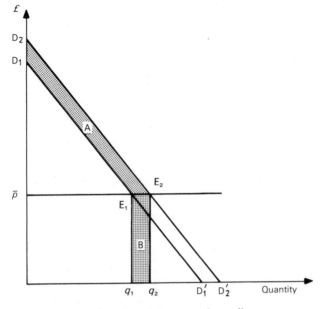

Figure 11.1   The effect of regulation on service quality

the regulated monopolist has incentives to choose suboptimally low levels of service quality. It can also be noted that the magnitude of the bias will tend to be greater the less price elastic is the demand curve, since steeper demand curves will tend to be associated with higher values for area A (in the limit of complete inelasticity area A becomes infinite).

Put more intuitively, the regulated monopoly has incentives to chisel on quality since, by so doing, it can reduce its costs. In a more competitive market this might lead to sharp reductions in volume sold as customers switch to other products, but the revenue penalties from volume reductions will tend to be much less where substitutability in demand is limited. The latter condition is satisfied in the water industry case, and quality reductions can therefore be expected to have relatively small effects on quantity demanded at the relevant price. Hence, the quality problem is potentially a serious one.

The European Community Drinking Water Directive lays down minimum bacteriological, chemical, and acceptability standards, covering about 60 parameters, with which the water authorities are required to comply and which will continue to be imposed on a privatized industry (although profit-seeking firms will have greater incentives to press for derogations and delays in meeting these standards). Nevertheless, overall service quality depends upon a host of factors not specified in the Directive, and the water authorities currently collect and publish information on an additional set of indicators relating to the following aspects of service.

Water supply availability: new connections, response times.

Water supply quantity: reliability, pressure, supply failure.

Sewerage availability: new connections.

Sewerage service quality: flooding, sewer collapses, storm overflows.

Environmental protection: river water quality, estuarial quality, sea outfalls, sludge disposal, effluent consents.

Land drainage and flood protection: standards, conditions of main rivers, tidal defenses, flood warning.

Customer contact: emergencies, correspondence, administration, billing.

In the event that the 1987 proposals to remove environmental functions from the WSPLCs go through, the burden of regulating several of these quality-of-service indicators would be passed to other public bodies. Similarly, if the British Telecom precedent is followed, withdrawal of the existing legal privilege of the water authorities, exempting them from proceedings in tort, will ease some of the regulatory problems: affected parties will be able to sue the WSPLCs for nuisances such as foul flooding. Nevertheless, the DGWS will still be confronted with the task of ensuring that profit-seeking monopolists devote sufficient resources to the maintenance and improvement of a number of important dimensions of service quality. This will impose a considerable information burden, since, in setting service standards, the DGWS will have to both determine the cost–quality trade-offs that are involved and form judgments as to consumer preferences over prices and quality. Finally, once service standard decisions have been made, there remains the problem of enforcement of the resulting targets.

The issue of service standards in the water industry is also intimately connected with the investment questions discussed in section 11.3.3, since many quality improvements are dependent upon additional capital expenditure on the pipeline infrastructure. Incentives to reduce service standards will therefore be reinforced by any biases toward underinvestment that result from the regulatory regime. However, it is possible that the quality regulation problem could be made less severe by the use of rate-of-return criteria when setting allowable prices. Thus, if rate-of-return regulation tends to encourage higher capital expenditures and if such expenditures are associated with improvements in service quality, it can be seen that the rate-of-return criterion tends to offset the incentives to reduce quality when the allowable price is fixed. The trade-offs involved have been explored by Spence (1975), and, while it is unlikely that the resulting outcomes will be socially optimal, the results serve to reinforce our earlier arguments that, as well as probably being inevitable, the development of explicit links between allowable prices and rates of return on capital would have a number of desirable consequences.

11.3.5 Yardstick Regulation

The opportunities for the use of yardstick regulation in the water industry follow from the fact that, when setting prices or target quality standards for any given firm, the performance statistics of other firms in the industry are likely to contain informative signals concerning the underlying economic trade-offs faced by the given firm's managers. The informativeness of the signals springs in turn from a variety of common features in the input and output markets of the several regional monopolists. As explained in chapter 4, it is a general principle of agency theory that incentive structures will be more efficient if rewards are made contingent upon such signals (where they exist). Hence, if feasible, the development of regulatory yardsticks would be highly desirable.

In paragraph 70 of the 1986 White Paper the choice of regulatory approach facing the Government was summarized as follows:

"In applying price controls and target standards, there is a choice between:

(i) tailoring standards and price controls individually to each WSPLC, taking account of its geography and investment needs; and

(ii) setting uniform standards and price controls throughout the industry.

The first allows for greater flexibility, but would involve the Director General in complex and repeated negotiation with each WSPLC, making it difficult to judge the success or failure of an individual company, and leading to the risk that the Director General would usurp some of the management's functions. It would also be difficult to demonstrate even-handedness between the regulated companies. The second method has the advantage of simplicity once it is in operation. The variations in their situation would be reflected in their capital structures and the prices they would command on the market. By encouraging direct comparisons between authorities by investors, it would also promote efficiency by means of competition. The normal disciplines of the capital market would become a direct spur to poor performers as would sanctions available to the Director General himself. If the price formula were set to reflect changes in the average performance of the industry as a whole, it would provide two further advantages: it would pass on to the customer the benefit of the average cost reduction, and would give WSPLCs an incentive to be more effective than the average, and so more profitable."

In terms of the choice posed, option (i) might be labeled the traditional cost-of-service approach, under which controls imposed upon a firm are based entirely, or almost entirely, on information specific to the firm and its own local markets while, to the extent that standards and prices are based on averaged national information, option (ii) can be considered to be a variant of yardstick regulation. Unfortunately, however, this passage from the White Paper contains a number of confusions, and a commentary upon it will serve to bring out the issues more clearly. In particular, we would draw attention to the following points.

(i) The choice facing the Government is less stark than the one cited. In setting price controls and standards for a given firm, available information can be partitioned into two sets: that deriving from the firm in question and its markets (labeled F) and that deriving from the set of other firms and their markets (labeled S). The general issue is how this available information is to be used in arriving at regulatory decisions. Yardstick regulation refers to any solution that conditions decisions on information in set S, irrespective of whether or not the decisions are also influenced by information in set F. In general, it will be optimal to rely on both sources of information, and there exist a large number of ways in which this can be done. Thus, setting uniform standards and price controls throughout the country is far from being the only alternative to traditional cost-of-service regulation. For example, in the basic version of Shleifer's model (see section 4.6.2), the allowable price for one firm is set equal to the averaged unit costs of all other firms. In that case the resulting prices will not, in general, be uniform unless the cost conditions of the various firms are identical.

(ii) Whatever form of regulation is ultimately implemented, the information requirements of regulators will be broadly similar; in all cases detailed information about the activities and performance of each and every firm in the industry will be required. Problems of judging success and failure, of complex and repeated negotiation with each WSPLC, and of demonstrating evenhandedness are therefore characteristics of all options. For example, if uniformity of prices and standards prevailed, a company with high costs arising from the geographic characteristics of its region might properly complain that it had not been treated in an evenhanded manner.

(iii) The relationship between the prices and costs of a particular company is not a matter that affects only its standing on the Stock Exchange and that can simply be dealt with by an appropriate choice of initial capital structure. Consider again the high cost WSPLC described in (ii). If allowable prices are very low in relation to its costs, the marginal return on investment is also likely to be low, leading to deficient capital investment and, given the practical impossibility of precisely controlling all dimensions of quality, lower service standards. On the other side of the coin, excessively high price–cost margins imply the exercise of market power that will impair allocative efficiency (at least with respect to metered supplies).

(iv) Rational investors will make direct comparisons between authorities irrespective of whether or not the latter face uniform price controls and quality standards. Given the public nature of regulated price and quality constraints, and provided that the general procedures for setting them in the future are known, there is little reason to believe that particular methods of calculation will significantly affect the efficiency of the capital market. Of rather more concern is the problem that, to date, U.K. policy has created uncertainty as to the conduct of future regulatory policy.

(v) The most important advantage of yardstick regulation, which is not dependent upon uniform constraints, is that it can improve the regulatory trade-off between allocative and internal efficiency. That is, as claimed in the final sentence of the quotation from the White Paper, prices can be adjusted to reflect cost movements whilst preserving incentives for cost reduction.

To illustrate the flexibility of yardstick regulation, consider the situation of a regulatory body faced with the question of how to reset the pricing formula at the end of the first indexation period (i.e. at the first review date). Suppose further, for simplicity, that $X = 0$, so that the issue at hand is simply the determination of the real price levels of the WSPLCs. Finally, assume that regulators are considering either one or other of two extreme options:

(a) setting prices for each WSPLC so that, with given real costs, each will be expected to earn the same rate of return R on capital assets;

(b) with respect to firm i, calculating the uniform increase or decrease in the prices of all *other* firms that would yield a rate of return of R on their collective assets and then applying this percentage increase or decrease to the allowable price for firm i.

Thus, option (a) is traditional rate-of-return regulation, while option (b) is the "rate-of-return equivalent" of the Shleifer model. Let the resulting prices be $p_i(a)$ and $p_i(b)$. Then the two options can be regarded as special cases of the more general rule that the allowable price should be set equal to

$$p_i = \mu p_i(a) + (1 - \mu)p_i(b),$$

where $0 \leqslant \mu \leqslant 1$. It can be seen that, by varying μ, it is possible to change the relative weights accorded to information specific to firm i and its markets and to information derived from other firms in the industry.

Under this scheme the most efficient weighting pattern would be determined by balancing off the effects of changes in μ on incentives for internal and allocative efficiency in the product market. When $\mu = 1$ (cost-of-service regulation) prices are kept closely in line with costs, but the incentives for cost reduction are weak and there will be a tendency towards overcapitalization. On the other hand, when $\mu = 0$, because the firm is unable to influence the regulatory decision via manipulation of its own cost structure, the incentives for cost reductions are strong. However, the fact that movements in a regulated firm's prices are completely unrelated to its own costs opens up the prospect of substantial losses in allocative efficiency, particularly in the longer term as the effects of review decisions cumulate.

Broadly speaking, as μ is decreased, the marginal (negative) impact on allocative efficiency will be greater in magnitude the less well correlated are those cost variations of the different firms in the industry that arise from exogenous changes in their economic environments. This occurs because the more the allowable price for a firm is made to depend on cost variations that are uncorrelated with its own the greater will be the expected value of the absolute magnitude of its price–cost deviation. It follows that the greater the similarity among the operations and market conditions of the firms the lower will tend to be the value of μ that maximizes overall economic efficiency. Note, however, that while complete similarity indicates that μ be set equal to zero, the fact that firms are not identical does not imply that yardstick regulation should be abandoned in favor of individualistic price setting (i.e. that μ should be set equal to unity). Even if each of the individual WSPLCs has significant idiosyncratic characteristics, regulatory effectiveness can still be improved by the proper use of comparative performance data.

Against these points in favor of yardstick regulation, it might be argued that its introduction would introduce unnecessary complexity into the policy process, and that it would be difficult to understand. We have little time for this position. Effective regulation is necessarily a complex business, and to pretend otherwise is likely to have damaging long-term consequences for the industries concerned. Undue simplification of the initial framework of regulation for privatized monopolies will, as we have argued throughout this book, very frequently lead to the emergence of much more serious difficulties in the longer term. Moreover, managements and investors alike have continuously to find solutions to difficult incentive and information problems, and it is hard to believe that they would for long be perplexed by the type of averaging formula described above.

11.4   Assessment of the Government's Privatization Proposals

Thus far, the Government has set forth its proposals for privatization of the water industry only in relatively general terms. Nevertheless, the central strands of policy are clear: the ten water authorities, most probably stripped of many of their environmental functions, will be turned into ten water supply public limited companies that will then be offered for sale on the stock market, privately owned statutory water companies are likely to be given the option of converting to public limited companies, the industry will be regulated by a new Director General of Water Services through licenses granted to the WSPLCs, and regulation to protect consumers from abuse of market power will take the form of price controls rather than profit or dividend controls. Given this general approach, and its similarity to many of the features of privatization in the telecommunications and gas industries, in this final section we will focus on three questions.

Do the proposals take full advantage of opportunities for increasing competition in the industry?

Is it likely that an effective regulatory regime will be established?

Taking into account the likely framework of competition and regulation, will ownership transfer improve economic efficiency?

Competition   Except at the unacceptably high cost of a spatially fragmented industrial structure, there is little prospect of substantially increasing competition in the core transportation services of water distribution and sewerage. However, the non-environmental activities of the water authorities extend beyond the areas of natural monopoly and, with respect to these other operations, the proposed flotations are likely to be less conducive to the development of competition than are alternative policies based on the organizational isolation of natural monopoly activities. In particular, it is possible to create organizational structures that would be more favorable to the development of competition in, for example, sewage treatment and the construction and maintenance of the pipeline networks. Such a policy could be based upon the retention of water authorities in the public sector, but with their roles constrained by compulsory franchising requirements in designated activities (such as sewage treatment and pipeline maintenance). Firms competing for these contracts could be either privately or publicly owned (e.g. local authorities).

In section 4.6.1 we examined some of the limitations of franchising as a solution to the natural monopoly problem. Most of these difficulties stem from the existence of sizeable sunk costs and, because of this, we would favor proposals that leave the ownership of the pipeline networks with the water authorities or their successors. That said, the scope for increased use of franchising in the water industry is still substantial.

As Littlechild points out, however, the WSPLCs will themselves be free to contract out parts of their businesses, or to franchise parts of their operations. Hence, outside contractors will be able to compete with each authority's in-house service units, and, to the extent that the authorities are cost minimizers, the performance outcome might be expected to be similar to that likely to emerge from compulsory franchising.

Our own view is less sanguine than Littlechild's. The WSPLCs will not be operating in a competitive product market, where pressures to serve consumers' interests more effectively than rivals feed back into pressures to reduce costs. The payoffs from cost reductions achieved by contracting out activities previously undertaken in-house will therefore depend heavily upon the effectiveness of the regulatory regime. Since, as we have seen, incentives for internal efficiency that are established by regulatory frameworks are likely to have significant imperfections, there are grounds for concern about the extent to which competition will, in fact, develop. Further, large organizations are prone to develop biases in favor of in-house activities (see Williamson, 1975). Given that there are no reasons to believe that the WSPLCs will be immune to these biases, we conclude that the Government's proposals are unlikely to produce the same effects as compulsory franchising and, in particular, that they are less favorable to the promotion of effective competition in the markets for supplies of inputs to the natural monopoly services.

Regulation On the assumption that the water authorities are to be privatized without restructuring of their principal operational activities, there are two aspects of the Government's proposals for the regulatory structure that are to be welcomed. The first is the 1987 decision, reversing earlier plans, to create a new environmental regulatory body to which many of the subsidiary functions of the water authorities will be transferred. The original proposal to retain the integrated river-basin management principle by allowing privately owned firms to act as environmental regulators would have created severe longer-term problems. While it is not impossible to envision the subcontracting of some regulatory functions to profit-seeking firms, the scope and variety of the environmental activities of the water authorities would, within the timescales usually associated with legislative preparations for privatization, have almost certainly led to a regulatory quagmire. For example, one effect would probably have been substantial duplication of effort, together with undue delay in finalizing decisions, as disgruntled third parties appealed to the Government against the judgments of the WSPLCs.

The second favorable development has been the apparent willingness of the Government, expressed in the 1986 White Paper, to contemplate the introduction of more explicit regulatory yardsticks into the control framework. Unfortunately, the White Paper also contains what appear to be a number of confusions about the underlying issues that are involved, and it remains to be seen whether or not the ideas will be taken any further. Since exogenous movements in demand and cost conditions for the water authorities *are* correlated, albeit imperfectly, yardstick regulation offers scope for improving the regulatory trade-off between internal efficiency and allocative efficiency, and it is therefore to be hoped that the tentative suggestions in the White Paper will indeed be developed and implemented.

The Government's intentions regarding other aspects of the regulatory framework for a privatized water industry have not yet been revealed. The multiproduct nature of the water authorities, the importance of unmetered supplies, the question of domestic metering itself, and the issues surrounding the control of water quality and levels of service will all raise serious problems for regulatory policy. The telecommunications and gas precedents do not give many grounds for hope that these issues will be satisfactorily handled in the initial licenses, and perhaps the best that can be anticipated is that the policy regime will give sufficient scope for the DGWS to correct some of the deficiencies later (as has been done by the Director General of Telecommunications).

Perhaps the most fundamental problem to be solved is how to ensure an adequate supply of finance from private investors for investment purposes. Existing rates of return in the industry are low and, unless the yield on new investment is increased, there is a danger that service quality will be damaged in the longer term. One method of offsetting any bias to underinvestment would be to create an industry structure that afforded protection to managements from capital market pressures (e.g. by rendering takeovers more difficult) in the hope of encouraging discretionary capital expenditures. Needless to say, we find this option unattractive, since it would also reduce the incentives for internal efficiency and, on earlier arguments, weaken competition in input markets. Instead, we would favor attempts to establish a long-term bargain between society and the WSPLCs which, to the extent that it is feasible, seeks to provide clearer assurances to investors that regulatory policy recognizes the importance of capital cost recovery. We can see no way of doing this without explicit recognition of the importance of rate-of-return criteria in the determination of allowable prices. While this may lead to some diminution in incentives for internal efficiency, it would be better to deal with this effect through the use of regulatory yardsticks rather than by abandoning the rate-of-return approach; maintenance of capital programs is simply too important for the future performance of the industry to risk serious supply failures in this area.

Ownership   It will be apparent from the above discussions that we believe that the existing proposals for privatization of the water industry will have several substantive detrimental effects on economic efficiency. Among the negative factors are the following:

(i) loss of economies of scope from the abandonment of the integrated river-basin management system, which abandonment is desirable if privatization is to be based on flotations of the existing water authorities but undesirable if alternative policies, such as compulsory franchising of some of industry's activities, are allowed on to the policy agenda;

(ii) the likely effects of using private, rather than social, decision criteria when assessing whether or not to meter domestic water supplies;

(iii) the establishment of an industrial structure less conducive to the promotion of competition than alternatives characterized by greater use of franchising;

(iv) the incentives of privately owned firms to lower service standards and the difficulties faced by regulators in preventing this effect;

(v) depending upon the precise form of the pricing rules that are adopted, the possible creation of incentives for cross-subsidization;

(vi) the danger that, in the absence of a clear long-term policy framework that protects the sunk investments of private shareholders and which commands general assent, capital expenditure in the industry will be suboptimally low.

This is a formidable list of problems, and it would be necessary to believe that the Government's proposals would lead to substantial gains in internal efficiency, over and above those available under alternative policy regimes, to conclude firmly that privatization of the water industry in the way that is planned is likely to have a net beneficial effect on economic welfare. In our view, the evidence does not support such a conclusion. Despite the deficiencies of the current framework of control for the nationalized industry, significant reductions in operating costs and significant improvements in productivity have already been achieved over the last few years, and this necessarily reduces the scope for further gains from the introduction of profit incentives. More importantly, stronger incentives for reductions in both operating and investment costs can be introduced through compulsory franchising. Since this can be achieved whilst retaining the public sector status of the water authorities, it is also consistent with the maintenance of the integrated river-basin management system, the retention of cost–benefit criteria for metering decisions, and the promotion of effective competition in input markets. In addition, it avoids the creation of incentives for lower service standards and lower investment that are likely to arise from an increased emphasis on profit criteria in decision making.

It is likely, of course, that a franchising solution would lead to a substantial increase in the level of involvement of privately owned firms in the water industry. Such firms would be free to compete with, say, local authorities for contracts and, given the evidence outlined in section 2.5, we believe that they would meet with a large measure of success. Thus, our conclusions should not be read as arguments against all forms of privatization in water supply and related activities. Rather, they point toward an industry containing a mix of public and private firms, with the former (the water authorities) responsible for regulatory functions, major investment decisions (e.g. with respect to pipelines, metering, etc.), and service standards, and the latter more prevalent in activities such as pipeline construction, pipeline maintenance, and sewage treatment.

Chapter 12

Conclusions

"Suppose a schoolboy was asked to observe the sale of British Gas and then explain the meaning of the term privatisation. What sort of an account would he give? His first intelligent guess might be that it was some kind of stunt organised by the advertising profession. What else could explain the frequency of the TV advertisements featuring his favourite soap opera stars or the number of colourful hoardings in city centres?

But then he might observe his parents raiding the building society and pleading with the bank manager to lend them money. He would deduce that privatisation was a serious matter involving something called 'investment.' What you do is send off a cheque and await what appears to be a guaranteed profit. Then you may well sell your shares as quickly as possible.

The boy, if really bright, would realise that privatisation also entails a change in status of a large and powerful company. Yet it is a change which seems to have few material consequences: the company does not get split up or experience a change in management. The crucial thing is that the process of 'going into the private sector' seems to make the chairman, government ministers, a place called the City and his parents very happy. It brightens up Christmas.

What the child would never guess is that privatisation is supposed to be a way of improving industrial efficiency."

(*Financial Times* editorial, 26 November 1986)

The British privatization program has been widely acclaimed as an economic and political success of the first order. It has led to a massive expansion in the number of shareholders, billions of pounds have been raised for the Exchequer, and state involvement in industrial decision making has been drastically reduced. But has the British privatization program really been a success? What lessons does it hold for the longer term?

To assess these questions we must first specify criteria for judgment. In this book we have taken the improvement of industrial efficiency to be the primary criterion. Many other goals have been associated with the privatization program—extending share ownership, raising revenue, and so on—but those objectives can be promoted more sensibly by other means, and we therefore attach only secondary importance to them. (However, as we have seen in the last few chapters, the Government's ranking of priorities seems to have been otherwise.)

We have stressed in this book that the economics of privatization cannot be separated from the economics of competition and regulation. Ownership arrangements—including shareholder monitoring and the possibilities of takeover and bankruptcy—are an important influence upon the incentives of decision makers in firms, but their behavior depends equally upon the stimulus of market forces and mechanisms of regulation. As well as its direct benefit in promoting allocative efficiency, competition between firms has the added advantage of improving internal efficiency by enabling managerial incentive structures to be based on comparative performance measurement. Competition serves to overcome asymmetries of information between owners and managers, and thereby diminishes inefficiency and slack. Despite these advantages, head-to-head competition can at times be wasteful and inefficient, for example when there are large scale economies or externalities between firms. Even so, potential competition in the form of entry threats or competition induced by regulatory mechanisms (e.g. franchising or yardstick regulation) can still play an important role in promoting allocative and internal efficiency.

Because ownership, competition, and regulation are such interrelated determinants of corporate incentives and behavior, it is impossible to assert very general propositions as to the respective merits of private and public ownership. Theoretical analysis and empirical evidence support the view that private ownership is most efficient—and hence privatization is most suitable—in markets where effective (actual or potential) competition prevails. Thus in the British privatization it was sensible to focus initially on companies such as Amersham, British Aerospace, Cable and Wireless, Enterprise Oil, and Jaguar, all of which operate in reasonably competitive conditions. In those cases the conflict between objectives that would become a feature of later privatizations did not emerge, because the discipline of market forces serves to channel private energies toward socially desirable ends.

Policy dilemmas became sharper when the Government's ambitions to privatize grew to embrace firms with extensive market power. Where monopoly exists—that "great enemy to good management" in Adam Smith's words—the case for preferring private ownership to public ownership weakens considerably: privately efficient profit seeking can no longer be expected to lead to socially efficient results. It is then imperative for privatization, if it occurs, to be accompanied by adequate measures to reduce and contain market power. Where feasible, the scope of competitive forces (actual or potential) should be expanded by the effective removal of barriers to entry and by restructuring the dominant enterprise. Where monopoly power still remains, the task is to devise regulatory mechanisms that encourage internal and allocative efficiency and discourage strategic behavior by the firm towards the regulatory authority. That can best be done if the firm's monopoly of information is broken, and the regulator has independent access to detailed information bearing on, for example, the potential for cost reduction and the relative costs of different services supplied by a multiproduct firm. Unless effective competition and/or regulation are introduced, the privatization of firms with market power brings about private ownership in precisely the circumstances where it has least to offer.

We have seen in the later chapters of this book that British privatization policy for firms with monopoly power (e.g. British Telecom (BT) and British Gas) has been seriously flawed. Important obstacles to competition have been left in place and, even where legal barriers to entry have been removed, mechanisms to guard against anticompetitive behavior are often weak (though Oftel has made strenuous efforts in this regard). The desire to limit the burden on regulators has often resulted in limiting the effectiveness of regulation. For example, the information available to Ofgas about the business of British Gas is minimal. RPI $-$ X price regulation has been introduced in several industries (telecommunications, gas, and airports to date) to hold the fort for the time being, but it leaves wide discretion to the regulated firms (e.g. regarding relative prices) and its longer-term efficiency properties are questionable unless the authorities have access to independent information of good quality. The energetic activities of Oftel in price regulation underline this point about information, and show the importance of a regulator going beyond the simple remit that RPI $-$ X lays down. However, nothing requires Oftel to adopt the active pro-competitive stance that it has taken. The effectiveness of regulation in the future will depend heavily upon the attitudes that regulatory bodies, the Monopolies and Mergers Commission and government ministers choose to adopt.

Although the main focus of regulatory activity is on pricing, we have emphasized in several chapters the importance of regulatory incentives for investment behavior. Whereas much of the theoretical literature has examined strategic motives for overinvestment, we have examined several dangers of underinvestment. First, private discount rates may substantially exceed social discount rates, especially in view of uncertainty about the future of regulation (existing regimes specify little beyond their initial five-year term) and longer-run political developments. Secondly, it is difficult for governments to commit their successors to allow the regulated firm its fair share of the gains from successful investment and innovation, and hence dynamic efficiency may suffer. These concerns are greatest in industries with long asset lives and sunk costs (e.g. water and gas pipelines).

Thus there are several grounds for concern about the prospects for the long-term industrial performance of the major privatized firms. Some difficulties (e.g. political uncertainty) are not within the Government's control, but their policies on competition and regulation have been faulty in many instances. In our view, Mrs Thatcher's Government has been guilty of just the sort of "short termism" that has colored policy toward nationalized industries in the past. The desires to privatize speedily, to widen share ownership quickly, and to raise short-term revenues have stood in the way of devising adequate measures of competition and regulation for the industries concerned. (In the event revenues have not been maximized either because of the underpricing of shares.) In the process, the Government has partly been captured by the managements of the firms being sold, since their cooperation is essential for rapid privatization. Short-term political advantage may have been won, but longer-lasting gains in economic efficiency have been lost.

In criticizing the Government's policies for competition and regulation in the privatization program, we do not wish to suggest that there are easy alternative solutions. On the contrary, the problems of organization and control in utility industries such as telecommunications, gas, electricity, and water are among the most difficult in the field of microeconomic policy. Indeed, our view is that under private ownership there are conditions in which they become so acute that public ownership is to be preferred. When there are massive economies of scale and scope, high entry barriers, or externalities, private ownership performs poorly. The incentive and opportunity to exploit consumers threatens allocative efficiency, and the lack of competitive benchmarks leads to internal inefficiency and slack. The fact that public ownership is also far from perfect in these circumstances reflects the inherent difficulty of economic organization in such industries.

The final question is whether it was right to sell the companies that have been privatized and whether it is desirable to press on with the privatization program. This question cannot properly be answered independently of the mechanisms of competition and regulation for the industries concerned (whether they are in public or private ownership), but our broad views are as follows. Privatization is appropriate where private ownership works best, and we therefore agree with the privatization of firms in reasonably competitive industries, including Amersham, Associated British Ports,

British Aerospace, British Petroleum, Cable and Wireless, Enterprise Oil, Jaguar, Rolls-Royce, and the TSB. Likewise, British Airways should be in private ownership provided that it is made to operate in a truly competitive environment. As to the future, there are good grounds for selling remaining state holdings in the car and steel industries if that becomes feasible.

In the utility industries we believe that a more piecemeal approach is warranted. Competition and private ownership are more suitable for BT's long-distance and apparatus supply businesses than for its local network operations. In the gas industry we believe that privatization would have been more advantageous if the national transmission system had been kept under public ownership. Regionalization of the area boards, and the privatization of some of them, would have allowed yardstick regulation and a direct comparison of public and private performance. Similarly, in the electricity supply industry, we would not privatize the national transmission grid. Nor do we favor the privatization of nuclear power stations, but we do not believe that the privatization of some other generating capacity would be a bad thing, provided that effective environmental regulation exists. As in gas, the regionalization and the privatization of some area electricity boards is an option with attractions.

In airports it is hard to see what advantages privatization has. Commercial activities at BAA airports are contracted out to private operators in any event, and Government is heavily involved in important decisions regarding traffic activities through its environmental and civil aviation policies. However, it is in the water industry where the dangers of privatization appear greatest, because of a combination of concerns about the environment, natural monopoly, and infrastructure investment. While there is scope for contracting out some operations (e.g. sewage treatment and pipeline maintenance), in general there is little to gain from privatization in the water industry, and great problems lie in store if it goes ahead. We would retain public ownership of the industry's assets and would maintain the principle of integrated river-basin management.

The razzmatazz associated with stock market flotations is the most immediately visible aspect of privatization, but in the long run the British privatization program will be judged in terms of its effect on economic efficiency. By failing to introduce sufficiently effective frameworks of competition and regulation before privatizing such industries as telecommunications and gas, the Government has lost a major opportunity to tackle fundamental problems experienced in the past under public ownership. By pushing the program too far and too fast, the Government is undermining the long-run success of privatization in Britain.

References

Alchian, A. and H. Demsetz (1972). Production, Information Costs and Economic Organization. *American Economic Review* 62: 777–795.

Ashworth, M.H. and P.J. Forsyth (1984). *Civil Aviation Policy and the Privatisation of British Airways*, IFS Report Series 12. London: Institute for Fiscal Studies.

Asquith, P. (1983). Merger Bids, Uncertainty, and Stockholder Returns. *Journal of Financial Economics* 11: 51–83.

Atkinson, A.B. and J.E. Stiglitz (1980). *Lectures on Public Economics*. Maidenhead: McGraw-Hill.

Atkinson, A.B. and L. Waverman (1973). Resource Allocation and the Regulated Firm: Comment. *Bell Journal of Economics* 4: 283–287.

Audit Commission (1984). *Securing Further Improvements in Refuse Collection*. London: HMSO.

Averch, H. and L. Johnson (1962). Behavior of the Firm under Regulatory Constraint. *American Economic Review* 52: 1052–1069.

Aylen, J. (1980). Britain's Steelyard Blues. *New Scientist* 26 June.

Bailey, E.E. (1973). *Economic Theory of Regulatory Constraint*. Lexington, MA: Lexington Books.

Bailey, E.E. (1974). Innovation and Regulation. *Journal of Public Economics* 3: 285–295.

Bailey, E.E. (1976). Innovation and Regulation: A Reply. *Journal of Public Economics* 5: 393–394.

Bailey, E.E. (1986). Price and Productivity Change Following Deregulation: The U.S. Experience. *Economic Journal* 96: 1–17.

Bailey, E.E. and R.D. Coleman (1971). The Effect of Lagged Regulation in the Averch–Johnson Model. *Bell Journal of Economics* 2: 278–292.

Bailey, E.E., D.R. Graham and D.P. Kaplan (1985). *Deregulating the Airlines*. Cambridge, MA: MIT Press.

Bailey, E.E. and J.C. Malone (1970). Resource Allocation and the Regulated Firm. *Bell Journal of Economics* 1: 129–142.

Baron, D.P. and D. Besanko (1984). Regulation, Asymmetric Information, and Auditing. *Rand Journal of Economics* 15: 447–470.

Baron, D.P. and D. Besanko (1987). Commitment and Fairness in a Dynamic Regulatory Relationship. *Review of Economic Studies* 54: 413–436.

Baron, D.P. and R.B. Myerson (1982). Regulating a Monopolist with Unknown Costs. *Econometrica* 50: 911–930.

Baumol, W.J. (1982). Contestable Markets: An Uprising in the Theory of Industrial Structure. *American Economic Review* 72: 1–15.

Baumol, W.J. and D. Bradford (1970). Optimal Departures from Marginal Cost Pricing. *American Economic Review* 60: 265–283.

Baumol, W.J. and A.K. Klevorick (1970). Input Choices and Rate of Return Regulation: An Overview of the Discussion. *Bell Journal of Economics* 1: 162–190.

Baumol, W.J., J. Panzar and R.D. Willig (1982). *Contestable Markets and the Theory of Industry Structure*. New York: Harcourt Brace Jovanovich.

Baumol, W.J. and R.D. Willig (1986). Contestability: Developments Since the Book. *Oxford Economic Papers (Supplement)* 38: 9–36.

Bawa, V.S. and D.S. Sibley (1980). Dynamic Behaviour of a Firm Subject to Stochastic Regulatory Review. *International Economic Review* 21: 627–642.

Beato, P. and A. Mas-Colell (1984). The Marginal Cost Pricing as a Regulation Mechanism in Mixed Markets. In Marchand, M., P. Pestieau and H. Tulkens (eds), *The Performance of Public Enterprises*. Amsterdam: North-Holland.

Beesley, M. (1981). *Liberalisation of the Use of British Telecommunications Network*. London: Department of Trade and Industry.

Beesley, M. and S. Littlechild (1983). Privatization: Principles, Problems and Priorities. *Lloyds Bank Review* 149: 1–20.

Benoit, J.-P. (1985). Financially Constrained Entry in a Game with Incomplete Information. *Rand Journal of Economics* 15: 490–499.

Boardman, A.E. and A.R. Vining (1987). *A Comparison of the Performance of Private, Mixed and State Owned Enterprises in Competitive Environments*. Working Paper 1206, Faculty of Commerce, Columbia University, New York.

Bös, D. (1986). *Public Enterprise Economics*. Amsterdam: North-Holland.

Bös, D. and W. Peters (1986). *Privatization, Efficiency, and Market Structure*. Discussion Paper A-79, Institute of Economics, Bonn University.

Boyfield, K. (1985). *Put Pits into Profit*. London: Centre for Policy Studies.

Breyer, S. (1982). *Regulation and its Reform*. Cambridge, MA: Harvard University Press.

Brock, G. (1981). *The Telecommunications Industry*. Cambridge, MA: Harvard University Press.

Brock, W.A. (1983). Contestable Markets and the Theory of Industry Structure: A Review Article. *Journal of Political Economy* 91: 1055–1066.

Bruce, A. (1986). State to Private Sector Divestment: The Case of Sealink. In Coyne, J. and M. Wright (eds), *Divestment and Strategic Change*. Oxford: Phillip Allan.

Bruggink, T.M. (1982). Public versus Regulated Private Enterprise in the Municipal Water Industry: a Comparison of Water Costs. *Quarterly Review of Economics and Business* 22: 111–125.

Buckland, R., P.J. Herbert and K.A. Yeomans (1981). Price Discounts on New Equity Issues in the U.K. *Journal of Business Finance and Accountancy* 8: 79–95.

Buiter, W.H. (1985). A Guide to Public Sector Debt and Deficits. *Economic Policy* 1: 13–61.

Bulow, J., J. Geanakopolos and P. Klemperer (1985). Multimarket Oligopoly. *Journal of Political Economy* 93: 488–511.

Caillaud, B., R. Guesnerie, P. Rey and J. Tirole (1985). *The Normative Economics of Government Intervention in Production in the Light of Incentive Theory: A Review of Recent Contributions*. Technical Report 473, IMSSS, Stanford University, Stanford, CA.

Caves, D.W. and L.R. Christensen (1980). The Relative Efficiency of Public and Private Firms in a Competitive Environment: the Case of Canadian Railroads. *Journal of Political Economy* 88: 958–976.

Charnes, A., W.W. Cooper and T. Sueyoshi (1985). A Goal Programming/Constrained Regression Review of the Bell System Breakup. Paper presented to the 7th Congress of European Operational Research, Bologna, June 1985.

Christensen, L.R. and W.H. Greene (1976). Economies of Scale in U.S. Electric Power Generation. *Journal of Political Economy* 84: 655–676.

Civil Aviation Authority (1984). *Airline Competition Policy*, Paper 500. London: CAA.

Collins, B. and B. Wharton (1984). Investigating Public Industries: How has the Monopolies and Mergers Commission Performed? *Public Money*, September 1984.

Cowling, K. *et al.* (1980). *Mergers and Economic Performance*. Cambridge: Cambridge University Press.

Crain, W.M. and A. Zardkoohi (1978). A Test of the Property Rights Theory of the Firm: Water Utilities in the United States. *Journal of Law and Economics* 21: 395–408.

Cremer, H., M. Marchand and J.-F. Thisse (1987). The Public Firm as an Instrument for Regulating an Oligopolistic Market. Paper presented at the 2nd Congress of the European Economic Association, Copenhagen, August 1987.

Crew, M.A. and P.R. Kleindorfer (1986). *The Economics of Public Utility Regulation*. London: Macmillan.

Culham, P.G. (1987). *A Method of Determining the Optimal Balance of Prices for Telephone Services*. Oftel Working Paper 1. London: Oftel.

Curwen, P.J. (1986). *Public Enterprise: A Modern Approach*. Brighton: Harvester Press.

Dasgupta, P., P. Hammond and E. Maskin (1979). The Implementation of Social Choice Rules: Some General Results of Incentive Compatibility. *Review of Economic Studies* 46: 185–216.

Dasgupta, P. and J.E. Stiglitz (1985). *Sunk Costs, Competition and Welfare*. Mimeograph, St John's College, Cambridge.

Davis, E.G. (1973). Dynamic Behaviour of a Regulated Firm with a Price Adjustment Rule. *Bell Journal of Economics* 4: 270–282.

Davis, E.H. (1984). Express Coaching Since 1980: Liberalisation in Practice. *Fiscal Studies* 5(1): 76–86.

De Alessi, L. (1977). Ownership and Peak Load Pricing in the Electric Power Industry. *Quarterly Review of Economics and Business* 17.

De Fraja, G. and F. Delbono (1986). Alternative Strategies of a Public Enterprise in Oligopoly. Paper presented at the 1st Congress of the European Economic Association, Vienna, August 1986.

Deloitte, Haskins and Sells (1983). *British Gas Efficiency Study*. London: Deloitte, Haskins and Sells.

Demsetz, H. (1968). Why Regulate Utilities? *Journal of Law and Economics* 11: 55–65.

Department of Energy (1986). *Authorisation Granted by the Secretary of State for Energy to British Gas under Section 7 of the Gas Act 1986*. London: HMSO.

Department of the Environment (1986). *Privatisation of the Water Authorities in England and Wales*, Cmnd 9734. London: HMSO.

Department of Trade and Industry (1982). *The Future of Telecommunications in Britain*, Cmnd 8610. London: HMSO.

Department of Trade and Industry (1984). *Licence Granted by the Secretary of State for Trade and Industry to British Telecommunications under Section 7 of the Telecommunications Act 1984*. London: HMSO.

Department of Transport (1984a). *Buses*, Cmnd 9399. London: HMSO.

Department of Transport (1984b). *Airline Competition Policy*, Cmnd 9366. London: HMSO.

Department of Transport (1985). *Airports Policy*, Cmnd 9542. London: HMSO.

Deutsches Institut für Wirtschaftsforschung (1984). *Economic Evaluation of the Impact of Telecommunications Investment in the Communities: A Study on Behalf of the Commission of the European Communities*. Berlin: DIW.

Diamond, P. and J.A. Mirrlees (1971). Optimal Taxation and Public Production. *American Economic Review* 61: 8–27, 261–278.

Dimson, E. (1983). The U.K. New Issue Market. In Broyles, J., I. Cooper and S. Archer (eds), *The Financial Management Handbook*. London: Gower.

Dixit, A. (1980). The Role of Investment in Entry Deterrence. *Economic Journal* 90: 95–106.

Edison Electric Institute (1985). *Analysis of the Differences among Alternative Forms of Utility Ownership in the U.S.A.* Washington, DC: Edison Electric Institute.

Ekern, S. and R. Wilson (1974). On the Theory of the Firm in an Economy with Incomplete Markets. *Bell Journal of Economics* 5: 171–180.

Englebrecht-Wiggans, R., P.R. Milgrom and R.J. Weber (1983). Competitive Bidding and Proprietary Information. *Journal of Mathematical Economics* 11: 161–169.

Estrin, S., P.A. Grout and S. Wadhwani (1987). Profit Sharing and Employee Share Ownership. *Economic Policy* 4: 14–62.

Evans, D.S. and J.J. Heckman (1984). A Test for Subadditivity of the Cost Function with an Application to the Bell System. *American Economic Review* 74: 615–623.

Fare, R., S. Grosskopf and J. Logan (1985). The Relative Performance of Publicly Owned and Privately Owned Electric Utilities. *Journal of Public Economics* 26: 89–106.

Farrell, J. (1986). Moral Hazard as an Entry Barrier. *Rand Journal of Economics* 17: 440–449.

Farrell, J. and G. Saloner (1985). Standardization, Compatibility and Innovation. *Rand Journal of Economics* 16: 70–83.

Faulhaber, B.C. (1975). Cross-subsidization: Pricing in Public Enterprises. *American Economic Review* 65: 966–977.

Findlay, C.C. and P.J. Forsyth (1984). *Competitiveness in Internationally Traded Services: The Case of Air Transport*. Working Paper, ASEAN–Australia Joint Research Project.

Firth, M. (1979). The Profitability of Takeovers and Mergers. *Economic Journal* 89: 316–328.

Firth, M. (1980). Takeovers, Shareholders Returns and the Theory of the Firm. *Quarterly Journal of Economics* 94: 235–260.

Forsyth, P.J. (1984). Airlines and Airports: Privatisation, Competition and Regulation. *Fiscal Studies* 5(1): 61–75.

Franks, J.R. and R.S. Harris (1986a). *Shareholder Wealth Effects of Corporate Takeovers: The U.K. Experience 1955–85*. Working Paper, London Business School and University of North Carolina at Chapel Hill.

Franks, J.R. and R.S. Harris (1986b). The Role of the Mergers and Monopolies Commission in Merger Policy: Costs and Alternatives. *Oxford Review of Economic Policy* 2(4): 58–76.

Freixas, X. and J.J. Laffont (1985). Marginal Cost Pricing versus Average Cost Pricing under Moral Hazard. *Journal of Public Economics* 26: 135–146.

Friedman, J. (1979). On Entry Preventing Behaviour and Limit Price Models of Entry. In Brams, S.J. *et al.* (eds), *Applied Game Theory*. Vienna: Physica.

Fromm, G. (ed.) (1981). *Studies in Public Regulation*. Cambridge, MA: MIT Press.

Fudenberg, D. and J. Tirole (1983). Learning by Doing and Market Performance. *Bell Journal of Economics* 14: 522–530.

Fudenberg, D. and J. Tirole (1984). The Fat-Cat Effect, the Puppy-Dog Ploy, and the Lean and Hungry Look. *American Economic Review Papers and Proceedings* 74: 361–366.

Gilbert, R.J. and D. Newbery (1982). Pre-emptive Patenting and the Persistence of Monopoly. *American Economic Review* 72: 514–526.

Gist, P. and S.A. Meadowcroft (1986). Regulating for Competition: the Newly Liberalised Market for Private Branch Exchanges. *Fiscal Studies* 7(3): 41–66.

Goldberg, V.P. (1976). Regulation and Administered Contracts. *Bell Journal of Economics* 7: 426–448.

Graham, D., D.P. Kaplan and D. Sibley (1983). Efficiency and Competition in the Airline Industry. *Bell Journal of Economics* 14: 118–138.

Greenwald, B.C. (1984). Rate Base Selection and the Structure of Regulation. *Rand Journal of Economics* 15: 85–95.

Grossman, S. and O.D. Hart (1980). Takeover Bids, the Free-Rider Problem and the Theory of the Corporation. *Bell Journal of Economics* 11: 42–64.

Grout, P. (1987). The Wider Share Ownership Programme. *Fiscal Studies* 8(3): 59–74.

Halpern, P.J. (1973). Empirical Estimates of the Amount and Distribution of Gains to Companies in Mergers. *Journal of Business* 46: 554–573.

Hammond, E.M., D.R. Helm and D.J. Thompson (1985). British Gas: Options for Privatisation. *Fiscal Studies* 6(4): 1–20.

Harris, R.G. and E.G. Wiens (1980). Government Enterprise: An Instrument for the Internal Regulation of Industry. *Canadian Journal of Economics* 13: 125–132.

Hart, O.D. (1983). The Market Mechanism as an Incentive Scheme. *Bell Journal of Economics* 14: 366–382.

Hartley, K. and M. Huby (1985). Contracting-out in Health and Local Authorities: Prospects, Progress and Pitfalls. *Public Money*, September 1985.

Hay, D.A. and D.J. Morris (1979). *Industrial Economics*. Oxford: Oxford University Press.

Hayek, F.A. (1945). The Use of Knowledge in Society. *American Economic Review* 35: 519–530.

Hazlewood, A. (1953). The Origin of the State Telephone Service in Britain. *Oxford Economic Papers* 5: 13–25.

Heald, D. (1980). The Economic and Financial Control of U.K. Nationalised Industries. *Economic Journal* 90: 243–265.

Henney, A. (1987). *Privatise Power: Restructuring the Electricity Supply Industry*. London: Centre for Policy Studies.

Herbert Report (1956). *The Electricity Supply Industry*, Cmd 9672. London: HMSO.

Heyworth Report (1945). *The Gas Industry*, Cmd 6699. London: HMSO.

HM Treasury (1961). *Financial and Economic Obligations of the Nationalised Industries*, Cmnd 1337. London: HMSO.

HM Treasury (1967). *Nationalised Industries: A Review of Economic and Financial Objectives*, Cmnd 3437. London: HMSO.

HM Treasury (1978). *The Nationalised Industries*, Cmnd 7131. London: HMSO.

HM Treasury (1985). *The Government's Expenditure Plans 1985–86 to 1987–88*, Cmnd 9428-II. London: HMSO.

HM Treasury (1986). *The Government's Expenditure Plans 1986–87 to 1988–89*, Cmnd 9702. London: HMSO.

HM Treasury (1987). *The Government's Expenditure Plans 1987–88 to 1989–90*, Cm 56. London: HMSO.

Holmstrom, B. (1982). Moral Hazard in Teams. *Bell Journal of Economics* 13: 324–340.

House of Commons (1968). Select Committee on Nationalised Industries, Session 1967–68. *Ministerial Control of the Nationalised Industries*. London: HMSO.

Huettner, D.A. and J.H. Landon (1978). Electric Utilities: Scale Economies and Diseconomies. *Southern Economic Journal* 44: 883–912.

Hunt Report (1982). *Report on the Inquiry into Cable Expansion and Broadcasting*, Cmnd 8679. London: HMSO.

Jackson, P.D. (1986). New Issue Costs and Methods in the U.K. Equity Market. *Bank of England Quarterly Bulletin* 26: 532–542.

Jaffer, S.M. and D.J. Thompson (1986). Deregulating Express Coaches: A Reassessment. *Fiscal Studies* 7(4): 45–68.

Jenkinson, T. and C.P. Mayer (1987). The Privatisation Process in Britain and France. Paper presented to the 2nd Congress of the European Economic Association, Copenhagen, August 1987.

Joskow, P.L. and R.M. Schmalensee (1983). *Markets for Power: An Analysis of Electric Utility Deregulation*. Cambridge, MA: MIT Press.

Kahn, A.E. (1970). *The Economics of Regulation*, Vols 1 and 2. New York: Wiley.

Katz, M. and C. Shapiro (1985). Network Externalities, Competition and Compatibility. *American Economic Review* 75: 424–440.

Katz, M.L. and C. Shapiro (1986). Product Compatibility Choice in a Market with Technological Progress. *Oxford Economic Papers (Supplement)* 38: 146–165.

Kay, J.A., C. Mayer and D. Thompson (eds) (1986). *Privatisation and Regulation: The U.K. Experience*. Oxford: Oxford University Press.

Kay, J.A. and Z.A. Silberston (1984). The New Industrial Policy—Privatisation and Competition. *Midland Bank Review* Spring: 8–16.

Kay, J.A. and D.J. Thompson (1986). Privatisation: a Policy in Search of a Rationale. *Economic Journal* 96: 18–32.

Keynes, J.M. (1936). *The General Theory of Employment, Interest and Money*. London: Macmillan.

Kilvington, R.P. (1985). *Lessons of the 1980 Transport Act*. Mimeograph, Transport Studies Unit, Oxford.

Kilvington, R.P. and A.K. Cross (1986). *Deregulation of Express Coach Services in Britain*. Aldershot: Gower.

King, M. 1986. *Takeovers, Taxes, and the Stock Market*. Mimeograph, London School of Economics.

Kitchen, H.M. (1976). A Statistical Estimation of an Operating Cost Function for Municipal Refuse Collection. *Public Finance Quarterly* 4(1): 56–76.

Klevorick, A. (1971). The Optimal Fair Rate of Return. *Bell Journal of Economics* 2: 122–153.

Klevorick, A. (1973). The Behaviour of a Firm Subject to Stochastic Regulatory Review. *Bell Journal of Economics* 4: 57–88.

Kreps, D. and R. Wilson (1982). Reputation and Imperfect Information. *Journal of Economic Theory* 27: 253–279.

Laffont, J.J. and J. Tirole (1986). Using Cost Observation to Regulate Firms. *Journal of Political Economy* 94: 614–641.

Leibenstein, H. (1966). Allocative Efficiency versus X-Efficiency. *American Economic Review* 56: 392–415.

Lesourne, J. (1976). Innovation and Regulation: A Comment. *Journal of Public Economics* 5: 389–392.

Littlechild, S. (1983). *Regulation of British Telecommunications Profitability*. London: HMSO.

Littlechild, S. (1986). *Economic Regulation of Privatised Water Authorities*. London: HMSO.

Loeb, M. and W. Magat (1979). A Decentralized Method for Utility Regulation. *Journal of Law and Economics* 22: 399–404.

Malatesta, P.H. (1983). The Wealth Effect of Merger Activity and the Objective Functions of Merging Firms. *Journal of Financial Economics* 11: 155–181.

Mandelker, G. (1974). Risk and Return: The Case of Merging Firms. *Journal of Financial Economics* 1: 303–335.

Mankiw, N.G. and M.D. Whinston (1986). Free Entry and Social Inefficiency. *Rand Journal of Economics* 17: 48–58.

Matthews, S. and L. Mirman (1983). Equilibrium Limit Pricing: the Effects of Private Information and Stochastic Demand. *Econometrica* 51: 981–996.

Mayer, C.P. and S.A. Meadowcroft (1985). Selling Public Assets: Techniques and Financial Implications. *Fiscal Studies* 6(4): 42–56.

McGowan, F. and C. Trengrove (1986). *European Aviation: A Common Market?* IFS Report Series 23. London: Institute for Fiscal Studies.

Meadowcroft, S.A. and L. Pickup (1987). *The Initial Effects of the 1985 Transport Act in the Metropolitan Areas*. Mimeograph, Transport Studies Unit, Oxford.

Meeks, G. (1979). *Disappointing Marriage: A Study of the Gains from Mergers*. Cambridge: Cambridge University Press.

Meyer, R.A. (1975). Publicly Owned versus Privately Owned Utilities: a Policy Choice. *Review of Economics and Statistics* 57: 391–399.

Milgrom, P. and J. Roberts (1982a). Predation, Reputation and Entry Deterrence. *Journal of Economic Theory* 27: 280–312.

Milgrom, P. and J. Roberts (1982b). Limit Pricing and Entry Under Incomplete Information: An Equilibrium Analysis. *Econometrica* 50: 443–459.

Millward, R. (1982). The Comparative Performance of Public and Private Ownership. In Roll, E. (ed.), *The Mixed Economy*. London: Macmillan.

Molyneux, R. and D. Thompson (1987). Nationalised Industry Performance: Still Third-Rate? *Fiscal Studies* 8(1): 48–82.

Monopolies and Mergers Commission (1980). *British Railways Board: London and South East Commuter Services*, Cmnd 8046. London: HMSO.

Monopolies and Mergers Commission (1981a). *Central Electricity Generating Board*, HC 315. London: HMSO.

Monopolies and Mergers Commission (1981b). *Severn–Trent Water Authority, East Worcestershire Waterworks Company and the South Staffordshire Waterworks Company*, HC 339. London: HMSO.

Monopolies and Mergers Commission (1982a). *Bristol Omnibus Co., Cheltenham District Traction Co., City of Cardiff District Council, Trent Motor Traction Co., West Midlands Passenger Transport Executive*, HC 442. London: HMSO.

Monopolies and Mergers Commission (1982b). *Anglian Water Authority, North West Water Authority*, Cmnd 8726. London: HMSO.

Monopolies and Mergers Commission (1983a). *Yorkshire Electricity Board*, Cmnd 9014. London: HMSO.

Monopolies and Mergers Commission (1983b). *National Coal Board*, Cmnd 8920. London: HMSO.

Monopolies and Mergers Commission (1983c). *Civil Aviation Authority*, Cmnd 9068. London: HMSO.

Monopolies and Mergers Commission (1984a). *The Post Office Letter Post Service*, Cmnd 9332. London: HMSO.

Monopolies and Mergers Commission (1984b). *South Wales Electricity Board*, Cmnd 9165. London: HMSO.

Monopolies and Mergers Commission (1984c). *London Transport Executive*, Cmnd 9133. London: HMSO.

Monopolies and Mergers Commission (1985). *British Airports Authority: A Report on the Efficiency and Costs of, and the Service Provided by, the British Airports Authority in its Commercial Activities*, Cmnd 9644. London: HMSO.

Monopolies and Mergers Commission (1986a). *British Telecommunications PLC and Mitel Corporation—a Report on the Proposed Merger*, Cmnd 9715. London: HMSO.

Monopolies and Mergers Commission (1986b). *The General Electric Company PLC and the Plessey Company PLC—a Report on the Proposed Merger*, Cmnd 9867. London: HMSO.

Mookherjee, D. (1984). Optimal Incentive Schemes with Many Agents. *Review of Economic Studies* 51: 433–446.

Moore, J. (1985). *The Success of Privatisation* (speech made when opening Hoare Govett Ltd's new City dealing rooms on 17 July). HM Treasury Press Release 107/85.

Morrison, H. (1933). *Socialisation of Transport*. London: Constable.

Mulley, C. and M. Wright (1986). Buy-outs and the Privatisation of National Bus. *Fiscal Studies* 7(3): 1–24.

Myerson, R. (1979). Incentive Compatibility and the Bargaining Problem. *Econometrica* 47: 61–74.

Nalebuff, B. and J.E. Stiglitz (1983). Prizes and Incentives: Towards a General Theory of Compensation and Competition. *Bell Journal of Economics* 14: 21–43.

National Audit Office (1985). *Report by the Comptroller and Auditor General on Sale of Government Shareholding in British Telecommunications plc*. London: HMSO.

National Audit Office (1987a). *Report by the Comptroller and Auditor General on Sale of Government Shareholding in British Gas plc*. London: HMSO.

National Audit Office (1987b). *Report by the Comptroller and Auditor General on Sale of Government Shareholding in British Airways plc*. London: HMSO.

National Economic Development Office (1976). *A Study of U.K. Nationalised Industries*. London: HMSO.

Newbery, D.M.G. (1985). Pricing Policy. In Belgrave, R. and M. Cornell (eds), *Energy Self-Sufficiency for the U.K.?* Aldershot: Gower.

Newbould, G.D. (1970). *Management and Merger Activity*. Liverpool: Guttistead.

Newman, K. (1986). *The Selling of British Telecom*. Eastbourne: Holt, Rinehart and Wilson.

Niskanen, W. A. (1971). *Bureaucracy and Representative Government*. Chicago: Aldine-Atherton.

Ofgas (1987). *First Report*. London: HMSO.

Oftel (1985a). *First Report*. London: HMSO.

Oftel (1985b). *BT's Price Changes, November 1985*. London: HMSO.

Oftel (1986a). *Annual Report 1985*. London: HMSO.

Oftel (1986b). *Review of BT's Tariff Changes, November 1986*. London: HMSO.

Oftel (1987). *Annual Report 1986*. London: HMSO.

Peltzman, S. (1971). Pricing in Public and Private Enterprises and Electric Utilities in the United States. *Journal of Law and Economics* 14: 109–147.

Peltzman, S. (1976). Towards a More General Theory of Regulation. *Journal of Law and Economics* 14: 109–148.

Perry, M.K. (1984). Scale Economies, Imperfect Competition and Public Policy. *Journal of Industrial Economics* 32: 313–333.

Pescatrice, D.R. and J.M. Trapani (1980). The Performance and Objectives of Public and Private Utilities Operating in the United States. *Journal of Public Economics* 13: 259–276.

Posner, R. (1971). Taxation by Regulation. *Bell Journal of Economics* 2: 22–50.

Posner, R. (1974). Theories of Economic Regulation. *Bell Journal of Economics* 5: 335–358.

Price, C.M. (1984). *Distribution Costs in the U.K. Gas Industry*. Discussion Paper 31, Department of Economics, University of Leicester.

Pryke, R. (1981). *The Nationalised Industries: Policies and Performance Since 1968*. Oxford: Martin Robertson.

Pryke, R. (1982). The Comparative Performance of Public and Private Enterprise. *Fiscal Studies* 3(2): 68–81.

Pryke, R. (1987). Privatising Electricity Supply. *Fiscal Studies* 8(3): 75–88.

Redwood, J. (1984). *Going for Broke*. Oxford: Blackwell.

Rees, R. (1984a). *Public Enterprise Economics*. London: Weidenfeld and Nicholson.

Rees, R. (1984b). A Positive Theory of the Public Enterprise. In Marchand, M., P. Pestieau and H. Tulkens (eds), *The Performance of Public Enterprises*. Amsterdam: North–Holland.

Rees, R. (1985). The Theory of Principal and Agent, *Bulletin of Economic Research* 37: 3–26, 75–95.

Robinson, C. and E. Marshall (1988). Liberalising the British Coal Industry. In Helm, D.R., J.A. Kay and D.P. Thompson (eds), *The Market for Energy*. Oxford: Oxford University Press.

Robinson, W. (1988). The Economies of Coal. In Helm, D.R., J.A. Kay and D.P. Thompson (eds), *The Market for Energy*. Oxford: Oxford University Press.

Robson, W.A. (1960). *Nationalized Industry and Public Ownership*. London: George Allen and Unwin.

Rowley, C.K. and G.K. Yarrow (1981). Property Rights, Regulation and Public Enterprise: the Case of the British Steel Industry 1957–75. *International Review of Law and Economics* 1: 63–96.

Salop, S. and D. Scheffman (1983). Raising Rivals' Costs. *American Economic Review Papers and Proceedings* 73: 267–271.

Sappington, D. (1980). Strategic Firm Behavior under a Dynamic Adjustment Process. *Bell Journal of Economics* 11: 360–372.

Savas, E.S. (1977). Policy Analysis for Local Government: Public Versus Private Refuse Collection. *Policy Analysis* 3: 49–74.

Scharfstein, D. (1986). *The Disciplinary Role of Takeovers*. Mimeograph, MIT, Cambridge, MA.

Schmalensee, R. (1978). Entry Deterrence in the Ready To Eat Breakfast Cereal Industry. *Bell Journal of Economics* 9: 305–327.

Schmalensee, R. (1979). *The Control of Natural Monopolies*. Lexington: D.C. Heath.

Schmalensee, R. (1982). Product Differentiation Advantages of Pioneering Brands. *American Economic Review* 82: 349–365.

Schmalensee, R. (1983). Advertising and Entry Deterrence: an Exploratory Model. *Journal of Political Economy* 90: 636–653.

Schwartz, M. (1986). The Nature and Scope of Contestability Theory. *Oxford Economic Papers (Supplement)* 38: 37–57.

Schwartz, M. and R.J. Reynolds (1983). Contestable Markets: An Uprising in the Theory of Industry Structure: Comment. *American Economic Review* 73: 488–490.

Selten, R. (1978). The Chain Store Paradox. *Theory and Decision* 9: 127–159.

Shapiro, C. (1985). Patent Licensing and R&D Rivalry. *American Economic Review Papers and Proceedings* 75: 25–30.

Sharkey, W.W. (1979). A Decentralized Method for Utility Regulation: A Comment. *Journal of Law and Economics* 22: 74–75.

Sharkey, W.W. (1982). *The Theory of Natural Monopoly*. Cambridge: Cambridge University Press.

Sharpe, T. (1982). *The Control of Natural Monopoly by Franchising*. Mimeograph, Wolfson College, Oxford.

Sharpe, T. (1985). British Competition Policy in Perspective. *Oxford Review of Economic Policy* 1(3): 80–94.

Shepherd, W. (1984). 'Contestability' vs. Competition. *American Economic Review* 74: 572–587.

Shleifer, A. (1985). A Theory of Yardstick Competition. *Rand Journal of Economics* 16: 319–327.

Singh, A. (1971). *Takeovers: Their Relevance to the Stock Market and the Theory of the Firm.* Cambridge: Cambridge University Press.

Singh, A. (1975). Takeovers, Economic Natural Selection and the Theory of the Firm. *Economic Journal* 85: 497–515.

Slater, M. and G.K. Yarrow (1983). Distortions in Electricity Pricing in the U.K. *Oxford Bulletin of Economics and Statistics* 45: 317–338.

Smith, A. (1776). *An Inquiry into the Nature and Causes of the Wealth of Nations* (edited in two volumes by Campbell, R.H. and A.S. Skinner (1976)). Oxford: Clarendon Press.

Spence, M. (1975). Monopoly, Quality, and Regulation. *Bell Journal of Economics* 16: 417–429.

Spence, M. (1977). Entry, Capacity, Investment and Oligopolistic Pricing. *Bell Journal of Economics* 8: 534–544.

Spence, M. (1981). The Learning Curve and Competition. *Bell Journal of Economics* 12: 49–70.

Spence, M. (1983). Contestable Markets and the Theory of Industry Structure: A Review Article. *Journal of Economic Literature* 21: 981–990.

Starkie, D. (1984). BR: Privatisation Without Tears. *Economic Affairs* 18(4): 16–19.

Starkie, D. and D. Thompson (1985). *Privatising London's Airports*, IFS Report Series 16. London: Institute for Fiscal Studies.

Starkie, D. and D. Thompson (1986). Stansted: A Viable Investment? *Fiscal Studies* 7(3): 76–82.

Stevens, B.J. (1978). Scale, Market Structure and the Cost of Refuse Collection. *Review of Economics and Statistics* 60: 438–448.

Stigler, G. (1971). The Theory of Economic Regulation. *Bell Journal of Economics* 2: 3–21.

Suzumura, K. and K. Kiyono (1987). Entry Barriers and Economic Welfare. *Review of Economic Studies* 54: 157–167.

Vass, P. (1986). The Water Industry. In *Public Domain*. London: Public Finance Foundation.

Veljanovski, C. (1987). *Selling the State*. London: Weidenfeld and Nicholson.

Vickers, J.S. (1985a). Strategic Competition among the Few—Some Recent Developments in Oligopoly Theory. *Oxford Review of Economic Policy* 1(3): 39–62.

Vickers, J.S. (1985b). The Economics of Predatory Practices. *Fiscal Studies* 6(3): 24–36.

Vickers, J.S. (1985c). Delegation and the Theory of the Firm. *Economic Journal* (Conference Papers) 95: 138–147.

Vickers, J.S. and G.K. Yarrow (1985). *Privatization and the Natural Monopolies*. London: Public Policy Centre.

Vogelsang, I. and J. Finsinger (1979). A Regulatory Adjustment Process for Optimal Pricing by Multiproduct Monopoly Firms. *Bell Journal of Economics* 10: 157–171.

Waterson, M. (1984). *Economic Theory of the Industry*. Cambridge: Cambridge University Press.

Watts Report (1985). *Joint Study of Water Metering: Report of the Steering Group*. London: HMSO.

von Weizsäcker, C.C. (1980). A Welfare Analysis of Barriers to Entry. *Bell Journal of Economics* 11: 399–420.

Williamson, O.E. (1968). Economies as an Antitrust Defense: Welfare Tradeoffs. *American Economic Review* 58: 18–36.

Williamson, O.E. (1975). *Markets and Hierarchies: Analysis and Antitrust Implications*. New York: Free Press.

Williamson, O.E. (1976). Franchising Bidding for Natural Monopolies—In General and with Respect to CATV. *Bell Journal of Economics* 7: 73–104.

Willig, R. D. (1985). *Corporate Governance and Product Market Structure*. Mimeograph, Princeton University.

Yarrow, G.K. (1988). The Price of Nuclear Power. *Economic Policy*, to be published.

Yarrow, G.K. (1986). Privatization in Theory and Practice. *Economic Policy* 2: 324–377.

Yarrow, G.K. (1988). The Price of Nuclear Power. *Economic Policy*, to be published.

Zajac, E.E. (1970). A Geometric Treatment of the Averch–Johnson Behavior of the Firm Model. *American Economic Review* 60: 117–125.

Author Index

Subject Index